SCOTTISH LITERATURE AND
THE SCOTTISH PEOPLE

SCOTTISH
LITERATURE
AND THE SCOTTISH
PEOPLE

1680–1830

DAVID CRAIG

*Organising Tutor, Workers' Educational Association
North Yorkshire*

1961
CHATTO & WINDUS
LONDON

PUBLISHED BY
CHATTO AND WINDUS LTD
42 WILLIAM IV STREET
LONDON WC2

★

CLARKE, IRWIN AND CO LTD
TORONTO

★
PRINTED IN GREAT BRITAIN
BY R. AND R. CLARK LTD, EDINBURGH

"National literature is the work of writers, who are moulded by influences that are moulding their countries, and who write out of so deep a life that they are accepted there in the end . . . I mean by deep life that men must put into their writing the emotions and experiences that have been most important to themselves. If they say, 'I will write of Irish country-people and make them charming and picturesque like those dear peasants my great-grandmother used to put in the foreground of her water-colour paintings', then they had better be satisfied with the word 'provincial'. If one condescends to one's material, if it is only what a popular novelist would call local colour, it is certain that one's real soul is somewhere else. Mr Synge, upon the other hand, who is able to express his own finest emotions in those curious ironical plays of his, where, for all that, by an illusion of admirable art, everyone seems to be thinking and feeling as only countrymen could think and feel, is truly a National writer, as Burns was when he wrote finely and as Burns was not when he wrote 'Highland Mary' and 'The Cottar's Saturday Night'."

W. B. Yeats, *Plays and Controversies.*

TO
JILL, MARIAN
AND
PETER

CONTENTS

FOREWORD

I owe thanks for priceless stimulus and help to the following people: Dr and Mrs F. R. Leavis, whose interest and critical hints, on a subject not their own, were constantly suggestive and encouraging; John Manson, who first showed me that the main concern of literary studies should be their relevance to the lives of the people around one; Mr David Murison, who gave me during the last year of my work, with tireless helpfulness, the benefit of his seemingly exhaustive knowledge of Scotland; Morris Shapira and my brother—conversation with them over the years amounted to the finest kind of education; and my wife, who drew up the Glossary, and reads my work with the keenest eye for the far-fetched and the dull. (We are also indebted to Mr Murison and to Sandy Fenton for help in glossing a number of words.)

Hugh MacDiarmid and Mr John Speirs are mentioned in this book mainly in disagreement. But we owe it to Mr Mac-Diarmid that Scottish literary culture in the 20th century exists at all; and Mr Speirs's *The Scots Literary Tradition* is the only book I know which shows a modern literary mind at work on Scottish literature. Q. D. Leavis's *Fiction and the Reading Public* and Van Wyck Brooks's histories of American literature and society were inspiring examples; these writers have shown that studies of the public behind a literature need not stop at un-critically accumulated facts about dead books, but can lead into the core of the society concerned.

This book has been completed in Ceylon, where Scottish books are not plentiful. As a result some references and other details are imperfect because they could not be checked or added to during rewriting.[1] I should also mention that more historically-minded readers may sometimes be dissatisfied with the treatment of a particular point. I could not of course treat every matter with a historian's fullness of detail. My aim was, rather, to suggest the essentials of Scottish culture during the period, in relation to the literature and its public. I can only hope that some themes touched on here may be thought worth exploring in greater detail by other writers.

My work on this subject was originally done for a thesis accepted for the Cambridge Ph.D. I must thank the University

[1] I am indebted to my father for doing some checking for me.

9

FOREWORD

of Aberdeen and the Carnegie Trust for Scotland, who financed
me during my research; and the staffs of various libraries,
especially Miss Balfour of the Edinburgh Room, Edinburgh
Central Public Library, Mr Blackett of the National Library
of Scotland, and Mr Marcus Milne, Chief Librarian of the
Aberdeen Public Libraries.

Parts of this book originally appeared in *Essays in Criticism*,
the *Spectator*, and *The Voice of Scotland*, and I thank their Editors
for permission to use them here.

D. C.

Peradeniya, Ceylon
January 1961

INTRODUCTION

THE approach and period of this book have been framed so as to form a 'social history' of literature for Scotland from the late 17th to the early 19th century. I have not aimed to *cover* the background. Social issues have been followed up only where questions of literary significance or, sometimes, of failure to develop uncovered what seemed to be key trends or traits in the life of the people. Thus the method used has had to be flexible. At some points one has to look closely into the layers of meaning in a particular novel or poem. At others one must discover who exactly was reading a book, whether judges as well as ploughmen. Here we have to study the kind of community behind the literature, down to the very town-plan or working conditions amidst which writer and readers led their lives; there, again, we have to study a period through key events—the trial of a trade unionist, waves of emigration, or the annual councils of a Church. Always the aim has been to find the particular facts and particular passages of poetry or fiction in which the life of the people seems to reveal itself most genuinely, and hence to give actuality to themes such as community, society, class, speech-idiom, tradition—which are so apt to remain vague.

Such work is liable to defeat itself unless it is controlled—indeed inspired in the first place—by a literary-critical sense of its subject. For very far from all facts of 'background' are relevant. We need a sense of where the main centres and lines of cultural force lie, what ways of life, milieux, and events had most to do with shaping the creative product. And unless this sense is based on a critically-formed idea of what literature in the field is valuable, one will easily be enticed by theories away from the facts of what was there in the society. A critic recently wrote (in an article with the impressively modern title ' *The Bride of Lammermoor:* A Novel of Tory Pessimism') that "Redgauntlet is a mature man whose devotion to the Pretender is so deep-rooted that no change of ideology is possible".[1] Now, we do naturally wish—as we gaze back and try to make out the features of 18th-century Scotland—that Scott had somewhere followed through such a theme. But attentive reading of *Redgauntlet* shows us that Redgauntlet, so far from being a mature man, is a stock villain-hero from melodrama. Scott, like Burns,

[1] Article by R. C. Gordon, *Nineteenth Century Fiction* (London: September 1957), Vol. 12, No. 2.

specially requires that what is deeply felt, consistently worked out, in his writings should be winnowed away from what is artistically lifeless: in Scott's case, the unassimilated anti-quarian interests and the stereotypes of Scottish character, relished though they were by his contemporaries. Again, the delicate work of defining the limitedness of the vernacular poetry—for example its preoccupation with local matters—without merging into the uncomprehending snobberies of the genteel critics brings home that it is the approach of a critical reader which can best, not only work out, but even bring to light the basic issues—questions of real or fake idiom, ample or cramped culture—which make up the 'social history of literature'.

The period I set out to cover, 1680 to 1830, is a long one, partly because it is a natural age (or sequence of phases), and partly because the kind of literary and social growth to be explored does not fully show itself inside brief periods. This period is natural in that it stretches from the point at which literary activities begin to pick up after the disorder, bloodshed, and tyranny of the religious wars to the point at which Scotland was all but emptied of native talents during the early Industrial Revolution and the increase of emigration. The literary evidence is simply very intermittent and scanty before the Glorious Revolution and after the Reform Acts, and in this it closely parallels the state of the nation. We may say (although any such time-division is partly arbitrary) that modern Scotland dawned around the Establishment of Presbyterianism (1690) and the Parliamentary Union with England (1707). Similarly, the abolition in 1832 of the separate Scottish representative system is regarded by historians as the end of our political history, and the Disruption in the Church of Scotland (1843) as the end of our ecclesiastical history, as far as they concern the national historian.[1] This span is distinctly a 'period', and it is also a natural phase in literature: it includes the last flowering of the vernacular poetry and the rise and hey-day of the native novel.

Secondly, a long period is needed to get long enough per-spectives of the evolution which took place. Scottish history has often been muddled by writers who have failed to understand how inevitable and how of a piece is the growth of a culture. For example, both G. M. Trevelyan and G. S. Pryde (a fore-

---

[1] E.g. W. L. Mathieson, *Church and Reform in Scotland, 1797–1843* (Glasgow: 1916), p. 373.

most living Scottish historian) can speak of our 18th-century literature as somehow a consequence of the 1707 Union, and a satisfactory one: characterful but barbaric Scotland, now behaving well in the leading-strings of the more civilised country to the south, settled down to supply the world with the appealing lyrics and stirring historical novels which her two great writers specialised in. Bigotry being dead, Scotland could turn to "romance and scenery rather than rebellion and gloomy wastes".[1] This glorification of Scotland's 'Golden Age' does not explain the cultural impasse which followed: the use of the native language became embarrassed, poetry ran shallow and dried up, the novel was provincial from the start, many of the most original minds emigrated. Hence the historian is left calling Victorian culture in Scotland "*strangely* rootless" (my italics [2]), whereas a more critical sense of the 18th century would have seen that some sort of disintegration was already visible even in the best Scots poetry and in the way the language was being used.

Run-of-the-mill histories, and 'common knowledge' about the subject, are riddled with such misapprehensions. But a more telling case is to be found in William Power's excellent *Literature and Oatmeal*. Power seizes on and diagnoses a great many crucial changes in the cultural tradition; but he does not see that they were historically inevitable. Thus, deploring the "liltings and facetiae of persons of poor temperament and inferior intellect" and the "genteel and touristic attitude to Scotland" which the imitators of Burns and Scott, respectively, have made notorious, he can be as unthinking as to say, "The pity is that both somehow lent themselves to exploitation by enemies of Scotland's all-round vitality as a nation".[3] Literature is hardly a battlefield, on which damage can be done by external 'enemies'. We must rather ask, Was the vitality of Burns and Scott themselves sufficiently all-round, that they should so readily have been vulgarised? On the novel Power writes: "With the deaths of Scott, Hogg, Galt, and Wilson [Christopher North], Scots literature fell at once from a national to a provincial level" (p. 117). "At once"—overnight! In fact the work of these novelists themselves, as we shall see, was deeply conditioned by provincialism; and to insist otherwise

---

[1] See G. M. Trevelyan, *Ramillies and the Union with Scotland* (London: 1932), pp. 285-6; G. S. Pryde (ed.), *The Treaty of Union of Scotland and England, 1707* (London: 1950), pp. 64-5.
[2] R. S. Rait and G. S. Pryde, *Scotland* (2nd ed., London: 1954), pp. 316-17.
[3] (London: 1935), pp. 81-2.

is merely to construct a golden age of Scottish literature for the sake of more dramatically lamenting or chiding the present.

The weaker literatures encourage ill-grounded speculations—there are fewer outstanding facts to resist loose theorising. They may also discourage both criticism and sociology because they give less purchase, less solid richness of material, to the reader who aims to get from literature "some notion of the difference involved in day-to-day living—in the sense of life and its dimensions and in its emotional and moral accenting".[1] But clear-sighted recognition, final level-headed acceptance of the quality and limitations of Scottish literature need not discourage. They should make all the difference to whether one comes to the literature, and the whole national life, with the right expectations, with a mind likely to understand. We cannot pretend that Scottish literature grows strongly and continuously alongside the national history—as do, say, Russian or English fiction. Scottish literature enforces more than English the truth in Leslie Stephen's opinion that literature is "a kind of by-product . . . too small a part in the whole activity of a nation, even of its intellectual activity, to serve as a complete indication of the many forces which are at work, or as an adequate moral barometer of the general moral state".[2] We need not, then, speak as though the comparative weakness of the literature of the 17th or the 19th century shows that the Scottish people was throughout those periods in a state of stupor. The actual state of the nation matters more than the very obvious butts of derision, the Burns cult and the like, which have made controversy so easy and constructive criticism rare; and it is the changing state of the nation which this book, from its particular viewpoint, tries to describe.

We have to recognise, then, that there did not emerge along with modern Scotland a mature, 'all-round' literature. Sheer social forces—centralisation, emigration, the widespread wasting away of the regional and the vernacular—were against the sustained output of anything like a *separate* literature for Scotland. By the close of this period that has become, simply, something it would be unreasonable to look for. In the 17th century the mental talents of Scotsmen had run to the intense but one-track activity of Church and theological debate. In the 18th, this talent was, apparently, released for wider work—

[1] F. R. Leavis, 'Sociology and Literature': *The Common Pursuit* (London: 1952), p. 203.
[2] *English Literature and Society in the Eighteenth Century* (London: 1904), p. 22.

research, study, and experiment in science, farming, technology, philosophy, poetry—as a result of peace, more rational religion, new markets and increased investment. As W. H. Marwick puts it, "internal peace and order encouraged a *secularisation* of interests" (my italics [1]). But though David Hume could marvel that "we should be the people most distinguished for literature in Europe",[2] all that the famous Golden, or Athenian, Age could show for imaginative literature was a very striking dearth.

Scotland's intellect blossomed out wonderfully in the 18th century—perhaps stimulated (as is often suggested) by that same theological activity: Carlyle and his father are typical individual cases.[3] All at once it was the native thinkers who were supplying the most read, most influential works. In the 1750's, Hume's *Essays* were "universally read" (and a normally unpopular professor was asked to repeat a lecture course designed to refute them). In the '80's, the chemistry lectures of Cullen and Black made the subject fashionable among young lawyers—a record typical of pre-specialist days. In the early '90's, says Lord Cockburn, "The young, by which I mean the liberal young of Edinburgh, lived upon" *The Wealth of Nations*.[4] It is a remarkable record, not achieved in Scotland before or since. But—literature? The failure of Augustan Edinburgh to bring forth anything distinctive or fine in the imaginative way will be one starting-point for the argument of this book. Burns, of course, was the fine flowering of a long tradition; and Scott was the centre of a literary hey-day of a sort. But in discussing these authors it is lapses and fallings short that we have to account for as much as achieved first-rate work.

The reading public is the main social field of my enquiry because the public *is* the people as far as it concerns itself with literature. What social conditions impinged most sharply on

---

[1] *Economic Developments in Victorian Scotland* (London: 1936), p. 15.

[2] *Letters*, ed. J. Y. T. Greig (Oxford: 1932), I, p. 255.

[3] E.g. Thomas Carlyle, *Reminiscences* (Everyman ed., London: 1932), on his father: "He has said of a bad Preacher: 'He was like a fly wading among Tar'. Clearness, emphatic Clearness, was his highest category of man's thinking power: he delighted always to hear good 'Argument'; he would often say, 'I would like to hear thee argue with him': he said this of Jeffrey and me,—with an air of such simple earnestness (not two years ago); and it was his true feeling" (p. 12). See also Hugh Miller, *First Impressions of England and Its People* (edition Edinburgh: 1889), pp. 339-40, and W. L. Mathieson, *Politics and Religion in Scotland* (Glasgow: 1902), I, pp. 181-2.

[4] Thomas Somerville, *My Own Life and Times, 1741-1814* (edition Edinburgh: 1861), pp. 16-17; *A Tour in England and Scotland in 1785*, by an English Gentleman [Thomas Newte] (London: 1787), p. 326; Henry Cockburn, *Memorials of His Time* (Edinburgh: 1856), p. 46.

writers; what were the resources of culture and language to which they had familiar access; whether incompletenesses in the literature reveal lack of fulfilment in the people; how far the literature produced was alive to the concerns nearest the heart of the people who made its public; what attitudes to literature, especially what expectations of a native literature, were working in the country; what books were read, how they circulated, and the type of society this involved—these are the matters dealt with here. In short, Scottish poetry and fiction between 1680 and 1830 are here interpreted as the literature which was *possible* in the conditions of life in Scotland at that time.

PART I

VERNACULAR LITERATURE:
THE POPULAR AND 'POLITE' PUBLICS

CHAPTER I

The Old Communal Culture

... a whole lifetime passed in the study of Shenstone would only lead a man further and further from writing the 'Address to a Louse'. Yet Burns, like most great artists, proceeded from a school and continued a tradition; only the school and the tradition were Scotch, not English. While the English language was becoming daily more pedantic and inflexible, and English letters more colourless and slack, there was another dialect in the sister country, and a different school of poetry tracing its descent, through King James I, from Chaucer. The dialect alone counts for much; for it was then written colloquially, which kept it fresh and supple; and, although not shaped for heroic flights, it was a direct and vivid medium for all that had to do with social life.—R. L. STEVENSON, *Familiar Studies of Men and Books* (Tusitala edition), pp. 50-1.

SCOTTISH poetry, as Stevenson suggests, is peculiarly rich in all that has to do with social life. In the 17th and 18th centuries it is taken up almost exclusively with that, but socialness of a kind very different from, say, the equally 'social' English poetry of that time. Dryden and Pope lived amidst and wrote for an upper-middle and upper class metropolitan world of coffee-house, town mansion, and country estate, a milieu of politicians and landowners growing rich (or bankrupt) on investments, and the artists to whom they gave commissions and hospitality. Pope especially writes as one accustomed to shine in the company of the sophisticated and important; this forms not only his subject-matter (the conditions of a genuine literary culture; 'the use of riches'), but his manner also, which turns to creative uses the poise of a conscious conversationalist. The Scottish contemporaries, Allan Ramsay, Robert Fergusson, and later, Burns, could hardly differ more. They inhabit the ordinary pubs and market places, centres of gaming, drinking, eating, small business deals, the coming and going of farmers, chapmen (pedlars), and lawyers looking for work—but not, apparently, of literary connoisseuring and the discussion of new publications which could seriously influence a central government. They write in the manner of popular wiseacres, masters of repartee, in a language little different from that of the mass of their countrymen, not in that of an educated upper crust. 18th-century Scotland is of course famous for such an 'élite': men of letters such as Hume, Adam Smith, Henry Mackenzie, and (a little later) Scott, and the cultured law lords (Kames,

19

Hailes, and later Jeffrey). But as far as these men were concerned, at least in the 18th century, the creative literature of the country—the poetry of Ramsay, Fergusson, and Burns—was virtually underground, or in the backwoods. Its comedy embodied a social life beneath the dignity of the 'polite' class. Yet that stratum of social life—lived out in the howffs (pubs), street markets, and tenement stairs—was in fact shared, even in the capital city, by all classes, aristocracy, bourgeoisie, and working folk alike, to an extent unthinkable in any later age. The society was close-knit in its physical conditions of life, if not in education, property, and outlook.

Why was it, then, that the expression of Scottish socialness was carried on so exclusively by the vernacular writers? why did the communications represented by the national poetry stay so insulated from the more refined manners and ideas which the educated classes were learning from France and England? The town of Edinburgh, in its expansion from a congested, narrow, filthy medieval settlement to a geometrically planned model city, is not only a symbol of this two-sided Scottish culture, it is the very soil in which it grew. In exploring the town and village communities of pre-19th-century Scotland, we are to a great extent examining the immediate conditions which made the literature what it was, and made it distinctive.

The line of poetry which culminates in Burns represents the last phase in Scottish history in which a distinctively native mode of expression held together through several generations. It will be as well to form a concrete sense of what that poetry was like, before going further into the social conditions behind it. This line of poetry got its nickname, 'the matter of Habby Simson', from Robert Sempill's poem of the mid-17th century, 'The Piper of Kilbarchan' (a poem which Grierson and Bullough were catholic enough to put into the *Oxford Book of Seventeenth Century Verse*). This poem seems authentically popular, with no taint of *arrière-pensée* about the ordinary village fun. It gives the effect, though written by a landed gentleman, of sharing directly and artlessly in a village life whose high moments were signalled by music:

> *Now who shall play, the Day it Daws?*
> *Or Hunts Up, when the Cock he craws?*
> *Or who can for our Kirk-town-cause,*
>   *Stand us in stead?*
> *On bagpipes (now) no body blaws,*
>   *Sen Habbie's dead.*

Or wha will cause our shearers shear?
Wha will bend up the brags of weir,
Bring in the bells, or good play meir,
    In time of need?
Hab Simson cou'd, what needs you spear?
    But (now) he's dead.

.   .   .   .

At Clark-plays when he wont to come,
His pipe play'd trimly to the drum,
Like bikes of bees he gart it bum,
    And tun'd his reed.
Now all our pipers may sing dumb,
    Sen Habbie's dead.[1]

Such sociable music seems to have been in the bones of the people. Allan Ramsay says affectionately of the popular song tunes: "They are, for the most part, so cheerful, that on hearing them well played or sung, we find a difficulty to keep ourselves from dancing . . . such as are not judges of the fine flourishes of new music imported from Italy and elsewhere, yet will listen with pleasure to tunes that they knew, and can join in the chorus".[2] The familiar rhythms, indeed, get into the very metre of the poetry. Such snatches as this from the probably 16th-century 'Peblis to the Play',

        Sum said the quene of may   *wes cumit*
        Of peblis to the play,

move with just the beat of the foot checking and setting off again in a country dance.

    Such a poem as 'The Piper of Kilbarchan' is still purely of the old village way of life, that enacted in 'Peblis to the Play' and 'Christis Kirk on the Green' (to name two of the early models for Ramsay, Fergusson, and Burns). By Ramsay's time, the vernacular poet—even if he thinks of himself as popular—is no longer immersed in the country life. When Ramsay imitates 'Christis Kirk', he forces his jocosity onto us:

        But mony a pawky look and tale
          Gaed round when glowming hous'd them;
        The ostler wife brought ben good ale,
          And bad the lasses rouze them . . .[3]

---

[1] *The Poems of the Sempills of Beltrees*, ed. James Paterson (Edinburgh: 1849), pp. 41-2.
[2] *The Tea Table Miscellany* (edition Edinburgh: 1768), Preface, p. v.
[3] *The Works of Allan Ramsay* with life by George Chalmers (Edinburgh & London: 1800), I, p. 320. The quotation is from the first of two pastiche cantos Ramsay added to the poem when he reprinted it in *The Ever Green*.

In contrast the poet of the 16th century (or earlier) loses himself in the momentum of the fun:

> *Stewin come steppand in with stendis*
> *No renk mycht him arrest*
> *Platfut he bobbit up with bendis*
> *ffor mald he maid requeist . . .*

> *Than thai come to the townis end*
> *withouttin more delay*
> *He befoir and scho befoir*
> *To se quha wes maist gay.*
> *all that luikit thame upon*
> *leuche fast at thair array*
> *Sum said that thai wer merkat folk*
> *Sum said the quene of may   wes cumit*
> *Of peblis to the play.*[1]

In this, much the better of these two festivity poems, the action is relieved from the monotonous wallowing in muck and brutal horseplay by the extraordinary vivacity of every movement, for example,

> *Be that the bargan was all playit*
> *The stringis stert out of thair nokkis . . .*[2]

And once an extra delicacy that the fun takes on is plainly in touch with a very old vein of folk symbolism, apparently related to the strange imagery of heavenly beauty in the Border ballad 'The Wife of Usher's Well':

> *The carline wife's three sons came hame,*
> *And their hats were o' the birk.*

> *It never grew in syke nor ditch,*
> *Nor yet in ony sheugh;*
> *But at the gates o' Paradise,*
> *That birk grew fair eneugh.*[3]

'Peblis to the Play' expands the motif into something like a Pan figure or god of growth, and the stanza springs like a green shoot out of the poem:

> *Ane young man stert in to that steid*
> *als cant as ony colt*
> *ane birkin hat upon his heid*
> *with ane bow and ane bolt*

---

[1] *The Maitland Folio Manuscript*, ed. W. A. Craigie (Scottish Text Society, Edinburgh: 1919), I, pp. 150, 178.   [2] *Maitland Manuscript*, p. 181.
[3] Quoted from *Border Ballads*, sel. and ed. William Beattie (London: 1952), p. 209.

Said, mirrie madinis think nocht lang
The wedder is fair and smolt
He cleikit up ane hie ruf sang
Thair fure ane man to the holt   quod he
of peblis to the play.[1]

The suggestion that there is some *arrière-pensée*, or self-conscious rusticity, in this poetry has been made by the recent editor of Fergusson, Matthew P. MacDiarmid. He calls 'The Piper of Kilbarchan' "a comic play with undignified language, a species of burlesque", and regarding 'Peblis to the Play' he speaks of "burlesque" and "clownish caricature".[2] But such poetry, in its rhythm and in the unforced flow of action, reads more like a perfectly straight celebration of unbridled community-fun in which the whole village is caught up. Allan Ramsay, who took up this poetry in the 18th century, reprinting, garbling, and imitating it, catches onto only its possibilities for pawky farce, for example he misses the running-on dance rhythm got by the bob that ends each stanza and cuts it down to one short line:

She'd gar them a' be hooly
Fou fast that day.[3]

His people are individuals, unlike the scarcely-differentiated villagers of the old anonymous poetry. But this is not pure gain, for, as we have seen, his jocosity is put in, not the spontaneous emotion of primitive village life. As David Daiches has noted, he is self-conscious, unintegrated, in his feelings about 'low life'.[4] For one thing, he cannot but feel that the sayings of the townsfolk at play are quaint—vernacular gems or plums. Thus his proverbial phrases are visibly forced into his poetry for their own sake, rather than turned into genuine metaphor, for example:

. . . Now they may mak a kirk and mill
O't, since he's dead,

or,

We drank and drew, and fill'd again,
O wow but we were blyth and fain!
When ony had the Count mistain,

[1] *Maitland Manuscript*, p. 177.
[2] *The Poems of Robert Fergusson* (Scottish Text Society, Edinburgh: 1954), I, pp. 119, 160.
[3] *Works*, I, p. 317.
[4] 'Eighteenth Century Vernacular Poetry', in *Scottish Poetry: A Critical Survey*, ed. James Kinsley (London: 1955), pp. 155-6.

O it was nice,
To hear us a' cry, Pike yer Bain
And spell yer Dice.[1]

Such phraseology—proverbs, favourite metaphors, gambling jargon—were indeed the natural idiom for Scots poetry, for they were the favourite usage of a country still accustomed to the old oral literature and vernacular habits of speech and thought. 'A round of Scots proverbs'—enjoyed for their "agreeable tartness"—was a regular amusement amongst parties of ordinary folk, who, according to J. M. Robertson (himself from the peasantry), retailed them "with a serious gusto impossible to describe".[2] The same fun was had at the tea- and dinner-tables of the middle and upper classes. There was a craze for repeating proverbs at the tea-tables of the Edinburgh gentlefolk in the 1820's—some people could quote dozens; and in Glasgow, in the early 19th century, at a dinner including William Motherwell, the folk-song collector, Henderson, a collector of proverbs, and Sir James Anderson, "Proverbs and lines of Scotch poetry, and songs and sentiments went round".[3] Ramsay, however, picks such sayings out of natural speech and exploits them for local colour. He edited a collection of proverbs which circulated very widely in the late 18th century, especially in the form of the chapbooks or pamphlets which the chapmen sold at the farmhouse door. In his Preface he even sells the country people their own speech, on the lines of a conversation course:

> Ye happy herds, while your hirdsels are feeding on the flow'ry braes, you may eithly make yoursells masters of the hale ware. How usefull will it prove to you (wha have sae few opportunities of common clattering) when you forgather with your friends at kirk or market, banquet or bridal?[4]

Although Ramsay thus belongs to an age in which an interest in Scottish culture was all too prone to turn it into (at best) folk-lore, nevertheless the vernacular, and the 'Habbie Simson' style, do supply the one mode which seems to suit his

[1] 'Elegy on John Cowper', *Works*, I, p. 292; 'Elegy on Maggy Johnstoun', *ibid.* p. 289.

[2] *Memoir of Robert Chambers with Autobiographic Reminiscences of William Chambers* (Edinburgh & London: 1872), p. 17; John M. Robertson, 'Thomas Carlyle', in *Modern Humanists* (London: 1891), p. 32.

[3] *Parties and Pleasures* (the diaries of Helen Graham, 1823–26), ed. James Irvine (Edinburgh: 1957), p. 54; Peter Mackenzie, *Reminiscences of Glasgow and the West of Scotland* (Glasgow: 1866), II, p. 309.

[4] Burns Martin, *Allan Ramsay* (Cambridge, Massachusetts: 1931), p. 101; Allan Ramsay (ed.), *A Collection of Scots Proverbs* (edition Edinburgh: 1797), pp. 6-7.

experience, in which he becomes at all interesting or vivid. Whereas in most of his other works he is blatantly aspiring to Literature, in his mock-elegies and verse epistles he is writing close to life. They give a sense of being in the thick of a social kind of life, not only in content but at those specially vivid points at which he expresses appreciation of simple convivial zest, as in "We drank, and drew, and fill'd again" or another couplet from the mock-elegy on Maggy Johnstoun, a popular pub-keeper:

> *Sae brawly did a pease-scon toast*
> *Bizz i' the queff, and flie the frost . . .*[1]

This is a characteristic feeling of the Scots poetry in this tradition. It is rich in passages in which food and drink are revelled in as part of the fellow-feeling and brisk, busy coming-and-going of pub celebrations, often worked up into a sort of extravaganza which we would call caricature if the poet were not so wholeheartedly *with* the feeling he evokes. In Fergusson's 'Caller Oysters', money whirls round with the party:

> *When auld Saunt Giles, at aught o'clock,*
> *Gars merchant lowns their chopies lock,*
> *There we adjourn wi' hearty fock*
> *To birl our bodles* [2]

Handing round the common cup is described in words which richly evoke a sort of ideal luxury:

> *Auld Reikie! thou'rt the canty hole,*
> *A bield for mony caldrife soul,*
> *Wha snugly at thine ingle loll,*
> *Baith warm and couth;*
> *While round they gar the bicker roll*
> *To weet their mouth.*[3]

In Burns, the drink itself takes on a super-animated life:

> *When Vulcan gies his bellows breath,*
> *An' ploughmen gather wi' their graith,*
> *O rare! to see thee fizz an' freath*
> *I' th' lugget caup!*
> *Then Burnewin comes on like death*
> *At ev'ry chaup.*[4]

---

[1] *Works*, I, p. 289.   [2] *Poems*, ed. MacDiarmid, II, p. 67.   [3] *Ibid.* p. 33.
[4] As Burns, unlike the other poets discussed here, is available in countless editions, I will give as reference only the titles of his poems. I have myself used thróughout *The Life and Works of Robert Burns*, ed. Robert Chambers, revised by William Wallace (Edinburgh & London: 1896). The stanza above is from 'Scotch Drink'.

Burns also, with his genius for making something poetic of the familiarity natural to the people in a small community, has striking phrases which concentrate the sense of accustomed well-being and comradeliness which are part of such life, for example his emphatic use of "stand":

> *At kirk or market, mill or smiddie,*
> *Nae tawted tyke, tho' e'er sae duddie,*
> *But he wad stand, as glad to see him,*
> *An' stroan'd on stanes an' hillocks wi' him.*[1]

Or, again, the passage at the beginning of 'Tam o' Shanter':

> *. . . Ae market night,*
> *Tam had got planted unco right,*
> *Fast by an ingle, bleezing finely,*
> *Wi' reaming swats, that drank divinely . . .*

In the weight of "stand" and "planted", we feel that the very posture embodies the heart of the contentment, the social rightness and well-being.

This characteristic socialness is seen at its best in the habit of making poetry from the high moments in the life of the community, whether ceremonies or festivities. Fergusson does the motley town scene almost for its own sake, or for its surface ludicrousness, as in 'The Election':

> *The* MAGISTRATES *fu' wyly are,*
> *Their lamps are gayly blinking,*
> *But they might as leive burn elsewhere,*
> *Whan fock's blind fu' wi' drinking.*
> *Our* DEACON *wadna ca' a chair,*
> *The foul ane durst him na-say;*
> *He took* SHANKS-NAIG, *but, fient may care,*
> *He* ARSELINS *kiss'd the cawsey*
> *Wi'* BIR *that night.*[2]

Burns, however, transforms such rollickings into a satirical image of Presbyterian extremist heat and sectarianism; the rhythm and extravagance of the mode are *used* to hit off, farcically, the other kind of extravagance indulged in by the bigot:

> *Kilmarnock wabsters, fidge and claw,*
> *An' pour your creeshie nations;*
> *An' ye wha leather rax an' draw,*
> *Of a' denominations.*

[1] 'The Twa Dogs.'
[2] *Scots Poems*, by Robert Fergusson, ed. Bruce Dickins (Edinburgh: 1925), p. 44.

Swith! to the Laigh Kirk, ane an' a',
An' there tak up your stations;
Then aff to Begbie's in a raw,
An' pour divine libations
For joy this day.

. . . Mak haste an' turn King David owre
And lilt wi' holy clangor;
O' double verse come gie us four,
An' skirl up 'the Bangor':
This day the kirk kicks up a stoure,
Nae mair the knaves shall wrang her,
For Heresy is in her pow'r,
And gloriously she'll whang her,
Wi' pith this day.[1]

We can see how much pointedness the social poetry has taken on since Ramsay's imitations of the old jocundity. A related characteristic is coining phrases which amount to a whole notation for the life of a community, for example Fergusson's "stair-head critics", Burns's "yill-caup commentators"— equivalent of 'bar-room politicians'—and Hamilton of Gilbertfield's "send them a' right sneaking hame / Be Weeping-Cross".[2] At every point in this poetry it is the focal points and familiar symbols of a community way of life that are used for the basic idiom.

It is true that the conviviality runs also to a dismayingly silly cult, for it is really too slight to give the impulse of a whole poetry, or of a poetry sufficiently removed from light verse. In the end one's heart sinks at the everlasting 'homely' moral-swopping about drink:

A wee soup drink dis unco weel
To had the heart aboon,

or the bravado of

Leeze me on drink! it gies us mair
Than either school or college;
It ken'les wit, it waukens lear,
It pangs us fou o' knowledge . . .[3]

We must remember that at that time a pre-occupation with drink was something like inevitable in the people's poetry.

---

[1] 'The Ordination.'
[2] From 'Auld Reikie', *Poems*, II, p. 110; 'The Holy Fair'; Hamilton's first 'Familiar Epistle' to Allan Ramsay, *Works of Allan Ramsay*, ed. Burns Martin and J. W. Oliver (Scottish Text Society, Edinburgh: 1945), I, p. 116.
[3] From 'Hallow-Fair': Fergusson, *Poems*, II, p. 93; from Burns, 'The Holy Fair'.

Engels (writing in 1872) refers very justly to "The fact that under the existing circumstances drunkenness among the workers is a necessary product of their living conditions, just as necessary as typhus, crime, vermin, bailiff and other social ills, so necessary in fact that the average figures of those who succumb to inebriety can be calculated in advance"; [1] and figures and comments from Scotland in the late 18th and early 19th century bear this out.[2] The literary fact, however, is that the very copious poetry of drink is usually inferior, seemingly a reaction part defensive, part self-surrendering to an evil social fact. I have concentrated on the feeling of pure convivial enjoyment because that is so often what is there at the most vivid points of wording in this poetry. Sometimes such feeling is self-conscious, and tries to rationalise itself. But when it is straightforward, it is one of the poetry's most genuine emotions. It seems to represent the amazing energy and animal spirits of the common people, coming out in a poetry which helps to put us in the thick of the life they led in public.

A literature so strongly 'social' brings home to us what it meant to live in a society so thrown upon its own devices as the Scottish—in particular, so compact a capital. Living conditions in Edinburgh before the modern replanning have often been described, but more often than not for the gossip, or for the sake of 'old Edinburgh' itself, than as a way to understanding the national culture. Here the make-up of the town is to be considered in so far as it directly influenced the literature, both as a positive inspiration and as a cause of the alienation of the Scottish cultivated class from the 'typically Scottish'.

Scotsmen were used to very small, close communities, even in their main cities. Glasgow's population had gone up from 12,700 at the Union (1707) to 20,000 by mid-century, and its commercial expansion had begun. Yet carriers still built their haystacks in front of their doors, and the town herd went round every morning with his horn calling the cattle from the Trongate and the Saltmarket (where early in the century the wealthiest merchants lived) to the common meadows nearby.[3] Edinburgh too was very compact, clustered round two parallel main streets, and it had, for a capital, unusually few com-

---

[1] Friedrich Engels, *The Housing Question* (Moscow: 1955), p. 73.

[2] See note 1. The reader should note that a good many points aside from the main line of the argument are discussed in fuller notes, indicated (as here) by arabic numbers, and arranged under chapters at the end of the book.

[3] George Eyre-Todd, *History of Glasgow* (Glasgow: 1934), III, p. 74; John Rae, *Life of Adam Smith* (London: 1895), pp. 87-8.

munications with the rest of the country. Roads were very bad, and settlements (unlike those of England) were set far apart from each other. The first Scottish bank, the Bank of Scotland, failed in several early attempts to circulate its paper money in the provinces because so little trade came and went between the capital and the country.[1] Cobbett later described this social arrangement in terms of satellite communities. On the Suffolk scale, there would have been thirty-two villages with their churches in the seventy-five square miles round Craigmillar Castle (south of Holyrood), whereas there was, in addition to Musselburgh, only one: "how much greater and more famous EDINBURGH would be, if it were surrounded, as it ought to be, with market-towns and numerous villages. . . ."[2]

Because of the way Edinburgh had grown up on a narrow ridge of volcanic rock, it had had to build perpendicularly, squeezing lofty, narrow buildings (as in Manhattan) onto the slim pier of building space available. The main streets, High Street and Cowgate, ran east and west along the ridge, and the poorer streets were tunnel-like wynds and closes piercing the ground floor of the lofty tenements or 'lands' and dropping in slopes and steps down the cliff to either side. Behind the lands— some of whose façades were well enough built and even, if inhabited by the aristocracy, carved with arms and decorations —were those courts, deep wells of dirty stonework, where nowadays old air-raid shelters stand surrounded by dustbins and the dwellers hang out their washing on gallows-like spars projecting from the upper windows. Thus Edinburgh was not quartered off between the classes until the end of the century. This Scottish town housing was until the 1780's unique in the way it mixed the classes. In England even the poor usually had separate dwellings, whereas old Edinburgh was the only important British town in which tenement dwelling had been normal time out of mind, a condition it shared at this time with other old walled towns such as Stirling, and also with Glasgow, where most of the well-known, well-off citizens lived in tenement flats.[3] As a result, leading tradesmen squeezed

[1] Robert Chambers, *Domestic Annals of Scotland*, From the Revolution to the Rebellion of 1745 (Edinburgh & London: 1861), p. 132.
[2] William Cobbett, *Tours in Scotland*, from *Rural Rides, etc.*, ed. G. D. H. and Margaret Cole (London: 1930), III, p. 769.
[3] Adam Smith, *The Wealth of Nations*, ed. Edwin Cannan (London: 1904), I, pp. 119-20; Friedrich Engels, *The Condition of the Working-Class in England* (1844): see Marx and Engels, *On Britain* (Moscow: 1953), pp. 67-9; J. H. Clapham, *An Economic History of Modern Britain* (2nd ed., reprinted, Cambridge: 1950), p. 37 and n. 5; Eyre-Todd, *History of Glasgow*, III, p. 105.

their families into quarters as cramping and unhygienic as the poor had elsewhere: one eminent goldsmith lived above his shop in Parliament Square, his nursery and kitchen in a cellar "where the children are said to have rotted off like flies".[1] The lands were such warrens that in places people could step from one upper window to another across the street. Early census-takers were unable to track down every family living in the maze of stairs, closes, and cellars. Yet in these buildings the wealthiest and most elegant people in the country had apart-ments. Sweeps or messengers and odd-job men from the High-lands lived in the cellars, aristocrats or professional people on the first floor, shopkeepers and clerks on the higher floors, and poor skilled workmen in the attics.[2]

So conditioned by this small community were the townsfolk that their social life, even that of the cultivated, was very close. As late as the '90's, the first planned extension to the old High Street nucleus, Brown and Argyle Squares, south of the Castle ridge, formed "a little world of their own, and had their own Assembly-rooms, and society of an excellent quality, in some degree apart from the rest of Edinburgh". Brown Square, indeed, was occupied by the set who produced the *Mirror*, Scotland's *Spectator*: Henry Mackenzie, William Craig (later a judge), Lord Woodhouselee, the 'great' Dundas (when an advocate), Islay Campbell, and Jeannie Elliot of Minto, author of 'The Flooers o' the Forest'.[3] A man could live and die on that south side of the town without seeing the New Town to the north, beyond the pit of the Nor' Loch which became Princes Street Gardens after drainage. Adam Ferguson the historian's house at Sciennes, a couple of miles from the Town Cross, was called by the other *literati* 'Kamchatka'; and lawyers were alarmed that the move to the New Town would lose them their *clientèle*.[4]

Primitive conditions would by their nature throw people together. An Englishman observed of the narrow main street: "So great a crowd of people are nowhere else confined in so small a space, which makes their streets as much crowded every day as others are at a fair".[5] There was no piped water until

---

[1] Robert Chambers, *Traditions of Edinburgh* (Edinburgh & London: 1868), p. 13.
[2] Marx and Engels, *On Britain*, p. 68; Henry Grey Graham, *The Social Life of Scotland in the Eighteenth Century* (London: 1906), p. 85.
[3] Sir Walter Scott, *Provincial Antiquities and Picturesque Scenery of Scotland* (London: 1826), I, p. 75; James Grant, *Old and New Edinburgh* (London: 1882), II, pp. 270-1.
[4] Rae, *Life of Adam Smith*, p. 326; Chambers, *Traditions of Edinburgh*, p. 16.
[5] Graham, *Social Life of Scotland*, pp. 89-90, quoting the *Gentleman's Magazine* for 1766.

the '70's. Water was drawn from five public wells, which must thus have been great gathering points for the working-class.[1] The gregarious habit was so strong that the modern Exchange, begun in 1754, was for some time little frequented because "the merchants always chuse standing in the open street, exposed to all kinds of weather". Although their stance, the Cross, was removed from the Canongate (the eastward extension of the High Street) in 1765, the lawyer-historian of Edinburgh, Hugo Arnot, writing in 1779, observed that "Public proclamations continue to be made there. There also company daily resort, from one to 3 o'clock, for news, business, or meeting their acquaintances, nobody frequenting the exchange".[2] Before the Bank of Scotland was founded, even important business would be done in little back shops or pubs and hardly any elsewhere. In Glasgow this was so widespread that the Council had to rule that town funds would not be liable for expenses incurred in this way.[3]

This hugger-mugger living affected the vernacular poetry through the kind of popular culture—the network of institutions, habits of mind and behaviour, styles of expression—engendered by the compact town. The celebrations and gatherings which so fascinated the poets were bound to be enacted in the very midst of the city. Funerals and processions were elaborate shows; and the Company of Archers, in gorgeous costume, and (till the Union) Parliament paraded through the High Street. Leith Races, celebrated in Fergusson's poem of that name, was "a species of carnival to the citizens of Edinburgh". Every morning one town officer walked down to Leith with the 'City Purse' on a pole richly decked with flags and streamers, accompanied by the City Guard in full uniform and their drummer. Quacks and mountebanks put up stages in the High Street itself to sell remedies with comic patter; acrobats performed there; and quakers preached at the Cross to large audiences.[4] The Edinburgh of Ramsay and Fergusson recalls, not contemporary London, but the London of Shakespeare and Ben Jonson.[5]

The arts, too, were carried on amidst the people's daily life.

[1] Hugo Arnot, *The History of Edinburgh* (Edinburgh & London: 1779), p. 341.
[2] *Ibid.* p. 311; Thomas Pennant, *A Tour in Scotland* (Chester: 1769), p. 49; Arnot, *History of Edinburgh*, p. 303.
[3] Chambers, *Domestic Annals*, p. 129; Arnot, *History of Edinburgh*, p. 354; Eyre-Todd, *History of Glasgow*, III, p. 109.
[4] Arnot, *History of Edinburgh*, pp. 195, 395; Grant, *Old and New Edinburgh*, III, p. 269; Chambers, *Domestic Annals*, p. 262; *ibid.* pp. 467-8.
[5] The modernisation and compartmentalisation of London, a century before Edinburgh's, are well described by Ian Watt, *The Rise of the Novel* (London: 1957), p. 178.

For example, Fergusson himself had fun seeing how many sheets of ballads he could sell in two hours in the High Street, plying as a street singer.[1] Before the Musical Society was formed, gentlemen met weekly in a pub whose proprietor was a great lover of music, and a good singer of Scots songs, and played Handel and Corelli. In the great hall of Parliament House which was used as a common promenade, there were bookstalls against one wall, just as there were jewellers' booths against one wall of St Giles's Cathedral. The better bookshops were, like the coffee-houses of Dryden's and Addison's London, the centres of literary society. James Donaldson's shop was the resort of the wits of Edinburgh during the time of Boswell. The leading bookseller in the '70's and '80's, William Creech, made his shop a 'lounge' and held literary breakfasts at his house. Its situation near the Parliament House was convenient as so many of the literary men were lawyers. (In contrast, the New Town, as Lockhart complained, had for some years only one "great lounging bookshop", Blackwood's.)[2] Also, the comparative poverty of the place tended to keep amusements popular and informal. Theatre after theatre failed, out of all proportion to the population, because trade around the mid-century brought in so little that even "ordinary gentle-women, or the wives and daughters of shopkeepers or mechanics" were reluctant to go to the theatre unless they heard that it was packing for some performance; and their menfolk preferred the pubs.[3]

Such conditions affected literature quite directly. Scots town literature of this period is, like English, highly social, but in a way very different from *Spectator* prose or Augustan poetry— products of a metropolitan fashionable society which, as F. R. Leavis puts it, "thought of poetry in general as of something that ought to be social . . . as belonging to the province of manners".[4] Not a hint of 'correct' behaviour, of the cultivated manner and clever wit that belong to it, or indeed of a *conscious* code of any kind appears in the Scots work of that time. Its impulse, as has been suggested, comes directly out of the *mêlée* of common life; and this life was so formed that the bourgeoisie and ruling-class were not aloof from popular amusements any

[1] Sydney Goodsir Smith (ed.), *Robert Fergusson, 1750–1774* (London: 1952), pp. 23-4.
[2] Arnot, *History of Edinburgh*, p. 379 and n.; *ibid.* pp. 293, 297; Thomas Constable, *Archibald Constable and his Literary Correspondents* (Edinburgh: 1873), I, p. 537; J. G. Lockhart, *Peter's Letters to His Kinsfolk* (marked 3rd, really 1st, edition, Edinburgh 1819), I, pp. 122-3; *ibid.* p. 186.
[3] Arnot, *History of Edinburgh*, p. 373.
[4] F. R. Leavis, *Revaluation* (London: 1936), p. 112.

more than from the popular haunts. Ramsay's vernacular
'elegies' were modelled on cheap broadside-verse, yet at least
one of them was handed round in manuscript among the gentry
who were fellow-members of the Easy Club. Fergusson speaks
familiarly of the various kinds of sociable group, the popular
debating and drinking clubs, as an essential part of his town:

> *Siclike in* ROBINHOOD *debates,*
> *Whan twa chiels hae a pingle;*
> *E'en-now some couli gets his aits,*
> *An' dirt wi' words they mingle,*
> *Till up loups he, wi' diction fu',*
> *There's lang and dreech contesting;*
> *For now they're near the point in view;*
> *Now ten miles frae the question*
> *In hand that night.*

Fergusson was himself the 'Precentor'—seemingly the recognised wit, singer, reciter—of the Cape Club, whose members
included smiths and barbers as well as advocates and middle-
class men of letters.[1] In his 'The Daft-Days' drinking is evoked
in rough vernacular—"While round they gar the bicker roll".
Yet Lord Kames records that in *any* company, as late as 1730,
one common cup was used by everybody for the whole evening,
and it was thought fussy when people began to wish for separate
glasses. Likewise Ramsay writes as a poor workman in 'Maggy
Johnstoun':

> *When in our pouch we found some clinks,*
> *And took a turn o'er Bruntsfield Links.*

In fact the *habitués* of Maggy Johnstoun's howff included a
judge (Lord Cullen) and a "well-employed advocate". In
contrast the English clubs of the period were the preserve of the
upper classes, whether literary or political, and the aristocracy
were beginning to split off into their own exclusive societies
with their own premises.[2]

It is never easy precisely to define how such social conditions
—so broad, so mixed, so varying in their effect on individuals—
impinge on literature, or the writers of literature. But it is not
uncommon for lines of force and limitations in the society to set
broad limits which literature will be at least likely to keep to.

---

[1] 'Leith Races', *Poems*, II, p. 166; Hans Hecht, *Songs from David Herd's Manu-
scripts* (Edinburgh: 1904), pp. 37-8 (I owe this reference to Smith, *Robert Fergusson*,
pp. 22-3).
[2] Graham, *Social Life of Scotland*, p. 103; Ramsay, *Works*, I, p. 288; Chambers,
Domestic Annals, p. 534. Stephen, *English Literature and Society in the Eighteenth Century*, pp. 38-9.

We cannot account for all there is to Metaphysical poetry simply by referring to the make-up of the Court and country-house circles in which so much of it was written. Yet consider its kind of satirical wit, its mingled courtliness and indecency, the sophistication which is so conscious of itself, the close co-presence (in poems like Donne's 'Sunne Rising' and 'Canonization') of an intimate personal passion and a busy, mercenary, place-seeking Court *milieu*, felt as surrounding almost oppressively the personal life. These features show plainly enough the marks of the Stuart court, with its community of cultured nobility and arranged marriages, diplomats who were also scholars and poets, and officials living on perquisites. The style of the courtly poets—Wyatt, Raleigh, Donne, Carew, Herbert of Cherbury, Ben Jonson, Wotton—is both dignified and idiomatic, combining "the candour and naturalness of conversation among equals with the grace of a courtly society". When they are wittily amorous, they often (notably Carew) give the effect of vying with their fellows in the tradition of the elaborate compliment so ready to turn into indecency. Here again we see the marks of the reading-public or social set in which the poets functioned: gentlemen writing for gentlemen, circulating their work in manuscript, and certainly not exposing it for public sale.[1]

The richer the literature, the less straightforward is the problem of making out the process whereby social forces had their conditioning effects. At the very least, however, a precise knowledge of history can forbid those covertly idealising speculations or assumptions about past communities to which modern critics often succumb. John Speirs, for example, has argued that Fergusson's poetry is "fundamentally rustic": the "town community . . . was still distinctly rural in character and speech", its legal side superficial. According to Mr Speirs the rural affiliations come out in a poem such as 'The Rising of the Session':

> . . . *The wylie* writers, *rich as Croesus,*
> *Hurl frae the town in hackney chaises,*
> *For country cheer . . .*[2]

This by itself, however, might be no more rustic fundamentally than London professional men holidaying on their dairy farms in Sussex. Lockhart describes how the judges and advocates

---

[1] Full references for this account of English early 17th-century poetry are given in note 2.

[2] John Speirs, *The Scots Literary Tradition* (London: 1940), pp. 116-17.

prepared for their summer week-ends in the country at farm or villa, wearing gorgeous informal clothes in court on Saturday, their horses lined up in parade in the Parliament Close.[1] It is hard to see how such habits connect with the hurly-burly of common folk which gave Fergusson his impulse, especially as many farming lawyers of those days were of the new 'improving', scientific type. Lord Auchinleck, Boswell's father, was an early cultivator of root crops in the south-west. Cockburn of Ormiston, father of the great farming pioneer and a Lord Justice Clerk of Scotland, gave his tenants long leases enabling them to drain and hedge their ground. Sir James Montgomery, a Lord Advocate, was an improver of crops and livestock and sponsored a Bill to alter the law of entail in favour of improvers. Lord Kames, author of the *Elements of Criticism*, experimented in every branch of farming, especially root vegetables, green crops, sown grass, summer fallowing, and drainage, and wrote an expert book on these subjects. An East Lothian advocate, Michael Menzies, invented a threshing machine.[2] Such legal landowners hardly belonged to the ancient country round Mr Speirs apparently has in mind. One judge, Lord Hermand, is described by Cockburn as spending whole days on his farm hoeing in his old clothes, but he was famous for his eccentrically broad and old-fashioned ways.[3] What we know of community life in the 17th and 18th centuries amounts to a strong presumption that the Edinburgh *town* community was, by itself, the natural basis for poetry such as Ramsay and Fergusson's. Certainly it is striking that their comedy should be so akin to the country-living Burns's. But that is surely because in Scotand at that time even the central cities were villagey in their smallness, their closeness, and their informal, rough-and-ready social habits.

We must also remember that old Edinburgh was in many ways a nasty warren, and so close-packed that none could get away from it. The sociable wells and stairheads made inevitably for filth. Workmen and lords alike had heaps of slops and excrement on the landings outside their flats; and shopkeepers sometimes had to cut a passage from shop door to street through piles of garbage. Much of the most brutal life of the place was

[1] *Peter's Letters to his Kinsfolk*, I, pp. 122-3.
[2] Chambers, *Domestic Annals*, p. 503; James E. Handley, *Scottish Farming in the Eighteenth Century* (London: 1953), pp. 111, 147 and n. 1, 202 n. 1; A. F. Tytler, *Memoir of the Life and Writings of the Hon. Henry Home of Kames* (Edinburgh: 1807), II, pp. 28-30 and n.; Handley, *Scottish Farming*, pp. 155-7, 138-41.
[3] Cockburn, *Memorials of his Time* (op. cit.), p. 132.

out there in the main streets. One of the marts, the Grassmarket, is succinctly called by Pennant (who toured in 1767) the place "where cattle are sold, and criminals executed"; and there are descriptions of the crowds buying and selling farm produce at one end of the Market while they watched the gallows being put up at the other. Yet in spite of the "inconvenience, and exceeding nastiness" of the market places, new ones were not begun till 1774.[1] At the end of the 17th century (fifteen years before Ramsay started to write), specimens were provided for the early anatomy classes from "unclaimed bodies of persons dying in the streets". In 1700 floggings were carried out at several points on the High Street; in 1709 there were beheadings at the great gathering-place, the Cross; and petty offenders stood in the jougs and pillory at the Tron. Cock-fighting on the streets had to be prohibited by the Town Council to stop the disturbances it caused. Although so much of the social life centred in the pubs, their "equivocal character" made it unwise for women of "delicacy and propriety" to go into them.[2] Scotland still suffers from the lack of a natural, inte-grated social life (in comparison with, for example, France and England) because there are so few pubs where women are welcomed on equal terms with the men.

Scott had good reason to know the miserable side of Old Town life—his parents lost four sons and two daughters in seven years, probably because the College Wynd at the foot of the Canongate, where they had their house, was so insanitary. Hence, perhaps, the actuality of his description, in *Provincial Antiquities*, of the wear and tear of that old close life. "Each inhabitable space was crowded like the under deck of a ship. Sickness had no nook of quiet, affliction no retreat for solitary indulgence." He emphasises the darkness of the interiors; the bother and labour for the porters who had to carry all water up many flights of stairs; and the lack of space for furniture in the cramped rooms.[3]

The buoyant energy which tided people through such a life is felt in the non-stop flow of action and the caricaturing idiom, hearty and familiar, of the vernacular poetry. But we must equally note the wear and tear, the loss and curtailment

[1] *Tour in Scotland*, p. 54; *Chambers's Edinburgh Journal* (Edinburgh & London: 1833), Vol. 1, No. 2, p. 11; Arnot, *History of Edinburgh*, p. 528.
[2] Chambers, *Domestic Annals*, p. 106; *ibid.* pp. 59, 327, 222, and 372; Arnot, *History of Edinburgh*, p. 195; *ibid.* p. 354.
[3] J. G. Lockhart, *Memoirs of the Life of Sir Walter Scott, Bart.* (Edinburgh: 1837), I, pp. 78-9; Scott, *Provincial Antiquities*, I, p. 73.

of life, and the brutal attitudes to one another inevitable in such
conditions. Much of the action in poems such as Ramsay's
'Christis Kirk', Fergusson's 'The King's Birth-Day in Edinburgh' or 'Hallow Fair', is horse-play, gross and dirty, and the
poet's attitude is to revel in the discomfiture of the butt who
falls down in the gutter or gets a swipe from a dead cat. Such is
the counterpart of a life in which the festivities at Leith Races
ended in a "promiscuous free fight" all up and down Leith
Walk as the crowds returned to Edinburgh on the last evening
of race week.[1] The real destructiveness and brutality of such a
life is, of course, lost sight of in Fergusson's or the old anonymous
poets' kind of rollicking comedy.

Such conditions were bound to cause a recoil. For one thing,
the bourgeois men of letters—the spokesmen of the 'polite'
culture which grew up as the century wore on—themselves
lived on top of the dirt and confusion. Grant, the historian of
Edinburgh, remarks that "within the narrow compass of this
wynd [the College Wynd, Scott's birthplace] . . . were representatives of nearly every order of society, sufficient for a whole
series of his Waverly novels". This also meant that there was a
filthy byre at the foot of the street (not far from the University),
and a well-known town idiot, Daft Bailie Duff, died in a "little
den" there, in 1788.[2] Yet late in the century the Cowgate, for
example, was still reckoned an aristocratic locality. Henry
Mackenzie, connected with the landed upper-class, was born
in a wynd off the Cowgate, and later lived with his wife and
family in a land at the junction of the Cowgate and the Grassmarket. Hume wrote his *History of England* in a land in the
Canongate before moving to James's Court in the Lawnmarket
(the continuation of the High Street towards the Castle), where
Boswell also lived. William Robertson, the historian and leader
of the Moderate clergy, lived in the Principal's house in the
College, near the foot of the Canongate. His house was stormed
by mobs rioting against the 1779 Bill to repeal the Catholic
Penal Laws, his library was burned, and he had to take refuge
in the Castle. Yet well on in the century the Canongate was still
the fashionable quarter for "the better aristocracy of letters
and science", including Adam Smith, Lord Kames, Lord
Hailes, Cullen, Dugald Stewart, Lord Monboddo, and Sir John
Dalrymple.[3]

[1] Grant, *Old and New Edinburgh*, III, p. 269.   [2] *Ibid.* II, p. 255.
[3] *The Book of the Old Edinburgh Club* (Edinburgh: 1925), XIV, p. 135: compare
Cockburn's description of elegant company frequenting the Cowgate, *Memorials of*

Such conditions were bound to force them out. When the English poet Rogers visited Edinburgh in 1789, Adam Smith told him that the Old Town "deserved little notice"—it had a bad name for filth, and he himself wanted to move to George Square (another of the model extensions to the south). Hugh Blair, the Moderate minister and fashionable writer on rhetoric, moved from the Lawnmarket to Argyle Square; Robertson moved to Grange (a near-rural district where the law lords built their villas, between Edinburgh and the Pentland Hills), for his health, not long before he died; and Hume died in the house he had built himself in St Andrew Square, then the most fashionable quarter of the New Town. St David's Street, still the name of the connection between the Square and Princes Street, is supposed to have got its name from a jibe chalked by a town humorist on the notorious atheist's front door.[1]

The *literati* thus participated in a general change. The town was becoming conscious of its obligations as a capital. By the 1780's hotels were being built to replace the "noisy, dirty, and incommodious" pubs in which travellers of all ranks had lodged like waggoners or carriers. Tradesmen's daughters "blushed to be seen in a market".[2] A new ideal of civic dignity came to the fore. The Exchange was founded to fill the want of "public buildings necessary for accommodating those societies which assemble in populous cities, to direct the business of the country, and provide for its general welfare". "Proper accommodation" was wanted for the Musical Society, it being "for the interest of the town to give countenance for such polite amusements as might encourage strangers of rank to reside in the city".[3] The final outcome was a clean split in the said city, for the New Town was not a plan for Edinburgh as a whole. The ruling-class simply moved out into their "brilliant aristocratic quarter" on the other side of the Nor' Loch (so grand that some at first feared it would be impracticably expensive) and left the Old Town to become, in the 19th century, a crammed slum of

---

His Time, p. 29; Grant, *Old and New Edinburgh*, I, p. 120; *ibid.* I, p. 97; *ibid.* I, p. 261; John Kay, *Original Portraits*, with Biographical Sketches (edition Edinburgh: 1877), I, p. 93; Rae, *Life of Adam Smith*, p. 325.

[1] Rae, *Life of Adam Smith*, p. 417; Grant, *Old and New Edinburgh*, I, p. 97; *ibid.* II, p. 271; Dugald Stewart, *The Life and Writings of William Robertson*, given before the Royal Society of Edinburgh, 1801, quoted from Robertson, *History of Scotland* (London, 12th ed.), I, p. 131; Ernest Campbell Mossner, *The Life of David Hume* (London: 1954), pp. 562-3, 603.

[2] Arnot, *History of Edinburgh*, p. 352; William Creech, *Edinburgh Fugitive Pieces* (Edinburgh: 1815), p. 92; *ibid.* p. 111.

[3] Arnot, *History of Edinburgh*, p. 311; *Book of the Old Edinburgh Club* (1933), XIX, p. 56.

80,000 people, living in quarters meant for nearer 30,000.[1] At precisely the same period Edinburgh ceased to have its own literature. Scott, living in the New Town, looked out to the whole of the country for his subject-matter; and the Edinburgh of his novels is either historical, intelligently so, as in *The Heart of Midlothian*, or indulged in for its bygone charm, as in *The Chronicles of the Canongate*. Ramsay and Fergusson had written out of the thick of Edinburgh. After the removal of the cultivated class from the Old Town, contemporary 'socialness' entirely ceases to figure in Scots literature. In this case the affiliations of literature and social change were decisive.

[1] Chambers, *Traditions of Edinburgh*, p. 16; Marx and Engels, *On Britain*, p. 67. For details of Edinburgh's changing population see note 3.

CHAPTER II

The Establishment of 'Polite' Culture

It is curious to remark that Scotland, so full of writers, had no Scottish culture. . . . Hume was too rich a man to borrow; and perhaps he reacted on the French more than he was acted on by them; but neither had he aught to do with Scotland; Edinburgh, equally with La Flèche, was but the lodging and laboratory, in which he not so much morally *lived*, as metaphysically *investigated*. Never, perhaps, was there a class of writers so clear and well-ordered, yet so totally destitute, to all appearance, of any patriotic affection, nay, of any human affection whatever.—THOMAS CARLYLE, *Burns*.

THE 18th-century *literati*—David Hume, Adam Smith, and their set—belong to the first intelligentsia that grew up in modern Scotland. As a class they strove to cultivate 'politeness', 'elegance', depreciation of the 'low', to a peculiarly intensive degree, for they were themselves anxious to get clear of the backward life which pressed them so close. The town culture of Edinburgh had not produced (it is scarcely surprising) any literature as socially adult or fine as its English equivalent. The Augustan-type culture which was enthroned in the New Town was nothing if not adult; its members believed strongly in the intellectual and mannerly code of the 18th-century gentleman. What, then, was responsible for its failure to develop its own imaginative literature—not, of course, in its raw days, but later? What can its potentialities have been?

The intelligentsia of the Scottish capital, in the generation of Hume, Smith, and the Moderate clergy, and again in the generation of Jeffrey, Cockburn, and Scott—the young Whigs of the *Edinburgh Review* and the Romantic Tories—formed *milieux* which were powerful as centres of literary culture, and also highly conscious of their prestige. Alexander Carlyle, the urbane Moderate minister of Inveresk (a few miles east of the capital), quotes approvingly in his *Autobiography* (a key document of this group of men) a remark by James Edgar, one of the Dundas family, who refused an offer to sit with a club of *literati* in Paris "as he had a club at Edinburgh, with whom he dined weekly, composed, he believed, of the ablest men in Europe".[1] We have already mentioned Hume's claim that the Scots were "the people most distinguished for Literature in

---

[1] *The Autobiography of Dr Alexander Carlyle of Inveresk, 1722–1805*, ed. John Hill Burton (London & Edinburgh, 1910), p. 442.

Europe" in spite of heavy social and political impediments. This Edinburgh, indeed, prided itself on having advantages over the more famous London milieu. Carlyle said of the Select Society, a semi-sociable, semi-learned gathering of the Edinburgh intelligentsia: "It was those meetings in particular that rubbed off all corners, as we call it, by collision, and made the *literati* of Edinburgh less captious and pedantic than they were elsewhere". Similarly, Henry Mackenzie disapproved of the Londoners' "prize-fighting of wit"—a fair comment on the 'Scriblerus' activities of Pope and Swift—which he explains on the grounds that their literary circle was "a caste separate from the ordinary professions and habits of common life. They were traders in talent and learning . . . with a jealousy of competition which prevented their enjoying, as much as otherwise they might, any excellence in their competitors".[1] That London literary world does surely strike us now as having been quite oppressive in its intensely inbred concern with a small range of disputes and personalities; and Pope himself felt this. There is more than a superior pose of detachment in the opening of the 'Epistle to Dr Arbuthnot':

> P. *Shut, shut the door, good John! fatigued, I said;*
> *Tie up the knocker, say I'm sick, I'm dead.*
> *The Dog-star rages! nay 'tis past a doubt,*
> *All Bedlam, or Parnassus, is let out:*
> *Fire in each eye, and papers in each hand,*
> *They rave, recite, and madden round the land,*

or in the heartfelt lines from the first 'Imitation of Horace':

> *. . . The world beside may murmur, or commend.*
> *Know, all the distant din that world can keep,*
> *Rolls o'er my grotto, and but soothes my sleep.*
> *There, my retreat the best companions grace,*
> *Chiefs out of war, and statesmen out of place. . . .*[2]

At the same time there are several comments by the Scotsmen which suggest that they may have been stung by Johnson's notorious attitude to Scotland and Scotsmen,[3] for they regularly stress

[1] *Autobiography*, p. 312; Mackenzie, *Life of John Home* (the Moderate minister who wrote the tragedy *Douglas*), given to the Royal Society of Edinburgh, 1812 (Edinburgh: 1822), pp. 22-4.
[2] Alexander Pope, *Collected Poems* (Everyman ed., London: 1924), pp. 253, 268-9.
[3] Not only the jokes in the *Dictionary*. Boswell records remarks of his on John Campbell, a minor Scottish writer settled in London: "'I used to go pretty often to Campbell's on a Sunday evening, till I began to consider that the shoals of Scotchmen who flocked about him might probably say, when anything of mine was well done, "Ay, ay, he has learnt this of Cawmell!"' "—*Life of Samuel Johnson*, ed. William Wallace (Edinburgh: 1892), p. 119.

his eccentricity and miss his rare distinction of character and mind. Scott, for example, is evidently aiming at the correct genteel opinion when he says in his *Lives of the Novelists* that Johnson was comparatively a "stranger to the higher society in which such restraint became necessary".[1] The Scottish *milieu* was likewise obtuse to its own Hume, blandly assuming that his scepticism about, for example, causality and revealed religion were mere indiscretions in an otherwise decent and creditable man of letters.[2] It is quite typical of their rather second-hand desire to conform and do the right thing that they should have been unequal to the demands of original men.

We must also remember that this Edinburgh had real, distinctive virtues. In the first place, Mackenzie is right in saying that Scottish men of letters did not form a 'caste' separate from the ordinary professions. Unlike such English literary men as Dryden, Pope, and Johnson, the Scotsmen, e.g. Hume, Smith, Robertson, Mackenzie, Jeffrey, and Scott, tended to have a professional job, often legal, in addition to their writing; and in the case of Smith, Robertson, Jeffrey, and Scott, at least, the jobs were full-time and not (as with Addison or Gibbon) little more than sinecures. An aspect of this is that they devoted their intellectual gifts to bettering the nation in a range of fields much wider than the arts (and more useful than the belles-lettres of some of them). The Select Society, the main forum of that first generation of Edinburgh intellectuals, helped the new drive to economic improvement by offering prizes for, among other things, the best samples of farm produce and rags for paper-making and for the best papers on physics and improvements in husbandry; and the Highland Society, whose *Transactions* Mackenzie edited, carried out an enquiry into possible improvements in the farming, fisheries, trade, manufactures, and communications of the Highlands and the preservation of the Gaelic language, poetry, and music.[3] It is only regrettable that these latter projects remained a pastime for gentlemen, and were never implemented. Again, the *Edinburgh Review*'s effective interests did not stop at books. Its practical

[1] World's Classics ed. (London: 1906), p. 160. Compare Henry Mackenzie, *Anecdotes and Egotisms*, ed. H. W. Thompson (Oxford: 1927), pp. 181, 189; and John Ramsay of Ochtertyre, *Scotland and Scotsmen in the Eighteenth Century*, ed. Alexander Allardyce (Edinburgh & London: 1888), I, p. 174.
[2] E.g. Ramsay, *Scotland and Scotsmen*, I, pp. 466-7; Mackenzie, *Life of Home*, p. 20; Carlyle, *Autobiography*, pp. 288-9.
[3] Hume, *Letters*, I, p. 219; Davis D. McElroy, unpublished Ph.D. thesis (University of Edinburgh: 1952), *The Literary Clubs and Societies of Eighteenth Century Scotland* and their influence on literary productions in the period from 1700 to 1800, pp. 146-8, 155-6 and n. 2.

function is indicated in a letter of Cockburn's on the move in
the 1820's to reform jury selection, then heavily weighted
towards getting a conviction whenever the public prosecutor
wanted it. Cockburn decided that the best place to print an
account of the constitution and practice of the Court of Justi-
ciary and of the usefulness of the Bill would be the *Review* (he is
writing to Kennedy, the M.P. who introduced the Bill):
". . . even though you fail this time, the very discussion is of
great use—especially as it prevents the people here from getting
habituated to their present horrid system . . ." [1] This is the
place to say that Cockburn is himself the flower of this ruling-
class culture. As we read through the range of his journals and
memoirs (his *Memorials*, his *Journals*, his *Life of Jeffrey*, and his
Circuit Journeys), there seems to be no issue or human type
(inside his social range) on which he does not make a central
comment, defined with a trenchant good-sense worthy of
Johnson. A notable instance is his passage in his journal for
March 6, 1847, arguing that the law of entail needs reform:

> Capital is clamorous for earth. A great majority of heirs of
> entail, fretted and degraded by debt, pant for emancipation;
> and our plan of entails, which allows every worm of the day
> to torment the most distant generations with the most
> pernicious conditions, is indefensible. Nothing can justify
> the eternising of individual caprice over the fixed national
> property . . . The result is that something like the English
> system of entails, limited to visible mortal interests, will
> probably be adopted; but not at once, or on principle or
> system. This will be thought too bold. The plan of only
> slackening the chains over the tight parts will be adopted,
> till, the popular mind being made up and irritated by delay,
> the whole system will, in some unexpected moment, dis-
> appear . . . What the Scotch call "*a yird hunger*" is a very
> strong passion. The tradesman's dream over the counter is of
> land; and if he once gets the acres, a single month of them,
> with "esquire", changes his nature. He is a laird, and his
> dreams are of the country gentleman. This is the natural
> aristocracy of land, and it needs no go-cart to help it. [2]

That prose, in the remarkably intense imagery and flow of
pointed speech—fusing the shrewdness of an experienced
lawyer and administrator with an intelligent specialist's
passion for his subject and a concern for humane law—shows

---

[1] *Letters Chiefly Connected with the Affairs of Scotland*, from Henry Cockburn to
Thomas Kennedy, M.P. (London: 1874), pp. 16-17.
[2] *Journal of Henry Cockburn*, 1831–1854 (Edinburgh: 1874), II, pp. 170-1.

at its best a class whose public life gave room for the mature and varied interests of its outstanding men.

Secondly, as is well known, that Edinburgh was rich in clubs and societies through which its ideas could be canvassed and its projects furthered. Detail and personalities are hardly necessary;[1] it will be enough to cite two statements of faith in what societies could do. Jeffrey wrote to a *Review* contributor, the economist Francis Horner, that the Friday Club "promises to unite the literature of the place more effectually and extensively than anything else"; and Cockburn wrote, on being engaged by the Edinburgh students to take up their case against the Senatus who were expelling debating societies from the University:

> Literary societies of students which have met academically for thirty or fifty years, are now in taverns. . . . I have done everything and convinced everybody, except some reptile of the Town Council, through whom the atrocity still endures . . . I have told the Provost plainly that you [Thomas Kennedy], Jeffrey, Murray, Palmerston, Lansdowne, and Brougham, were all educated in Societies. . . .[2]

The same names figure again and again in these societies, for the Scottish intelligentsia made a very compact group. This was an advantage of their small cities. Scott says that the small-scale Edinburgh society meant that people could meet at short notice, and the closeness of neighbours to each other "gave a tone of social enjoyment to the whole system". He also mentions the low income on which a family could keep up a "very creditable rank in society", and William Robertson makes the same claim: "You know with what ease women of a middling fortune mingle with good company in Edinburgh; how impossible that is in London; and even how great the expence is of their having any proper society at all".[3] According to Lockhart an advantage for literature was that "No book can be published there [in Edinburgh, around 1819], and totally neglected. In so small a town, in spite of the quantity of books published in it, the publication of a new book is quite sure to attract the attention of some person, and if it has the least interest, to be talked of in company." An example of this is

---

[1] Mr McElroy has left little to discover regarding the habits of meeting, membership, and aims (on paper) of these clubs and societies.

[2] Henry Cockburn, *Life of Lord Jeffrey* (Edinburgh: 1852), I, p. 147; *Letters . . . Affairs of Scotland*, p. 440.

[3] Scott, *Provincial Antiquities*, p. 74: ibid. pp. 74 and (figures of income) 82; Dugald Stewart, *Life of Robertson* (*op. cit.*), p. 48.

Robert Chambers's *Traditions of Edinburgh*: no sooner had he, then a literary novice, brought out the first edition than men of letters such as Scott, Mackenzie, and John Wilson ('Christopher North') rallied round, with typical patriotism for their town, and supplied him with further sources and information on 'old Edinburgh'.[1]

Finally, these *milieux* had their own ethos or community outlook, one seemingly representative of Scottish minds at that time. Visitors to Henry Mackenzie regularly found that he had a sharp wit—not at all what they had expected of an Edinburgh 'man of feeling'. Cockburn writes:

> Strangers used to fancy that he must be a pensive sentimental Harley; whereas he was far better—a hard headed practical man, as full of worldly wisdom as most of his fictitious characters are devoid of it; and this without in the least impairing the affectionate softness of his heart. In person he was thin, shrivelled and yellow, kiln-dried, with something when seen in profile, of the clever wicked look of Voltaire.[2]

Again, Hume wrote from Fontainebleau in 1763 yearning for "the plain roughness of the Poker [a club comprising his set], and particularly the sharpness of Dr Jardine, to correct and qualify so much lusciousness". Although in his writings 'politeness' (in one place "mutual deference and civility") is to him so important an ideal that it can even stand for something like 'culture' or 'civilisation', he yet feels a need for the Scottish intellectual downrightness.[3] The habit of taking up arguments directly, and often literally, even in what is meant to be polite conversation seems to me typically Scottish;[4] but in that Edinburgh it was perhaps the lawyers who were specially responsible for it. The Faculty of Advocates (which around the turn of the century had many members with poor practices, waiting for the Tory monopoly to break down) formed the "chief community of loungers and talkers in Edinburgh"; and we have some close descriptions of the talk whose tone they set.

---

[1] Lockhart, *Peter's Letters to his Kinsfolk*, II, p. 167; *Memoir of Robert Chambers* (*op. cit.*), pp. 176-83.

[2] *Memorials*, p. 265; see also Lockhart, *Life and Letters*, by Andrew Lang (London: 1897), I, pp. 302-3, and *The Journal of Sir Walter Scott* (Edinburgh: 1890), I, p. 35.

[3] *Letters*, I, pp. 410-11; 'Of the Rise and Progress of the Arts and Sciences', *Essays, Moral, Political, and Literary* in *Philosophical Works* (Boston and Edinburgh: 1854), III, pp. 127, 130, 136.

[4] See Yeats's account of John Davidson's introduction to the Rhymers Club—that group of sensitive '90's poets—of four Scotsmen who "excelled in arguments"; *Autobiographies* (London: 1955), pp. 316-18.

Scott writes of Sir Samuel Shepherd, "There is a neatness and precision, a closeness and truth, in the tone of his conversation, which shows what a lawyer he must have been"; and Lockhart writes of the younger set in the days of the *Edinburgh Review*:

> The best table-talk of Edinburgh was, and probably still is, in a very great measure made up of brilliant disquisition—such as might be transformed without alteration to a professor's note-book, or the pages of a critical Review—and of sharp word-catchings, ingenious thrusting and parrying of dialectics, and all the quips and quibblets of bar pleading.[1]

Such passages suggest that the law life was less superficial to the town than Mr Speirs makes out.[2]

Such a bent for talk must have helped engender the periodical writing of which Edinburgh was then so influential a centre (the base at first of both leading British reviews, the *Edinburgh* and the *Quarterly*), for what the reviews retailed was the opinions, on the books and events of the day, of the cultured gentlemen, an amateur of many subjects, with a mind equipped and sharpened by public life. I have stressed the lawyerly *idiom* because it might seem to be the kind of expression or style native to that society which could have been put to use in a literature of its own. In fact such a literature did not emerge. Histories, philosophies, sermons, treatises were produced in plenty, and supplied the country with much of its standard serious reading. But of the more personal, imaginative kinds of writing, giving expression to the more intimate values and the day-to-day living of that educated class, there is next to nothing. There is no Pope to take up the cultivated talk into his style of poetic wit—creating rich poetry out of such materials as the arts, institutions, and general environment of his class and capable of being imaginatively inspired by the economic order which it controlled (as at the close of his fourth 'Moral Essay'). There is not even an Addison to turn the attitudes of the educated classes into a neat (or glib) prose currency. Partly this may have been because this currency sufficed Scotsmen too, as we can see by the great popularity of the *Spectator*. In the early 18th century, when Perthshire gentlemen met after church to discuss the news of the week, the *Spectator* was read over as closely as the newspapers (it was staple reading through-

---

[1] Lockhart, *Peter's Letters*, I, p. 214; Scott, *Journal*, I, p. 57; Lockhart, *Life of Scott*, IV, pp. 152-3.
[2] See Chapter I, p. 34.

out the country); and at the end of the century Addison's works were still the most popular English items in the Edinburgh bookshops and auction rooms.[1] But there seem also to have been peculiarities in the Scottish situation itself which damped down creative responses to it.

The main force causing this was probably language—the confusing transition from Scots to English, which affected personally both Hume and Scott. In this chapter we must consider rather the way in which drive to correctness of culture tended to overlay the true experience of the country. Some such process was almost bound to overtake a small country living in the shadow of England. Hume himself, in the essay 'Of the Rise and Progress of the Arts and Sciences', defines the danger (though without reference to Scotland) of having "the arts imported from their neighbours in too great perfection"; he instances the Italianising of English painting, and the prestige of French hindering the German and other northern nations from cultivating their own language.[2] Ramsay of Ochtertyre raises the specifically Scottish question when he speculates on what might have been gained for literature if we had kept our independence. He remembers conversing with a member of the Union Parliament who spoke the old upper-class Scots that "differed as much from the common dialect as the language of St James's from that of Thames Street", and he comments: "Had we retained a Court and Parliament of our own, the tongues of the two sister kingdoms would, indeed, have differed like the Castilian and the Portuguese; but each would have had its own classics, not in a single branch, but in the whole circle of literature".[3] That is only an 'if'. But in several places we can see inhibition, arising from consciousness of being provincial, actually at work. Robert Chambers wrote in a collection of his editorials from *Chambers's Journal*: "These papers were written under some difficulties, particularly those of a provincial situation . . ."—the Scottish critic of manners felt he had no native source or authority to appeal to. Amongst the cultivated classes, the anxious urge to refine led almost inevitably to conscious modelling on England, in spite of the differing deeper experience of the countries. Lord

[1] Hurd's *Addison*, quoted by Alexandre Beljame, *Men of Letters and the English Public in the Eighteenth Century* (edition London: 1948), p. 274 n. For the Scottish book sales see below, Chapter VII, p. 210.

[2] *Essays (op. cit.)*, p. 148.

[3] Letter to James Currie, printed in Currie (ed.), *The Works of Robert Burns* (London: 1800), I, pp. 280-2.

Woodhouselee, of the *Mirror* set, assumed that London was the only conceivable cultivated milieu:

> The habits of polite life, and the subjects of fashionable conversation, were become familiar at this time to the citizens of Edinburgh, from the periodical papers of Addison and Steele; and the wits of Balfour's Coffee-house [the names he gives include three of the leading contributors of Scots songs to Ramsay's *Tea Table Miscellany*] . . . were a miniature of the society to be met with at Will's and Button's.[1]

"The habits", "the subjects"—Lord Woodhouselee assumes that there is one correct code, which should be practised by the best circles in whatever country. Lockhart comes close to the actual behaviour involved in this modelling process:

> . . . the Dandies of the North are chiefly of the imitative description. They want that boldness of character, and strength of outline which distinguish their more accomplished prototypes in the South. They have none of that redeeming elegance—that visible consciousness of superior bon-ton— that calm and nonchalant assurance of manner—that complacent look of contemptuous self-approbation. . . .[2]

My point is not of course that it was a positive, hampering deficiency in Scottish culture that it lacked smooth men-about-town but that, being rather preoccupied with such *politesse*, it lacked a proper self-sufficiency and was condemned to self-consciousness, forcing, and wishful thinking in its aspiration to be 'polite'. The 'politeness' of the imitative dandies might afford butts for the supercilious, thinly Augustan criticism of manners in the *Mirror* and *Lounger* (Scotland's *Tatler* and *Spectator*) but it could hardly have gone to feed any such *ideal* of urbane civilisation as gave character to Augustan literature in England. In the final *Mirror* essay Mackenzie mentions disadvantages of that very Edinburgh compactness as though they had seriously jeopardised his kind of journalism. A wit, he says, cannot have the prestige to succeed because his audience all know him too well to take him as any kind of authority; and Edinburgh as a place does not have the *cachet* of a London:

> With us, besides the danger of personal application, these local characters and public places are hardly various enough for the subject, or important enough for the dignity of writing. There is a sort of classic privilege in the very name of places

---

[1] *Memoir of Robert Chambers*, p. 9; Allan Ramsay, Works (essay on his 'Genius', by Woodhouselee), I, p. 49.   [2] *Peter's Letters*, III, pp. 113-15.

in *London*, which does not extend to those of *Edinburgh*. The *Canongate* is almost as long as the *Strand*, but it will not bear the comparison upon paper; and *Blackfriars-wynd* can never vie with *Drury-lane* in point of sound. . . .

Mackenzie might have had an unusual inferiority complex, yet that is what he writes in a paper offered to the *literati* of his own town, and he does say clearly that he has suffered from an unreceptive public: "Hence the fastidiousness with which, in a place so narrow as *Edinburgh*, home productions are commonly received; which, if they are grave, are pronounced dull; if pathetic, are called unnatural; if ludicrous, are termed low".[1] We might have lost little if we had had no *Mirror*, it is true, yet any modern culture wants its own moral critiques, and these can, too, stimulate a native novel, as in England. This Scotland lacked till late on, and when it finally came with a rush, it was preoccupied with the past.[2]

The split between the standpoint of the cultivated Scotsman and the mass of life in his country is nowhere more overt than in this attitude to the past. Any country wants to expand and to clear its feet of ancient miseries, but in Scotland this meant that a great deal in recent history had to be disowned or censored away because it was so coarse and violent and its mark still so deeply felt. Even one of the Covenanting ministers, Cargill, had to warn his flock, with the experiences of the 17th century fresh in their memories, against making a cult of 'sufferings for the testimony'—"whoever rested upon them would have a cald Coal to blow at in the end"; and in the 18th century, once Presbyterian was Established, we find a minister hoping that his congregation do not find themselves regretting the past stirring days when their religion was on trial.[3] As late as Burns's day this past had its effects in Ayrshire. His friend Gavin Hamilton, who was hounded by the Kirk Session for breaking the Sabbath, was anyway suspect in the neighbourhood for his descent from an Episcopalian curate who had helped to bring the Highland Host into the district to hunt Presbyterians late in Charles II's reign. This was remembered against him in a district supposed to have only recently recovered from this savage plundering. And Burns's father, an incomer to Ayrshire from the North-east (Kincardineshire) and

---

[1] *The Mirror*, No. 110 (Edinburgh & London: 1783), III, pp. 317-18, 316.
[2] See below, Chapters V-VII.
[3] Patrick Walker, *Biographia Presbyteriana* (edition Edinburgh: 1827), II, p. 31; W. L. Mathieson, *The Awakening of Scotland* (Glasgow: 1910), p. 235.

rather stately and reserved in manner, was suspiciously received in the South-west. The community there got at him by rumouring that he had been 'out'—with the Jacobite army —during the 'Forty-five.[1]

Such is the friction between the sectors of a nation left by civil war. As a result, Scotsmen wished urgently for peace, order, civility—a polite civilisation. It is a reaction equivalent to England's in the 17th century. Men such as Falkland and Chillingworth—the humanist aristocrats and preachers of the Great Tew milieu—were driven by sectarian bigotry and the Civil War to form an ideal of sceptical detachment and, before all things, tolerance. This reaction seems to have been a seed of that rational deism and general esteem for order which were at the core of the 18th-century Augustan ethos.[2] Scottish Augustanism did learn from England; but it would hardly have turned that way had it not been for social pressures inside itself similar to the English. Just as Falkland disliked what he called "great mutations", so the Earl of Mar hoped that the Union of 1707 would enable Scotsmen "to live at peace and ease, and mind their affairs and the improvement of their country—a much better employment than in the politics".[3] The country, broken up by war and persecutions, wanted to consolidate and modernise itself in peace; and it was typical that the 'Forty-five should have been followed by a wave of pamphlets, subscriptions, and projects for the improvement of the capital.[4] Robert Chambers, in his essay 'A Trait in Public Affairs', was content that Scotland should get a little attention from the southern newspapers and be just a "tax-fertile appanage of the British crown which gives no trouble". He was satisfied with the silent, uneventful "progress in the materials by which a people are supported, and in their ideas, feelings and manners . . . more important to it than victories in stricken fields, or struggled for the change of dynasties". He was glad to end his *Domestic Annals* on an event "in which we find the associations

---

[1] J. G. Lockhart, *The Life of Robert Burns*, revised by W. Scott Douglas (London: 1882), pp. 56-7; Currie, *Works of Burns*, I, p. 81.

[2] There are illuminating passages on this phase of English history in Matthew Arnold's 'Falkland', which quotes extensively from Clarendon: *Mixed Essays* (London: 1879), esp. pp. 214-15, 218, 223, 230-1, 234; Marjorie Cox, in *From Donne to Marvell* (*op. cit.*), pp. 31-2; and in Trevelyan, *England Under the Stuarts*, which shows how to some extent the Augustan belief in order and urbanity was merely a paper ideal (*op. cit.* pp. 475-6).

[3] Arnold, 'Falkland', p. 230; H. W. Meikle, *Scotland and the French Revolution* (Glasgow: 1912), p. xvii. See also H. T. Buckle, *Introduction to the History of Civilisation in England*, ed. J. M. Robertson (London: 1904), pp. 724 and n., 733, for further details of this new ambition.   [4] Arnot, *History of Edinburgh*, p. 231.

of the lawless times of the Highlands inosculating with the industrial proceedings of a happier age".[1] Although this points to the same complacency in face of the misery, exploitation, and economic disasters of the 19th century as disfigured the journal he published for the good of the working classes,[2] he is, nevertheless, obviously quite right to say that the settlement achieved in the 18th century was for the good of the country.

This same recoil from disorder seems, however, to have emasculated the literary culture. The prevailing outlook and taste were tamely genteel. The *Quarterly Review* took exception to Scott's *Lord of the Isles* because it imitated the "rude vehemence of barbarous chiefs"; and Jeffrey likewise objected to *The Lay of the Last Minstrel* for its

introduction . . . of those worthies who
> Sought the beeves that made their broth,
> In Scotland and in England both,

into a poem which has any pretensions to seriousness or dignity. The ancient metrical romance might have admitted these homely personalities; but the present age will not endure them: and Mr Scott must either sacrifice his Border prejudices, or offend all his readers in other parts of the Empire.[3]

Again we see that Scotland is embarrassed by the gaze of the outer world. A more important example is the squeamishness of the *literati* at discussing controversial subjects—that is, subjects that mattered. The Philosophical Society resolved to keep out theology, morals, and politics:

> The great delicacy of the subject, the imperfections of human understanding, the various attachments and inclinations of mankind, will for ever propagate disputes with regard to those parts of erudition. And it is the peculiar happiness of geometry and physics, that as they interest less the passions of men, they admit of more calm disquisition and inquiry.

Lord Meadowbank threatened to have a check kept on the Speculative Society (the students' debating union) "if they interfered with questions of modern politics"; and the Select Society ruled "That every Member may propose any subject of debate, except such as regard Revealed Religion, or which may give occasion to vent any Principles of Jacobitism".[4]

[1] *Memoir of Robert Chambers*, pp. 320-1; *Domestic Annals*, p. 618.
[2] See below, Appendix C, 'The Centralisation of Scottish Periodicals'.
[3] *Quarterly Review* (London: July 1815), Vol. XIII, No. 26, p. 295; Francis Jeffrey, *Contributions to the Edinburgh Review* (2nd ed., London: 1846), II, p. 234.
[4] McElroy, *Literary Clubs and Societies*, pp. 106, 383-4, 142; and see also note 1.

Only people unaffected by real issues and comfortably in charge of society could have afforded so sublime a detachment.[1] We shall see that the correctness and the studious shunning of the low which made up the ideal of the cultivated class could be kept up only by indifference to much in the life of their country.

To sum up: the several generations of the 'great Edinburgh' made a body of remarkably talented men, working and living together as a conscious intelligentsia who led their country in many fields of thought and professional work. Moreover, they had a character or ethos of their own, distinctive in idiom and social attitude. The manners and idiom of their milieux did not feed a polite literature of any quality, and this correlates with their anxious awareness of a powerful culture near by, very different from their own yet appealing to them as a model civilisation—a culture less tied than their own to a backward country and one, too, which had a much more articulate character and powers of expression, for all the Scotsmen's readiness to criticise its shortcomings in politeness. There is no law according to which one could expect *any* such culture to produce its literature: seemingly the more personal kinds of imagination just were not the *métier* of that cultivated class. But it did aspire to be literary: it was proud to have its tragedy in Home's *Douglas*, its epic in Wilkie's *Epigoniad*, its elegant essay in the *Mirror* and *Lounger*, its romantic novel in *The Man of Feeling*. Yet these are all unreadable now, lifeless side by side with the literature of that 'low' popular culture—from which, inevitably, the *literati* were striving to shake themselves clear.

The developments that I have traced show themselves fully, and affected people most personally, through the contemporary ideals of expression. Scotticisms, naturally, were censored as such—they voiced the uncouth life of the people; and the terms in which this censorship was justified suggest the powerful drives to correctness and polite manners which were at work.

The organ of Adam Smith's set, the first *Edinburgh Review* (a short-lived periodical of the mid-1750's), was one of the early attempts to regularise Scottish letters. It repeatedly censures 'vulgarity' of language. The Preface to the first number explains the uphill "progress in knowledge" in "North Britain" by the "difficulty of a proper expression" in a country without a refined standard of language. Adam Smith

[1] See note 2 for details of a later opposite of this outlook.

himself, in his review of Johnson's *Dictionary*, advocates excluding improper words even more rigorously than Johnson.[1] The criteria underlying this standard are exposed in all their wincing gentility in Jardine's reviews of sermons by Secession (i.e. Presbyterian extremist) ministers. Ebenezer Erskine's style is "very *familiar*, and in our opinion most indecently familiar"; ". . . the sublime doctrines of Christianity are treated of, in such a low and ludicrous manner, and are so disfigured with obscure and sometimes indecent allegories". He is scandalised that a certain sermon on 'The Redeemer's Ability to Save Sinners to the Uttermost' should have been preached in an Edinburgh church (the Tolbooth): its vulgarisms would have been indecent even in conversation, let alone the pulpit. What he quotes includes "[Satan] lying *nibbling* at the *heels of the Saints*", "the soul's *minting* to depart out of the spiritual Egypt, the Redeemer's paying the *dyver's debt*", "human nature, which is like a back to the Godhead".[2] Yet "minting" (aiming, having an urge to) and "dyver" (bankrupt) are just Scots words;[3] and in "nibbling at the heels" nasty, covert temptation is realised as it could not be in Augustan English.

Jardine is here setting his face against the vernacular idiom of the class which contained the most whole-hearted believers —those whose whole experience, including the physical and emotional, entered into their religion. There are old Scots hymns, special favourites of the village handloom weavers of the Mearns and Angus in the late 18th century, which address God with the intimate directness of a negro spiritual; and there are many stories, often comic, which show how literal and whole-hearted was Christian belief amongst the lower classes who still used Scots naturally.[4] Jardine also objects to Ebenezer Erskine's gloss on *Psalms*, 40, 8, "I delight to do thy will":

> I consent to it, and am heartily willing and content; a bargain be it; let it be registered in the volume of thy book; i.e. let it be entered into the records of Heaven, and an

---

[1] *Op. cit.* (Edinburgh: July 1755–March 1756), Vol. I, p. ii; *ibid.* p. 62.
[2] *Ibid.* Vol. II, pp. 37, 27.
[3] It must be said also that likening the redemption to paying off a bankruptcy belongs to the anthropomorphic trick of evangelical preachers which the Moderates, in both Scotland and England, specially disliked: see Leslie Stephen on Wesley, *History of English Thought in the Eighteenth Century* (3rd ed., London: 1902), II, p. 418.
[4] A. F. Mitchell (ed.), *The Gude and Godlie Ballates* (Scottish Text Society, Edinburgh: 1897), p. lxii. For the traditional fervour of lower-class believers see John Hill Burton, *History of Scotland, 1689–1748* (London: 1853), I, pp. 189-90, 203-4, and Mathieson, *Church and Reform in Scotland* (*op. cit.*), p. 305. For stories of such belief see note 3.

extract thereof be given out in the scriptures of truth unto
sinners of mankind, that they may have their thoughts
about it.[1]

This is certainly rather an arbitrary piece of Biblical interpretation, and verbally strained as Scottish pulpit analogies from
law, trade, and the like typically were. But the idea of men
having their thoughts about God's will is a main bent of
Presbyterianism, that urge to thorough debate of everything
in their belief which Knox provided for in the *First Book of
Discipline*. He quotes the text "Ye may, one by one, all prophesy"
in laying down that a congregation shall be a community of
minds, all able to interpret and expound Scripture at a high
standard of relevance and seriousness.[2] Here Moderatism
seems to lose more than it gains by refining popular belief: the
independent thought and the emotions of the whole-hearted
believer are censored away.[3]

This urge to enforce conformity to the 'proper' is of course
Augustan. Hugh Blair's analyses of Addison and Swift in his
very fashionable *Lectures on Rhetoric and Belles Lettres* are close to
Johnson's strictures on Shakespeare's English. Analysing the
prose of *Spectator* No. 414 (on landscape) Blair writes: "we
return with pain from those pleasing objects [trees, orchards],
to the insignificant contents of a nurseryman's shop". Johnson
is recognisably appealing to the same sense of the proper when
he writes in his *Rambler* note on *Macbeth*: "this sentiment is
weakened by the name of an instrument used by butchers and
cooks in the meanest employments; we do not immediately
conceive that a crime of importance is to be committed with
a *knife*".[4] The Scotsmen 'however, were driven to Augustan
constraint by motives rather different from the English. The
Preface to Smith's *Review* reveals the social urge at work. The
ancient state of Scotland is being obliterated as a result of
the Glorious Revolution and the Union and with the help of
the "more mature" England:

> The communication of trade has awakened industry; the
> equal administration of laws produced good manners; and

[1] *Op. cit.* p. 37.
[2] John Knox, *The History of the Reformation*, ed. W. Croft Dickinson (London:
1949), II, pp. 315-6.
[3] See also note 4 for further details of the censorship of 'vulgarisms'. See note 5
for the corresponding anti-Moderate mistrust of ministers who spoke good English,
and their support for Scots.
[4] *Op. cit.* (London: 1783), I, p. 474; Samuel Johnson, *The Rambler and The Idler*,
with *The Adventurer* and *The Connoisseur* (London & Edinburgh: 1876), p. 289
(essay No. 168, 'Poetry debased by mean expressions').

the watchful care of the government, seconded by the public spirit of some individuals, has excited, promoted, and encouraged, a disposition to every species of improvement. . . .[1]

The entire professional class was to co-operate in the great work of self-improvement. To Jardine reformation of manners should even be the "great object of every preacher's attention". Hugh Blair, lecturing in Edinburgh, directed students to analyse Addison "as a proper method of correcting any peculiarities of dialect"; and James Beattie in Aberdeen compiled a book of *Scotticisms* to help country students who had had "no opportunity of learning English from the company they kept". The ministers who wrote the accounts of parishes for the *Old Statistical Account* regularly note with satisfaction any 'improvement', i.e. Anglicisation, of the language in their district. In 1761 the Select Society ran lessons in 'correct' (i.e. English) pronunciation, given by an Irish elocutionist, intended to help Scotsmen "to avoid many gross improprieties". An Aberdeen Moderate and scholar has a typical passage against the "coarseness" and "vulgarity" of "provincial dialect" ("ridiculous" to "men of knowledge and taste") in his lectures for Divinity students; and a magazine writer of the time advocated "just pronunciation" as a test for the ministry and a qualification to be "scrupulously exacted" from all teachers of English.[2]

'Correctness' was of course what all Augustans—whether American, French, English, or Scottish—were out to impose. But in Scotland it was made the more constrained and all-embracing by the deference to England and the awareness of the uncouth at home. Henry Mackenzie and Jardine (whom Hume loved for his "sharpness") show far less character in their writings than they evidently had in life, which is hardly true of Addison or Steele. The Scottish *literati*, indeed, out-Augustan the Augustans, as when Adam Smith says, in his review of Johnson's *Dictionary*, that humour is "something which comes upon a man by fits, which he can neither command

---

[1] *Op. cit.* p. ii; compare also William Robertson's exactly similar attitude to the automatic cultural benefits of the Union, *History of Scotland* (*op. cit.*), II, pp. 306-307.
[2] Jardine, *op. cit.* p. 37; Blair, *Rhetoric and Belles Lettres*, I, p. 430, n.; Beattie: Sir William Forbes, *Account of the Life and Writings of James Beattie* (Edinburgh: 1806), II, p. 47; *Old Statistical Account*, ed. Sir John Sinclair (Edinburgh: 1792–6), III, p. 114 (Ayrshire), XV, pp. 294-5 and XVI, p. 592 (Aberdeenshire); Select Society: *The Scots Magazine* (Edinburgh: 1761), Vol. XXIII, p. 440; George Campbell, *On Pulpit Eloquence: Works* (edition London: 1840), VI, p. 142; correspondent in Ruddiman's *Weekly Magazine* (Edinburgh: 1772), p. 361.

nor restrain, and which is not perfectly consistent with true politeness . . . a man of wit is as much above a man of humour, as a gentleman is above a buffoon". So paralysing an ideal of dignity could be matched by several imitators of Addison in an age when Augustanism was becoming sclerosed. But it is significant in this case that humour was precisely the type of what Scotsmen felt inhibited from expressing because they were blocked off from their native speech. This was a constant complaint of the time, for example Alexander Carlyle's direct statement that "Since we began to affect speaking a foreign language, which the English dialect is to us, humour, it must be confessed, is less apparent in conversation". The same was said by William Craig, in his *Mirror* paper on the 'Scarcity of Humourous Writers in Scotland': "The *Scottish* dialect is our ordinary suit; the *English* is used only on solemn occasions. When a Scotsman therefore writes, he does it generally in trammels", and this stifled comic writing because there the writer's "language must be, as nearly as possible, that of common life, that of the bulk of the people"—an idea fully borne out by the comedy of Fergusson and Burns, as well as that of Scott. One of the most inward and psychologically exact accounts of the language difficulty is contained in a note on this same subject, the frustration of Scots humour. John Wilson, a Greenock schoolmaster who wrote a pedestrian Augustan-Miltonic poem *The Clyde*, was noted for his comic stories—which he told in Scots. His biographer goes on to say that Scotsmen have been thought obtuse to humour because "in polite companies" they are "prohibited, by the imputation of vulgarity, from using the common language of the country, in which he expresses himself with most ease and vivacity, and, clothed in which, his earliest and most distinct impressions always arise to his mind. He uses a species of translation, which checks the versatility of fancy, and restrains the genuine and spontaneous flow of his conceptions."[1] This indeed applies not only to humour in everyday talk but also to the *creative* effort to use a language, the effort of finding words for feelings and ideas as they start up half-formulated from the depth of the consciousness. Thomas Carlyle seems to have spotted this very process in action in Jeffrey's telling of Scots stories, "Which he did with a greatness of *gusto* quite peculiar to the topic; with a fine and deep sense of humour, of real

---

[1] *Autobiography*, p. 232; *The Mirror* (*op. cit.*), III, pp. 74-5, 76; John Leyden (ed.), *Scotish Descriptive Poems* (Edinburgh: 1803), pp. 13-14.

comic mirth, much beyond what was noticeable in him otherwise; not to speak of the perfection of the mimicry, which
itself was something".[1] The fact that it is in such light, un-
buttoned expression that the old native idiom can still break
out should not blind us to how genuine and powerful a thing it
is. At such points we seem to catch the whole organism of
feelings and attitudes which language embodies, in the very
act of being canalised off from the main-stream of the man's
usage, still alive and flowing—very likely a peculiar relief to
the speaker—yet moving irretrievably out of touch with his
standard usage. The problem was quite personal for the
Scottish Augustans. Hume, Jardine, Robertson (and later
Scott and Cockburn) all spoke broad Scots; yet the polite
standard obliged them to expunge it from their formal usage.[2]

The testimony of these men themselves shows that they felt
their difficulty as a social matter, a matter of poise, presence,
manner, and the other qualities necessary to unworried extra-
version if one was not to show oneself up as an outsider or
commit a *gaffe*. Sir John Sinclair treats de-Scotticising as a
piece of etiquette. Scotticisms are "uncouth" and "unintelligible", "equally conspicuous, at the table, in the pulpit, and
at the bar", and a handicap when visiting the capital—
London. James Beattie says in his *Scotticisms*: "where purity of
language is concerned, it is, in *my* opinion, more safe to be too
scrupulous, than too little so". But in a letter he confesses the
embarrassment that results:

> . . . when an easy, idiomatical phrase occurs, [we] dare not
> adopt it, for fear of Scotticisms. In a word, we handle
> English, as a person who cannot fence handles a sword; con-
> tinually afraid of hurting ourselves with it, or letting it fall,
> or making some awkward motion that shall betray our
> ignorance . . .[3]

This typical wording is sufficient evidence of how acute were
the feelings at work—"conspicuous", "safe", "betray".

Thus the general 18th-century concern with correct manners
was, in Scotland, aggravated by anxiety over language. The
Scottish policy of refining language has something in common
with the ideal of English for correct intellectual usage stated by

---

[1] *Reminiscences (op. cit.)*, p. 340.
[2] For recorded examples and contemporary descriptions of their speech see
note 6.
[3] Sinclair, *Observations on the Scottish Dialect* (London & Edinburgh: 1782), p. 142;
Beattie, *Scotticisms* (second ed., Edinburgh: 1787), p. 3; Forbes, *Life and Writings of
Beattie*, II, p. 17.

Bishop Sprat in his *History of the Royal Society of London*. In the section 'A Proposal for Electing an English Academy', he links "purity of Speech" with "greatness of Empire", and he wants language to develop away from the "outlandish" and "fantastical" idiom used by the religious sects. Thus the social background of his ideas is very similar to that of the Scotsmen in the 18th century. But his ideal speech was not one which they could have allowed themselves:

> They [the Royal Society] have exacted from all their members a close, naked, natural way of speaking, positive expressions, clear senses, a native easiness, bringing all things as near the Mathematical plainness as they can, and preferring the language of Artizans, Countrymen, and Merchants, before that of Wits or Scholars.[1]

Native easiness—or, in a phrase of Beattie's, a "vernacular cast"—was just what these Scotsmen felt themselves helpless to get through to; and the language of their artisans and countrymen was the disreputable Scots.[2]

It was only natural that the upper educated class should have been indifferent or hostile to much in the native literature: it had behind it so uncomfortably different a social world from what they were building up. Such an aversion to the native is perhaps typical of a culture forced into a provincial frame of mind by the influence of some great centre. It seems that before Pushkin Russian colloquial idiom required rehabilitation, the cultivated gentry affecting French. In America, early in the 19th century, the Anglophil culture of Boston was akin to that of Augustan Edinburgh, and their intellectual life, according to Mr Van Wyck Brooks, was timid, cautious, and derivative: "English culture had a right of way that no one thought of challenging, and every Boston boy was taught to regard Pope and Burke as unapproachable." The New England versifiers ignored the folk literature of the New England coast and the hinterland of Vermont and Connecticut; and the South Carolina novelist William Gilmore Simms was thought to be wasting his time writing about the history of his own country.[3] The Scottish case is very similar, but specially unfortunate

---

[1] Quoted from *Critical Essays of the Seventeenth Century*, ed. J. E. Spingarn (Oxford: 1908), II, pp. 112-13, 117-18.
[2] *Life and Writings of Beattie*, II, p. 17.
[3] Brooks, *The Flowering of New England, 1815-1865* (Cleveland & New York: 1946), pp. 15-16, 47, 56; *The World of Washington Irving* (London & New York: 1944), p. 234.

because the popular poetry was, until the arrival of Scott and the break-through of the national subject-matter, the only native literature that mattered.

To be sure, the upper classes did not ignore Scots songs; they themselves composed them, and sang them at their parties.[1] This, like their taste for proverbs, is a sign of the comparative unsophistication of the Scottish upper class, its homely natural-ness despite its aspirations to the polite. But songs were light; they could not affect that class either in its serious literary taste or in its understanding of the mass of the people. Woodhouselee, for example, wrote of Allan Ramsay:

> . . . he wrote with more ease in the Scottish dialect, and he preferred it, as judging, not unreasonably, that it conferred a kind of Doric simplicity, which, when he wished to paint with fidelity the manners of his countrymen, and the peculiarities of the lower orders, was extremely suitable to such subjects.[2]

For such taste, the vernacular has no intrinsic value, as best able to express what is felt personally by a man of creative talent—let alone qualities from which the life of the higher classes might have benefited. Scots is only the appropriate vehicle for the given social stratum. Furthermore, the polite notion of this stratum is unreal. The usual line of Edinburgh critics of Burns was to treat the working-class poet as a prodigy (although poetry in fact flourished amidst his daily life [3])—a "Heaven-taught ploughman", or "common ploughman" of "untutored fancy", whose work, though naturally defective, was wonderfully good considering. In the *Lounger* paper with which Edinburgh first greeted Burns's *Poems*, Henry Mackenzie says that Burns, "from his humble and unlettered station, has looked upon men and manners" with wonderful sagacity. According to Currie, Burns's first editor, educated readers marvelled that a simple peasant should have been able to depict high life so vividly (the lairds and young bucks in 'The Twa Dogs') and supposed he must have come by his observa-tions at the Ayr Races.[4] It is as though they thought of the

[1] Song—literature meant for oral currency—is a massive field which has been set aside from the literature (art-poetry and fiction) considered in this book. See note 7.

[2] *Works* of Ramsay, I, p. 151; Ramsay himself fell dutifully in with this class attitude, pretending that his 'Christis Kirk' was moral propaganda meant to clean up the immorality of the lower orders: *ibid.* p. 333.

[3] See below, Chapter IV.

[4] *The Edinburgh Magazine* or Literary Miscellany (1786), pp. 284-5; *The Lounger* (2nd ed., Edinburgh: 1787), III, p. 287; Currie, *Works of Burns*, I, p. 30, n.

working man as looking out from a burrow, not moving about in a society in the same world as themselves.

Jeffrey, in 1809, distinguished better than the early critics between Burns's Scots poetry and English versifying; yet he still shies away, treating Burns's peasant spirit of directness or "equality", the want of "respectfulness" in his "gallantry" (i.e. in his love poems), as a failing, not as a source of strength. What he means is such poetry as this:

> At kirk or at market, whene'er ye meet me,
> Gang by me as tho' that ye cared na a flie;
> But steal me a blink o' your bonie black e'e,
> Yet look as ye were na lookin' to me,
> Yet look as ye were na lookin' to me.

> O whistle an' I'll come to ye, my lad,
> O whistle an' I'll come to ye, my lad,
> Tho' father an' mother an' a' should gae mad,
> O whistle an' I'll come to ye, my lad,

with its vigorous 'equality' between woman and man; or the equally straight and spontaneous directness of 'The Braw Wooer':

> He spake o' the darts in my bonie black een,
> And vow'd for my love he was diein',
> I said he might die when he liket—for Jean—
> The Lord forgie me for liein', for liein';
> The Lord forgie me for liein'!

or

> This is no my ain lassie,
> Fair tho' the lassie be;
> Weel ken I my ain lassie . . .[1]

Today we might be readier to see that such qualities are valuable regardless of class, that they make for a whole-hearted emotional strength which is a mainstay of life, whereas the code of 'manners' only encourages stagnation, failure of nerve, and the confinement of men and women to petty roles. It is no wonder that Lawrence was always fond of Burns "as a sort of brother", and admired the sincerity of 'A man's a man for a' that' as against the condescension of "Those damned middle-class Lockharts".[2]

Burns is a specially important case, because his poetry so concentrates the virtues of the 'popular'. But other responses to

[1] Jeffrey, *Contributions to the Edinburgh Review*, II, p. 147. Note that 'Whistle and I'll come to ye, my lad', 'The Braw Wooer', and 'This is no my ain lassie' were all written for music.
[2] D. H. Lawrence, *Letters*, ed. Aldous Huxley (London: 1932), pp. 84, 694-5.

the native literature reveal the same attitudes. Perhaps we could hardly have expected a polite minister like Hugh Blair— a soft dean who "never mentions Hell to ears polite"—to look on Burns's free, satirical references to salvation and damnation as anything other than profane (whether or not he himself, a Moderate and anything but Calvinist, really cared about the guying of hell or salvation [1]). But Adam Smith disapproved even of so innocuous a Scots work as Ramsay's pastoral play, *The Gentle Shepherd*: "It is the duty of a poet to write like a gentleman. I dislike that homely style which some think fit to call the language of nature and simplicity and so forth"; and he likewise pooh-poohed a pioneering collection of folk poetry, Bishop Percy's *Reliques of Ancient English Poetry*.[2] Blair could not approve the *Shepherd* partly because he was so conscious of a public outside Scotland: "it is so entirely formed on the rural manners of Scotland, that none but a native of that country can thoroughly understand or relish it",[3] and partly because he was so ready to believe that the vernacular was near dead: "the old rustic dialect of Scotland, which, in a short time, will be entirely obsolete, and not intelligible".[4] (History has been disproving this typically assured Augustan pronouncement for two centuries. The Scots 'dialect' in use since the 18th century consists of about 50,000 words.) It was the opinion of such critics that the *Shepherd* verged on the ludicrous because Scots was of its nature incompatible with deeply-felt experiences. Beattie wrote that

> ... to a Scotsman who thoroughly understands it, and is aware of its vulgarity, it appears *ludicrous*; from the contrast between *meanness* of phrase, and *dignity* or *seriousness* of sentiment. This gives a farcical air even to the most affecting parts of the poem.[5]

There was indeed an incongruity in the poetry of the *Shepherd*, which tries to present the farmyard in tidy heroic couplets:

> *What needs the bairn this gate sae air at morn?*
> *Is there nae muck to lead? to thresh nae corn?*

But Beattie can make *his* criticism only because he cannot grasp that Scots was the actual language of a mass of people whose

[1] When Burns came to Edinburgh in 1787, Blair went through his *Poems*, censoring the profanities: J. DeLancey Ferguson, 'Burns and Hugh Blair', *Modern Language Notes* (Baltimore: 1930), XLV, pp. 441-2.
[2] Conversations quoted by Rae, *Life of Adam Smith*, p. 369.
[3] For details of such catering for the British public see note 8.
[4] *Rhetoric and Belles Lettres*, II, pp. 252-3.
[5] 'On Laughter and Ludicrous Composition', *Essays* (London: 1779), p. 382.

feelings and opinions were as serious as anyone else's.

Finally it must be said that these critics were enabled to stay fortified in their class standards because they met a comparatively weak challenge from the native work. It was all too easy for the run of vernacular poetry to be slighted or overlooked by an educated reader—taken for no better than a kind of light verse or lampoon—because though at best it has the breath of life in it, it is sadly mingled with juvenility and moronic dirt. Before Burns, nothing had been done in modern Scots which would have compelled an educated man to take it as seriously as he would the best in any language. Indeed, the critics felt the lack of first-rate work in Scots. John Pinkerton, one of the first scholars to turn his attention to the native literature, complained that our "really great poets" (such as Barbour, Dunbar, and Drummond of Hawthornden) were neglected in favour of Ramsay because the *Shepherd* "is our only drama in the Scottish language"; and William Robertson, Ramsay of Ochtertyre, and a later scholar, Sibbald, had theories of language—to the effect that Scots had been stopped in its development by the Union of 1603—to account for the dearth of modern Scottish literature.[1]

We have seen that at the start of the 18th century the cultivated classes were very close to even the most primitive life in the country. One symptom in the poetry is those exercises in the vernacular which were a peculiar ploy of the Scottish gentry, for example 'The Flyting of Polwart and Montgomerie'—a 17th-century revival of Dunbar's kind of virtuoso abuse—and deliberate extravaganzas of low life such as the Sempills' 'Epitaph on Sanny Briggs' or 'The Blythsome Bridal', with its fantastic revelling in the local foods. Of course such mud-slinging and slumming is just a game with words, but it is rather a gross and silly one, a weakness caught from a backward society in which dirt and knockabout existed in the shape of real general hardship. Lord Hailes's comment on the 'Flyting', typical of the Augustan fastidiousness, is perfectly just: "It is equally illiberal and scurrilous, and shews how poor, how very poor, Genius appears, when its compositions are debased to the meanest prejudices of the meanest vulgar".[2] No 18th-century gentry anywhere could be unaware of the coarse side of life. Pope and Swift indulge in dirt, not just in

[1] Pinkerton (ed.), *Ancient Scotish Poems* (London: 1786), p. cxxxv; for the historical theories regarding Scots see note 9.

[2] *Ancient Scottish Poems* from the manuscript of George Bannatyne, ed. Lord Hailes (Edinburgh: 1770), p. 239 (note on Dunbar's 'Sevin Deidly Synnis').

private *graffiti* but also in their main poetry (e.g. the early books
of *The Dunciad*). But it is perhaps better for wholeness of culture
that such low life should intermingle openly with the polite.
The result of the Scottish language split was that the upper
classes in effect disowned a great deal of what went on in their
own country.

This alienation from things native also affected Scottish
thought, the classic works of the *literati* on religion, philosophy,
history, economics. Their alienation is perhaps less in evidence
here because, especially in the latter two fields, the writer is
bound to attend to practical necessities, he cannot just disdain-
fully avert his gaze from the life around him. Yet here too these
men tended to be blinkered by the exclusive outlook of a ruling-
class. This is not the place to criticise such thinkers as Adam
Smith and Hume for the main bodies of thought which make
up their value for us. But some sketch of their positions is
needed to complete our idea of what the polite culture made of
the life of the country.

The polite attitude to devoted, or bigoted, religion is revealing. Hume especially detests bigotry, fanaticism—almost a test
of sanity in a country with that history, in a town whose
presbytery had forced the hanging of a young free-thinker
fifteen years before Hume was born, and which during his lifetime tried to forbid visiting on Sundays—called by the ministers
"useless communications"—and looking out of the window
on a Sunday—"beholding vanities abroad".[1] The *Edinburgh
Review* of Adam Smith was stopped (according to Tytler)
because of the opposition aroused by Jardine's reviews of
extreme-Presbyterian sermons; and it was proposed to the
Church of Scotland's General Assembly in 1755 by some of the
country ministers (and evaded only by the strategy of Hume's
Moderate friends) that he should be summoned to answer for
his *Inquiry Concerning the Principles of Morals*, the book censured,
and the author excommunicated. Adam Smith was execrated
after Hume's death for suggesting an atheist could have died
peaceably and for calling him the type of "a perfectly wise
dan virtuous man".[2]

It is thus natural that Hume, in his *Essays* and his *History of*

[1] Chambers, *Domestic Annals*, pp. 160-6; Arnot, *History of Edinburgh*, p. 204, n. 2.
[2] Tytler, *Life of Kames* (*op. cit.*), I, p. 233; Rae, *Life of Adam Smith*, pp. 126, 331-2.
The ministers tried to suppress the free-thinking Kames at the same time: see
Mackenzie, *Life of John Home*, pp. 39-41; J. Y. T. Greig, *David Hume* (London:
1931), pp. 219-22.

England, should be so severe on 'superstition' and 'enthusiasm'. In his essay 'Of Superstition and Enthusiasm' he has a splendid rationalist passage on enthusiasm so presumptuous that "it thinks itself sufficiently qualified to *approach* the Divinity, without any human mediator" (Hume is not of course really solicitous about the Divinity) and whose "rapturous devotions are so fervent, that it even imagines itself *actually* to *approach* him by way of contemplation and inward converse". And in his *History* he calls the Covenanters "madmen, who should be soothed, and flattered, and deceived into tranquillity".[1]

His arguments, however, suggest that he does not fully understand either his country's history or its present state. After quoting the bond or manifesto issued by Knox's Congregation of 1559, he suggests that the Protestants went too far in demanding that prayers should be said in the "vulgar tongue" in all churches, and preaching and interpretation of scripture legalised in the meantime in private houses. That is, he does not realise that this desire for a universal opportunity for religious debate was one of the best and most characteristic bents in the Scottish Reformation, and at the root of its revolt against the old Church thought. He does not mention, for example, that preaching in later Catholic times had sunk to "fables" on purgatory and addresses on the virtues of pilgrimage and the merits of the saints, delivered by the lowest and most illiterate order of monks.[2] Hume indeed ignores the popular movement behind the Reformation. He does not even mention its considered programme—the *First Book of Discipline*—and he would rather blacken the 'mob', the "illiterate multitude", and judge the Reformers by their outrages and zeal to persecute, than give any consideration to whatever was natural in their turning against the medieval Church or to their underlying aims. Knox is "this rustic apostle", so uncouth that he would not even soften his rebukes or his obdurate heart in face of Mary's royal grace and feminine tears. It is of a piece with this that he should rationalise away the drive of the Reformers against riches and privilege—a radical move comparable to that of the Diggers and Levellers after the English Civil War—as envy of the Crown finances from which they got no subsidy. He even

[1] *Essays (op. cit.)*, p. 82; *History of England* (last corrected ed., reprinted, London: 1793), XII, p. 131. Hume wrote a special preface for the second volume of his *History* justifying himself against attacks on his critique of Protestant and other fanaticism, but it was not published. (Mossner, *Life of Hume*, pp. 306-307).
[2] *History*, VII, p. 26; Robertson, *History of Scotland*, I, p. 125.

considers that their "furious zeal for religion, morose manners, a vulgar and familiar, yet mysterious cant" was affected, an opinion he repeats in a note on the character of priests in his essay 'Of National Characters', where he stresses the "appearance of fervor and seriousness" which they keep up and their promotion of superstition "by a continued grimace and hypocrisy".[1] No-one nowadays would wish, any more than Hume, for a Knoxian theocracy; but (to consider the sociological aspect alone) Hume can have had no sense of the actual background—the living conditions, speech, and outlook of the people among whom the Reformers found their most devoted followers, or he could not have doubted their sincerity. Adam Smith plainly dislikes fanaticism; but in the section in *The Wealth of Nations* on 'Institutions for Religious Instruction' he does not make Hume's mistake of rationalising away the austerity of the Reforming ministers, and he realises that the Presbyterian clergy's exceptional influence over the minds of the common people was founded on moral leadership as well as on violent proselytising.[2] That is, he recognises the important fact that in Scotland, until well into the 18th century, devotion to religion was so all-embracing that it acted as the main framework or channel of activity for the able men of the country—as do, say, education and politics today.

Hume's narrow base in Scotland comes out continually. When he is considering what produces variety of "manners and characters" in a nation, he rules out climate because Scotland has the same climate as England yet not its variety of manners. Here he ignores the marked differences between, say, Hebridean Islanders, Glaswegians, folk from Buchan (the North-east farming area) and folk from Edinburgh—the obvious equivalents of the Londoners, Midlanders, Cornishmen, and the rest who make up the English variety. Again, more central to his position, he says that Scotsmen, once rampant enthusiasts, "are now settled into the most cool indifference, with regard to religious matters, that is to be found in any nation of the world".[3] Now, it is true that in Hume's day Moderatism was at its peak. Evangelicalism had succumbed to it, or been driven out into Secession. The General

---

[1] *History*, VI, p. 179; VII, pp. 27, 30, 42; *ibid.* pp. 54-6, 60; *Essays*, p. 219, n. 2.
[2] *The Wealth of Nations*, II, pp. 290, 295.
[3] *Essays*, p. 227; *ibid.* Compare his remark in 'Of Superstition and Enthusiasm' that "our sectaries, who were formerly such dangerous bigots [his instances include Covenanters and other Presbyterians], are now become very free reasoners" (*ibid.* p. 83).

Assembly was having to enjoin ministers to "make Gospel subjects their main theme"—to prevent mere moral homilies from the pulpit—and in Edinburgh a professed Calvinist was so acceptable to a Moderate congregation that he shared the church with Hugh Blair. It has been said that religion "bore the stamp of mediocrity throughout the whole period" from 1745 to 1780, roughly Hume's heyday.[1] This is doubtless the background Hume has in mind, that is, the church-going of his own class. Yet devoted religion still carried on amongst the people, its traditional domain. Jardine had had to criticise sermons preached in an Edinburgh church which were phrased to appeal to the common people. Chambers, the publisher, describes the usual talk in an Edinburgh lodging-house, at the end of the century, among packmen, masons, and old women, discussing in their ordinary language the works of Boston (a famous Presbyterian minister from the Borders) or going over last week's sermon—the interest of the Old Testament book from which the text came or how the exposition compared with others on the same text. According to the Moderate Thomas Somerville, recalling the 1740's,

> Any books read by the working people . . . were such as they themselves possessed; and a select number of treatises of popular divinity, like Boston's *Fourfold State*, the same author's *Crook in the Lot*, and Bunyan's *Pilgrim's Progress*, might be found in almost every cottage.[2]

Such facts, along with the constant activities in the Assembly of the Presbyterian extremists, suggest a whole life Hume is unaware of. He is taking one small class to stand for the country.

Often it is not so much errors of fact as the manner or tone of the Moderates which shows their indifference to those under their charge. Thomas Reid, the 'common-sense' philosopher, called the Glaswegians "Boetian in their understanding, fanatical in their religion and clownish in their dress and manners".[3] Alexander Carlyle ridicules his parishioners for doubting whether he had "the grace of God, an occult quality which the people cannot define, but surely is in full opposition to the defects they saw in me". Carlyle is here standing out stoutly for a liberal ministry. His congregation had mistrusted him "as too young, too full of levity, and too much addicted to

[1] Mathieson, *Church and Reform in Scotland*, pp. 43-50; P. Hume Brown, *History of Scotland* (Cambridge: 1911), III, p. 265.
[2] *Memoir of Robert Chambers*, pp. 85-6; Somerville, *Life and Times* (*op. cit.*), p. 350.
[3] Quoted by Ian Hislop, 'Scottish Presbyterianism'; *Blackfriars* (English Dominican Journal: April 1946), p. 137.

the company of my superiors", as one who danced, dressed carelessly, "and had been seen galloping thro' the Links one day between one and two o'clock". It was he and his group who had set out to win for ministers the liberty of going to the theatre, when certain of them were had up before the Assembly for the enormity of going to the first performance of John Home's tragedy *Douglas* in a public playhouse. (The play itself was a collaborative work of the *literati*, rehearsed in their houses while it was being written, with themselves taking parts.) The scandal became for Edinburgh a thorough battle of enlightenment versus puritanism; and in Carlyle's summary of the affair his liberal ideals are stated seriously:

> . . . it was of great importance to discriminate the artificial virtues and vices, formed by ignorance and superstition, from those that are real, lest the continuance of such a bar should have given check to the rising liberality of the young scholars, and prevented those of better birth or more ingenious minds from entering into the profession.[1]

Yet for all that, his comment on 'grace'—"an occult quality which the people cannot define"—is both supercilious and shallow, for many amongst the common people were thoughtful, trained believers, as well as caring more than he for the fundamentals of the faith out of which he nevertheless made his profession. When Daniel Defoe visited Scotland on a secret service mission from London to sound the state of opinion before the Union, he found that every church-goer had a Bible in his hand: "if you shut your eyes when the minister names any text of Scripture, you shall hear a little rustling noise over the whole place, made by turning the leaves of the Bible"; and when Gilbert Burnet, the Scottish Episcopalian, toured the Western counties with Archbishop Leighton's 'evangelising' mission in the 1660's, he was "amazed to see a poor commonalty, so capable of arguing upon points of government, and on the bounds to be set to the power of Princes, in matters of religion: upon all these topicks they had texts of scripture at hand; and were ready with their answers, to anything that was said to them. This measure of knowledge was spread even amongst the meanest of them, the cottagers, and their servants."[2]

---

[1] *Autobiography*, pp. 216, 339-40. The clash was really acute: some ministers who had gone to the play defended themselves to their indignant parishioners on the grounds that they had hidden behind pillars in the theatre so as not to bring the ministry into disrepute.

[2] Defoe, *Memoirs of the Church of Scotland*, ed. Rev. William Wilson (Perth: 1844), pp. 354-5; Burnet, *History of My Own Time* (edition London: 1753), I, p. 410.

The Moderates may, then, have pointed the way to the final civilising of popular belief; yet in their attitude to the people they show too little of the understanding and responsibility which are obligatory on the thinkers or legislators who take it on themselves to lead the public. Few of them had the openness to the needs of the people which is shown by the Whig Cockburn in his comments on the Disruption (the 19th-century Church dispute), even when he does not feel personally for the beliefs at stake:

> Be it desirable or not, the taste of the serious Presbyterian portion of the people is the same now that it was then [in the 16th and 17th centuries]; and the legal constitution of their Church, as well as the phrases in which it is embalmed, have undergone no change whatever. Accordingly this taste, where it exists, absorbs every other feeling. Among the religious population of Presbyterian Scotland no difference of opinion upon any other subject disturbs the unanimity with which they all cling to the old subjects of the Church's spiritual independence, and the popular hostility to unmitigated patronage. . . . The mere critic of manners may be allowed to sneer; but the statesman is bound to manage a people in reference to their hereditary feelings.[1]

William Robertson and, as we have seen, Adam Smith both wrote more understandingly on the popular religion. In his *History of Scotland* Robertson discriminates well between the devoted and the brutal strains in the Reformers. He dislikes the deliberate wrecking of Catholic church art, but he notes that the idol-smashing and looting of monasteries after Knox's sermon to the Congregation of 1559 was "an accidental eruption of popular rage". He understands the historical force behind idol-breaking: the "speculative errors of popery" were less easy for the mass of the people to see whereas public worship, "by striking the senses, excited more universal disgust". He gives value to the fact that so high a proportion of the country rallied to the forces of the Reformers, the Congregational army, and he notes (what is ignored by Hume) that an ardent love of liberty, protecting the subject's rights against the encroachments of the monarch, typically went hand in hand with Protestantism.[2]

Yet both Robertson and Smith turn against democracy when it comes to that great testing-ground—contemporary events.

[1] *Journal*, I, pp. 181-2; compare Jeffrey's similar opinions, *Life of Jeffrey*, I, pp. 390-1.
[2] *History of Scotland*, I, pp. 153, 218; 157; 159, 155.

Both are quick to depreciate or discount the 'prejudices' of the people in questions of government. Robertson, for all his Wordsworthian enthusiasm for the dawn of the French Revolution, later exploited the worst side of the anti-Revolution atmosphere for Church ends. He got up a scare about political 'unrest' to block appeals to Parliament by congregations wanting to be relieved of ministers imposed on them against their choice; and he aimed to crush the popular spirit of Presbytery by enforcing patronage—the privilege of the landowner to choose a minister for the district (or to decide on the short-list of candidates) regardless of what the congregation wanted.[1] These were the issues which, until the growth of Parliamentary representation, represented the class struggle. How anti-democratic the resistance to popular choice of minister could be is shown in a remark of Sir John Clerk of Penecuik (one of the commissioners who worked out the Act of Union earlier in the century): "Is it not an absurd thing that a tenant or servant who may be removed at a certain term should have a vote in choosing a minister for life to his master?"[2] This virtually feudal attitude better enables us to understand the social passions aroused over the issue of the ministry.

Smith had in some ways as narrow a base in Scotland as Hume. Arguing to the humane end of correcting "whatever was unsocial or disagreeably rigorous in the morals of all the little sects into which the country was divided"—an end typical of his class—he proposes, for their enlightening effects, the study of science and philosophy. But teachers will not be paid, which would make them idle. Hence, inevitably, higher training in science and philosophy will have to be restricted to people "of middling or more than middling rank or fortune".[3] On that showing Smith might as well not have belonged to a country in which the sons of crofters and shepherds were constantly educating themselves to be ministers, doctors and surgeons, teachers, philologists. (The crofter counties still produce a higher proportion of university graduates than any other area in the country.) Smith's argument about 'idleness' is in fact no more than a rationalisation of his ruling-class tendency to confine advantages to those who already have them. For example (a point specially relevant in a small nation which had

---

[1] Mathieson, *Church and Reform in Scotland*, p. 13; Meikle, *Scotland and the French Revolution*, pp. 39-40.
[2] *Memoirs of the Life of Sir John Clerk of Penecuik*, ed. John M. Gray (Scottish Historical Text Society, Edinburgh: 1892), pp. 247-8.
[3] *The Wealth of Nations*, II, pp. 280-1.

united with a larger one and given up its capital), he was against the separation of the American colonies: they should stay united with "the best of mother countries", and send representatives to the British capital. There are no *real* obstacles to such a union: "The principal perhaps arise, not from the nature of things, but from the prejudices and opinions of the people both on this and on the other side of the Atlantic".[1] Thus the member of the 'élite' takes it for granted that popular feeling can always be managed—here, that the opinions of the people are something less than 'the nature of things'—i.e. the convenience of the larger power. Smith had but a dim idea of how popular forces persist and gather momentum, in spite of controls from above. McCulloch, the first editor of *The Wealth of Nations*, was struck that Smith had had no prescience of the French Revolution.[2] Similarly Hume took it for granted that peoples grew steadily away from religious belief. Yet not long after his death the popular stir at the time of the Revolution had the effect of breaking the hold of Moderatism. Evangelicalism (even apart from such hysterical spasms as the Cambuslang 'warks', when thousands of frantic people flocked to be 'saved' at open-air meetings) and, along with evangelicalism, democratic church government came back with such force that they dominated the General Assembly and led to the breakaway of over 470 ministers from the Church (in a total of 1,100) at the Disruption over the patronage issue in 1843.[3] In this as in other things Hume and Smith maintained their serene Augustanism by excluding from their notice the major part of society.

Leslie Stephen suggests that the position of Hume and Smith is typical of 18th-century thinkers. Hume was limited by "inadequate appreciation of the true value of the great moral forces", for example in thinking that he could analyse away the natural faculty of conscience and the general aversion to suicide. And Smith did "all that can be done without bringing a theory of commerce into actual contact with the underlying social problems". In particular he ignored, in a book purporting to deal with the bread and butter of society, some of the most clamant problems of his own day—the poor laws, the mush-

---

[1] *The Wealth of Nations*, II, p. 124.
[2] Rae, *Life of Adam Smith*, p. 229.
[3] Cockburn, *Life of Jeffrey*, I, p. 388; Thomas Brown, *Annals of the Disruption* (Edinburgh; 1893), pp. 97-8. Brown's figure is based on the number of ministers who signed the Deed of Demission resigning the position and stipend of the Established Church.

rooming of population.[1] The liberalism of the Moderates, Mathieson suggests, was superseded at the end of the 18th century because it sought to do for the people what the people claimed the right to do for themselves. Being fastidious and exclusive, it sought "not to emancipate the people but to place them under better, if no less absolute, government than that of courtiers, mistresses and priests". That is indeed a decisive comment on all bourgeois reformism, not only on the Moderates but also on Whigs like Cockburn and Jeffrey who worked for the Reform Acts of 1832 as though they would bring a reign of social justice—but of course called a halt to extending the franchise to the 'mob'. Mathieson will go no further than to call the growth of Whiggism the development of a class "sufficiently experienced and organised to interpose between the aristocracy and the people as the exponent of moderate reform".[2] As far as literature is concerned, we shall see that there also developed at this time a less disdainful attitude to the native country. The period of growing Whiggism and the 'diffusion of knowledge' was also one in which Scottish fiction fostered a rather wider understanding and acceptance of its own country than had been usual under the polite culture.

[1] Stephen, *Eighteenth Century Thought*, II, pp. 102, 96; I, pp. 324-5, 326. Compare Engels: "When we study the real economic relations in various countries and at various stages of civilisation, how singularly erroneous and deficient appear the rationalistic generalisations of the 18th century—good old Adam Smith who took the conditions of Edinburgh and the Lothians as the normal ones, of the universe!" (Marx and Engels, *Selected Correspondence*, Moscow: n.d., p. 518).
[2] Mathieson, *The Awakening of Scotland*, p. 214; *Church and Reform in Scotland*, p. 12.

CHAPTER III

Vernacular Poetry and 'Country Wit'

> The star that rules my luckless lot,
> Has fated me the russet coat,
> An' damn'd my fortune to the groat;
> But, in requit,
> Has blest me with a random-shot
> O' countra wit.
> BURNS, *Epistle to James Smith.*

SCOTTISH poetry was poorly developed as a cultivated art; but to say this barely gets below the surface of the life that went into it. No literature can exist without embodying the human nature and habits of life actually there in the country it comes from. Scots vernacular poetry is, indeed, in its strengths and in its typical deficiencies, an eloquent representative of the people. We can, if we take its hints, gather much about the quality of life they led—their powers and how far they were fulfilled.

The line of poetry leading to Burns expresses much of what came to be thought of as 'Scottishness'—'the Scottish character'. The poets in this tradition are totally devoid of interest when writing outside their Scots idiom, and their poetry almost never, when it is at all original or considerable, brings in any element from outside their own society. Appreciation of this line, which is mainly comic, was for long debased into a relish for the 'Kailyaird'—sly farce or nostalgic escapism in which social life is brought exclusively inside the range of country ways and values, and these values (as in S. R. Crockett, J. M. Barrie, or Iain Maclaren) become more and more unreal as the main initiative of the nation sets in from the towns. The belittling sense of country life as dream-worldy or farcically uncouth and backward got its start partly from a broken-down idea of the vernacular poetry itself. For generations such words as 'couthy' or 'pawky' have been used to hit off essential Scottish qualities,[1] and such words—making self-consciously explicit, as a cult of the rural, the stock peasant traits—came in with the imitation country poetry that became popular

---

[1] Needless to say, such qualities could be matched amongst the country, village, and small-town folk of other countries.

during the Burns vogue, for example James Hogg's 'The Village of Balmaquhapple':

> There's Johnny the elder, wha hopes ne'er to need ye,
> Sae pawkie, sae holy, sae gruff, an' sae greedy;
> Wha prays every hour as the wayfarer passes,
> But aye at a hole where he watches the lasses—

here Hogg draws not from life but, unconsciously perhaps, from Burns's 'Holy Willie's Prayer'—or, still more remote, R. L. Stevenson's *Ille Terrarum*, where country feelings are put in from the outside, and sentimentally selected at that:

> An, noo to face the kirkward mile:
> The guidman's hat o' dacent style,
> The blackit shoon, we noo maun fyle
>   As white's the miller:
> A waefu' peety tae, to spile
>   The warth o' siller . . .
>
> The solemn elders at the plate
> Stand drinkin' deep the pride o' state:
> The practised hands as gash an' great
>   As Lords o' Session . . .[1]

It is typical of the backwater nature of this cult that a writer of Stevenson's gifts should waste himself on subject-matter so far from his own experience.

Although 19th-century taste thus debased the original vernacular idioms and subjects, it was at least in closer touch with them than that 18th-century educated public, dedicated to the English-Augustan. Jeffrey quotes the close of Burns's 'Address to the Deil' as one example of his "delicate and tender feeling, indicating that softness of heart which is always so enchanting". Yet his quotation includes the final stanza with its characteristic familiarity or humorously ironic fellow-feeling:

> But fare-you-weel, auld 'Nickie-ben'!
> O wad ye tak a thought an' men'!
> Ye aiblins might—I dinna ken—
>   Still hae a stake:
> I'm wae to think upo' yon den,
>   Ev'n for your sake![2]

Here the polite critic of the early 19th century—his taste beginning to melt into Victorian sentimentality—does not even catch the vernacular tone for what it is.

---

[1] Hogg, *Songs and Ballads*, p. 67; Stevenson, poems in Scots from *Underwoods: Poems* (London: 1909), p. 52.

[2] *Contributions to the Edinburgh Review*, II, pp. 159-61.

Yet while the polite critics merely armoured themselves in an attitude which they could not justify, there were real deficiencies in the way of life which was ingrained in the vernacular. Mr John Speirs writes thus of Ramsay's Scots: "The strength of his idiom in the epistles and elegies is shown in its power to subjugate satisfactorily heroes and gods". He quotes from the third 'Familiar Epistle' to Hamilton of Gilbertfield:

> *That bangster billy, Caesar July,*
> *Wha at Pharsalia wan the tooly,*
> *Had better sped had he mair hooly*
> *Scamper'd thro' life,*
> *And 'midst his glories sheath'd his gooly*
> *And kiss'd his wife.*

Mr Speirs also says in his chapter on Burns: "The world of Vienna and Versailles [in 'The Twa Dogs'], because balanced against the more immediate 'local' world of

> *He rives his father's auld entails,*

suffers satiric depreciation. . . ." [1] That adequately defines the effect of those passages, but this effect, one of *reduction* or simplifying caricature, seems dangerous to take as an unquestionable poetic strength, both because of the very quality of intrinsic feeling it embodies and because of the limitations of range it suggests in the tradition as a whole.

If we are to use literature as a touchstone of the moral qualities of a society, we must keep in mind some sensitive critical criterion, such a one, perhaps, as T. S. Eliot's implies in his essay on Marlowe: "blank verse within Shakespeare's lifetime was more highly developed, the vehicle of more varied and more intense feeling than it has ever conveyed since". Tennyson's blank verse "is cruder . . . because less capable of expressing complicated, subtle, and surprising emotions".[2] Explanations of what has happened to Scottish life since the Reformation, or since the Unions, have too often treated the cultural tradition as though it were something which could be turned on and off, channelled this way or that, like a water-supply. For example, it is almost an axiom of Scottish Renaissance criticism (to be found in such books as William Power's *Literature and Oatmeal*, Edwin Muir's *Scottish Journey*, and on all sides in the work of Hugh MacDiarmid) that what the Scottish imagination mainly suffered from after the Reformation was some

[1] *The Scots Literary Tradition*, pp. 101, 131.
[2] *Selected Essays* (edition London: 1948), pp. 118-19.

suppression of profane art and worldly feelings by a Calvinist
Church. But if we read the literature, in the light of Eliot's
ideas of the subtle and the crude, we find that what is happening
is not so much censorship or suppression as the bringing out, by
Calvinism, into full potency of a native trait which itself tended
to thwart or curtail imagination. For example, there are a good
many poems of the mid-16th century which take up the
Calvinist condemnation of imagery laid down by Knox:[1]

> They lute thy lieges pray to stocks and stanes
> And paintit papers, wats nocht what they mean;
> They bade them beck and bynge at deid men's banes,
> Offer on knees to kiss, syne save their kin:
> Pilgrims and palmers passes them between
> Sanct Blais, Sanct Boit, blate bodies' een to blear.
> Now, to forbid this great abuse has been,
> God give thee grace agains this guid new year.
>
> They tyrit God with trifles, toom trentals,
> And dazit him with daily darigies,
> With owklie abits to augment their rentals,
> Mantand mort mumlingis mixed with money lees. . . .[2]

This poetry of Alexander Scott's is typical of Reformation satire
in that effect whereby making the subject concrete, bringing it
to realisation, thereby reduces it to the common terms in which
it can be felt as absurd. So in the *Gude and Godlie Ballates*:

> The haly matines fast thay patter,
> Thay gif yow breid, and sellis yow watter,
> His cursingis on yow als thay clatter,
> Thocht thay can hurt yow not,
> Gif ye will geve thame Caip or Bell,
> The clink thairof thay will yow sell,
> Suppose the Saul suld ga to hell,
> Ye get na thing unbocht,

and

> To rottin banis ye gart us kneill,
> And sanit us from neck to heill . . .[3]

The satire is similar to the Pardoner in Chaucer's 'Prologue'
("And in a glas he hadde pigges bones") but the poetic effect

[1] See *The First Book of Discipline* on ritual and imagery, "inventions devised by
men", "honouring of God not contained in his holy Word", which "accuseth the
perfect institution of Jesus Christ of imperfection". (*History of the Reformation*, II,
pp. 282-3.)
[2] 'Ane New Year Gift to Queen Mary'; *The Poems of Alexander Scott*, ed. Alexander Scott (Saltire Society, Edinburgh: 1952), pp. 14-15.
[3] *Ballates* (*op. cit.*), 'Remember man, remember man', pp. 201-2; 'Hay now the
day dallis', p. 194.

is one natural to the Scots vernacular, the caricaturing of any action through its physical presence, as in "sanit us from neck to heill" with its ludicrous suggestion of 'made a good job of us, blessed us good and proper'. Such a style can achieve seriousness, as in this on ostentatious communicants:

> Gif God was maid of bittis of breid,
> Eit ye not oulklie sax or sevin,
> As it had bene ane mortall feid . . .

But usually this idiom expresses a downrightness, crude and summary, which seems to limit in the very act of affirming, as in

> Albeit they be now Tulchin bischops stylit,
> Having proud kingis and counsalis to decoir the,
> Auld God is God, and will not be begylit . . .[1]

"Auld God is God" is a tone very different from anything in the religious poetry of, say, Henryson. It expresses a peculiarly Protestant sense of being face to face with God, a Protestant scorn of concocted rites. But, as expressed, this is emptied of any richness; the affirmed belief is barely felt at all.

The style used for this plainly draws directly on spoken, unliterary Scots. That kind of sceptical, ironic downrightness is in fact what came to be the standard idiom of Scottish poetry. It is always present, suggesting a kind of norm of commonsense (what Burns called "countra wit"), even in the most abandoned comic flights. My point here is that it is through such processes in the sensibility, rather than in any outward censorship, that 'Calvinism' mainly affected the deeper life of the country. To make Calvinism itself a simple scapegoat merely smooths the path of that kind of nationalism which lives by pure antipathies—concealing its own lack of positive ideas by raging at convenient bugbears, whether in England or at home. Yeats's *Autobiographies* records most memorably how a nationalist cultural movement can be dragged down into chauvinism and pettiness by such attitudes. Another commonplace has been to suggest that literature, and free imagination generally, failed because the energies of the nation were, simply, channelled off into the Kirk: the Kirk became Scotland's true domain. What I suggest is that the peculiar Presbyterian frame of mind got an impulse from, and in turn singled

---

[1] *Ballates*, 'Knaw ye not God Imnipotent', p. 210; Robert Sempill, Preface to 'The Legend of the Bischop of St Androis Lyfe', *Satirical Poems of the Time of the Reformation*, ed. James Cranstoun (Scottish Text Society, Edinburgh: 1891), I, p. 349.

out and reinforced, an existing national bent, and that it is this bent which we find expressed in most of the significant vernacular poetry.

The effect of 'subjugation' described by Speirs is common to a great deal of this poetry. Ramsay reduces Caesar's battle to a scrap or tussle, and the Church struggle at the Reformation to a brawl—Lyndsay's satires

> . . . gave the scarlet whore a box
> Mair snell than all the pelts of Knox.[1]

We can imagine these very words spoken by an old-fashioned congregation zestfully recalling, as they file out of church, the minister's fine digs at the enemies of Presbyterianism. Again, Alexander Wilson, the Paisley weaver poet, has similar lines on the part played by Paine's *Rights of Man* in the struggle against tyranny:

> . . . Tammy Paine the buik has penned,
> And lent the courts a lounder.[2]

It is this same trick of popularising, bringing down into the streets, the affairs of the great which Burns deliberately works up into such rich comedy in, for example, 'The Ordination', both in the whole idea of making over a solemn Presbyterian ceremony into a village festivity, and in the poetic turn whereby the Presbyterian aggressiveness and denunciatory preaching turn the Old Testament into a pub brawl:

> . . . Zipporah, the scauldin' jad,
> Was like a bluidy teeger,
> I' th' inn that day.

Burns's uses of such idiom *are* deliberate. He is in delicately-balanced control of the bold and, as it were, bare-faced impropriety of his speech—it creates much of his satirical effect. Thus he can bring high life to the test of the commonsense of the working man, living close to the streets where the mass of the people must live and the ground where the basic work on which all depend is done. This is the spirit of the Grand Tour passage from 'The Twa Dogs':

> At operas an' plays parading,
> Mortgaging, gambling, masquerading,
> Or maybe, in a frolic daft,
> To Hague or Calais takes a waft,

[1] 'Epistle to James Clerk, Esq.', *Works*, III, p. 106.
[2] 'Address to the Synod of Glasgow and Ayr', *The Poems and Literary Prose of Alexander Wilson*, ed. Rev. A. B. Grosart (Paisley: 1876), II, p. 73.

To mak a tour an' tak a whirl,
To learn bon ton, an' see the world'.
*   There, at Vienna, or Versailles,*
He rives his father's auld entails;
Or by Madrid he takes the rout,
To thrum guitars an' fecht wi' nowt;
Or down Italian vista startles,
Wh-re-hunting amang groves o' myrtles:
Then bowses drumlie German-water,
To mak himsel' look fair an' fatter,
An' clear the consequential sorrows,
Love-gifts of Carnival signoras.

This is not all broad: some of the poetic turns release a considerable charge of meaning ("takes a waft", "Carnival
signoras"). But "To thrum guitars, an' fecht wi' nowt" moves
with the effect of a sneer and then a blow; it gets its force from
country wit, as though to say with a hoot of scorn, "Fight with
cattle!" Similarly, in 'The Author's Earnest Cry and Prayer to
the Scotch Representatives in the House of Commons', the tone
is of natural honest impatience with jerrymandering; it reduces
the Members of Parliament in London to local lads saying their
piece at a village meeting:

In gath'rin votes you were na slack;
Now stand as tightly to your tack:
Ne'er claw your lug, an' fidge your back,
*   An' hum an' haw;*
But raise your arm, an' tell your crack
*   Before them a'.*

These last two examples, however, must also make us
question the validity of such an idiom for a whole literature
(as that poetry, in Scotland, had to be). Ramsay's poetic
criticism of the professional soldier ends up in a shrug:

And 'midst his glories sheath'd his gooly,
*   And kiss'd his wife.*

Such reductive criticism seems too easily arrived at—it simply
writes off its subject. No sense of the physical nature, or the
complexities, of war and politics can be evoked, for these
are not given the full intelligent understanding which might
become 'criticism' as it penetrated its subject. We feel, indeed,
that a people confined to so simple-minded an outlook would be
disabled in the struggle for social development. Similarly in
'The Twa Dogs' Burns is content to sneer and hit at the young

blood from a distance; whereas Pope, in the passage from Book
IV of *The Dunciad* on which it was presumably based, creates a
wonderfully rich poetry in which the *attractions* of Europe are
potently evoked, along with the young man's foolishness:

> *Intrepid then, o'er seas and lands he flew:*
> *Europe he saw, and Europe saw him too . . .*
> *To happy convents, bosomed deep in vines,*
> *Where slumber abbots, purple as their wines:*
> *To isles of fragrance, lily-silvered vales,*
> *Diffusing languor on the panting gales:*
> *To lands of singing, or of dancing slaves,*
> *Love-whisp'ring woods, and lute-resounding waves.*
> *. . . Led by my hand, he sauntered Europe round,*
> *And gathered ev'ry vice on Christian ground;*
> *Saw ev'ry court, heard ev'ry king declare*
> *His royal sense of operas or the fair;*
> *The stews and palaces equally explored,*
> *Intrigued with glory, and with spirit whored:*
> *Tried all* hors-d'oeuvres, *all* liqueurs *defined,*
> *Judicious drank, and greatly-daring dined . . .*

Further, Pope has deep feeling for what is being allowed to
degenerate:

> *Spoiled his own language, and acquired no more;*
> *All classic learning lost on classic ground;*
> *And last turned air, the echo of a sound!*
> *See now, half-cured, and perfectly well-bred,*
> *With nothing but a solo in his head . . .*[1]

and it is because he has this feeling that his evocation of
degeneracy is so fully-imagined, and so decisive a 'criticism'.

Burns's dealings with this wider world are, in contrast, rather
prone to the too-obvious plain man's sarcasm of the 'Elegy on
the Year 1788' (a poem published in several local newspapers):

> *The Spanish empire's tint a head,*
> *An' my auld teethless Bawtie's dead;*
> *The tulzie's teugh 'tween Pitt an' Fox,*
> *An' oor gudewife's wee birdy cocks.*

The social implications of this deficiency in the Scottish poets
come into the open in 'The Author's Earnest Cry'. The poem
reminds us that the crofter Burns, like anyone else in any class,
was committed to relations with the ruling class, with the
aristocracy and bourgeoisie. With them he had to do business,

---

[1] *Poems*, pp. 171-2.

mingle, converse, correspond. His business with them is satirised in 'The Inventory', written on getting an assessment form from the surveyor of taxes in 1786 when extra taxes were being levied by Pitt:

> *Wheel-carriages I hae but few,*
> *Three carts, an' twa are feckly new;*
> *An auld wheelbarrow, mair for token,*
> *Ae leg an' baith the trams are broken;*
> *I made a poker o' the spin'le,*
> *An' my auld mither brunt the trin'le.*

This tone of light, off-hand contempt is kept up; the homely actuality of crofting life is, as it were, used against the government which addresses the masses in the language of property-owners:

> *For men, I've three mischievous boys,*
> *Run-deils for rantin' an' for noise;*
> *A gaudsman ane, a thrasher t'other:*
> *Wee Davock hauds the nowt in fother . . .*

In 'The Author's Earnest Cry', an imaginary appeal against extortionate excise regulations imposed from London, Burns creates irony by simulating the professional emotion of the beggar, alternately piteous and indignantly abusive:

> *God bless your Honors! can ye see't—*
> *The kind, auld, cantie carlin greet,*
> *An' no get warmly to your feet*
>   *An' gar them hear it . . .*

> *For G-d-sake, sirs! then speak her fair,*
> *An' straik her cannie wi' the hair . . .*

This tone is of course a humorous device; but it brings home to us that it came naturally to Burns—a Scots-speaking small farmer, remote from the centres of power—to write as one without a share in the full resources of wealth, goods, power, opportunity, or range of job available in his country, one whose privation was to the advantage of those who were in power.

Wherever we look at the social system under which Burns lived, we see that a sense of being 'on the outside' was inevitable for the poor man—if he was not content to live (actually or imaginatively) within the bounds of the village. It is the experience so memorably incarnated in *Jude the Obscure*. In Burns's day the ruling-class, alarmed by the people's new militancy, was making no bones about its position. The enlightened Cockburn assumed that to have some *millions* of starving people was inevitable under industrialisation: such "visitations" were "heartrending", but more for the "political danger" than for the "misery". A practising industrialist went much further: "The late stagnation has been exceedingly useful to our trade, and if it does not go too far it will be attended with the most beneficial consequences to men of real capital . . ." He deplored high wages because they encouraged workmen to gather in the ale-houses "where they became politicians and government-mongers, restless and discontented".[1] The 'discontents', of course, arose out of pub talk, not from the objective state of the people. . . . In fact the common people in Burns's Scotland were peculiarly deprived, especially of power to run their own life. To mention only the aspects which are immediately relevant: the Scottish Members of Parliament to whom Burns addressed his 'Cry' were indeed out of touch with the country, as we can see from the reports of how they performed in the House of Commons. They cared nothing for the mind of the people, and (some years later) belittled the orderly and determined Reform movement as an agitation for free whisky and no more gaugers, dismissing the petitions as put-up jobs signed in the gin-shops.[2] The electorate has been described as 'feudally' run. In 1788 there were 2,662 voters on the freeholders' roll (for a country of over a million); one or two lords controlled hundreds of paper votes; and in Burns's own county in 1788, 205 could vote out of a population of 65,000.[3] In the later days of Reform agitation, the historian Archibald Alison, who was no Radical, could write in the reactionary *Blackwood's* that "Cornwall and Scotland are the great fortresses of the aristocratic . . . factions".[4] The result (apart from the practical consequences of a minority government) was that the common people were less inclined to express themselves in political work and thinking. Most of the early Radicals were "of humble rank", it is true, and J. M. Robertson has written well of the advantage in humanity which such a spirit gave Burns over a patrician-minded man like Stevenson: "In spontaneously sympathising as he did alike with the American Revolution and the French Revolution, he

[1] Cockburn, *Journal*, II, pp. 4-5; Tom Johnston, *History of the Working Classes in Scotland* (Glasgow: 1920), p. 272.
[2] Hansard's *Parliamentary Debates*, 3rd Series (London: 1831), III, cols. 1243-4, 1320-1.
[3] Meikle, *Scotland and the French Revolution*, p. xvii; Mathieson, *Church and Reform*, p. 208; Snyder, *The Life of Robert Burns* (New York: 1932), p. 19.
[4] 'On the French Revolution, and Parliamentary Reform', III: *Blackwood's* (1831), Vol. XXIX, p. 440.

showed himself to be morally far above the average of the respectable people of his generation".[1] But this militancy, finally stirred by the American War and the French Revolution, had been slow to rouse. The people were less active than the Irish, generally not knowing the names of the government or what business it transacted; and at the Reform period petitions to Earl Grey's government were far less numerous proportionally from Scotland than from England and the Members of Parliament were especially reactionary, a clique any Tory government could rely on.[2]

Farming also reveals the undeveloped state of the people. Apart from backwardness in agriculture, the system was such that peasant folk had little opening for initiative and betterment in their own occupation. In the early 18th century English travellers remarked on (and Scotsmen admitted) the feudal and economic servitude of the Scottish farmer. "'Without those long and kind leases the tenants of England have, they are not encouraged by their lords in improvements.'" The heavy, and increasing, levies of corn which went with the compulsory use of the local mill (owned by the landlord) tended to discourage any attempt at increase of yield.[3] That was in the early 18th century. By Burns's day the Crown Commissioners for the estates forfeited by Jacobites had advised that leases should be extended and the more exorbitant landlord's rights done away with. Improving landlords were picking tenants for their ability, and discussing and advising with them on new kinds of farming. But the old constricting habits died hard;[4] and mental habits themselves get ingrained and are slow to dislodge, as we can see in such permanent deficiencies of Scots as the reductive idiom and the poor man's defensive pose, there in both Ramsay and Burns.[5] Furthermore, the gains resulting

[1] Mathieson, *Church and Reform*, p. 9; Robertson, *New Essays Towards a Critical Method* (London: 1897), pp. 290, 298.
[2] Meikle, *French Revolution*, pp. xviii-xix, 36-7, 41; Mathieson, *Church and Reform*, pp. 209, 213, 204.
[3] G. M. Trevelyan, *Ramillies and the Union with Scotland* (*op. cit.*), pp. 188 and n.; Mathieson, *Awakening of Scotland*, p. 287.
[4] Handley, *Scottish Farming*, pp. 240-2; John Sinclair, *General Report of the Agricultural State of Scotland* (Edinburgh: 1814), I, p. 174; Clapham, *Economic History*, p. 109; Handley, pp. 230-2.
[5] With Ramsay's 'Hame Content' compare Burns's 'Epistle to Davie':

> It's no in titles nor in rank;
> It's no in wealth like Lon'on bank,
> To purchase peace and rest:
> It's no in makin' muckle, mair;
> It's no in books, it's no in lear,
> To make us truly blest . . .

from improved farming were nullified, as far as quality of living was concerned, by the remorseless process, which shortly began, of converting the mass of small 'independent' producers into a propertyless proletariat. Burns himself often remarked that "the more highly cultivated he found an agricultural district, the more ignorant and degraded he almost always found the people", and that fine observer of society, the stone-mason geologist Hugh Miller, explains the process. The crofter, "in accordance with the distinguishing characteristic of the species as rational creatures", had "to look both before and after him. He had to think and act; to enact by turns the agriculturist and the corn-merchant; to manage his household, and to provide for term-day. He was alike placed beyond the temptation of apeing his landlord, or of sinking into a mere ploughing and harrowing machine. But, in many instances, into such a machine the farm-servant [the new country prole-tarian] sunk".[1] When Cobbett toured in Scotland, he found major frustrations blocking the development of the people. In the South-east especially, farm-workers had to stay in their bothies (the barracks put up to house the unmarried workers on the new large farms); they could not, as in England, set foot in the farmer's house. (The advantage which could result in culture, human relations, satisfaction from work, and co-operative communal and family spirit is finely shown by George Eliot in the scenes on the Poyser farm in *Adam Bede*.) Scottish country workers were utterly dependent on higher classes for their livelihood in that when they changed jobs they had to get a 'character' or reference from the farmer and also the minister of the parish they were leaving.[2] Lord Braxfield alleged in 1793 that in Scotland any man, "however low-born", could rise by ability "to the highest honours of the state".[3] But this was only in theory. Any sample of the men then in power shows that they tended to come from a small class favoured in birth, land, and wealth [4]—even apart from the cruel hobbles on the lower classes in the way of mortality-rate, health, opportunities to save for advanced education, and the like. Most liberal people would now agree to some

---

[1] *Essays* (3rd ed., Edinburgh: 1869), pp. 201-2. Compare Marx on "the expro-priation of the self-supporting peasants, with their separation from their means of production": *Capital*, Part VIII, ch. 30 (Vol. I, trans. Samuel Moore and Edward Aveling: Modern Library, New York: copyright 1906), pp. 819-21.

[2] Cobbett, *Tours in Scotland* (*op. cit.*), pp. 763, 851, 762.

[3] Johnston, *History of the Working Classes*, p. 223.

[4] See below, Chapter VII, note 3.

such account of those times. But what has not been well enough understood is the effects on the *quality* of ordinary life.

Serious frustration and friction could not but have resulted from such drags on the ordinary man's power of expanding his life. One result visible in the poetry is that sheer hostility and resistance to anything beyond their familiar range, the withdrawal into the local atmosphere, the grudge, suspicion, and lack of free sympathy and imagination which come out in the reductive idiom and that not wholly sound, throw-away wit which is so common in Burns, for example:

> Gie dreepin' roasts to countra lairds,
> Till icicles hing frae their beards;
> Gie fine braw claes to fine life-guards,
>   And maids of honor;
> An' yill an' whisky gie to cairds,
>   Until they sconner.

> 'A title, Dempster merits it;
> A garter gie to Willie Pitt;
> Gie wealth to some be-ledger'd cit,
>   In cent. per cent.;
> But give me real, sterling wit,
>   And I'm content . . .'

> O ye douce folk that live by rule,
> Grave, tideless-blooded, calm an' cool,
> Compar'd wi' you—O fool! fool! fool!
>   How much unlike!
> Your hearts are just a standing pool,
>   Your lives, a dyke!

('Epistle to James Smith')

Historically, what Burns there represents is the 'feudal Socialism' defined by Marx and Engels; their definition of it might have been written of Burns: "half lamentation, half lampoon; half echo of the past, half menace of the future; at times, by its bitter, witty, and incisive criticism, striking the bourgeoisie to the very heart's core; but always ludicrous in its effect, through total incapacity to comprehend the march of modern history".[1]

It is not only the poetry on specifically social themes which reveals these deficiencies. "It is always difficult to give an example of an absent quality" (in Henry James's phrase); but consider some passages from Fergusson.

---

[1] *Manifesto of the Communist Party* (Moscow: 1957), p. 90.

> *Death, what's ado? the de'il be licket,*
> *Or wi' your stang, you ne'er had pricket,*
> *Or our* AULD ALMA MATER *tricket*
>   *O' poor John Hogg,*
> *And trail'd him ben thro' your mark wicket*
>   *As dead's a log.*[1]

This audaciously *common* way with the conventional symbolism of death—the concreteness of the idiom which makes it possible —is felt at such points to come from a whole language peculiarly at home in a disabused, direct familiarity with the facts of life.[2] Historically, it fitted the Scots poets to avoid the unrealities of 'poetic diction' at a time when the language of English poetry had set into its most rigid forms.[3] Yet we feel at the same time a limitation at the heart of this strength. It is plainer if we put beside the elegy Fergusson's adaptation of Horace's Ode XI, Lib. I :

> *Now moisten weel your* geyzen'd wa'as
> *Wi' couthy friends and* hearty blaws;
> *Ne'er lat your* hope *so'ergang your* days,
> *For* eild *and* thraldom *never stays;*
> *The day looks* gash, *toot aff your* horn,
> *Nor care yae* strae *about the* morn.[4]

The downrightness of the Scots, so summary and practical, is an interesting equivalent for Horace's "carpe diem". Yet the off-hand attitude natural to Scots, even more marked at the beginning—"Ne'er fash your *thumb* what *gods* decree"—seems to preclude any realisation of the remorseless ageing ("invida aetas") which the poet is supposedly grappling with. Horace's poem has an alternating rhythm which evokes in turn the urge to dwell on pleasures and a realisation of inevitable fate:

> *. . . sapias, vina liques, et spatio brevi*
> *spem longam reseces. dum loquimur, fugerit invida*
> *aetas: carpe diem, quam minimum credula postero.*[5]

In contrast, Fergusson is at home in just the one feeling, that downrightness, as much impatient with fuss as savouring the pleasures ("toot aff your *horn*").

The effect of such Scots, as of the solid emphasis of 'John Hogg' ("As dead's a log"), is stultifying—it comes down hard

---

[1] 'Elegy on John Hogg, late Porter to the University of St Andrews': *Poems* (*op. cit.*), II, p. 191.   [2] See note 1, on Scots poetry about death.
[3] It also fitted Burns to be (as other writers have noted) an agent in weaning English poetry from the Augustan, by way of Wordsworth's *Lyrical Ballads.*
[4] *Poems*, II, p. 223.
[5] *Horatii Opera*, ed. Edward C. Wickham, revised by H. W. Garrod (Oxford: 1947): unpaged.

and bites off short, as does "Auld God is God".[1] In this it seems to reflect the way in which expression of feeling tended to be repressed or bitten off among peasant folk leading a desperately hard life amidst bleak conditions, or townsfolk whose finer feelings could not readily survive, or at least get outlet, in such conditions as were described in Chapter I. Hardship had even been rationalised into a moral advantage, for example by the extreme Presbyterians. Peden, a leading Covenanter minister, prophesied: "As long as the Lads are upon the Hills, and in Glens and Caves, you will have Bonnocks o'er Night; but, if once they were beneath the Beild of the Brae, you will have clean Teeth [i.e. nothing to eat], and mony a black and pale Face in Scotland".[2] Patrick Walker, who wrote down the histories and sayings of the Covenanters, was glad of his own sufferings because they had kept him from "wanton" dancing, "carnal vain springs".[2] It may be that this had entered deeply into certain of the peasantry as a curb of emotion. Carlyle said of his father (a Dumfriesshire stone-mason and crofter, and member of a Burgher or extreme-Presbyterian meeting house) that "he had not the free means to unbosom himself". A similar quality is found in a larger section of the peasantry by a Buchan minister writing in the *Old Statistical Account*: he associates their 'vulgarity' of language (defined, that is, in Augustan terms) with a want of "liveliness of imagination" and "warmth of feeling".[3] He equally warns against expecting of such folk the agreeable and polished expression which are "rather the effect of a cultivated taste, than of a cultivated understanding": that is, he recognises their distinctive character. Dialect speakers often excelled in powers of speech; their culture was strongly oral.[4] Yet there is also that marked vein of grippy constraint upon expression, which is specially relevant when literature is at issue, and relevant to an account of the difficulties and deficiencies of a popular culture.

The grippy and dinging type of speech is prominent in the work of the best Scottish novelists, men who were themselves thoroughly familiar with the small community. There is the speech of Gourlay and the Bodies in Brown's *The House with the Green Shutters*:

[1] Examples could be multiplied, esp. from the pithy end-lines which give the character of the 'Burns stanza', e.g. the end of Ramsay's 'Maggy Johnstoun':

> Guess whether ye're in heaven or hell,
> They're sure ye're dead!

[2] *Biographia Presbyteriana*, II, pp. 24-5; I, pp. 210-11.

[3] *Op. cit.* Vol. XV, p. 295.

[4] See below, Chapter VIII, on the oral basis for Ramsay, Fergusson, and Burns.

"It'th a fine morning, Mr Gourlay," he simpered.

"There's noathing wrong with the morning," grunted Gourlay, as if there was something wrong with the Deacon.[1]

And there is the whole run of the vernacular narrative in Lewis Grassic Gibbon's *A Scots Quair* (1932–4), as when the minister is supposed to have been caught out because he has been seen making love: "And *Oh, my dear, maybe the second Chris, maybe the third, but Ewan has the first for ever!* she was saying, whatever she meant by that; and syne as Dave Brown still looked the minister bent down and kissed her, the fool".[2] This grudging idiom seems also to have been provincial, affecting all classes in a backward country. Boswell characteristically recoils from Scottish familiarity, "the sarcastical Scotch humour" with its "jocularity and freedom"; and he imagines in Scots the digs which Rousseau's lack of dignity would expose him to in Scotland: "'Hoot, Johnnie Rousseau man, what for hae ye sae mony figmagairies? Ye're a bonny man indeed to mauk siccan a wark; set ye up. Canna ye just live like ither fowk?'"[3] What is interesting is that Boswell knew such Scots in his father, Lord Auchinleck, a judge and landowner; his speech is recorded in Scott's table-talk: "'There's nae hope for Jamie, mon . . . Jamie is gane clean gyte. What do you think, mon? He's done wi' Paoli—he's off wi' the land-louping scoundrel of a Corsican; and whose tail do you think he has pinned himself to now, mon? . . . A *dominie*, mon—an auld dominie! he keeped a schule, and caud it an acaadamy.'"[4]

Such speech is that of a people too much confined to one set of habits and one district, without ready outlet into or an open attitude towards other habits, other peoples. Carlyle himself was acutely aware of how such conditions could stultify. In his *Reminiscences* he constantly remarks on how such people may fail to 'develop'. He knew this well amongst his relatives; and he remarks on it whenever he has to comment on working-class literature. Robertson sees a similar want or strain in Carlyle himself; he suggests that his "spleen was largely the expression of an inherited need for hand labour, a need inhering in muscle and nerve; and indeed the Carlylean gospel of work, which inconsistently enough makes labour a virtue in itself,

[1] 1901 (edition Collins Classics, London: n.d.), p. 54.
[2] One-volume edition (London: 1952): *Sunset Song*, p. 190.
[3] *Boswell in Holland*, ed. F. A. Pottle (London: 1952), p. 378; *Boswell on the Grand Tour*, ed. F. A. Pottle (London: 1953), p. 254. I am not suggesting that Boswell's forced, sycophantic gentility is *preferable* to Scottish "jocularity and freedom".
[4] Lockhart, *Life of Scott*, II, p. 317.

irrespective of its direction, implies such a bias".[1] Of course such effects of society would tell only on certain temperaments; but it is clear that at a time when village Miltons were still likely to be bound to the village, the strain was liable to take toll, sometimes of health, sometimes of the very nerve of talent and outlook. Anyone who has read Maxim Gorky's *My Apprenticeship* and *My Universities* or a short story such as 'Konovalov' will agree that such strain, and an urgent concern for the better development or fulfilment of people born into such conditions, is likely to be at the core of literature produced by working-men.

In Scots vernacular poetry this shows also in the number of poems concerned with the simple living-needs of crofters, labourers, weavers, the people generally. James Thomson, the weaver poet of Kenleith (near Edinburgh), is typical of this kind, for example, his 'On the Times (in 1799)', a poem against farmers' exorbitant prices:

> *I winna ca' them a' blackguards,*
> *For ill they'll tak it;*
> *But in a wee they'll a' be lairds,*
> *Gif they can mak it. . . .*
>
> *To ha'd them right we strain ilk nerve*
> *O' hands or shanks;*
> *An' yet for a', I maun observe,*
> *We've little thanks.*

Thomson's attitude is entirely one of humble decency. In 'To the Masters' he appeals to farmers not to scrimp shearers of their rations,

> *For it's the meat, I hae heard say,*
> *That works the wark, not length o' day,*

and in 'Potatoes' (written in 1796 in prospect of a good crop) he accuses corn-hoarders of keeping up the price of meal:

> *For bodies poor they'll no respeck,*
> *But look like stink.*

The difficulty of his position comes out in the conclusion of 'On the Times'. He warns the exploiters to remember Hell, he wishes he could hang them, he moralises:

> *For ay the further ye gang in,*
> *Ye'll find it deeper.*[2]

[1] Carlyle, *Reminiscences*, esp. on his father, pp. 10-11; also pp. 130, 171, 227; on Burns, *Essays on Burns and Scott*, introd. Henry Morley (London: 1906), p. 60; on Ebenezer Elliott, the Corn Law poet, see *Critical and Miscellaneous Essays* (edition London: 1899), III, p. 154; Robertson, *Modern Humanists*, III, p. 9.

[2] *Poems*, ed. R. B. Langwill (London: 1894, reprinted from edition published for the author at Leith: 1801), pp. 24, 13, 151 and n., 26. For Thomson's typical career see note 2.

In short, he himself is helpless. Alexander Wilson of Paisley has a similar series of poems, based on the business side of his craft. He achieves much more than Thomson's utterly unliterary simplicity. 'The Shark' describes grinding bosses who build fortunes by skimping the workman's rewards and perquisites; and 'Hollander, or Light Weight' and 'Hab's Door' describes buyers' practices of bullying and gulling the ignorant workmen who are in their hands and paying short price by spoiling the cloth they are offered. Touches suggest the intensity of his moral feelings:

> *The mair we get by heuk and cruk*
> *We aften grow the greedier;*
> *Shark raiket now thro' every neuk*
> *To harl till him speedier;*
> *His ghastly conscience, pale and spent,*
> *Was summoned up, right clever;*
> *Syne, wi' an execration sent*
> *Aff, henceforth and for ever,*
> *Frae him that day.*

His natural emotion at dishonesty gives rise to a broad, soap-box kind of lampooning:

> *Wha cou'd believe a chiel sae trig*
> *Wad cheat us o' a bodle?*
> *Or that sae fair a gowden wig*
> *Contained sae black a noddle?*

He hits off the would-be genteel speech of the cunning buyer:

> *Dear man!—that wark'll never do;*
> *See that: ye'll no tak tellin',*

and he appeals to a sense of community:

> *What town can thrive wi' sic a crew*
> *Within its entrails crawlin'* . . .

The weird, nightmarish atmosphere of the buyer's shop in 'Hab's Door' suggests the ordeal of the dependent workman.[1] Such poetry succeeds, on its level of simple propaganda which here and there becomes something more, because its style is so direct, so close to facts. In the English equivalents we often feel that a quite inappropriate language from formal literature is getting in the way, for example in Elliott the Corn Law poet's

---

[1] *Poems and Literary Prose*, II, pp. 59, 60, 62, 66, 66-9.

'Steam in Sheffield' or in the poem by a Birmingham factory worker which Engels quotes as typical of this kind:

> There is a King, and a ruthless King,
> Not a King of the poet's dream;
> But a tyrant fell, white slaves know well,
> And that ruthless King is Steam. . . .
>
> The sighs and groans of Labour's sons
> Are music in their ear,
> And the skeleton shades, of lads and maids,
> In the Steam King's Hells appear.[1]

In contrast the Scotsmen have the great advantage of an idiom which is itself close to experience, as in *Whisperings to the Unwashed* by another weaver, William Thom from Aberdeen:

> And dead, the session saints begrudge ye
> The two-three deals in death to lodge ye,
> And grudge the grave, wherein to drop ye,
> And grudge the very muck to hap ye.[2]

Such poems cannot usually do much more than offer parallels to social history proper (Wilson's stanza on Shark's conscience is exceptional). Wilson was fined for libel, commanded to burn his poems at Paisley Cross, and imprisoned because he was too poor to afford the fine—a main cause of his decision to emigrate.[3] In this he was a victim of the police atmosphere which gripped Scotland during the French Revolution. Tradesmen of Jacobinical leanings had their credit stopped at the bank, housewives bought only from shopkeepers of proved 'loyalty', manufacturers dismissed workers suspected of disloyalty, even charitable work was looked on with suspicion.[4] Wilson's editor says that his poems were, on the facts, strictly justified; and we know that the weavers, "once the aristocracy of labour", suffered specially from the slump waves of the early Industrial Revolution. They could not even benefit from owning their own means of production, the loom, and from working their own hours, because prices were at the mercy of the buyers.[5] Wilson's helplessness, like Thomson's, comes out

[1] Marx and Engels, *On Britain*, pp. 219-21.
[2] Quoted by W. A. Gatherer, 'The Flyting Scotsman': *Lines Review*, ed. J. K. Annand (Edinburgh: Spring 1958), No. 14, p. 10.
[3] *Poems and Prose*, I, p. xxxvii.   [4] Meikle, *French Revolution*, p. 155.
[5] Wilson, *Poems and Prose*, I, p. xxxvii; Marwick, *Economic Developments in Victorian Scotland*, p. 20; Mathieson, *Church and Reform*, p. 148: a weaver convicted of sedition, who quoted *Hamlet* when speaking in his own defence, said that working fifteen hours a day he could make 5s. a week and a less expert man 3s. a week; p. 152: in the slump of 1819 the Ayrshire weavers were making 3s. 6d. for a 96-hour week and many were "literally starving": Johnston, *Working Classes in Scotland*, p. 271.

in his conclusions—"Wha cou'd believe . . .", "What town can thrive . . .", and the prayer that the devil will carry off the crooks. Robert Fergusson is not so firmly associated with the people as a whole (he was in fact a lawyer's clerk); but his inclination, whenever it comes to the test, is to identify himself with popular feeling. His satire 'The Ghaists', written near the end of his short life, suggests that he was coming onto a mature style and leaving behind the slapstick of his early work. The poem is about proposed legislation to empower, indeed to oblige, trustees of Scottish schools endowments to invest their funds in government stock—resented in Scotland because, among other drawbacks, it would take Scottish capital out of the country. Some of 'The Ghaists' is just versified argument, but at its best it is felt with the intense immediacy of poetry:

> *Hale interest for my fund can scantly now*
> *Cleed a' my callants backs, and stap their mou'.*
> *How maun their weyms wi' sairest hunger slack,*
> *Their duds in targets flaff upo' their back,*
> *Whan they are doom'd to keep a lasting Lent,*
> *Starving for England's weel at* three per cent.

> *. . . They'll sell their country, flae their conscience bare,*
> *To gar the weigh-bauk turn a single hair.*
> *The government need only bait the line*
> *Wi' the prevailing flee, the gowden coin,*
> *Then our executors, and wise trustees,*
> *Will sell them fishes in forbidden seas,*
> *Upo' their dwining country girn in sport,*
> *Laugh in their sleeve, and get a place at court.*[1]

Here the natural bite of the vernacular works perfectly within the metre of the heroic couplet ("wi' sairest hunger *slack*"); and the final image of the venal Establishment suggests that Fergusson was learning from Pope in composing a poetry in which the business of society could be felt as immediately as his 'personal experience'.

Of Burns it is sometimes said that he was not really 'a man of the people' (especially by clergymen, in January). But his poetry, whenever it refers beyond his immediate community, accepts the part of spokesman for the oppressed or ill-used, and in doing so often achieves rare quality. Burns often felt ill at ease inside his own class; he is far from a simple working-men's representative, like Thomson or Wilson. Yet his social position is unmistakable. In the 'Address of Beelzebub' (suppressed

[1] *Poems*, II, pp. 143-4, 287.

from the Kilmarnock volume) he speaks for the highlanders of Glengarry whose landlord, Macdonald, wanted to stop them emigrating to Canada:

> They, *an' be d-mn'd! what right hae they*
> *To meat or sleep, or light o' day?*
> *Far less—to riches, pow'r, or freedom,*
> *But what your lordship likes to gie them?*
>
> *But hear, my lord! Glengary, hear!*
> *Your hand's owre light on them, I fear;*
> *Your factors, grieves, trustees, and bailies,*
> *I canna say but they do gaylies;*
> *They lay aside a' tender mercies,*
> *An' tirl the hallions to the birses;*
> *Yet while they're only poind't and herriet,*
> *They'll keep their stubborn Highland spirit:*
> *But smash them! crash them a' to spails,*
> *An' rot the dyvors i' the jails!*
> *The young dogs, swinge them to the labour;*
> *Let wark an' hunger mak them sober!*
> *The hizzies, if they're aughtlins fawsont,*
> *Let them in Drury-lane be lesson'd!*
> *An' if the wives an' dirty brats*
> *Come thiggin' at your doors an' yetts,*
> *Flaffin' wi' duds, an' gray wi' beas',*
> *Frightin' away your ducks an' geese;*
> *Get out a horsewhip or a jowler,*
> *The langest thong, the fiercest growler,*
> *An' gar the tatter'd gypsies pack*
> *Wi' a' their bastards on their back!*

Here Burns's usual mingling of geniality with his irony is quite absent. The double-edged way in which he seems to take the landlord's part is akin to Mark Twain's treatment of slave-owner psychology in *Huckleberry Finn*, only it is ferocious instead of comic. In fact the Highland Society was meeting in London to raise a subscription to help the farming and fisheries of these highland emigrants and induce them to stay.[1] Burns's almost hysterical fury of sarcasm must be taken as a permanent feeling, ready to rise to the surface at any seeming exploitation, and natural to a man of his economic status. He was bound to feel it, for clearances were not only highland, they had also affected Burns's own district. Numerous families were evicted in Galloway in the 1720's to clear the land for the more profitable sheep pasture, and gangs of 'levellers and dyke-breakers' gathered in

[1] Chambers-Wallace, *Burns*, I, p. 347.

Dumfries to resist the landlords.[1] Again, in the 'Epistle to Davie' Burns evokes in sharp detail the hardship which was commonplace to the labourer:

> *To lie in kilns and barns at e'en,*
> *When banes are crazed, and bluid is thin. . . .*

It is often implied that human beings, who as we know are endlessly adaptable, can get used to any living conditions, however hard. The first-hand evidence often points the other way. When Hugh Miller and some mates, skilled stone-workers, arrived in Wester Ross to do a job, they were housed in a derelict outbuilding, "merely a roof-covered tank of green stagnant water, about three-quarters of a foot in depth". "'That a dwelling for human creatures!'", one of the men said. "'If I was to put my horse intil't, poor beast! the very hoofs would rot off him in less than a week.'" [2] Nor was wretched housing unusual. A "very considerable number" of farm-workers were housed in bothies, and Miller has this account of the wear-and-tear and self-corrupting hatred of the employer which such accommodation produced: "We never heard the name of the farmer mentioned among his servants without some accompanying expression of dislike; we never saw one of them manifest the slightest regard for his interest. They ill-treated his horses, neglected his cattle, left his corn to rot in the fields. Some of them could speak of his approaching ruin with positive glee." [3] Burns makes a simple summary comment on the situation of those with very little to come and go on which reminds us that he was writing shortly after a season of great scarcity and that his own means were so scanty that he could not bring out a second Kilmarnock edition for want of £27 to pay for the paper: [4]

> *They're no sae wretched's ane wad think,*
> *Tho' constantly on poortith's brink,*
> *They're sae accustomed wi' the sight,*
> *The view o't gies them little fright.*

('The Twa Dogs')

Generally, where other poets in the line can only render their own situation and express their helplessness, Burns rises

---

[1] Johnston, *Working Classes in Scotland*, pp. 182-5.
[2] *My Schools and Schoolmasters* (edition Edinburgh: 1907), p. 259.
[3] 'The Bothy System': *Essays* (*op. cit.*), pp. 200, 205. All the 'Political and Social' essays are relevant, esp. 'Our Working Classes', 'Peasant Properties', 'The Cottages of our Hinds', 'The Highlands', and 'The Scotch Poor-Law'.
[4] Handley, *Scottish Farming*, p. 12; Snyder, *Life of Burns*, p. 152.

to all the feelings of a man of great sensitivity pitting his whole imagination against the obdurate system, with all kinds of irony and sarcasm released as a result. Two stanzas on the (bourgeois) social life which was remote from him, touched off by his own poverty and insecurity, give rise to passages of rare quality in which the words come together into one rich compound metaphor.

> Do ye envy the city gent,
> Behind a kist to lie an' sklent;
> Or purse-proud, big wi' cent. per cent.
> An' muckle wame,
> In some bit brugh to represent
> A bailie's name?

('Second Epistle to J. Lapraik')

*   *   *

> Had I to guid advice but harket,
> I might, by this, hae led a market,
> Or strutted in a bank and clarket
> My cash-account;
> While here, half-mad, half-fed, half-sarket,
> Is a' th' amount.[1]

Burns constantly gets his effect by singling out details of simple living conditions. Thinking of Robert Fergusson's miserable end, he says to the "E'nbrugh gentry":

> The tythe o' what ye waste at cartes
> Wad stow'd his pantry!

('Epistle to William Simson')

Similarly he echoes the common prayer for 'food and raiment' in the closing lines of 'The Author's Earnest Cry' with their trenchant double effect—flinging at Parliament with the tone of both a cocky insult and a deliberate and bitter reminder of how most people have to live:

> God bless your Honors, a' your days,
> Wi' sowps o' kail and brats o' claise. . . .

His passages on living conditions are not always militant. Generally, ordinary working life is what supplies his subjects, his *dramatis personæ*, his very metaphors. The first few stanzas of both the second epistle to John Lapraik and 'The Vision'

---

[1] From 'The Vision'. The poem was praised by contemporary critics for the fustian English allegory of which it mainly consists; but the first six stanzas, in Scots, make up a fine self-contained poem on Burns's domestic work and leisure.

are admirably-realised poetry of country work, and it is this that he constantly draws on to create a comic point.[1] But rankling, radical dissatisfaction is always near at hand when he enters on a specifically social subject.

Such a situation, as we may judge from Burns, could not give rise to a complete and mature poetry, however fine the spirit visible in it. The trenchant satire I have quoted crops up in snatches only. It is incomplete and ill-developed beside Pope, who found an integrated form for his whole social experience. The *form* of 18th-century Scottish poetry tends to be incommensurate with wholeness of experience, as well as the reductive idiom. The range of the forms used is rather restricting—the 'Habbie' or Burns stanza (its short lines suited to the favourite pithy moralising), the couplet of four-beat lines (Ramsay's 'Fables', Fergusson's 'Auld Reikie', Burns's 'Twa Dogs'), the rollicking stanza taken from the 16th-century 'The Cherry and the Slae' through Ramsay's 'The Poet's Wish' and used in Burns's 'Epistle to Davie', and the rollicking 'Christis Kirk' stanza taken through Ramsay's pastiche and used in Fergusson's 'Leith Races' and Burns's 'Holy Fair' and 'Ordination'. A result of the taste for forms based on social festivities is to limit the kind of life, and the attitude to it, that can be expressed. Conviviality, the drink, music, and good-fellowship of the pub, the fun and knock-about of the public holiday—such things form the situation and state of mind from which much of the vernacular poetry at least starts. One cannot but feel that it is at the expense of the more inward feelings and settled and abiding concerns of the people. No Scots poet of common life goes so deep as Chaucer in his 'Wife of Bath's Prologue'. Chaucer is saturated in the ways of common folk, yet his poetry is not in the least dragged down by it. Common fun figures in it all right:

> *For evere yet I loved to be gay,*
> *And for to walke in March, Averill, and May,*
> *Fro hous to hous, to heere sondry talys—*
> *That Jankyn clerk, and my gossyb dame Alys,*
> *And I myself, into the feeldes wente.*
> *Myn housbonde was at Londoun al that Lente;*
> *I hadde the bettre leyser for to pleye,*
> *And for to se, and eek for to be seye*
> *Of lusty folk . . .*

[1] See also note 4.

95

But the Wife also rises to a pitch of *awareness* of her own situation which is almost tragic:

> *But, Lord Christ! whan that it remembreth me*
> *Upon my yowthe, and on my jolitee,*
> *It tikleth me aboute myn herte roote.*
> *Unto this day it doth myn herte boote*
> *That I have had my world as in my tyme.*
> *But age, allas! that al wole envenyme,*
> *Hath me biraft my beautee and my pith.*
> *Lat go, farewel! the devel go therwith!*
> *The flour is goon, ther is namore to telle;*
> *The bren, as I best kan, now moste I selle . . .*[1]

The poem is in sum an excellent presentment of the whole life of an uneducated woman from the common people. The Wife is stout-hearted, triumphantly practical, gossipy, bawdy, mercenary, her mind a rag-bag of medieval superstition and scraps of learning—in which she is well able to stand up to her clerical adversaries—and her wayward speech is perfectly got. The poet's art is such that something like the fullness of his own vision of life can be mediated through so vernacular style.[2] Beside such art Scots poetry indeed seems 'incomplete'.

It is true that Burns puts the 'rollicking' genre to original uses; and the 18th-century 'festive' poetry (for example Fergusson's 'The Daft-Days', Ramsay's 'Elegy on Paty Birnie', a comedy of a roving fiddler, or Burns's 'Jolly Beggars') is not as primitive as, say, 'Christis Kirk on the Green', which has little room for any but the one feeling of brutal abandon in which the whole village loses itself. But a popular style originating in brutal knockabout is still limiting when used for satire of 18th-century life. The result may be comic but finally trivial or careless, as in Burns's political poems, for example the 'ballads' for the Kirkcudbright election of 1795:

> *Fy, let us a' to Kirkcudbright,*
> *For there will be bickerin' there . . .*

> *And there will be* Douglasses *doughty,*
> *New christening towns far and near;*
> *Abjuring their democrat doings,*
> *By kissin' the —— o' a Peer . . .*[3]

---

[1] *The Works of Geoffrey Chaucer*, ed. F. N. Robinson (2nd ed., London: 1957), pp. 81, 80.

[2] Compare Yeats on Synge in my epigraph: "by an illusion of admirable art, every one seems to be thinking and feeling as only countrymen could think and feel".

[3] 'Ballads on Mr Heron's Election, 1795: Ballad First.' Considered as political satire, it is as though Yeats had written no poems on such subjects apart from 'The Ghost of Roger Casement' and 'Come Gather Round Me, Parnellites' (from *Last Poems*).

The result may, again, be to reduce the significance even of so good a poem as 'The Ordination'. The comic idea of making the solemn ordination a village rough-and-tumble is certainly telling, yet we feel that to bring it off the poet has had to immerse himself in the parodied crudity, and so to sacrifice any means of conveying some finer attitude of his own. Or again the result may be offensively feckless, as in Hogg's slapstick version of Culloden, 'Bauldy Frazer':

> *Sic hurly-burly ne'er was seen,*
> *Wi' huffs, an' cuffs, an' blindit een . . .*[1]

This constant resort to communal festivity reads like a literary counterpart of the abandoned fun, turned to as a release from hardship, which is typical of a people in that undeveloped state. Taine speaks of Burns's "strange gaiety, savage and nervous, and which, in better style, resembles that of the *Ça ira*",[2] and this kind of emotion seems to have had something to do with his way of life. An early 19th-century account of coal-mining in the Forth Valley and Midlothian describes the women who carried the 170-lb. loads of coal up the pit stairs for shifts of eight, twelve, or more hours at a time, "weeping most bitterly, from the excessive severity of their labour; but the instant they have laid down their burden on the hill, they resume their cheerfulness, and return down the pit singing". The author shows, quoting a remark by one of them, that they were "fully sensible, and feel the severity of their labour";[3] yet the sheer strain of the job was distorting their feelings from moment to moment, forcing them from strain to release to strain again, shortening as it were the whole mental horizon. Marx's description of overworked engine-drivers is similar: "At a certain point their labour-power failed. Torpor seized them. Their brain ceased to think, their eyes to see."[4] The coal-heaving, at least, is a lower kind of labour than that of any of the worker poets discussed above. But not only did Burns feel for the plight of any worker; also, in his own life the most wearing heavy work (which irreparably damaged his heart when he was a growing boy and led to his early death) is associated with troughs of depression, for example:

[1] *Songs and Ballads (op. cit.)*, p. 53.
[2] *History of English Literature*, trans. H. van Laun (Edinburgh: 1874), III, p. 397.
[3] Robert Bald, *A General View of the Coal Trade of Scotland* (Edinburgh: 1812), pp. 132, 141.
[4] *Capital (op. cit.)*, p. 279.

The thresher's weary flingin'-tree,
The lee-lang day had tired me;
And when the day had clos'd his e'e,
Far i' the west,
Ben i' the spence, right pensivelie,
I gaed to rest . . .

All in this mottie, misty clime,
I backward mus'd on wasted time . . .

('The Vision')

A related outlet for hard-pressed feelings was evangelical religion. D. H. Lawrence describes in the opening pages of *Apocalypse* how a religion which prophesies doom to the worldly and rich is a bitter vicarious satisfaction to poor folk; they throw themselves into its tirades. In Scotland there were actual counterparts to the violent abandon of the festivity poetry, for example evangelical outbursts such as the open-air preachings at Cambuslang in 1742, accompanied by convulsions, prostration, groaning, nose-bleeding; or the services of the Seceders, where (according to one of their leading ministers, Ralph Erskine) the preacher could often "scarcely be heard for the weeping noise that surrounds him".[1] Such hysteria (now unknown) is the other pole to the unquenchable animal spirits which show in the rhythm and action of such poems as 'Peiblis to the Play' or Burns's 'Hallowe'en'. Again we may remember equivalent things in Gorky, the elaborate conventions of brutal fun, half-believed comforting sayings, fables, and images of escape (which made up his grandmother's religion), and moment-to-moment forgetfulness, by which such people as his relatives and workmates tided themselves through their cruel life.

As the workers got outlets into a wider life, and organised themselves for political work, study, negotiation on wages and working conditions, and buying and distributing food, their state of mind *vis-à-vis* society could begin to change.[2] Cockburn noticed that workers congregated in the towns, even if there was a better chance of work elsewhere: "They are gratified by appearing in their corporate character, not merely from pride, but because they see that number and unity best secure relief, and, if carried far enough, make them irresistible".[3] Their

[1] W. L. Mathieson, *Scotland and the Union, 1695–1747* (Glasgow: 1905), pp. 264, 266-7.

[2] See, e.g., Meikle, *French Revolution*, p. 155; Mathieson, *Church and Reform*, pp. 144 ff., 239-43; Johnston, *Working Classes in Scotland*, pp. 303-6, 382-4. The corresponding change in reading habits is discussed in Chapter VII.

[3] *Journal*, I, pp. 2-4.

quite new kind of communal gathering, for example to press the government for Reform, Cockburn calls "one of the most impressive marks of their state"; and he describes a Glasgow meeting in 1831, attended by 100,000 people, in which Glasgow and the near-by towns walked in procession to the Green, divided into crafts, societies, villages, and parishes, with their colours and emblems.[1] Thus something of the old community ceremony persisted under the new economic order. It is at about this time, just after Burns, that the old kind of popular poetry peters out. A late survival is a poem ridiculing a Chartist hunger march during the '40's, from Dundee to Forfar. The march is ridiculed as a grand spree:

> *For some young imps, wi' squib and preen,*
> *Caused such a great commotion*
> *That lasses crushed, cuist up their een,*
> *Like zealots in devotion,*
> > *An' scriegh'd that day.*[2]

There the anti-piety of Burns is taken up along with one of his styles. This poem is not (unlike, say, Ramsay's 'Christis Kirk') self-consciously popular; it is straightforward local lampoon. But obviously it can do no more than lampoon, or caricature. It cannot take the full measure of the popular movement it is criticising (as Burns could with 18th-century Kirk life), and its imagery, e.g. the "zealots", is no longer truly contemporary.

Scotland thus lacks a poetry which develops on into the modern or industrial age, and it is surely related to this that it rarely brings serious powers of *mind* to bear on experience from the point of view of the working-class. The Scottish worker poets are a more spontaneous off-shoot of this class than anything in England's Corn Law poet, Ebenezer Elliott. But poems of Elliott's such as 'The Village Patriarch' and 'Steam at Sheffield' do have the merit of suggesting intelligent, disinterested thought about their subjects from 'low life', for example the ironical passage from 'The Village Patriarch' which sees the habits of a lord in the poacher:

> *. . . Honest Jem works not,*
> *Begs not, but thieves by plundering beggars here.*
> *Wise as a lord, and quite as good a shot,*
> *He like his betters, lives in hate and fear,*
> *And feeds on partridge, because bread is dear . . .*

[1] *Ibid.* pp. 9, 15.
[2] George Mudie, 'The Rebels' Rout': see Leslie C. Wright, *Scottish Chartism* (Edinburgh: 1953), p. 227.

See how magnificently he breaks down
His neighbour's fence, if so his will requires! . . .
Jem rises with the moon; but when she sinks,
Homeward, with sack-like pockets, and quick heels,
Hungry as borough-mongering ghoul, he slinks.
He *reads not, writes not, thinks not—scarcely feels* . . .[1]

Elliott is plainly drawing some of his thoughtfully and seriously ironic manner from Crabbe; and that is just the kind of influence from a more 'complete' poetry by which Scottish popular poetry failed to benefit. The work and career of John Clare (often compared with Burns) makes a relevant contrast. John Speirs remarks that though he became a 'literary' poet (a follower of Pope), "he continued to share even as such a poet the traditional life of the countryside". He also differs from the Scotsmen in having educated himself poetically through reading 18th-century art poetry. As with them, the Bible and the ballads were staple literary food amongst the people from whom he came; but whereas the Scots poets were dependent on a medieval art poetry and very limited oral work,[2] Clare considered the ballads recited by his almost illiterate father rather trash and it was to the ampler poetry of the recent English classics that he turned for suggestions.[3] Scottish poetry, in contrast, became sidetracked onto the lines of the comic poems from Watson's *Choice Collection*. A convention arose of deliberately or unconsciously ludicrous *genre* scenes of domestic or 'low' life, and the seriously original poet had to rise through this inferior medium if he was to reach a level worthy of his talent.

What 'might have been' in the way of a more inclusive Scots poetry is perhaps glimpsed in a poem to the Sempills' name in Watson which is very different from 'The Piper of Kilbarchan', Francis Sempill's 'The Banishment of Poverty'. It is a little allegory of the author's hardships during the religious troubles, set in "Fernyier, when Whigs were ill mischiev'd", that is, when the Presbyterians were routed at Bothwell Bridge. The poet is shown as dogged by "that pultron Povertie":

> *There we shook hands, cauld be his cast;*
> *An ill dead may that custron die;*
> *For there he gripped me full fast,*
> *When first I fell on cautionrie.*

[1] *The Poetical Works of Ebenezer Elliott*, ed. Edwin Elliott (London: 1876), I, pp. 229-30. [2] See below, Chapter IV, pp. 119-20.
[3] Speirs, review of *The Poems of John Clare*, ed. J. W. Tibble: *Scrutiny* (June 1935), Vol. IV, No. 1, p. 85.

The narrative has touches that suggest a ballad: a later line is given by Watson as "I had not tarried an hour or two", on the lines of "They hadna sail'd a league, a league".[1] But the sense the poem gives of a modern society, traversed and contacted at representative points by the teller, is quite unballad-like. He scours the country for "forrage":

> No man would open me the door,
> Because my comrade stood me by.
> They dread full ill I was right poor,
> By my forcasten company.

In Edinburgh:

> I grein'd to gang on the plain-stanes,
> To see if comrades wad me ken:
> We twa gaid pacing there our laines,
> The hungry hour 'twixt twelve and ane.
>
> Then I ken'd no way how to fen,
> My guts rumbl'd like a hurle-barrow;
> I din't with saints and noblemen,
> Even sweet St Giles and Earl of Murray.
>
> · · · ·
>
> I slipt my page and stour'd to Leith,
> To try my credit at the wine;
> But foul a dribble fil'd my teeth,
> He gript me at the coffee sign.[2]

The rest of the poem allegorises his suits to various noblemen, ending with the Duke of Albany,

> Where one blink of his princely eye,
> Put that foul foundling to the flight . . .

The poem as a whole is uneven, and rather thin, but it is an original experiment in the styles which it brings together: the ballad narrative, touches of alliterating abuse from the old flyting style, the easy use of community imagery ("the coffee sign") such as was typical of the social poetry, and also echoes of a 17th-century gentlemanly dignity—"No man would open me the door, Because my comrade stood me by". We are familiar with this measured simplicity from the poetry of Lovelace and Marvell's 'Horatian Ode', and, in Scotland, the poetry in English collected by Watson, for example the poems

---

[1] James Watson (ed.), *A Choice Collection of Comic and Serious Scots Poems* (Edinburgh, 1706, 1709, 1711; ed. used, Glasgow: 1869), I, p. 16.
[2] Quoted from Paterson (ed.), *Poems of the Sempills*, pp. 51-5.

of Sir Robert Aytoun and the few by Montrose that survive:
the 'Lines on the Execution of King Charles I':

> *Great, good, and just, could I but rate*
> *My grief, and thy too rigid fate . . .*

or "My dear and only love, I pray":

> *He either fears his fate too much,*
> *Or his desert is small,*
> *Who puts it not unto the touch,*
> *To gain, or lose it all.*[1]

The Sempills' editor notes the traditional fact that Francis
was "intimate with many of the English officers in the army of
the Commonwealth at Glasgow, who are said to have highly
appreciated his acknowledged wit and humour".[2] In his poem
this element is able to co-exist with the vernacular at the centre
of his sensibility. The "idea of vulgarity" which poisons a
language had not yet made the overtly Scottish side of the
gentleman's culture improper for literary use.[3]

The Scots poems of Dr Alexander Pennecuik (1652–1722)
have similar implications. 'Peter's Many Obligations, given in
to King James VI' and the more substantial 'Truth's Travels'
are partly archaic exercises, with their Morality-like personifications 'Truth' and 'Vanity'. But they too suggest an effort to
find some form for the experience of the whole society, and here
and there they achieve some moral subtlety:

> *The Judge was first put in his place,*
> *And Warldly gain crap in behind him,*
> *Who durst not come before his face*
> *For fear her golden glance should blind him.*[4]

I do not mean to suggest that Sempill and Pennecuik are anything but greatly inferior to Fergusson and Burns, in social
interest and in liveliness of language. Burns's type of poetry
develops right away from that attempted mixture of the colloquial and the older formal style, and the popular, comic vein
was apparently what Burns needed for his experience. Nevertheless, this popular vein could not be more than a partial one for

---

[1] *Choice Collection*, III, pp. 107-12.
[2] *Poems of the Sempills*, p. 116.
[3] The "idea of vulgarity" is a phrase of Cockburn's from his *Life of Jeffrey* (I,
p. 48), where he is describing how by the later 18th century educated people had
become irretrievably self-conscious about Scots speech.
[4] *The Works of Dr Alexander Pennecuik* (edition Edinburgh & London: 1815),
p. 395.

the whole culture of the country, and this was felt by the poets themselves, as we see in their many efforts to extend their range.

The major case of this lies in the extraordinary change that came over Burns's poetry once the early creative burst at Mossgiel was over. Extraordinary because, as I contend, Burns was in a wonderfully original and rich vein in the poems that may be called his satires (they include more personal poetry, such as epistles and the opening of 'The Vision'); yet there is precious little to compare with that group, for serious creative quality, in his whole work from the Edinburgh visit of 1786-7 to his death in 1796.[1] Leslie Stephen calls him "a poet who has left behind him an impression of power quite astonishing when compared with the fragmentary character of his work".[2] Only, I should say, in 'Holy Willie's Prayer', 'To a Louse', 'The Ordination', 'The Holy Fair', and 'The Twa Herds' does he seem to have braced and concentrated himself to write up to the fullness of what was in him and in the life he knew. After 1786 one finds a parallel in his production between mediocre versifying with no creative core (apart from the job of arranging songs) and spasmodic efforts to get through to more satisfactory forms of writing. Mr Speirs writes on this point:

> It was probably a positive advantage to Burns that he was compelled to work within these narrowly defined limits. It was a condition probably of his success. But the three years of poetic productivity at Mossgiel, which resulted in the Kilmarnock volume, were, it seems, sufficient practically to exhaust the possibilities. It is difficult to see what else was left him to do, if he was not simply to repeat himself, except turn for the remainder of his life to the songs.[3]

To explain this 'exhaustion' requires more emphasis on the deficiencies of the vernacular tradition than Mr Speirs might admit. For surely creative possibilities are not a finite repertoire, to be simply 'exhausted' or 'repeated'. The tradition at this point lived in the man and poet, Burns, with his own experiences. In particular he has an urge to master subjects outside his own immediate way of life. It is this that comes out in his constant experiments from 1786 to 1796.

[1] Justification of this point is meant to emerge piecemeal from the passages of strong Burns quoted in this and the following chapter. It has been made before in one way or another by various critics.

[2] *Eighteenth Century Thought*, II, p. 454.

[3] *Scots Literary Tradition*, p. 125.

There persists after 1786 what is recognisably the old vein of social satire, for example the 'Elegy on the Year 1788'. Its sorry crudity may or may not represent a loss of power in this vein, but what is certain is that he did not again find in local activities any such positive suggestions as he had found in the Kirk and community of his early days. The best songs stand out as being still fed by his whole experience, for example 'Whistle and I'll come to ye, my lad' or 'A man's a man for a' that', written as a song but very close in its imagery to the early poems on the theme of peasant self-reliance:

Ye see yon birkie ca'd 'a lord',
Wha struts, an' stares, an' a' that . . .

But most of the songs are unsustained. Often the direct, dramatic opening runs out into literary padding, moralising in the abstract as the impulse fails, for example 'O let me in this ae night' or 'Oh way ye wha's in yon town'. Precisely the same applies to Ramsay (for example 'An thou were my ain thing', 'This is no my ain house', and 'For the sake of somebody'[1]). We must conclude that touching up songs was a second-rate job for an 18th-century poet of any quality.

Burns's preoccupation with songs started up very soon after the first edition of his poems. His first letter to James Johnson, the first song publisher he had to do with, is dated 4.5.1787.[2] In October of that year he wrote to the Rev. John Skinner, inviting him to help in collecting songs: "I have been absolutely crazed about it, collecting old stanzas, and every information respecting their origins, authors, etc, etc."[3] There is no call to belittle the asset Burns's songs have been to Scottish and other people; but the acute feeling of "crazed" is painful if we think of the slightness, as nourishment for *his* talent, of what he thereafter spent himself on. On the whole he is not aware enough of the curtailment he is suffering to be effectively critical of his own production.[4] But in the letter to the song-collector Thomson containing 'A man's a man' he writes sarcastically: "A great critic, Aikin on songs, says that love & wine are the exclusive

---

[1] *Works*, II, pp. 254, 271, 292.
[2] *The Letters of Robert Burns*, ed. J. DeLancy Ferguson (Oxford: 1931), I, pp. 89-90.
[3] *Letters*, I, p. 134.
[4] We may recall what Yeats said of Douglas Hyde: "He had no critical capacity, having indeed for certain years the uncritical folk-genius, as no educated Irishman or Englishman has ever had it, writing out of an imitative sympathy like that of a child catching a tune and leaving it to chance to call the tune; and literature permitted the ruin of that genius. . . . I mourn for the 'greatest folklorist who ever lived', and for the great poet who died in his youth." (*Autobiographies*, pp. 218-19.)

themes for song-writing.—The following is on neither subject,
& consequently no Song; but will be allowed, I think, to be
two or three pretty good *prose* thoughts, inverted into rhyme."[1]
"*Prose* thoughts" is said ironically; yet it also reflects a view of
poetry Burns shared with Pope and Johnson.

In a letter of 1787 to his genteel arbiter, Dr John Moore (in
which he says that his main aim is to please his "rustic compeers" but he is glad to be "noticed in such a manner, by judges
of the first character"), he admits to being "not vain enough to
hope for distinguished poetic fame" in "a language where Pope
and Churchill have raised the laugh, and Shenstone and Gray
drawn the tear; where Thomson and Beattie have painted the
landscape, and Lyttelton and Collins described the heart".[2]
Yet it was inevitably in some of those directions that he tried to
extend his range. It is often objected that this kind of influence
on Burns was just pernicious Anglicising, and this is indeed the
right reaction to the patronising advice he got from the most
unintelligent pundits, such as the self-important Earl of Buchan:
"These little doric pieces of yours in our provincial dialect are
very beautiful, but you will soon be able to diversify your
language, your Rhyme and your subject, and then you will
have it in your power to show the extent of your genius and to
attempt works of greater magnitude, variety and importance".[3]
Yet we cannot deny that what Burns had so far brought out was
bound to seem slight to readers whose taste had formed on
Dryden, Pope, and Johnson.

Burns himself thought of writing Augustan satires. He constantly quoted Pope, and in 1788 and 1789 he produced such
'satires' as the 'First Epistle to Robert Graham' and 'The
Poet's Progress'. The latter he sent to the Edinburgh philosopher Dugald Stewart, with a note explaining that it was to
be the first of several 'verse-portraits': "I intend it shall be the
work of my utmost exertions ripened by years".[4] But he is here
(unlike Clare) far from his *métier*. His 'Augustan' wit is simple
antithesis or bathos:

> Foxes and statesmen subtle wiles ensure;
> The cit and polecat stink, and are secure . . .
> ('The Poet's Progress')

Nothing is 'created' (as, say, the student's life is created in
'The Vanity of Human Wishes'), and the passage on critics

[1] *Letters*, II, p. 284.
[2] *Letters*, I, p. 70.
[3] Chambers-Wallace, *Burns*, II, p. 46.
[4] *Letters*, I, p. 288.

only shows up, in contrast with its obvious model in *The Dunciad*, Burns's lack of inwardness with the literary world. Ramsay made similar attempts, and what he says of them in a Preface shows his publicist's kind of awareness that Scots poetry needed defending: "There are some of the following, which we commonly reckon *English* Poetry, such as the *Morning Interview*, *Content*, &c, but all their Difference from the others is only in the Orthography of some words, such as *from* for *frae*, *bold* for *bauld*, and some few Names of things: and in those, tho' the Words be pure *English*, the idiom or Phraseology is still *Scots*".[1] But those poems are, in subject, imagery, movement, tone, pure Dryden, Pope, and Swift, in spite of references locating them in Scotland and words like 'plaid' and 'haughs' put into the Augustan pastoral. The poetry of *The Gentle Shepherd* is little different, for example the peasant dialogue:

> *E'en twining out a thread with little din,*
> *And beaking my cauld limbs afore the sun.*
> *What brings my bairn this gate sae air at morn?*
> *Is there nae muck to lead? to thresh nae corn?*[2]

The first couplet is both poetic and Scots, but in the last line the vernacular wages hardly a struggle with the alien style clamped onto it. It is a case more revealing than any English one could be of the weakness T. S. Eliot finds in 18th-century minor poetry: "it merely applies the magniloquence of Milton or the neatness of Pope to matter that is wholly unprepared for it; so that what the writers have to say always appears surprised at the way in which they choose to say it".[3]

Various suggestions for new modes were made to Burns, for example by the laird and man of letters John Ramsay of Ochtertyre. He suggested, for example, a Scottish *Georgics* and another *Gentle Shepherd*. His reason for Burns's failure to carry out these projects is the usual moral-pointing ("steadiness and abstraction were wanting, not talents"[4]), and indeed it is not unlikely that Burns's talents would have come to more if he had had more leisure and relief from bread-winning wear and tear: "A life of literary leisure, with a decent competence, is the summit of my wishes".[5] But we must also remember his natural limits. In a letter saying how much he admires the *Georgics* ("far the

---

[1] *Poems*, ed. Martin and Oliver, pp. xix-xx.
[2] Act II, Scene iii: *Works*, III, p. 75.
[3] *English Critical Essays: XX Century*, ed. Phyllis M. Jones (World's Classics, Oxford: 1950), p. 307.
[4] Currie, *Works of Burns*, I, p. 289.   [5] *Letters*, II, p. 292. See also note 4.

best of Vergil"), which "filled my head with a thousand fancies of emulation", he is also crestfallen at his own stature beside Vergil's—"like the idea of a Shetland pony, drawn up by the side of a thoroughbred hunter".[1] And in any case his own way with 'rural life and manners' lay in the other direction from the pastoral—the mode which suited the tastes of the cultured gentry.[2]

John Ramsay also transcribed for Burns a Highland legend of chivalry, set in medieval times, which had attracted the poet on his visit to Ochtertyre, and suggested he might make a play of it: "An imagination so varied and forcible as yours may do this in many different modes". Burns had himself hankered after the Highlands in the manner of his period: "My journey through the Highlands was perfectly inspiring; and I hope I have laid in a good stock of new poetical ideas".[3] But the history of efforts by Lowland writers to make something of Highland life is all unfavourable to the notion that it was at all germane to their concerns. The Highlands were a *terra incognita* to Lowlanders at that time and the Highlanders were supposed to be barbaric warriors and thieves. Most Lowlanders could know the Highlanders only as the raiders who operated on the marches of the two Scotlands. They were only dimly aware of the mass of ordinary Highland life with its subsistence farming, oral literature (falsified by 'Ossian' Macpherson), and once highly-developed religion.[4] As for the drama itself, Burns wrote finely only in a syntax, vocabulary, and turn of phrase which were thoroughly Scots, certainly not easily intelligible to ears more used to following English in public speaking. Scott suggested in his review of Cromek's *Reliques of Robert Burns* that "The Scotch dialect would have rendered such a piece"—a projected play by Burns on Bruce—"wholly unfit for the stage".[5] In some cases Scots had succeeded on the stage, but the idiom of *The Gentle Shepherd*, for example, is less broad than

---

[1] *Ibid.* I, p. 221.
[2] Fergusson, who had had a grammar school and university education, had plans for doing classical material into Scots. He aimed to "imitate Gaw. Douglass by translating the Eclogues and Georgics, and then publishing the Aeneid with it" (i.e. in Gavin Douglas's translation); and at the same time, two years before his tragically early death, he called what he had already done "juvenile productions". But these plans came to nothing, possibly discouraged by the poor sales of his 1773 *Poems* and the rebuff and failure of 'Auld Reikie' (*Poems*, ed. MacDiarmid, I, pp. 34, 38, 40-1; for his education see Douglas Young, 'The Making of a Poet': *Robert Fergusson*, ed. Smith, pp. 78-84).
[3] Currie (ed.), *Works of Burns*, II, pp. 92, 101; Burns, *Letters*, I, p. 106.
[4] See note 5, the Highlands in literature.
[5] *The Quarterly Review* (February 1809), Vol. I, No. 1, p. 33.

Burns at his best and much of the dialogue is in English. The Waverley Novels were later to succeed on the stage, but the evidence suggests that Scots was kept for the comic and 'character' parts, an artificial split which would have been disastrous for Burns. The place of Scots in the theatre was anything but secure,[1] and it seems likely that it would have forced Burns to some dilution of his best talent. He thought seriously of it himself, believing that "a Scotish audience would be better pleased with the Affectation, Whim, & Folly of their own native growth, than by manners which to by far the greatest of them can be only second hand", and he set himself to master the leading French and English dramatists.[2] But the Sheridan-Goldsmith kind of comedy he seems to be envisaging, and the laborious preparatory reading, suggest that he would have been stretching as far beyond his *métier* as in Augustan satires. All he says on fiction (apart from appreciative comments on his favourites, Smollett and Henry Mackenzie) is a remark prompted by John Moore's *Zeluco*: "I have been revolving in my mind some kind of criticisms on novel-writing; but it is a depth beyond my research".[3]

A final possibility that must be mentioned was raised by Alexander Tytler regarding 'Tam o' Shanter': "Go on—write more tales in the same style—you will eclipse Prior and La Fontaine; for, with equal wit, equal power of numbers and equal naivete of expression, you have a bolder and more vigorous imagination".[4] Now, we can well imagine that Burns might, if he had lived, have made more of this genre. In 'Tam' a strength of impulse reappears which he had lacked since Mossgiel, notably in the realism of the opening and in the fine humour which later interrupts the ghost story:

> *Now Tam, O Tam! had thae been queans,*
> *A' plump and strapping in their teens!*
> *Their sarks, instead o' creeshie flannen,*
> *Been snaw-white seventeen hunder linen!—*
> *Thir breeks o' mine, my only pair,*
> *That ance were plush, o' guid blue hair,*
> *I wad hae gien them aff my hurdies,*
> *For ae blink o' the bonie burdies!*

The idiom is wonderfully *practical*, and the language rises perfectly to the full flow of emotion, the sentence interrupting itself, pausing, setting off again—"Thir breeks o' mine"—as

---

[1] See note 6. [2] *Letters*, I, p. 380.
[3] *Letters*, I, p. 360. [4] Chambers-Wallace, *Burns*, III, p. 256.

though words were at a loss to contain the rich sensuality. Yet in the burlesque so deliberately emphasised throughout we feel a lack of tension, or grip on central concerns. Burns is only going as deep as his material (the local witch tale he wrote down for Grose the antiquarian) allows. Tytler himself suggests the weakness: "The preparation is fine, but the result is not adequate. But for this, perhaps, you have a good apology—you *stick to the popular tale*" (my italics).

It seems, then, that the vernacular at least tends to limit possibilities of expression, however powerfully it is used from time to time. An implicit criticism of its scope is made by Burns's own 'Holy Willie's Prayer'. Its satire is created by using *two* styles, the lofty English of the Authorised Version and the pulpit (both imitated straight and shown swelling into every kind of egotism) and frank, coarse, chapbook Scots— hitting off the everyday life of the self-righteous:

> *O L—d! yestreen, Thou kens, wi' Meg—*
> *Thy pardon I sincerely beg,*
> *O! may't ne'er be a livin' plague*
> *To my dishonour,*
> *An' I'll ne'er lift a lawless leg*
> *Again upon her.*[1]

The result is his most remarkable poem, one that lives in our minds as the classic of its subject. His poetry here surpasses the one-track rhythm and feeling unavoidable in 'The Ordination' and 'The Holy Fair', and he so commands his subject that he achieves an impersonality far stronger than the mere blowing-off of private discomfiture which is so common in his satires on conventional virtue. In 'Holy Willie' arrogant piety reveals itself in one dramatic utterance, with every change of tone, every symbol and idiom that would be natural to it in life, yet so subtly pointed that the most intelligent satirical 'criticism' is created. Particularly fine is the dramatic blend of the sanctimonious, the self-pitying, and the puffed-up, all cast in the devotional idiom:

> *Maybe Thou lets this fleshly thorn*
> *Buffet Thy servant e'en and morn,*
> *Lest he owre proud and high shou'd turn,*
> *That he's sae gifted:*
> *If sae, Thy han' maun e'en be borne,*
> *Until Thou lift it.*

[1] DeLancy Ferguson points out that "lift a lawless leg" is actually borrowed from the chapbook author Dougal Graham: 'Some Notes on Burns's Reading', *Modern Language Notes*, XLV, p. 371.

Here, as very rarely, the vernacular poet does not have to rise through the crudity of a popular form to register his own insight. He has created a style commensurate to the whole life, personal, social, cultural, of his subject.

'Holy Willie', then, is an important poem; and it is perfectly original and perfectly of its own culture. This must be stressed; for although Burns is fragmentary, yet to define his 'incompleteness' without invoking standards far removed from what is relevant to him is a delicate undertaking. It is perhaps true in a sense that, "with culture", with the background of "a well-trained, intellectual workman", he 'might have' better fulfilled his genius.[1] Yet to think of him as a classically-accomplished poet *manqué* is just irrelevant—to him and to the history of the people he stands for. If one thinks of the life of, say, a Pope, Hume, or Scott, one realises how solid an advantage it is to a writer to be given 'security', plenty company of like minds, the kind of recognition that can help. I would not myself exchange one Burns for a dozen Humes or Scotts; but it is surely also important to follow home the question, How integrated a literature was possible in the half-developed state of the mass of Scottish people then? Leslie Stephen places Burns in 18th-century history as the exemplar of the strength of a common man, the country peasant, in an age of revolution.[2] But the impression of fragmentary achievement also noted by Stephen concerns life as well as poetry. Burns and his kind remind us of struggle and thwarted progress as well as of sturdy, rooted vitality.

[1] J. M. Robertson, *New Essays*, p. 271; Carlyle, *Burns and Scott*, p. 60.
[2] *Eighteenth Century Thought*, II, p. 455.

CHAPTER IV

Scottish Poetry: The Communal Public

> But, first an' foremost, I should tell,
> Amaist as soon as I could spell,
> I to the crambo-jingle fell;
>   Tho' rude an' rough—
> Yet crooning to a body's sel,
>   Does well eneugh.
>   BURNS, *First Epistle to John Lapraik*.

IT has been said that the political awakening of Scotland in the days of the French Revolution was "divorced from its intellectual life"—the 'leaders of thought' had little sympathy with the popular stirrings.[1] Much, however, of the popular poetry was at the root of that awakening. Folk poets such as Fergusson and Burns were naturally democratic. We have also seen that the significant Scottish literature of that time *was* popular, entirely so, and furthermore, that the polite public tended to hold aloof from such work. We have now to consider the reaches of society in which this literature circulated by channels very different from those of the ruling-class with its formal culture.

The vernacular poetry typically came out in cheap, popular form, for hand-to-hand circulation, rather than in books for sale to a well-off educated class. The leading poets all brought out volumes, some of which did well;[2] but their natural, and most appreciative, public—those whom we *know* to have seized on their work and read it with great pleasure—got hold of their reading matter through something like a comprehensive system of cheap publishing and casual passing round. Sempill's 'Piper of Kilbarchan' had a wide circulation in broadsides or pamphlets in the later 17th century. According to tradition, Ramsay's mock-elegies on well-known town characters were

---

[1] Mathieson, *Church and Reform in Scotland*, p. 11.

[2] Ramsay's subscribers to an early book of poems included leading English men of letters—Pope, Steele, Hogarth, Gay (for subscription lists see *Poems*, ed. Martin and Oliver, I, pp. xxx-xxxvii). Fergusson published a book two years before his death, and originally dedicated his separate publication of 'Auld Reikie' (unfinished at his death) to Scotland's leading banker, Sir William Forbes (*Works*, ed. Robert Ford, Paisley: 1906, p. 82, n.; *Poems*, ed. MacDiarmid, I, pp. 40-1). Burns always sold well with all classes, e.g. the Caledonian Hunt, an "association of nobility and gentry", subscribed for a hundred copies of the 1787 Edinburgh *Poems* (*Works*, ed. Chambers-Wallace, I, pp. 23, 91).

sold for pennies in the streets of Edinburgh. It has been shown that these broadsides were most probably pirated reprints of poems he had published singly himself; and this is of course still stronger evidence of his popularity. Fergusson's poems came out in a weekly magazine before they were collected into books; and he himself on one occasion plyed up and down the High Street of the Old Town selling sheets of ballads. Burns's first book is almost unique among influential modern books in that it was put out not from one of the big centres but from a small country town, Kilmarnock. His poems, in addition to many subsequent book editions, came out in cheap weekly tracts in Glasgow late in the 1790's. Indeed some of his most notable poems—'The Jolly Beggars', 'The Twa Herds', 'The Kirk's Alarm', 'Holy Willie's Prayer'—did not appear in book form till the Glasgow edition of 1801; and 'The Jolly Beggars' had circulated as a chapbook up to that time.[1] Alexander Wilson the Paisley weaver poet's 'Watty and Meg', a vernacular pastoral (later a model for Hector MacNeill's 'Will and Jean', a poem that sold extremely well in literary Edinburgh), was first published anonymously as a chapbook, and ascribed by some to Burns; and his 'Loss o' the Pack' was an "immensely popular" chapbook which sold in thousands.[2] It is a strong, continuous tradition, the more remarkable in that some of these works were poetry of some art and complexity, not obviously suited for handing round, like songs. Such was, moreover, the one line of creative expression indigenous to Scotland.

It was communications of this kind, as well as his natural appeal, that enabled Burns's poetry to run right through the bloodstream of the people as soon as it appeared. A critic writing in 1815 (to defend him against Jeffrey's accusation of uncouthness) says that "the writings of Robert Burns, are in Scotland the most popular of any works of fancy, antient or modern . . . there is scarcely a house in the kingdom which does not contain a copy of his poems . . . there are few individuals elevated above the clods of the valley, who are not familiar with

[1] Sempill: T. F. Henderson, *Scottish Vernacular Literature* (Edinburgh: 1910), p. 392; James Watson, *Choice Collection of Comic and Serious Scots Poems*, 1706, 1709, 1711 (edition Glasgow: 1869), p. xiv. Ramsay: Burns Martin, *Allan Ramsay (op. cit.)*, pp. 124-5; Andrew Gibson, *New Light on Allan Ramsay* (Edinburgh: 1927), ch. 7, esp. p. 88, and pp. 114-15. Fergusson: the magazine was Ruddiman's *Weekly Magazine*; see *Scots Poems*, ed. Dickins, pp. ix-xi, 91-2. Burns: *The Bibliography of Robert Burns* (Kilmarnock: 1881), p. 12; *ibid.* p. 9; Nancie Campbell, catalogue of the Murison Burns Collection (Public Library, Dunfermline: 1953), p. 16.
[2] *The Poems and Literary Prose of Alexander Wilson*, ed. A. B. Grosart (Paisley: 1876), II, p. x; *Archibald Constable and his Literary Correspondents*, II, p. 235; *Poems . . . of Wilson*, I, p. xxxvi; *Book of the Old Edinburgh Club*, I, p. 53.

the products of his muse".[1] This is of course an enthusiastic exaggeration. There can hardly have been enough copies in print to supply every household in a country of over one and a half million. But the number available was astonishingly high. By 1815 at least eighty-two editions of his works, both complete and selected, had come out, thirty-one in Scotland, and in Ireland and Northern England, where he was specially well served, seven and eight respectively; and seven more editions followed in the year Peterkin wrote.[2] The numbers of copies, so far as we know, were not large,[3] but the booksellers in Scotland, England, Ireland, the United States were busily pirating his works, and the passing of copies from hand to hand among the poor people must greatly have increased his circulation. Fully as important as the figures is the eagerness with which people of his own class swarmed to get his poems. A contemporary wrote:

> I was at that time resident in Galloway, contiguous to Ayrshire, and I can well remember, how that even ploughboys and maidservants would gladly part with the wages they earned the most hardly and which they wanted to purchase the necessary clothing, if they might but procure the works of Burns.[4]

Four months after the issue of his first small edition, Burns set out for Edinburgh, and he was already a celebrity. His way lay past Covington Mains, where the farmer had subscribed for twenty copies of the first edition. "All the farmers in the parish had read with delight the poet's then published works", and they were called to meet him by a sheet on a pitchfork planted on a corn-stack in the barn-yard: "Instantly was the white flag hoisted, and as instantly were the farmers seen issuing from their houses, and converging to the point of meeting", where they spent an evening and night talking with Burns.[5] There was his natural public; his outlook, his style, his public and private personality all fitted him for it.

The poorer workers had to pick up their reading matter as they chanced to find it, sometimes in the middle of work. In the 1830's the poet Allan Cunningham told the Chamberses,

[1] Alexander Peterkin, *A Review of the Life of Robert Burns and of Various Criticisms of his Character and Writings* (Edinburgh: 1815), pp. xiii-xiv.
[2] Kilmarnock *Bibliography*, pp. 5-23.
[3] For details see note 1.
[4] Article on Burns, *Biographical Dictionary of Eminent Scotsmen* (Chambers, Edinburgh: 1835), I, p. 433.
[5] Chambers-Wallace, *Burns*, II, pp. 9-10, 19.

the pioneers of cheap publishing, that their *Journal* was popular among the shepherds of Galloway. The first man who got a copy would read it and then leave it under a stone on a certain hill-top, where the next shepherd would collect it when he could and in his turn leave it on another·hill.[1] Alexander Somerville (author of the *Autobiography of a Working Man*), a stone-worker from a very poor Berwickshire family, describes Burns circulating among harvest workers: "We had some spare time between the departure of the emptied cart and the arrival of the loaded one; and James Wilson, who was a reader of books, asked me as we sat on the stack together, if I knew Burns's poem of Hallowe'en". Somerville, then a boy of nine, did not know what a poem was (he knew Burns's 'Auld Lang Syne', 'Of a' the airts the wind can blaw', and 'My Nannie O' as anonymous songs), so Wilson recited the whole of 'Hallow-e'en' and 'Death and Dr Hornbook' and finally lent him a Burns, a tattered book which had fallen apart and been sewn together again. Somerville was so enraptured that he started "eagerly laying hold of every printed poem, song, ballad, or verse, that could be reached"; and his father finally spent half a week's wages on the only poetry a rigid Presbyterian could approve—a book of *Gospel Sonnets*.[2] James Hogg, a Border shepherd, stumbled on literature in a similar way:

> The first time I ever heard of Burns was in 1797. . . . One day during the summer a half daft man, named John Scott, came to me on the hill, and to amuse me repeated Tam o' Shanter. I was delighted! I was more than delighted—I was ravished! I cannot describe my feelings; but, in short, before Jock Scott left me, I could recite the poem from beginning to end, and it has been my favourite poem ever since.

Hogg had lapsed into illiteracy at 18 after some rudimentary schooling, but within a few years he was writing songs himself and hearing them sung by the local girls, who jeered at him as "Jamie the Poeter".[3] Burns was handed on in this way well into the 19th century, in England as well as Scotland. The first book owned by George Douglas Brown (author of *The House with the Green Shutters*) was a Burns given him by an old herd. Samuel Bamford says that Burns inspired him to emulation,

---

[1] *Memoir of Robert Chambers*, p. 237.

[2] Somerville, *The Autobiography of a Working Man*, ed. John Carswell (London: 1951), pp. 42-4.

[3] Autobiography prefixed to *Songs and Ballads* (edition London: 1852), pp. xx-xxi.

as he did Hogg, by the thought that another working man had done well at poetry; and Thomas Cooper, the Radical, was lent Burns by the shoemaker to whom he was apprenticed.[1] So Burns circulated from hand to hand, and if copies were lacking, the extraordinary oral memory of a people not used to print kept him current by word of mouth.

Burns's pithy phrases (from such poems as 'Address to the Unco Guid', 'To a Louse'—"to see oursels as ithers see us"—'Auld Lang Syne', and 'A man's a man for a' that') entered at once into the language. Yet he had no sooner aroused such a following than he showed himself, privately, discomfited by it. In 1786 (the year of the Kilmarnock volume) he wrote to William Niven, one of the successful canvassers for the book: "In the mean time, remember this, never blow my Songs among the Million, as I would abhor to hear every Prentice mouthing my poor performances in the streets.—Every one of my Maybole friends are welcome to a Copy, if they chuse; but I wish them to go no further."[2] This is a passing qualm. Burns was also dedicated to his own people, as we can see in the poetry [3] and in such avowals as the following, to one of his genteel critics, Dr John Moore: "For my part, my first ambition was, and my strongest wish is, to please my Compeers, the rustic inmates of the Hamlet, while everchanging language and manners will allow me to be relished and understood". Yet it is an acute qualm, and it was repeated. He wrote to a local lady: "A little, a very little while ago, I *had scarce a friend but the stubborn pride of my own bosom*; now I am distinguished, patronised, befriended by YOU".[4] "Scarce a friend"—yet by far the most successful canvassers of the Kilmarnock volume were, not his gentry acquaintances, but his friends from his own class, some of them recipients of his verse epistles, and the heaviest subscribers, too, were the farmers and small townsfolk, not the aristocracy.[5] What Burns is thinking of is people of influence and prestige from the ruling-class. But such relationships had unhappy effects on his intensely touchy pride, forever falling over itself not to be slighted, as we can see, graphically given, in the poem on the meeting with Lord Daer which Dugald Stewart arranged for him. The aristocrat is first

[1] James Veitch, *George Douglas Brown* (London: 1952), p. 21; Bamford, *Early Days* (London: 1849), pp. 289-90; Cooper, *Life* (*op. cit.*), pp. 42-3.
[2] Burns, *Letters*, I, p. 39.   [3] See above, Chapter III.
[4] *Letters*, I, pp. 70, 80.
[5] F. B. Snyder, *The Life of Robert Burns*, p. 151; Chambers-Wallace, *Burns*, II, p. 191.

treated with characteristic extravagant caricature of social attitude:

> *But wi' a Lord!—stand out my shin,*
> *A lord—a Peer—an Earl's son,*
> *Up higher yet, my bonnet;*
> *An' sic a Lord!—lang Scotch ells twa*
> *Our peerage he o'erlooks them a',*
> *As I look o'er my sonnet.*

But in the next stanza this caricature, the poet seeing himself from outside, is acutely uncomfortable, the comic pose is used to carry off embarrassment:

> *But O for Hogarth's magic pow'r,*
> *To show Sir Bardy's willyart glow'r,*
> *An' how he star'd an' stammer'd,*
> *When goavin, as if led wi' branks,*
> *An' stumpin' on his ploughman shanks,*
> *He in the parlour hammer'd.*[1]

People of Burns's class who at all hankered after better status would obviously be prone to such self-consciousness,[2] or at least to some questioning of their status. Among the subjects Burns made speeches on at the Tarbolton Bachelors' Club are questions such as 'Whether is the savage man or the peasant of a civilised country in the most happy situation?', and 'Whether is a young man of the lower ranks of life likeliest to be happy who has got a good education, or he who has just the education and information of those around him?'[3] It was also inevitable that Burns should be uneasy about the status of his literature, partly because, like Hugh Blair, he could not be sure whether the oral culture of his people would last—"while ever-changing language and manners allow me to be relished and understood" —and partly because of his doubts about his social standing: sometimes he was over-proud and suspicious of slights, sometimes he was quite ready to advertise himself as a peasant poet.[4]

He had, however, some good reasons to be dissatisfied with

---

[1] 'On Meeting with Lord Daer.'

[2] That a writer of more integrated genius could rise clear of it is shown by the unforced assurance with which Lawrence moved about among his upper-class friends in Cambridge, London, and the Home Counties. Moreover, Lawrence was able to work experience of class embarrassment into the perfectly balanced art of stories such as 'Daughters of the Vicar', 'You Touched Me', 'Jimmy and the Desperate Woman', and 'The Fox'.

[3] Currie (ed.), *Works*, I, p. 118 n.

[4] E.g. the Preface to the Kilmarnock volume, facsimile edition (London: 1911), pp. iii-vi; and the avowed aim of his first Commonplace Book: see R. H. Cromek (ed.), *Reliques of Robert Burns* (London: 1809), pp. 315-16.

how he fitted into his community. For one thing, his grappling with Church affairs inspired much of his best poetry—but at the cost of having to suppress 'The Twa Herds', 'The Ordination' (first published in the Edinburgh edition of 1787), 'Holy Willie's Prayer', the 'Address to the Unco Guid', 'Dr Hornbook', and the 'Address of Beelzebub' from his first edition, which was a local one. Those poems account for much of the core of his finest work—and they would have scandalised his own community. Secondly, soon after his own success Burns was advising an editor that it would be risky to bring out a book of Scots poems by one Robert Mylne: "the very term, Scots Poetry, totters on the brink of contempt", the Kilmarnock volume having inspired a host of shoddy imitators—"an inundation of nonsense over the land".[1] Much of this work was explicitly in tribute to him. In a letter he complains, after returning to Ayrshire from Edinburgh, of "the servility of my plebeian brethren (who perhaps formerly eyed me askance)"; and this is borne out by those tributes, for example:

> *Fair fa' you, Robie, canty callan . . .*
> *Wha rhym'st a'maist as weel as Allan . . .*
>
> *Cou'd I, O! Rob, but brak my tether,*
> *And ony whare wi' you forgether,*
> *I'm sure we'd souple baith our leather,*
>   *I'd pawn my lugs,*
> *We'd mak our hearts as light's a feather*
>   *Wi' reaming jugs.*

This kind of attitude, at once patronising and familiar, was what the versifiers of the day felt licensed to do by the much more tough-minded colloquialism of Burns himself. Even the decent John Skinner (an educated minister who admired Scots literature) could address Burns thus:

> *An hour or sae, by hook or crook,*
> *And may be twa some orrow ouk,*
> *That I can spare frae haly beuk,*
>   *For that's my hobby,*
> *I'll slip awa' to some bye neuk,*
>   *And crack wi' Robie.*[2]

This convention of familiarity shows up the habit of treating a Scots-speaking poet as aside from the main stream of national

---

[1] *Letters*, I, p. 326.
[2] *Letters*, I, p. 96. *Robert Burns and His Rhyming Friends*, ed. J. D. Ross (Stirling: 1925), pp. 35, 38.

life, as a mere crony. It is not surprising that Burns, with his independent force, shied away at times from the familiarity of his own folk.

On the whole, however, this circulation of modern Scots literature represents a flourishing tradition of long standing. Native songs were, of course, common currency amongst the people, not only old ballads but the new songs of the Edinburgh wits, Ramsay and Hamilton. Burns's brother Gilbert, discussing their early reading of poetry, singles out "those excellent new songs that are hawked about the country in baskets, or exposed on stalls in the streets".[1] There was also a great deal of the older art poetry in circulation. Pinkerton might complain that Dunbar and the like had been neglected, but they had never died amongst the people. The Middle Scots poetry existed as popular classics from the time it was published up until the 18th-century revival of educated interest in it.[2] Lord Hailes published a selection of the *Gude and Godlie Ballates*, poems of propaganda for the Reformation, in 1765; but they had already circulated widely in the 17th century, with a great influence among the middle classes and "especially among the substantial burghers of the cities and trading communities". During the same period the works of Sir David Lyndsay, author of the *Satyre of the Thrie Estaitis*, were extremely popular (fourteen complete editions between 1558 and 1614); and people commonly appealed to him, as late as 1800, as a standard of correctness: "'There is na sic a word in a' Davie Lyndsay.'" [3]

This old art poetry was known by heart and recited. According to the scholar John Leyden (himself the son of a Teviotdale shepherd), the shepherds could repeat much of Barbour's *Brus*, Blind Harry's *Wallace*, and Lyndsay's poems. No doubt the 'nationalism' of the two former and John the Commonweal's indictment of the rule of the wealthy in the *Thrie Estaitis* had a permanent appeal. A popular Edinburgh poet, Pennecuik, describes peasants in their cottage passing a winter evening— the grandfather retelling the Covenanters' Battle of Bothwell Bridge, the aunt reading *Pilgrim's Progress*, the foreman telling "blads of William Wallace", and a son reciting Lyndsay by

[1] *Memoir of Robert Chambers*, pp. 28, 41; Currie, *Works of Burns*, I, p. 66.
[2] Gavin Douglas's *Aeneid* with Ruddiman's Glossary was published in 1710; Ramsay's *Ever Green* with poems from the Bannatyne MS. in 1724; Hailes's *Ancient Scottish Poems* from the Bannatyne in 1770; Pinkerton's *Ancient Scotish Poems* from the Maitland MS. in 1786.
[3] *Gude and Godlie Ballates*, ed. Mitchell, pp. xv, xl; Mathieson, *Politics and Religion in Scotland*, I, p. 208; George Chalmers (ed.), *The Poetical Works of Sir David Lyndsay* (London: 1806), I, p. 149.

heart.[1] Some accounts of peasant reading perhaps idealise. For example we are told that the Middle Scots classics were in "almost every cottage", "in every Scotish hamlet, and in every hand".[2] One wonders how many hamlets these writers had penetrated into, for there are very popular kinds of reading matter which they say nothing about. According to William Motherwell, the folk-song collector, chapbooks (many of which, for example Dougal Graham's, the most popular of all, are witlessly dirty) were to be found

> . . . on every stall, and in every cottage. They are essentially the Library of Entertaining Knowledge to our peasantry, and have maintained their ground in the affections of the people, notwithstanding the attempt of religious, political, or learned associations, to displace them, by substituting more elegant and wholesome literature in their stead.[3]

The Pilgrim's Progress and the "big ha' Bible" are usually prominent in pictures of peasant reading matter, yet the chapbooks were everywhere and it seems that the strictly religious kind were fewest in number. The truth in sum is that, under the old conditions, trash (much more real and tough-minded than the equivalent modern pulp) and the classics mingled freely in popular reading. In the middle of the 19th century chapbooks and the old Presbyterian works were together in the cottages, the old people reading sermons and theology and the young the chapbooks.[4]

The old poetry was thus an important part of the literary background for the 18th-century vernacular poets. Burns says in his autobiographical letter: "The first two books I ever read in private, and which gave me more pleasure than any two books I ever read again, were *The Life of Hannibal*, and *The History of Sir William Wallace* . . . the story of Wallace poured a Scottish prejudice in my veins, which will boil along there till the flood-gates of life shut in eternal rest".[5] It is typical that his

[1] Leyden (ed.), *The Complaynt of Scotland* (Edinburgh: 1801) pp. 224-5; *A Collection of Scots Poems on Several Occasions*, by Alexander Pennecuik and others (Leith: 1756), p. 7.

[2] Pinkerton, *Ancient Scotish Poems*, I, pp. xvii-xviii; R. H. Cromek (ed.), *Remains of Nithsdale and Galloway Song* (London: 1810), p. v. Lord Hailes called Blind Harry's *Wallace* the Bible of the common people, "he being their great favourite next to the Scriptures"; and Ramsay of Ochtertyre, as a youth, often heard country folk reading or reciting "the exploits of Wallace or Bruce against the Southrons" (Currie, *Works of Burns*, I, p. 284).

[3] John Fraser, *The Humorous Chapbooks of Scotland* (New York: 1873), pp. 213-14.

[4] *Amusing Prose Chapbooks*, ed. R. H. Cunningham (London: 1889), p. 7; R. K. Webb, 'The Victorian Reading Public: *Universities Quarterly* (London: 1957), XII, 1, p. 42. For quotation from the chapbooks see the account of Scots prose in Chapter VIII. [5] Chambers-Wallace, *Burns*, I, p. 11.

Wallace came to him not from his educated teacher but from one of his own class; his brother records that "he borrowed it from the blacksmith who shod our horses". Likewise Hogg says in his 'Autobiography' that when eighteen, working as a herd, he first "got a perusal of 'The Life and Adventures of Sir William Wallace' and 'The Gentle Shepherd'. . . . I thought if they had been in the same kind of metre with the Psalms, I could have borne with them. . . . The little reading that I had learned I had nearly lost, and the Scottish dialect quite confounded me." [1]

This reading matter had its uses, then, for a public many of whom had to educate themselves on whatever came to hand. But it must strike us as a rather backward staple of classics, not in its level of art, which was quite high, but because it dates so far back. It embodies a life largely medieval, remote from anything in contemporary Scotland, and is in quality hardly capable, unlike Chaucer, Shakespeare, or Bunyan, of refreshing one's sense of the life around one.[2] The painter Sir David Wilkie, the son of a Fife minister, who must have had some books around him, was captivated by Lyndsay, the *Wallace*, and the *Brus*, and by stories of the wars of the Covenant told him "by some worthy of the parish dropped into the manse". He was thus well bogged down in the old Scotland; and his enlightened patron, Sir George Beaumont, had to advise him some years later in London to take up the reading of *Don Quixote* and the 18th-century English novels to enrich his mind.[3] Again, Ramsay, Fergusson, and Burns obviously had ample access to modern English poetry, but they almost never take it up into their own work as a fruitful influence, and this accords with the predominance of old-fashioned work which was current in their own communities.

To some extent the development of Scottish reading was held up by the dearth of native work. The majority of the most humorous and characteristic chapbooks came out during the period from the death of Ramsay at the middle of the century to the time when Burns's poems began to get a firm hold in the country. Thus the Scots comic genius went underground during a time when there was a lack of distinguished individual talent. In 1800 it was observed that Ramsay's works (*The Ever Green*,

[1] Currie, *Burns*, I, p. 38; Hogg, *Songs and Ballads*, p. xvii.
[2] For discussion of which *Wallace* was in circulation, the old poem or the stilted modern rehash, see note 2.
[3] Allan Cunningham, *The Life of Sir David Wilkie* (London: 1843), I, pp. 17, 148.

the songs, *The Gentle Shepherd*) were "universally read" by the
peasantry and had partly superseded the *Brus* and the *Wallace*.[1]
Thus when modern Scots work did appear, it was welcomed,
and it entered into the entertainments of the community as well
as into its reading. Lady Anne Lindsay's famous song 'Auld
Robin Gray' was mimed by dancing dogs in the streets.[2] The
Shepherd was recited by the farmer's family at his fireside in the
evening, and the Lowland milkmaids, ploughmen, and shepherds could go through whole scenes from memory. In spite of
the disapproval of the *literati*, and James Beattie's opinion that
it had never given general satisfaction upon the stage, it was,
inevitably, accepted by the people as their drama, for it was
at one time the only stage work that reflected their life. In
Edinburgh it was repeatedly performed, by journeymen and
apprentices, before crowded houses, as a benefit for a printer
banished for printing Jacobite poems. Geikie, the great geologist, saw it played by peasants in the Pentland Hills in the
1850's: "The Scottish language of the dialogue was given by
the rustic actors with full Doric breadth, and even sometimes
with creditable dramatic power"; and it was regularly played
at the same period by the weavers of Carlops and the paper-
makers of Penicuik.[3] Again, Alexander Ross, an Angus schoolmaster whose songs were sung by the local peasants, was
inspired by *The Gentle Shepherd* to write *Helenore*, and it is said
to have become as popular in his district as Burns and *The
Pilgrim's Progress*.[4] Ross was no poet, and his 'drama' is pain-
fully wordy and lame. Yet he often achieves perfectly the
freshness of country life that is conventionally claimed for
Ramsay's play, for example:

> *You could na look your sairing at her face,*
> *It was so cheery an' so fu' o' grace;*
> *Her cherry cheeks you might bleed with a strae;*
> *Syne she was swak an' souple like a rae;*
> *Swack like an eel an' calour like a trout;*
> *An' was become a fairly round about . . .*[5]

[1] Fraser, *Humorous Chapbooks*, p. 110; Currie, *Burns*, I, p. 285.
[2] Lord Lindsay, *Lives of the Lindsays* (London: 1858), II, p. 333.
[3] Ramsay, *Works*, I, p. 114; Beattie, *Essays (op. cit.)*, p. 383; Arnot, *History of Edinburgh*, p. 368. These performances were so popular partly because the libellous poems against Butcher Cumberland and "certain zealous Whigs" had fired Jaco-bite enthusiasm. But the fact remains that it was the *Shepherd* that was chosen for such an occasion. Sir Archibald Geikie, *A Long Life's Work* (London: 1924), p. 55 (I owe this reference to Martin, *Allan Ramsay*, p. 85); Martin, *Ramsay*, pp. 82–90.
[4] Ramsay, *Works*, III, p. 26.
[5] Ross, *Scottish Works*, ed. Margaret Wattie (Scottish Text Society, Edinburgh: 1938), p. 16.

Remembering Ross, it is difficult to believe that the stilted
Shepherd would have attained the popularity it did if Ramsay
had been, like Ross, isolated from the centres of the public
in the remote braes of Angus, serving a tiny school in one of the
wildest glens in the central *massif* of Scotland.

This popular habit of bringing literature into the midst of
everyday life enabled the poets to participate directly, *as* poets,
in their communal life. Their poems could work as immediate
social events, both in their way of circulating and as a result of
how the poet treated the events of the day. Ramsay wrote
poems echoing the sort of broadside elegy which commonly
celebrated a well-known citizen or beauty who had just died,
the sort he himself ridiculed in his English lines, 'The Scribblers
Lashed':

> *An honest burgess cannot die,*
> *But they must weep in elegy . . .*[1]

Ramsay's poems are about real people—a Canongate bawd, a
Bruntsfield inn-keeper—and have little epitaphs and intro-
ductory verses to add to the air of popular pieces. But they are
not artless like the real elegies, for example a broadside poem
on a watchmaker who died in the 1690's:

> *Since none can well describe his worth that in this land doth dwell,*
> *He'll waken at the trumpet's blow, and answer for himself.*[2]

Ramsay's 'elegies' are 'Habbie Simson' poetry arranged to
suggest the common coin of the town. Fergusson too was close
to events; he wrote and published poems on the date of the
events they celebrated—the beginning and end of the legal
term, local holidays such as Leith race-week and the Hallowe'en
fair; and his finest poem, 'The Ghaists', was an immediate, as
though journalistic response to a topic then being publicly discussed.[3] Alexander Wilson, the Paisley weaver poet, tells in his
journal how on his rounds peddling as a packman he carried
prospectuses of his poems and canvassed for subscribers in
lodging-houses and at the lodge gates of big houses. His satires
on the merchant class were so directly aimed as to be libellous,
and they were keenly discussed in the weaving-shops and street
corners of Renfrewshire.[4]

[1] *Works*, II, p. 316.
[2] Chambers, *Domestic Annals*, p. 140.
[3] See *Scots Poems*, ed. Dickins, *passim*. For 'The Ghaists' see Chapter III,
p. 91.
[4] *Poems and Prose (op. cit.)*, I, p. xxxvi; Journal *(ibid.)*, p. 5.

Few of the poems in those examples are above the level at which such participation in the community would simply be expected: most of them are occasional or light. But Burns's participation in Ayrshire life was what awoke the poetry of his peak, during the years he lived at Mossgiel, and the stimulus he got from his community engendered not only the obvious local currency—the epigrams, epistles, and election songs at which he was a dab hand—but also some of his most serious poetry. Early in the vein which should be known as the essential Burns (the satirical comedy of community, often Kirk life, written from 1784–6), there appeared 'The Twa Herds'. It is the first of those very original poems in which he seized on and, as it were, transposed a Kirk event as the form of his comedy and the most graphically revealing aspect or scene of the local life. Moodie and Russell, the ministers in the case, are imaged as the shepherds of

> a' ye pious godly flocks,
> Weel fed on pastures orthodox.

The associations this calls up—rough husbandry, greedy feeding, and proprietorial pride and grippiness—create the satire:

> What flock wi' Moody's flock could rank,
> Sae hale and hearty every shank,
> Nae poison'd sour Arminian stank
>   He let them taste;
> Frae Calvin's well, ay clear, they drank,—
>   O, sic a feast . . .
>
> He fine a mangy sheep could scrub,
> Or nobly fling the gospel club,
> And 'new-light' herds could nicely drub,
>   Or pay their skin;
> Could shake them o'er the burning dub,
>   Or heave them in.

The poem names many real people, but there is no need (any more than with *The Dunciad*) to read it with footnotes. Its effect depends on masterly poetry.

> A' ye wha tent the gospel fauld,
> There's Duncan deep, an' Peebles shaul',
> But chiefly thou, Apostle Auld,
>   We trust in thee,
> That thou wilt work them, hot an' cauld,
>   Till they agree.

The modulation from "chiefly thou", unctuously devotional, to the biting emphasis on "work them", which catches the dinging manner of sectarian feuds, is admirable as poetry; and he further shows his mastery of tone—this time nearer the triumphant point-making of the soap-box orator—in endings such as

> *I doubt he's but a grey nick quill,*
> *An' that ye'll fin',*

and

> *Then Orthodoxy yet may prance,*
> *An' Learning in a woody dance,*
> *An' that fell cur ca'd 'common-sense',*
> *That bites sae sair,*
> *Be banish'd o'er the sea to France:*
> *Let him bark there.*

The natural appeal of such a style is described by Heron, who had seen the people buying Burns:

> They were written in phraseology, of which all the powers were universally felt. . . . Those topics of satire and scandal in which the rustic delights; that humorous delineation of character, and that witty association of ideas, familiar and striking, yet naturally allied to one another, which has force to shake the sides with laughter.[1]

'The Twa Herds' was thus perfectly fitted for use as a weapon in the feud itself. This was a dispute over parish boundaries, given a public hearing in the Presbytery of Irvine before a crowd of local people (including Burns), in which Moodie and Russell lost their tempers and abused each other "with a fiery virulence of personal invective, such as had long been banished from all popular assemblies".[2] This touched off Burns's local career. He writes in his autobiographical letter:

> I now began to be known in the neighbourhood as a maker of rhymes. The first of my poetic offspring that saw the light [i.e. circulated in manuscript] was a burlesque lamentation on a quarrel between two Reverend Calvinists, both of them *dramatis personæ* in my 'Holy Fair'. I had an idea myself that the piece had some merits; but, to prevent the worst, I gave a copy to a friend who was very fond of these things, and told him I could not guess who was the author of it, but I thought it pretty clever. With a certain side of both clergy and laity, it met with a roar of applause.[2]

---

[1] *Eminent Scotsmen* (*op. cit.*), I, p. 432. The "witty association of ideas, familiar and striking" still occurs in the speech of original-minded country folk.
[2] Lockhart, *Life of Burns*, p. 60.

He goes on to say that "'Holy Willie's Prayer' next made its appearance, and alarmed the kirk-session so much, that they held three several meetings to look over their holy artillery, if any of it was pointed against profane rhymers". His early satires, that is, were a campaign against narrow puritanism just as was the stand of the Moderates on the *Douglas* issue. Burns says of the background to this kind of dispute in his district:

> Polemical Divinity about this time was putting the country half-mad, and I, ambitious of shining on Sundays, between sermons, in conversation parties, at funerals, etc, in a few years more, used to puzzle Calvinism with so much heat and indiscretion, that I raised a hue-and-cry of heresy against me, which has not ceased to this hour.[1]

In this his district was showing what had been the character of the South-west for centuries—at the Reformation, in the mid-17th century, at the Covenanting period, and in the 18th-century disputes on election of ministers.[2] Burns, of course, is explicitly Moderate and common-sense, opposed to the heat of sects and theological logic-chopping, as he often sarcastically conveys. But it is significant that he got so strong an impulse from grappling with the extremists in religious argument. It confirms the ambiguity of his passage on the "cauld harangues" of the Moderates in 'The Holy Fair';

> *Smith opens out his cauld harangues,*
> *On practice and on morals;*
> *An' aff the godly pour in thrangs,*
> *To gie the jars an' barrels*
> *A lift that day.*

> *What signifies his barren shine,*
> *Of moral pow'rs an' reason?*
> *His English style, an' gesture fine,*
> *Are a' clean out o' season . . .*

We never doubt that the poet detests irrational bigotry, but— "barren shine"? . . . The phrase (like "Morality's demure decoys") cannot but stick in our minds as a drastic *criticism* of Moderatism (the religion of Hugh Blair and William Robertson), and Burns could hardly have arrived at images so fine and telling had he not himself felt the vigour (however harsh) of the older Presbyterianism and the mediocrity (however enlightened) of the new. He here points forward, in fact, to the age when

[1] Chambers-Wallace, *Burns*, I, pp. 19, 11.
[2] See Mathieson, *Politics and Religion in Scotland*, I, p. 361; *ibid.* II, p. 346; Burnet, *History of his Own Time*: see above, p. 67; Snyder, *Life of Burns*, p. 11.

religion, bereft of its old force, was to cease to command the serious attention of the more original minds (Carlyle, for example, and the Mills). Burns's two-edged meaning here is an example of how penetrating was his instinct for the movements of life in his community.

The following he got, the effect he had locally, arose directly from a poet's kind of gifts. Lockhart remarks that somebody who could talk like Burns could count on "the applause and countenance" of the local factions; and he says of his life at Dumfries, when his reputation was established: "All men's eyes were upon Burns. He was the standing marvel of the place; his toasts, his jokes, his epigrams, his songs, were the daily food of conversation and scandal."[1] It used to be said that John Wilson, the original of the apothecary Dr Hornbook in 'Death and Dr Hornbook', was forced to leave the district because Burns's poem had made him notorious. It is unlikely that this is true; what the story rather shows is the power of the reputation which gave rise to such gossip.[2] More important is the traditional notion that 'The Holy Fair' caused the mass field-communions to die out. This was part of a general change. According to a Victorian minister of Burns's old parish, Mauchline, an immediate cause of the drop in attendance at the field communions (from 1,400 in 1786, Burns's day, to 400 in 1819) might have been the death of "apostle Auld", the Mauchline minister for over fifty years. Furthermore customs were changing "and the better way had come in, or was coming in, of people contenting themselves with their own parochial ministrations".[3] In fact the 'holy fair' kind of communion—with relays of ministers preaching to hundreds in the open air, while crowds drank and picnicked on all sides—had been part of the old sociable coarseness. In Perthshire, for example, it was notorious for "fighting and other indecencies", and the time was "often made a season for debauchery".[4] Burns's satire on the crudity of the old Kirk is unexpectedly borne out by one of his own opponents. That same minister Mackinlay whom he takes off in 'The Ordination'—

> *Mackinlay, Russell, are the boys*
> *That heresy can torture—*

---

[1] *Life of Burns*, pp. 60, 223. How Burns's powers of speech flowed straight through into his poetry is discussed in Chapter VIII.

[2] Lockhart, p. 71; J. C. Ewing, 'Prototype of Dr Hornbook', *Burns Chronicle*, 2nd Series (Kilmarnock: 1941), XVI, p. 33.

[3] Rev. Andrew Edgar, *Old Church Life in Scotland* (Paisley: 1885), I, pp. 171-2, 179.   [4] Pennant, *Tour in Scotland*, p. 83.

was to write in 1792, in the *Old Statistical Account*:

> It must be observed, however, that notwithstanding so many divisions [the secessions and other splits], the people in general of all denominations, live together in the best habits of friendship, as Christians ought to do; and that ecclesiastical rancour, has fortunately given place to the milder dispositions of forbearance, benevolence, and charity.[1]

Burns's (rather different) expression of this is one sign that he was abreast of the better conscience of his time. In this as in other ways he stands at the division between the traditional and modern phases of Scottish public opinion.

The other or non-popular poetry of Scotland was for long a woefully disorganised art, and the conditions behind this show the difficulties Scotland had in forming a broad, enlightened culture representative of, and accessible to, the whole people. This disorganisation lasted from the time of the Sempills until the heyday of Edinburgh. As the period of the 17th-century religious troubles was a blank in Scots poetry, this takes us back in effect to the minor descendants of the Middle Scots makars—Hume, Montgomerie, Boyd, Alexander Scott, counterparts of Wyatt, Surrey, and the other gentleman poets of the English 16th century. The Scots tradition lacked major poetic forms used by writers of distinction, as we can see from the collections that cover this period. Watson's *Choice Collection of Comic and Serious Scots Poems*, a pioneering collection of the nation's scattered poetry, is a scrappy miscellany, showing a marked split between the popular and cultivated elements. Also, both there and in the 17th-century 'fugitive poetry' collected by David Laing, the Scots language is used mainly in songs, extravaganzas, and skits, and rarely in the more studied and would-be complex work which parallels English poetry (Donne, Cowley, Dryden).[2]

This confusion of influences and modes goes with the fact that around the turn of the century the literary public was scattered, barely extant. This seems to have been due to the severe conflicts which split the country throughout the later 17th century. The effective area of the Lowland-Scottish culture was so small that the whole of it could easily be embroiled by any troubles, and there were enough of these. The capital itself—seat of so much cultural activity—was threatened

---

[1] Volume II, p. 90.　　　　[2] See note 3.

by the Covenanters in 1666, up in arms and under siege at the Revolution, attacked by Jacobite troops at the 'Fifteen and the 'Forty-five and in the latter rising occupied. During and for a while after the 'Forty-five, Edinburgh's newspaper, the *Caledonian Mercury*, was suspended by the government for reprinting a supposedly subversive item from an English paper. For safety it was published anonymously from September 1745 to November 1746 and even so the proprietor, Thomas Ruddiman, was imprisoned and died of 'prison illness'. At the same time the editor of the *Glasgow Journal* was alienating readers by playing safe and leaving out news of the rising, and he finally gave up the editorship until peace returned. In 1723 copies of the Whig paper, the *Edinburgh Evening Courant*, had been seized for criticism of a current law case, and the proprietors gave their fear of censorship as their reason "why we have been so sparing all along of home news".[1]

Poverty and narrowness themselves bore hard on literature. It is said that in 1702 ministers were so poor and books so scarce that "few of them possess property of that kind to the value of 20/-"; and in a life of Wodrow, a historian and extremist Presbyterian minister, the country's poverty is given as a reason why so few books were published in Scotland and those that there were sold so poorly.[2] Literary work such as editing was poorly paid as publishers could not rely on goodly returns "while in Scotland every house [i.e. big house] had not yet a library".[3] The very means of publishing were scanty. As late as the Revolution printing was still struggling to establish itself. It had fallen into decay during the Civil War, and then in 1671 one Andrew Anderson (a son of Glasgow's first printer) was given a forty years' monopoly as printer to the King. "By this gift," says Watson, editor of the *Choice Collection* and himself a printer, "the Art of Printing in this Kindgom got a dead stroke; for by it no printer could print anything, from a Bible to a Ballad, without Mr Anderson's Licence." Printers in Glasgow, Aberdeen, and Edinburgh were imprisoned for infringing on Anderson's right. Yet he (and his widow after him) were shoddy profiteers, and specimens of their Bible show they were content to issue work so full of misprints that it was literally gibberish. This did not prevent its being for some time

---

[1] George Chalmers, *The Life of Thomas Ruddiman* (London: 1794), pp. 187, 206; *Notices and Documents Illustrative of the Literary History of Glasgow*, ed. Richard Duncan (Maitland Club, Glasgow: 1886), p. 4; Chambers, *Domestic Annals*, p. 439.

[2] Chambers, *Domestic Annals*, pp. 250-1; *Literary History of Glasgow*, p. 4.

[3] Chalmers, *Life of Ruddiman*, p. 66.

one of the most-used schoolbooks for teaching children English.[1]
Until the second decade of the 18th century, little was published in Scotland beyond newspapers, schoolbooks, law papers,
and Church pamphleteering. Finally, reprinting of English
books came in, and more authors arose—the growing repute of
the *literati* gradually enabled them to make good sums from
their histories, etc., after a scanty beginning. But at the start
of the century there were only four thinly-employed printers in
Edinburgh (in London there seem to have been 75 by 1724),
and they had to contend with tyrannical authorities. After
the Revolution, all the Edinburgh printers were imprisoned
because pamphlets had been issued reflecting on the government (they were rescued from prison by a mob); and Watson
was imprisoned in 1695 for printing a pamphlet on Scotland's
grievances over England's sabotaging of the ill-starred Darien
Expedition.[2]

Freedom to cultivate literature itself was limited by dicta-
torial authorities, although, as usual, such repression had to
fight an uphill struggle. The annalist Fountainhall records that
in 1686 printers and stationers were "discharged ather to print
or sell books reflecting on Popery"—one man said he had just
one, the Bible; and nothing was to be printed or sold "without
a licence from the Chancelor, or the Ordinar, or the Clerks of
Privy Counsell". The next year, when James II was making
his last efforts to hold his régime together, the Privy Council
commanded printers and booksellers to declare on oath what
books they had imported, printed, or sold in the last twelve
months and to produce their catalogues. It was alleged that
they had been selling "sundry scandalous and seditious
pamphlets", "meaning, it's like, Dr Gilbert Burnet's Travells,
and the books from England against Poperie". All printing and
selling without "licence or approbation" from the Chancellor
or the Archbishop of Glasgow was prohibited.[3]

After the Establishment of Presbyterianism, this suppression
was replaced by the censorship of the other side. The theocracy

---

[1] Watson, Preface to *History of the Art of Printing* (1713), quoted in *Choice Collection*, pp. v-vi; Arnot, *History of Edinburgh*, p. 435; *Domestic Annals*, p. 364. I have
concentrated on the matters most relevant to literature and public opinion, but we
may note also that printing was technically backward in Glasgow: type-setters'
wages were very low, machines were primitive, proof-readers were not employed.
No type-founding was done locally before 1718. (*Literary History of Glasgow*, pp. 3, 5.)
[2] Arnot, *History of Edinburgh*, pp. 437, 443; Creech, *Edinburgh Fugitive Pieces*,
pp. 70-1; *Choice Collection*, p. vii; A. S. Collins, *Authorship in the Days of Johnson
(1726–1780)* (London: 1927), p. 236.
[3] Sir John Lauder of Fountainhall, *Historical Notices of Scotish Affairs* (Bannatyne
Club, Glasgow: 1848), II, pp. 619, 816.

mistrusted literature as such. Wodrow complained that "young people, Merchants, and others . . . never wait on catechising; they have multitudes of corrupt books among their hands".[1] In 1696 and 1712 the Edinburgh magistrates searched the book-shops for "atheistical, erroneous, profane, or vicious" literature, and seized books; and in 1712 they were persuaded to inspect the borrowers' book at Allan Ramsay's lending library to stop the importing of "villanous profane and obscene books and playes printed at London". His stock was inspected but he was found to have withdrawn "a great many of the worst".[2] The triumphant persistence of free literary taste is shown on all sides by the spread of reading, the popularity of English books, the success of libraries. But such conditions can hardly have encouraged men to venture into literature in Scotland.

Church censorship bore hard on literature itself. The often-mentioned effects of 'Calvinism' on Scottish art are perhaps hard to pin down; but there are several cases of ordinary suppression. The attempted persecution of Hume and Lord Kames in 1755 and the victimisation of the Moderates over Home's *Douglas* in 1756 have already been mentioned.[3] When John Logan, a minister, had a tragedy, *Runnymede*, produced in Edinburgh in 1783, he was at once charged by the Leith parish and church courts, and he finally left the country, writing to Adam Smith, "[I] cannot easily submit to the puritanical spirit of this country". John Wilson had published his innocuous descriptive poem, *The Clyde*. When he applied for the post of master at the Greenock grammar school, the magistrates of the city, which was notoriously zealous, stipulated that he give up "the profane and unprofitable art of poem-making" (a significant pair of adjectives), and he did not dare to write again.[4]

Culture had indeed been injured at many points, especially by the dictatorship resorted to by both sides in the 17th-century struggle. The universities, for example, as in England, were disrupted by partisanship. In James II's reign their staffs were split between King and Protestants. According to a historian of Edinburgh University,

the Scottish nation was in the most distressing and pitiable situation that can be imagined. . . . The state of society had

[1] Wodrow, *Analecta* (Maitland Society, Edinburgh: 1843), IV, p. 31.
[2] *Domestic Annals*, pp. 146-7, 363; *Analecta*, III, pp. 575-6.
[3] See above, Chapter II, pp. 63, 67.
[4] Rae, *Life of Smith*, pp. 396-7; Leyden (ed.), *Scotish Descriptive Poems*, p. 8.

now become such that in Edinburgh attention to ordinary business was neglected, and every one jealous of his neighbour.

After the Revolution, Episcopalians on the University staff were put under surveillance:

> Their private and public conduct was to be submitted to the discretion of the Visitors. Their conversation,—the books taught,—the dictates they delivered to the students,—and, in short, their whole demeanour, was to be exposed to the most severe investigation.

In 1690 the Principal and four professors were expelled for not conforming to the Presbyterian tests; and David Gregory, an early Scottish follower of Newton, finally left to take a Chair at Oxford. The writer stresses that Edinburgh and its university were all along especially exposed to the fluctuating laws, hardships, confusion, and periodic policing of that time.[1]

Scotland also suffered from having given up her court and capital. Deference to the British public and uncertainty about the value of her own language and 'manners' have already been discussed. Readers of Alexandre Beljame's *Men of Letters and the English Public in the 18th Century* will know the advantage it was to English literary men to live near a court and seat of government which gave them direct employment, sinecures, pensions, and other support. These were by no means usually for literary achievement as such.[2] But the fact remains that such a system gave literary men encouragement, and the means, to subsist in their homeland. In contrast, Scottish writers such as James Thomson, John Home, and David Malloch did not get their paid places from the Crown till they had settled in London.[3] David Hume and Sir Gilbert Elliot wanted William Robertson to go to England after the success of his *History of Scotland* because his own country was a "narrow field" for ambition; but fortunately the position of King's Historiographer (at a salary of £200) was made for him, and this with other inducements decided him to stay.[4] Such cases show the beginnings of that emigration of talent which was almost to empty Scotland of notable writers in the 19th century.[5]

Finally, we must remember that some of the writers were

---

[1] Alexander Bower, *The History of the University of Edinburgh* (Edinburgh: 1817), I, pp. 307, 313-16, 381-5. The English situation is summarised by Majorie Cox: *From Donne to Marvell*, p. 34.

[2] Leslie Stephen, *English Literature and Society*, pp. 39-42.

[3] Douglas Grant, *James Thomson* (London: 1951), pp. 139, 169-70; Mackenzie, *Life of Home*, pp. 50-2; *James Thomson*, pp. 171-2.

[4] Stewart, *Life of Robertson*, p. 33.　　　　[5] See Chapter IX.

themselves caught up in the wars of that time. Montrose, Lord Gordon (both represented in Watson's *Choice Collection*), and Robert Sempill were embroiled in the Civil War, and Francis Sempill in the campaigns against the conventicles (the open-air services held by the Covenanters). Robert Sempill had fought for Charles I, forfeited Irish lands, and failed to recover them at the Restoration. Heavy debts and mortgages were transmitted to his son, Francis, who remained loyal to the Crown and almost lost his life fighting the Covenanters. Lord Gordon was killed at the Battle of Alford fighting under Montrose.[1] The poet and song-writer Hamilton of Bangour, a Jacobite, had to take refuge on the Continent after the 'Forty-five, and returned to die broken in health through lurking on the moors after Culloden.[2] The country had for long been so gravely weakened by such losses of able men—younger sons of nobility and gentry going abroad as 'soldiers of fortune', men staying abroad after the Revolution—that, not long before the 1707 Union, Andrew Fletcher of Saltoun, the famous anti-Unionist M.P., proposed to the Parliament in Edinburgh that they should grant an amnesty to such people—men "only fitted to involve others in the same uneasy and distracting circumstances under which they themselves live", when they might have been employed "to the improvement of their country, and increase of their patrimony".[3]

One would imagine that the cultivation of literature could hardly have come unscathed through such troubles; and in fact we find that even the non-popular poetry of the time is thoroughly disorganised, existing in bitty, semi-oral forms. Francis Sempill's 'The Banishment of Poverty', the work of a cultured gentleman, circulated in broadsides. His editor refers to it as one of the best and longest of his poems "which has been preserved"; and among the fugitive poetry Laing prints as "probably" Francis Sempill's a poem in the mode of the Metaphysical dialogue, a 'Discourse Between Law and Conscience'.[4] In the preface to Dr Alexander Pennecuik's *Works* it is explained that, before he had collected his poems, "they had been so much sought after, that surreptitious copies of his verses handed about the country, and much disfigured, were constantly

---

[1] Paterson (ed.), *Poems of the Sempills*, pp. l, lv; *Choice Collection*, p. xxi.
[2] *The Poems and Songs of William Hamilton of Bangour*, ed. James Paterson (Edinburgh: 1850), pp. xxx-xxxiii.
[3] 'First Discourse on the Affairs of Scotland' (1698): *Political Works* (Glasgow: 1749), pp. 75, 68.
[4] *Poems of the Sempills*, p. lii; David Laing (ed.), *Fugitive Scotish Poetry*, Principally of the Seventeenth Century, First Series (Edinburgh: 1825), p. xx and Poem 23.

presenting themselves to him in the course of his professional visits as a physician, and calling for corrections, and publication under his own eye".[1] The pioneers of fine printing on Scotland, the Foulises of Glasgow, published Hamilton of Bangour's poems before he had returned to Scotland after the 'Forty-five, in the hope that this would draw a correct edition from him when he did come, and because his friends were worried at the circulation in manuscript of incorrect versions of his work.[2] Such hand-to-hand circulation was natural to the popular culture. But these poems were comparatively sophisticated, not necessarily suited for only casual circulation. As access to them was so uncertain in the late 17th and early 18th centuries, they could not accumulate into a heritage of literature, recognised as the kind of work indigenous to that culture, on which writers could rely for their primary suggestions.[3]

The Sempills' editor says of Robert, "It is to be regretted that so few of his productions have been preserved. The great Civil War, which raged during the prime of his life, would no doubt interrupt the flow of his muse."[4] That is, it is possible that 'The Piper of Kilbarchan' was no more than the light-verse side of his work. Laing likewise suggests that the "remarkable dearth of Genius" (compared with the English 17th century) must be explained by the long train of "troubles, dissensions, and oppressions" of the time, "alike unfavourable to the prosperity of the Country, and the manifestation of the National Character in its Literary Pursuits".[5] Now, Scotland and England were then anything but so alike that great literatures could have been expected from each. It is as possible that, in Scotland, there was little poetry then as that much good work was lost in the troubles. This is indeed suggested by a contemporary poem, 'A Satyre Against the Prelats' (1638), which opens:

> Doe all pens slumber still, dare they not try
> In tumbling tymes to let their Pasquils fly?
> Each hour a Satyre craveth to display
> The secrets of this Tragick-Comick Play. . . .[6]

---

[1] *Works (op. cit.)*, p. v.   [2] *Literary History of Glasgow*, pp. 28-9.
[3] This hand-to-hand circulation of cultured poetry is obviously very different from that of Donne's milieu. Donne and his poet friends at Court, the great houses, and the Inns of Court were a compact group who could readily benefit from seeing each other's work in MS., whereas the Scottish poets were scattered and cut off from each other.
[4] *Poems of the Sempills*, p. 1.   [5] *Fugitive Scotish Poetry*, First Series, p. xxxii.
[6] *Fugitive Scotish Poetry*, Second Series (Edinburgh: 1853), Poem 13. The poem has been ascribed to Drummond of Hawthornden: see his *Poetical Works*, ed. L. E. Kastner (Scottish Text Society, Edinburgh: 1913), II, pp. 293 and 413-14 n.

Hume Brown, however, goes so far as to say that the troubles *cannot* have been the reason why Scotland in that period, in spite of her abundance of learned men, produced "no poet or prose-writer whose works have taken their place among British classics" because similar troubles in England "did not prevent the production of works of literary genius by both Puritans and Cavaliers".[1] This is hardly a sound analogy. While one cannot point definitely to any Scottish genius who came to nothing under the conditions of the 17th and early 18th centuries, there was that crowd of evils, peculiarly unfavourable to letters, which could have discouraged creative work at the root, and for various reasons they were likely to be more deadly in Scotland than in England.

It has been argued that "The political and religious disturbances which preceded the revolution of 1689 tend to distract attention from the intellectual ferment of late 17th-century Scotland". This writer instances the founding of the Botanic Garden in Edinburgh in the '70's and of the Royal College of Physicians and the Advocates' Library in the '80's; the number of distinguished doctors, jurists, and mathematicians then practising; and the publication of Stair's *Institutions of the Laws of Scotland*, "perhaps the greatest achievement of the age", which gave the country "in definitive form a reasoned and systematic code of law".[2] But we must also consider how far such work fertilised the country as a whole; that must indeed be the prime criterion of any cultural achievement. The larger and better-printed books which the writer also mentions can hardly have spread widely when printing and publishing were so primitive and there were only four printers in Edinburgh. And of what use in its day was a 'reasoned and systematic' legal code which allowed starving workmen to be sent to Botany Bay for stealing a sheep, juries to be chosen so as to get a conviction for the Crown whenever it was wanted, and Radicals to be sentenced to death by a hanging judge (Braxfield) who openly exulted in such work?

The evils I have described do not all belong to the abnormal troubles of one period. Some of them are bound always to affect a country which is small, poor, and finally dependent. Any evil may overrun the mass of it and leave few parts unaffected; and it has, too, the fewer resources to fall back on if it loses man-

[1] *History of Scotland*, II, pp. 451-2.
[2] *Four Hundred and Fifty Years of Scottish Printing* (National Library of Scotland: 1958), p. 8.

power, money, and equipment. Scotland had been in no condition, for example, to build many of the large country houses which were the natural bases for the culture of Ben Jonson's milieu and of Marvell.[1] Nor had she had the economic and political conditions for accomplished journalism such as prepared a public for Addison and the London prose-writers. No doubt such conditions were not solely responsible for the falterings in Scotland's literary tradition. But it must certainly have been cruelly hard for individuals at this period to free their minds sufficiently from forced thought and blighting hardships to ponder their condition like artists.

[1] See Appendix A, 'Scottish Great Houses as Literary Centres'.

PART II

SCOTTISH FICTION AND SOCIETY

CHAPTER V

The Age of Scott

Although, perhaps, it is not now the cue of Scotland to dwell very much on her own past history (which that of England has thrown too much into the shade), yet she should observe what fine things have been made even of this department, by the great genius of whom I have spoken above [Scott]—and learn to consider her own national *character* as a mine of intellectual wealth, which remains in a great measure unexplored. While she looks back upon the history of England, as upon that of the country to which she has suspended and rendered subordinate her fortunes, yet she should by no means regard English *literature*, as an expression of her mind, or as superseding the examination of what intellectual resources remain unemployed within her own domains. . . .—LOCKHART, *Peter's Letters to his Kinsfolk*, II.

R. L. STEVENSON's *Weir of Hermiston* (a novel which, in the range of its material, makes a natural close to this period in fiction) contains these sentences in its first chapter:

It was a common practice of hers (and strange to remember now) that she would carry the child to the Deil's Haggs, sit with him on the Praying Weaver's stone, and talk of the Covenanters till their tears ran down. . . . "Are not two sparrows", "Whosoever shall smite thee", "God sendeth his rain", "Judge not, that ye be not judged"—these texts made her body of divinity; she put them on in the morning with her clothes and lay down to sleep with them at night; they haunted her like a favourite air, they clung about her like a favourite perfume. Their minister was a marrowy expounder of the law, and my lord [her husband, the Judge] sat under him with relish; but Mrs Weir respected him from far off; heard him (like the cannon of a beleaguered city) usefully booming outside on the dogmatic ramparts; and meanwhile, within and out of shot, dwelt in her private garden which she watered with grateful tears.

Such writing strikes me as typifying one kind of thing that we may expect the novelist to make of history. Stevenson's sense of national religious history gets the best expression it could through that presentment of the individual character—so chosen that the humanising of the harsher Presbyterian doctrine and readiness to condemn the 'enemy' can be shown as partly a result of her temperament, partly of time passing and the old struggle becoming just a memory. Mrs Weir's religion does not

function in any important way in the novel as we have it.[1] Yet
there are not many passages in this body of Scottish fiction
which so well represent that fabric of feelings and symbols,
interwoven at all levels throughout the life of the country,
which the novel is specially fitted to render. We have to
consider, then, how far the approach to life of the leading
Scottish novelists enabled them to produce intelligent fiction,
and how far their work was charged with the life lived in their
place and time.

In comparison with the incomplete poetic tradition the
fiction may seem an ample thing. Scott, Galt, Hogg, Lockhart,
Stevenson—do they not together render a great range of the
national life? Yet such social coverage is not the only—or
indeed, by itself, a satisfactory, criterion of whether fiction is
living up to its full powers. We do not expect of a novel that we
should be able to use it as a book of history. We do expect of it
some rare sensitivity and constructive power of art, called into
being by some strong original feeling for life, which can,
according to the breadth of the writer's interests, direct and
deepen our sense of history as no other medium can.

Scottish fiction starts during an age when 'modern Scotland'
was developing fast. The poetry (with a few exceptions in
Fergusson and Burns) deals with nothing not conditioned by a
type of community that had been going for centuries. Partly as
a result of this, the poetry is comparatively homogeneous—
there is something like a medium there in the culture, for
inspiration and use. In contrast, the fiction is rather a rag-bag,
out of which any kind of art may tumble. It is uncertain, for
one thing, in its sense of what was essential in the life then
going forward. To formulate such a lack is delicate. Yet surely,
faced with a literature so bitty as the Scottish, we find ourselves,
willy-nilly, compelled to keep referring to the sense of history
we have accumulated from sources outside the literature. We
wonder, 'Did no novelist see anything in *that*, or *that*?' For the
Scottish novelists did evidently see little in the main social
changes of their time.

By the time the Scottish novel appeared in force, in the
second decade of the 19th century, industrialisation had taken
root and deeply altered the living of the country. In 1801 the

---

[1] Those interested will find in my article 'Stevenson and the Vanished Scotland'
an account of the radical reasons, visible even in the fragment, why Stevenson
probably could not have completed the novel as a satisfactory whole: see *The Voice
of Scotland*, ed. Hugh MacDiarmid (Edinburgh: 1958), Vol. VIII, Nos. 3-4, pp.
33-4.

population was half again as big as it had been at the Union. Glasgow, the big town most familiar to Galt, had multiplied its population six times in the same period. From a slow-growing country town whose chief class still included many aristocrats, it had turned into a teeming centre dominated by merchants who had made money quickly. It was looked down on by the Edinburgh circles who took it upon themselves to set the taste of the country. But Glasgow had its own type of citizen, vigorous, self-confident, well aware that he was not classy but not in the least abashed.[1] Apart from slight work—such as that of the weaver poet Wilson, Dougal Graham, the most popular chapbook writer, and Robert Tannahill of Paisley, who wrote insipid but well-liked songs—this new culture in the area of Glasgow, Paisley, Renfrew threw up no notable literature, although it was activated by a surge of new interests.[2] The intellectual rather than imaginative talent of the country comes out again here. It was this Glasgow which helped to make Adam Smith so eminent an economist. When he was a professor there in the 1750's, he discussed economics and got first-hand information from Andrew Cochrane, a pioneer of Glasgow's booming trade, and he could learn from the "thickening problems of the rising trade of the Clyde".[3] But the ascendancy of Edinburgh in purely literary culture was complete. Edinburgh itself, in 1707 an obsolete late-medieval capital and still dependent on the institutions and *cachet* of a capital for much of its prestige, had become also a banking centre and site of industries such as paper-making and printing. It had also changed itself into a well-planned modern metropolis, the upper classes living well separated from the lower in houses suited to their dignity and wealth. In the country, the primitive peasant tilling for subsistence crops (done by Burns) was giving way (especially in the Lothians) to intensive raising of cash crops by methods which demanded of the farmer a whole new skill. In some regions the peasant himself was changing into an industrial worker, often croftless, living in a bothy on one of the corn-factories (as Cobbett named the new large farms), and helping at the steam threshing. In the Lowlands the 'middle class' of peasant, the man who combined crofting with another trade, such as that of blacksmith, was beginning to die out, and the comparatively independent small producer was turning into an

---

[1] See, e.g., Lockhart, *Peter's Letters*, III, pp. 148, 169-70 (with which compare his description of the Edinburgh dandies); Thomas Carlyle, *Reminiscences*, p. 214.

[2] For Tannahill's community of literary tradesmen see note 1.

[3] Rae, *Life of Adam Smith*, pp. 87, 90.

employee.[1] The 1820's, part of Scott's heyday (though not his formative period), saw the consolidation of many of the industrial changes. By the repeal of the Combination Acts, trade unionism moved towards acceptance. The proportion of workers employed in industry was increasing fast every year. A poor rate was accepted by tax-payers; and organised philanthropy set itself to provide for the town poor, whose shadow, falling right across the transformed countryside, could no longer be ignored.[2]

These are mostly raw facts, which might or might not figure in a literature. But we can also see changes which were working in the deeper life of the people. Working-class life was being transformed. Cockburn's journal is full of accounts of their condition—factory work during the booms, with quick money as a main incentive, and, during slumps, crammed starving in smoke, insanitary towns, competing for jobs with the tough Irish immigrants and others of the helplessly floating population —all quite unaccustomed to such a way of life. One result was demoralisation.[3] For years to come working-class folk felt it degrading to be employed in a mill; and Hugh Miller speaks of this Scotland as a mass of people who are "not simply ignorant of religion" but have "broken loose" from it.[4] Miller is writing as a highly self-reliant country workman, from a family of well-read, intellectually-given peasants, affronted and appalled by much of what bore on him personally when he came down to Edinburgh from Easter Ross, and incapable of the readjustment necessary even to understand the new town life. For example, he condemns combinations—trade unionism —out of hand, on the grounds that any grouping of men is bound to drag all down to the level of the lowest of them. But he does also, in a number of memorable passages, testify to the influence on the wider life of their country which the workers were at last beginning to exert:

> . . . there is scarce a change that can come over opinion, or affect the people in even their purely physical concerns, which does not more or less fully index itself in the statute-book. The autumn of 1845, in which I travelled over England, was ungenial and lowering, and I saw wheaten fields deeply

[1] Cobbett, *Tours in Scotland*, pp. 762-3; Leyden (ed.), *Scotish Descriptive Poems*, p. 2; and see also Hugh Miller's comment, quoted in Chapter III, p. 83.
[2] See note 2 for composite reference.
[3] See above, Chapter 1, note 1.
[4] Edmund Wilson, *To the Finland Station* (edition New York: 1955), p. 91; *First Impressions of England and its People*, p. 41.

tinged with brown—an effect of the soaking rains—and large tracts of diseased potatoes. A season equally bad, however, twenty years ago, would have failed to influence the politics of the country . . . But the storms of 1845 proved greatly more influential. They were included in the cycle of rapid change, and annihilated at once the Protectionist policy and party of the empire.[1]

The changed position of the bourgeoisie has already been suggested: they were learning to "interpose between the aristo-cracy and the people", building on the material basis of their prosperity new ideas of social dignity, and moving in their manners nearer and nearer to those of the English centres which were now so much easier to reach. They could no longer stay entrenched in the belief that they alone were responsible for the mind and management of the country. They had become responsive to the general stir of thought. Usually they could not think through to a position beyond the paternalism of Whigs like Cockburn—concerned rather to keep the lower orders tidy and obedient than to admit them to the full oppor-tunities for development that the country afforded. Yet changes in their outlook (of a kind relevant to the state of 'the public') are revealed in the many remarks inspired by the new quick communications and the 'diffusion of knowledge'. Cockburn was quick to seize on and approve the spread of information by newspapers. *The Scotsman* had a series of articles on the rail-ways, looking forward to the improvement they would work on the provincial towns: "Commodities, inventions, discoveries, opinions, feelings, would circulate with a rapidity hitherto unknown; and above all the personal intercourse of man with man would be prodigiously increased". And Francis Horner, the Whig lawyer, Member of Parliament, and Edinburgh Reviewer, interested himself in "that remarkable traffic in books round Glasgow by itinerant retailers": there was no better protection against enemies of reform than "the effects of knowledge readily and solidly diffused through the great body of the people", "nothing in the interior economy of our country so important to know, as the progress of instruction among the industrious classes".[2] Many such remarks show no more than premature excitement at media and machinery the use of

---

[1] *My Schools and Schoolmasters* (edition Edinburgh: 1907), pp. 308-9, 336-8; *First Impressions of England*, pp. viii-ix.
[2] Cockburn, *Some Letters*, ed. Harry A. Cockburn (Edinburgh: 1932), pp. 29-30; *The Scotsman* (Edinburgh: 11.12.1824), p. 876; Horner, *Memoirs and Corre-spondence*, ed. Leonard Horner (London: 1853), II, pp. 304-5.

which still had to be learned. Yet they are worth recalling, and reaffirming, in an age when an unreasoning reaction against literacy and mental development generally has set in, often from apparently enlightened quarters.[1] To react thus is, in a word, unconstructive, criminally irresponsible, and the faith of the 19th century reminds us of what we should keep before us.

One disappointment of contemporary Scottish literature—that is, fiction—is that it responded so little to these changes. It may be that they do not in themselves offer themes for a novelist deeper than a Dickens or a Disraeli. But Dickens, especially, is not lacking in passages pregnant with 'essential history'.[2] In *Dombey and Son* the merchant's passion for goods, property, the physical actuality of money-power, is finely symbolised, at a level deeper than satire, in Dombey's devotion to his house and furniture—he feels for them more, and they have a richer presence in the novel, than his family. Scotland, too, had an important merchant class, for example the many who made careers in India in positions got through the influence of Dundas (Lord Melville), made fortunes, and returned as *nabobs*. But the *nabobs* in Scott's *St Ronan's Well* or Galt's *The Last of the Lairds* do not begin to be dramatic symbols at the level of Dombey (or Bounderby). In the strong half of *Bleak House* the realities of law-court 'justice' are terribly figured, especially in the poignant Miss Flyte. By comparison Scott's Peter Peebles (in *Redgauntlet*) is no more than a grotesque fitted into a loose ensemble of the author's memories of Parliament House. Scotland did not have her Dickens, or even her Disraeli.

It is often claimed, especially by historians, that Galt's *Annals of the Parish* is as valuable as any history or statistical account—perhaps because historians are pleased to find literature so like what they are accustomed to themselves.[3] But *The Annals*, though full of interesting footnotes to social history, does not work these into a medium which interests us for the livingness of the humanity in it. It is very restricted literature, both in the kind of action presented, a single typical event chosen for each year, and in its point of view—that of the old minister entering his charge in 1760 and surviving into the era sketched above,

[1] E.g. Yeats's unpublished pamphlet *On the Boiler*: "Forcing reading and writing on those who wanted neither was the worst part of the violence which for two centuries has been creating the hell wherein we suffer" (Joseph Hone, *W. B. Yeats, 1865–1939*, London: 1942, p. 467).

[2] The phrase is from F. R. Leavis's chapter on Lawrence's *Rainbow*: see *D. H. Lawrence: Novelist* (London: 1955), p. 135.

[3] E.g. W. Croft Dickinson's Galt Lecture to the Greenock Philosophical Society: 'John Galt, *The Provost* and the Burgh' (Papers of the Society, Greenock: 1954).

which he naturally cannot understand. We suspect, indeed, that the outlook of the canny, parochial, backward-looking Rev. Micah Balwhidder substitutes in some way for Galt's inability to grapple with contemporary life at a level beyond the imitation of types. Scott's sense of the contemporary will be considered shortly; here I will remark only on his weakness—his lack of 'all-roundness'[1]—as he approaches the contemporary scene. In *St Ronan's Well* (the novel prompted by William Laidlaw's assurance that he would 'exceed himself', i.e. excel himself, if he set a novel in the present) he is distinctly ill-at-ease amongst the upper classes of the country town: "Sir Walter always fails in well bred men and women,—and yet who has seen more of both? and who in the ordinary intercourse of Society is better bred?"[2] Again, *The Antiquary* was meant to bring up to Scott's own age his presentment of the 'manners of Scotland'. David Daiches regards it as among Scott's greatest and most characteristic novels, and sees it as belonging to his work on the theme of past and present: "He was a lover of the past combined with a believer in the present, and the mating of these incompatible characters produced the tension which accounted for his greatest novels".[3] But I should have thought that to be credited with historical insight at the level of art, Scott would have had to produce something more than the *idea* of the antiquary (the modern man who can only dabble in the storied past)—for Jonathan Oldbuck does not figure in a drama which is plausible, internally coherent, or humanly interesting. Scott's modern works cannot compare with those to which he had been fired by history, so long as it was fairly recent history and not a backcloth for remote adventures.

This defect in the range of Scottish fiction was hardly made good as the century wore on. The Kailyard fiction lies beyond my scope; but we may note here that as the country grew into a modern town-centred nation, Scottish fiction even recoiled, immersing itself in the country ways which the sensitive soul (whether *émigré* or minister at home still hankering after the old ways) could use to gratify his nostalgia for that homely, rural past. We must surely count it a large defect that Scotland

[1] See William Power's phrase, Introduction, p.13.

[2] Sydney Smith, *Letters*, ed. Nowell C. Smith (Oxford: 1953), I, p. 405; Lockhart, *Life of Scott*, V, pp. 284-5.

[3] Scott's Introduction, written for the Waverley Edition and always included subsequently. So many editions of Scott are available that, as with Burns, I will dispense with detailed references. Daiches, 'The Writing of Scottish Literary History': *Saltire Review*, ed. Alexander Scott (Edinburgh: Autumn 1955), p. 63; 'Scott's Achievement as a Novelist': *Literary Essays* (Edinburgh: 1956), p. 94.

can show so few serious town novels.[1] By the second half of the century Russia had her Tolstoy, with his intimate knowledge of Moscow and St Petersburg (as well as of the country), and England her George Eliot and Dickens, with their knowledge of the provincial town and of London. My point is not to match literatures against each other, or to expect the same of each, but to reveal this gap in the Scottish range as one example of a lacking sense of the contemporary.

To be sure contemporary life does not necessarily take direct effect in literature. Scott's interest in the common people in *The Heart of Midlothian* and *Old Mortality* might be considered as valid an expression of the change from the aloof attitude to 'low life' as anything overtly modern or democratic would have been. Yet it is only a small sector of this life which Scott can feel as immediately present, not distanced in history, or picturesque. We may find a standard in George Eliot, who knew her country so well. In such scenes as the birthday feast in *Adam Bede* or the Arrowpoints' Archery Meeting in *Daniel Deronda*, a large variety of people, representing many classes, is brought together with all their interrelations rendered in a drama which allows a full, an unstereotyping imaginative interest to each. That, we may say, is one type of a comprehensive, intelligent regard for the present life of one's society. In contrast, the Scottish intellectual class nowhere produces work which we may take as embodying its way of life; nothing in the fiction yields the wealth of contemporary interest, expressed in a prose charged at every point with a lively sense of fact, that is to be found in Cockburn's various memoirs. In the fiction itself, too often the higher classes are modelled on the run of British romances and novels of 'highlife' and the ordinary people are 'characters', that is, the only *personæ* in whom the ripe peculiarities of 'Scottish manners' can be vested.[2]

The Scottish novelists themselves inclined, as we shall see, towards social history, and they explicitly singled out many modern matters seemingly ripe for their art. Scott again and again shows himself preoccupied with the co-existence of an older, more violent state and the settled modern society he lived in himself.[3] He would have us think of Morton, the hero of *Old Mortality*, as a young Scot wearied beyond bearing by incessant warfare:

... And yet, who shall warrant me that these people, rendered wild by persecution, would not, in the hour of victory, be as

[1] See note 3. [2] See note 4.
[3] E.g. *Waverley*, Scott's note 29; *Redgauntlet*, first chapter of the 'Narrative'.

146

cruel and intolerant as those by whom they are now hunted
down? . . . I am weary of seeing nothing but violence and
fury around me—now assuming the mask of lawful authority,
now taking that of religious zeal. I am sick of my country, of
myself, of my dependent situation, of my repressed feelings,
of these woods, of that river, of that house . . .

[chap. 6]

Touches there have a personal rhythm unusual in Scott's
speech, and we feel that the theme it suggests might have
become something of permanent interest, regardless of period.
Again, *Rob Roy* verges at several points on an admirable
presentment of the tension between modern commercial
efficiency and the glamour of old families with their adven-
turous ways, for example in the masterly dramatic speech of
Bailie Nicol Jarvie in chapter 26 and the rather less natural
suggestion of his Glasgow business attitude to 'scenery' in
chapter 35. And one or two touches in the otherwise farcical
Laird of Dumbiedykes (*The Heart of Midlothian*) suggest that
the 'yird-hunger' described in Cockburn's passage on entail
could have been a theme for Scott—if he could have risen to
any such awareness of what were, as Abbotsford showed, his
own motives.

All these things arouse one's curiosity; yet it is too rarely
satisfied by what is done in the literature. The surface of various
themes is touched in passing, but they are not embodied
through and through in every detail of the particular drama
or fable (as Scott himself admitted).[1] The action in which
Bailie Jarvie has to play a part breaks down into a sequence of
adventures; and the history in *Old Mortality* comes over with
an effect of simplifying propaganda: we can believe neither in
the heavily-caricatured Covenanter extremists nor in the lay-
figure Morton in whom the author's reason and moderation
are vested.

Of the main social forces I have traced there is little in
Scottish poetry (with one or two exceptions such as Fergusson's
'The Ghaists' and Burns's 'A man's a man for a' that'), little
compared with such English pieces as Goldsmith's 'The
Deserted Village', Blake's 'London', or Shelley's 'The Mask
of Anarchy'. What is more surprising is that these forces make
so little of a showing in the novel, a form so suited to deal

---

[1] See the self-deprecating remarks in *The Antiquary*, Introduction; and in *Chronicles of the Canongate* he thinks of the real history in his novels as distinct from the
romance side: "There can be but little amusement in winnowing out the few
grains of truth which are contained in this mass of empty fiction".

comprehensively with social life. Must we, then, accept Henry James's *caveat*, "This moral is that the flower of art blooms only where the soil is deep, that it takes a great deal of history to produce a little literature, that it needs a complex social machinery to set a writer in motion"?[1] Simply to demand social history only exposes one to fallacies of judgement: George Eliot's *Felix Holt*, in spite of the study of blue-books, newspapers, and Radicals' lives which went into it, is not the novel which shows her most penetrating knowledge of England. Furthermore, there are natural lags between event and felt consequence. It was some time before emigration from Scotland, working on the existing cult of the rural, produced the full Kailyard and 'Canadian Boat Song' nostalgia, fixated on the auld hame, the wee hoose, and the whaups crying on the moor; just as the forcing of mankind into mechanical systems was not presented by Dickens in *Hard Times* till decades after the industrial system, and even utilitarianism, had got a hold in England. But in Scotland we are bound to feel with special acuteness any such lapse from the novelist's 'historical' function, for the end of the 19th century was reached and still an aware Scotsman could not feel that his country had found its literature. J. M. Robertson's essay 'Belles Lettres in Scotland' (1888) defines so many essentials of the situation I have been considering that it may be left to speak for itself. Writing on Mrs Oliphant, George MacDonald, and William Black, he says:

> Between treatment and choice of theme they have contrived to avoid any convincing reproduction of the life of their time, and to live for us in Scotland as agreeable or suggestive romancers, who happened to lay the scene of their romances more or less in Scotland, and to give their characters Scotch names. To realise how entirely destitute we are of real contemporary Scotch fiction, we have but to contrast the treatment of American life by Mr Howells and Mr James with the Scotch work of our Scotch novelists. In the American cases we feel we are at least partially introduced to a living society . . . if Bostonians knew when they were well off they would be grateful for the element of culture involved in the possession of a school of fiction which makes their normal life an art subject. A composition of normal Boston experiences has become a matter that can interest, more or less, an instructed reader in any civilised country . . . we in Glasgow and Edinburgh have to turn back to Scott to get a similar

[1] *Hawthorne* (pocket ed., London: 1909), p. 3.

sensation . . . our whole human polity will die unremembered, or dimly inferred from the faint cartoons of our idealistic novelists. . . .[1]

The worthwhile achievement of Scottish fiction lies mainly in the novels that deal with its dominant subject-matter, religion.[2] But the fiction may be characterised more generally, in the light of 'essential history' and 'the contemporary', by considering the qualifications as novelists of the most substantial of the early writers—Scott and Galt. What kind of fiction did they, impelled by their kind of interest in their country, aim to create? what stance did they take before the life of their time?

Scott is famous for having rendered the past in fiction, both 'bringing alive' past times and showing how something in the present has been formed by past forces.[3] Those were indeed his interests; but of such a novelist we must always ask, Does his past lead on, with no change in the degree of reality, into the life of his own time? is history to him more than a mass of convenient 'subjects', there for the doing, easy to handle because time has set them into a mould and removed the contradictions, personal depths, and general bewildering swarm of facts that we cannot avoid in the life around us? Now, Scott was by no means torpid in his contemporary interests. After acknowledging (in the 'General Preface' to the Waverley Novels) the lead he got from Maria Edgeworth's Irish fiction, he says characteristically:

> I thought also, that much of what I wanted in talent might be made up by the intimate acquaintance with the subject which I could claim to possess, as having travelled through most parts of Scotland, both Highland and Lowland, having been familiar with the elder as well as more modern race, and having had from my infancy free and unrestrained communication with all ranks of my countrymen, from the Scottish peer to the Scottish ploughman. Such ideas often occurred to me, and constituted an ambitious branch of my theory, however far short I may have fallen of it in my practice.

Certainly Scott strikes us, from his life, as being as experienced as Crabbe, say, or George Eliot; and his varied experience was

[1] *Criticisms* (London: 1903), II, pp. 61-3. Further relevant sentences from this essay (which is apparently unknown, and difficult to obtain) are given in note 5.
[2] See Chapter VI.
[3] See especially Leslie Stephen, *English Literature and Society*, p. 221, and (more fully expounded) *Hours in a Library* (edition London: 1909), I, pp. 160-3. Balzac's similar criticism of Scott is quoted in Chapter VI, p. 172.

put to use in that 'gallery of portraits' which stood in contemporary reviews as one of his main excellencies and is presumably what kept him in favour as a family classic.[1] Further, he was not without distinctively modern experience, which he had felt strongly for himself. A passage in the *Journal* shows that industrialisation had impinged sharply on him: "We have accumulated in huge cities and smothering manufactories the numbers which should be spread over the face of a country . . .".[2] Modern experience can even appear fleetingly as the motive of his best work, as in the figure of Bailie Nicol Jarvie. *Rob Roy* is set soon after the Union of 1707, but a passage from L. J. Saunders's *Scottish Democracy, 1815–1840*, shows that the Bailie could have been a type known by Scott at first hand. He is explaining Glasgow's class flexibility: "This was partly because the middle class was now too large to be homogeneous, but also because there already existed an attractive tradition of breeding and culture which received and educated the newcomers. Many of the 'better sort' in the town claimed kinship with the territorial families of the locality."[3] The divided attitudes this must have given rise to are beautifully caught by Jarvie's direct speech in chapter 26 of *Rob Roy*, with its shifting nuances: "'I ken his lineage: indeed he is a near kinsman, and, as I said, of guid gentle Hieland blude, though ye may think weel that I care little about nonsense . . . waste threads and thrums, as we say . . .'"[4]

In spite of such first-hand experience, the varied humanity Scott drew from the life typically got into his fiction more as colouring and 'relief' than as the ground of the main actions. It is only in *The Heart of Midlothian* that we are deeply interested in the heroes and heroines—characters who have behind them his experience of "all ranks of my countrymen". Three of his richest, and most celebrated, figures, Meg Merrilies (*Guy Mannering*), Wandering Willie (*Redgauntlet*), and Edie Ochiltree (*The Antiquary*), are none of them central to the drama of the novel. They wander around the main life, turning up when needed to pass off coincidences and surprises. What they are,

---

[1] Lockhart says revealingly that Scott "peopled all our firesides with inexpensive friends" (*Life*, VI, p. 88); *Tait's Magazine* says that themes such as Presbyterianism or the struggle between monarchy and people "lends a higher flavour to the dish, and nothing more": it is the characters "that we care for" (Edinburgh: Sept. 1832, VI, p. 663); and the *Edinburgh Review* values the Waverley Novels for the "gallery" of "breathing, acting, speaking individuals" (Jan. 1832, LV, pp. 65-6). The standard comparison was with Shakespeare.

[2] *Op. cit.* II, pp. 126-7.   [3] *Scottish Democracy*, p. 112.

[4] This speech is quoted in full in the section on language, Chapter VIII, p. 254.

of course, is vehicles for the author's 'good Scots' and his miscellaneous lore. Beside them, the official heroes and heroines shrink into puppets; but neither can such vehicles of idiom, lore, and 'character' get the status as human beings which they would if they could enter into relationships which affected the main course of the drama. Edie Ochiltree is Stephen's example of how Scott showed "by concrete instances, most vividly depicted, the value and interest of a natural body of tradi- tions";[1] but such themes come to nothing if the *dramatis persona* in question is no more than a character-actor called in to perform racily from time to time by way of eking out a melodrama.

Scott's interest in humanity was perhaps too little an artist's; it was more like an antiquarian's or annalist's, or (in his life) an anecdotalist's. His commonest word for the subject he finds in history is 'manners'. *Waverley* is a "slight attempt at a sketch of ancient Scottish manners". In his *Lives of the Novelists* he credits Fielding with "familiarity with the English character, in every rank and aspect" such as he had claimed for himself and sees this as equipping him to be "a painter of national manners".[2] 'Manners' was a period word, capable of meaning much—though it is plainly more suited to a Fanny Burney than to a Jane Austen. But in the Scotland of that day, and in Scott's usage, it was liable to connote an attitude which set the life so named—often past life—aside from the life felt as affecting one vitally. 'Manners' tended to mean the ways of a people now distanced from one, whether in time or socially, interesting because picturesque, characterful, part in fact of the typicalities and oddities of a way of life, now melting away, which the Scottish writer had to fix if he was to create something native to the country he still felt himself to represent. Cockburn suggests the whole process:

> The prolongation of Scotch peculiarities, especially of our language and habits, I do earnestly desire. An exact know- ledge and feeling of what these have been since 1707 till now would be more curious five hundred years hence than a similar knowledge and feeling of the old Greeks. But the features and expression of a people cannot be perpetuated by legislative engraving. Nothing can prevent the gradual disappearance of local manners under the absorption and

[1] *Hours in a Library*, I, p. 152.
[2] *Waverley*, Introduction; *Lives (op. cit.)*, p. 2. In *The Antiquary* Scott aimed rather to "describe manners minutely" than to compose an "artificial and combined narrative" (Introduction).

assimilation of a far larger, richer, and more powerful kindred adjoining kingdom. Burns and Scott have done more for the preservation of proper Scotland than could ever be accomplished by laws, statesmen, or associations.[1]

"Manners" and "preservation" go together significantly. In his devotion to Scotland Cockburn cherishes the language (and manners) above all; but in his political realism he cannot conceive of any social plan that could put such devotion into practice. This was a central dilemma of that Scotland, and to transcend it, even to bring it into focus, would perhaps have taken the rare wisdom of a great artist who can do justice to both the inevitability of a process and the losses involved, while minimising or evading neither.

In his interests, Scott verged on filling that function. But the feeling for past life which was content to skim off manners—idiom, costume, furniture, raw history—prevented him from getting far in that vein. His idiosyncrasy was to be confined to a fascination with the historical *objet* in itself: this really happened here, so-and-so is the real descendant of a famous family.[2] Stendhal seizes on an anecdote of Scott's rather snobbish Toryism which expresses it as a judgement of his literary value. He says that "*les personnages du romancier écossais manquent d'autant plus de hardiesse et d'assurance, qu'ils ont a exprimer des sentiments plus elevées*", and he follows this up with the story of Scott horrified at breaking the glass he had requested as a souvenir of George IV's visit to Edinburgh in 1822: "*il jette sa redingote, le verre se brise; il est au désespoir. Le vieux Corneille ou le bon Ducis auraient-ils compris ce désespoir?*"[3] The effect of such an idiosyncrasy is to keep Scott's eye on the picturesque, and prevent him from having his drama realise through and through the theme he has perceived in history. For example, we are told that he could imagine no subject so perfectly suited for fiction as the 'Forty-five.[4] Yet that event was surely more of an outbreak or flare-up, which passed off without seriously affecting Scott's society, than something fundamental in his past. We can see that he, in particular, would be bound to seize on the 'Forty-five for its possibilities as a glamorous romance (the last flourish of the tartan). But a more intelligent

[1] *Journal*, II, pp. 301-2.
[2] Lockhart is full of examples from life, e.g. IV, p. 119; V, p. 300; VI, pp. 100-1; VII, pp. 363, 399.
[3] 'Walter Scott et la Princesse de Clèves': *Mélanges de Littérature* (Paris: ed. 1933), III, pp. 310-11.
[4] Lockhart, *Life*, III, p. 131.

grasp of Jacobitism is shown by Hugh Miller, writing on the centenary of the 'Forty-five:

> The class of true Jacobites,—the men in whom Jacobitism was a solid principle,—died with the generation that fought at Culloden, and they were succeeded by the class to whom Jacobitism formed merely a sort of laughing-gas, that agreeably excited the feelings . . . Their principle was ineffective as a principle of action: it was purely a thing of excited imaginations, and of feelings strung by the aspirations of romance. . . .[1]

That suggests both the seductions of the subject and that it was hardly a serious theme for an intelligent novelist of the contemporary.[2] Similarly in *Redgauntlet* we cannot feel that political moves of any moment hang on the escapes and hurried journeys of the characters; and at the opening of *Old Mortality*, for example, Scott seems more interested in exactly what wappenschaws were like than in the historical bearings of his characters—the Cavalier aristocrat, the Covenanter skulking in disguise, maintaining a kind of fifth column, and the humane young man with no party allegiance.

The question of how successful is the art Scott makes of the issues he glimpses is, foremost, a critical one. But it is also relevant to consider the recoil from the present which occurred constantly in his life. Hogg wrote that Scott's only foible was his prodigious devotion for titled rank, "in such an illustrious character, altogether out of place", and accompanying that,

> the Whig ascendancy in the British Cabinet killed Sir Walter. Yes, I say and aver, it was that which broke his heart, deranged his whole constitution, and murdered him . . . a dread of revolution had long preyed on his mind; he withstood it to the last; he fled from it, but it affected his brain, and killed him. From the moment he perceived the veto of democracy prevailing, he lost all hope of the prosperity and ascendancy of the British Empire. He not only lost all hope of the realm, but of every individual pertaining to it . . .[3]

Hogg probably overstates the results, but his diagnosis of motive seems correct. Scott took serious alarm at the 'Radical War'—trouble threatening among the working-class during

---

[1] 'The Centenary of "The 'Forty-five"': *Essays*, p. 85.
[2] On the 'Forty-five, see note 6.
[3] James Hogg, *Domestic Manners and Private Life of Sir Walter Scott* (Edinburgh: edition 1882), pp. 17, 95-6.

the farming and industrial slumps of 1819–20. Even the Tory Lockhart describes as ridiculously exaggerated the rumour, believed by Scott, that "upwards of 50,000 blackguards are ready to rise between Tyne and Wear". To Scott, the trade unions were so many underground gangs:

> You are quite right in apprehending a *Jacquerie*; the country is mined below our feet—[this after hearing that] the Manchester Weavers' Committee corresponds with every manufacturing town in the South and West of Scotland, and levies a subsidy of 2s. 6d. per man—(an immense sum)—for the ostensible purpose of petitioning Parliament for redress of grievances, but doubtless to sustain them in their revolutionary movements.[1]

Certainly some unions at that time resorted to serious terrorism —assassination and vitriol-throwing.[2] But there were enlightened people outside the working-class who did not get up scares—they felt for themselves too much of the real grievance and helplessness of the workers. Thomas Carlyle's finely-observed passage on the 'Radical War' notes the sympathetic crowds and the "old powdered gentlemen in silver spectacles talking with low-toned but exultant voice about 'cordon of troops, Sir'"; and Cockburn's memoir of it (as an Edinburgh gentleman he had been obliged to mobilise) is a perfect example of his trenchant sarcasm at lack of social good-sense:

> The perfect facility with which a party of forty or fifty thousand weavers could march from Glasgow, and seize upon the Banks and the Castle of Edinburgh, without ever being heard of till they appeared in our streets, was demonstrated. . . . On entering the large room I found at least 400 or 500 grown gentlemen, pacing about, dressed coarsely, as if for work, and armed, according to taste or convenience, with bludgeons, fowling pieces, dirks, cane-swords, or other implements. A zealous banker laboured under two small swivels set on stocks, one under each arm.

And on the subsequent trial and execution of some of the rebel workers he writes:

> They were all guilty of high treason, no doubt; as any old woman is who chooses to charge a regiment of cavalry.[3]

[1] *Life*, IV, p. 335 and n.; letter to Southey, *The Letters of Sir Walter Scott*, ed! H. J. C. Grierson (London: 1933), III, p. 125.
[2] Mathieson, *Church and Reform*, pp. 239-41.
[3] Carlyle, *Reminiscences*, pp. 212-13; Cockburn, *Memorials*, pp. 365-6.

There is contemporary life; but it had little interest for Scott. In 1816 he told Lockhart that he would have been glad to write the historical article in the *Edinburgh Annual Register* "if the war had gone on"—wars were enthralling and colourful— "but that the prospect of having no events to record but radical riots, and the passing or rejecting of corn bills and poor bills, sickened him".[1] So far from 'believing in the present' (in Dr Daiches's phrase), Scott recoiled from it disgusted; and such a revulsion, in a novelist, is unlikely to affect only day-to-day politics and economics.

There were strong propensities in Scott which made for something less than full intelligence about the course of history. He would not have been content with 'manners' if he had had a more compelling sense of what mattered in the older life; and he could hardly have been so preoccupied with the older life if he had been more aware of the life around him. Edwin Muir has a theory that these deficiencies belonged to Scott's society:

> Scott's heroes escape unscathed because they exist in a No Man's Land very like the Scotland of his day, which was civilised but without that living spirit of civilisation which creates its own centre of life and goes on nourishing society from it. To offend against that civilisation was therefore only a conventional transgression, unless it took the universally contemned forms of theft and murder. One has only to compare Fielding's attitude to lawlessness with Scott's to see the difference in instinctive outlook between a man living in an organic society and a man living in a sort of law-abiding limbo. . . .[2]

This sounds persuasive, and implies some sound criticism of the novels. But it is also vague. In fact Radical workers and gentlemen were being executed or transported for 'sedition' in that Scotland; and though in the 18th century the gentry could get away with a few years' exile for murdering each other, the lower classes could not. Further, Muir is implying that Scott's novels register more of contemporary civilisation than they seem to me to be capable of. Heroes escaping unscathed is surely an ordinary feature of the 'romance'. The born antiquary who, boy-like, enjoys himself in the bloody past is perhaps a prevalent Scottish type; but there were distinguished Scottish types—Burns, Cockburn—who felt their civilisation as anything but a limbo. If Scott had been more aware of the society

---

[1] *Life*, IV, pp. 147-8.
[2] *Scott and Scotland* (London: 1936), p. 172.

around him, he might have been less prone to the irresponsibility of romance-writing and plot-making; and a proper
awareness need not have precluded a deep feeling for the past.
In her essay 'Hawthorne as Poet' Q. D. Leavis has a memorable account of what the past may be to a novelist. Hawthorne,
she writes, was never "an imaginative recreator of the romantic
past", he had always "very clearly in view the *criticism* of the
past" and he worked "through the external forms of a society
to its essence and its origin". His dominant theme from early
America is the conflict between the Puritans who became New
England and the non-Puritans who were "merely the English
in America and whom he partly with triumph but partly also
with anguish sees as being cast out . . . a symbolic recurring
struggle". "It is a kind of spiritual and cultural casting-up of
accounts: what was lost and what gained, what sacrificed to
create what? he is perpetually asking and showing".[1] We will
have to recognise later, in the case of *Old Mortality*, that that is
just the function Scott could not rise to in his recreation of
Scotland.

Galt's idea of 'manners' raises different issues. In his *Literary
Life* he writes that he meant *The Last of the Lairds* to contribute
to that "series of fictions of manners, of which the Annals of the
Parish is the beginning".[2] In all his accounts of what he aimed
to do in fiction a simple idea of 'the real' is to the fore. He says
in his *Autobiography* that in all his works he had "kept the
instructive principle more or less in view . . . restraining the
scope of inventions entirely to probabilities":

> The novels would be more properly characterised as theo-
> retical histories, than either as novels or romances . . . I do
> not think I have had numerous precursors, in what I would
> call my theoretical histories of society, limited though they
> were required [*sc.* to be] by the subject necessarily to the
> events of a circumscribed locality.[3]

He is here an old man rationalising about the works of some
decades back. Yet the aim he states is, as an idea, a praiseworthy
effort to do something more serious than plot-spinning. He
seems to have been helped to form the aim of 'theoretical
history of society' by a prevailing attitude of Scotland to itself.

[1] 'Hawthorne as Poet', I: *Sewanee Review* (Tennessee: 1951), Vol. LIX, pp.
186-7.
[2] John Galt, *The Literary Life and Miscellanies* (Edinburgh: 1834), I, p. 270.
[3] *Autobiography* (London: 1833), II, pp. 210, 219-20.

Galt, first recognised and published by Blackwood, headed a squad of writings, centred on Blackwood's publishing house and *Blackwood's Magazine*, which set out to publish writing in Scots and to 'do' provincial Scotland.[1] This indeed implies a reversal of the 18th-century literary attitude (still there in Jeffrey) that 'low life' was disqualified as a subject, perhaps colourful enough in its own way, and redeemable by a Burns, but really outside the proper domain of literature.

This new taste came in time to set the image of Scotland for the Victorian public, and what is behind it is plain already in Galt. For example, at the start of *Sir Andrew Wylie of that Ilk* he speaks, with an air of acceptable commonplace, of "one of those clachan carlins who keep alive, among the Scottish peasantry, the traditions and sentiments which constitute so much of the national character".[2] Here we have again the linking of 'manners' and 'preservation', for by "national character" Galt obviously means that character as it had *hitherto* been. We have considered already the narrow exclusiveness of the 'polite' attitude to the life of the clachan carlins. Yet it did have, contrasted with Galt, an Augustan strength— the character of a class which knew its own mind and what it wanted culture to be. Galt has no motive beyond the imitation of the immediately available surface life. It is true that *The Annals of the Parish* does what Scott cannot do: by its idiom, and of course subject-matter, it evokes a contemporary ethos. Events are brought up to date, to the American and French wars and the coming of factories to the Ayrshire countryside. The Kirk life is decidedly later than the heyday of the Presbyterian extremists who took over from the Covenanters. The minister narrator, Micah Balwhidder, has got his church through a patron, against popular resistance; and his kind of Scots registers contemporary usage: for example in chapter 17, when the minister preaches a "touching discourse" against war and enlistment (which were enticing the able-bodied young men from the villages), Galt modulates into his thickest Scots for the evocation of the family and the deserted home—"the feckless wee bairns laid on a bed of sickness, and their poor forlorn mother sitting by herself at the embers of a cauld-rife fire; her tow done and no a bodle to buy more".[3] And this is perfectly true to the broad Scots for professional pathos which

---

[1] See below, Chapter VII, p. 219.
[2] Blackwood's Standard Novels (Edinburgh: n.d.), p. 3.
[3] *Annals*: Nelson's Classics (London: n.d.), pp. 13-17, 116.

we know to have been used by, for example, advocates in court at that time.[1]

Galt has, however, no particular attitude to the way of life he imitates, no effort of art goes into the selection of events to render; the only effort in the novel goes into creating the (unsatisfactory) medium of the minister's character—easy-going, and devoid of any attitude more sharply-defined than his canny belief that his own douce, practical piety will always have the last word. Because the minister is as conservative and credulous as many of his parishioners, and because everything is felt through his mentality, all other possible life is diminished to his kind of understanding. Here, for example, is his passage (under 1788) on political interests awakening among the spinners and weavers in the new country industries:

> But, in the midst of all this commercing and manufacturing, I began to discover signs of decay in the wonted simplicity of our country ways. Among the cotton-spinners and muslin-weavers of Cayenneville were several unsatisfied and ambitious spirits, who clubbed together and got a London newspaper to the Cross Keys, where they were nightly in the habit of meeting and debating about the affairs of the French, which were then gathering towards a head . . . they confounded me with their objections, and used my arguments, which were the old and orthodox proven opinions of the Divinity Hall, as though they were the light sayings of a vain man. So that I was troubled, fearing that some change would ensue to my people, who had hitherto lived amidst the boughs and branches of the Gospel unmolested by the fowler's snare, and I set myself to watch narrowly, and with a vigilant eye, what would come to pass.

Galt is deliberately 'fair' to the Radicals—even to the extent of making them turn into decent citizens who do well for themselves in London. . . .[2] But the effect is to give nothing of them beyond the fact of their existence and the minister's comically blinkered view of them; no sense emerges of what they were in themselves or of their real impact on society. The other pole of his theme is of course the older way of life itself; but we must conclude that to choose a medium so immersed in the older ways is an unnecessarily self-limiting way of writing a modern novel.

Such limitations are more oppressive in *The Provost* than in

---

[1] See Lockhart's description of Cockburn's language in court: *Peter's Letters*, II, pp. 69-73.   [2] P. 178.

The Annals. Balwhidder is at least a conscious student of his community, whereas Provost Pawkie, as standardised as his name, is concerned only with whatever shows him cannily dominating. That is the point of this novel of local government, but it is all the point, and the exhibition is monotonous. To be sure Galt does not mean us to accept the local as the sum of the experience he offers. He repeatedly nudges the reader to remind him that the local is rather absurd. *The Provost* is surrounded by an apparatus of mock-editorship supposedly done by a sophisticated outsider, and a similar figure intrudes as the 'I' in *The Last of the Lairds*.[1] Again, the characters in *Sir Andrew Wylie* are pointedly made to find the little Scottish climber much more ludicrous than anything Galt in fact shows us; and the emphasised self-importance of the church officer in *The Betheral* reminds us that his world is more parochial and insignificant than the man himself can realise.[2] Yet, as Galt's very medium—the imitation of local speech and outlook—is bound to immerse him in just that parochialism, all he can contrive to suggest, as the dissociating satirical standpoint he feels the need of, is a superciliousness which conveys nothing more than his own self-conscious superiority and hankering after a more important society.[3]

Such literature results from the writer aiming, not to work out his own experience—whatever its social provenance—but to hit off the social subject, the 'manners', for its own sake. To take an example from another vernacular: *Castle Rackrent* is Maria Edgeworth's most original work; beside it her English society novels are as nothing. Using a thin Anglo-Irish (the speech of the old servant), she can suggest ironies about the Irish gentleman—his fecklessness about his wife, his estates, his dependents—which are natural to that language. But the effect is also to limit the total significance by immersing, in the outlook she is supposedly criticising, whatever values she might have suggested by means of a style she had developed from *herself*. In Galt this comes out also in his ticketing names: in *The Annals*, Byres the farmer, Graft the gardener, Given the

[1] The 'editor' of the provost's 'memoirs' writes ironically of "the addition we are thus enabled to make to the stock of public knowledge": Galt, *Works*, ed. D. Storrar Meldrum (Edinburgh & London: 1896), *The Provost*, I, pp. 3-4. For *The Lairds* see chaps. 1 and 40.

[2] E.g. "It is very needful that I should state this here, for the commonalty might think, if I did not expound what a betheral was in the Bleakrigs . . . that I had been no better than one of the clanjamphry . . .": included in *Literary Life and Miscellanies*, III, p. 6.

[3] Galt left Greenock for London at the age of twenty-five; he was supposed to have alienated the townsfolk by his 'high ideas'.

minister, Mutchkins the spirit-dealer, Jenny Gaffaw the idiot;
in *The Provost*, Pawkie himself, Swapkirk, a minister, Shuttle-
thrift who owns a mill; in *The Last of the Lairds*, the gentry with
names like Mailings (Scots for a farm or holding), Custocks of
Kailyards, Moss o' Peats. It is as though Galt thought it perfectly simple to give a comprehensive picture of all there was to
parish life in Scotland—typical trades, typical events, and the
few typical traits which make up 'the Scottish character'—the
mercenary, the canny, the sly, the homely.[1] The individuals he
chooses to dramatise do not so much have lives of their own as
fill stock communal parts.

Galt, it is true, is a minor novelist; but the form taken by his
second-hand images of life is one which typifies the *morale* of the
small nation whose culture is all too easily 'covered' by a few
labels or set roles. Gorky, writing on anti-semitism, criticises
the Jews for themselves putting about a kind of repertoire of
'typical' Jewish funny stories; and Yeats constantly stresses the
danger for Irish nationalism in thinking that the only culture
that can benefit the nation is the overtly and defiantly Irish—
what he symbolises in *The Trembling of the Veil* by Harps and
Pepperpots.[2] By the time fiction grew up, this Scottish self-
typing was ingrained. To take their nationality for granted was
just what the more aware Scotsmen of the age could not do.
They had to represent a country much more confined than its
neighbour, with no very extensive recent or classic literature
to enrich its sense of itself, and this sense, this national idea,
had been kept down and kept in by the narrow opportunities
of a poor country. The character of such a culture might be
strong in itself—with the self-reliance, directness, and unquenchable vitality of a Burns or the responsibility and good-
sense of a Cockburn—and yet falter when faced by a world
larger and more naturally sophisticated.

Galt's trick of writing as though he could sum up the traditional life in a few stock types and mannerisms is vastly different
from George Eliot's standpoint in, say, *Scenes of Clerical Life*.

[1] Galt seems to have been of the Provost Pawkie kind himself. According to one
of Carlyle's trenchant sketches of Scotsmen in London, Galt "has the air of a sedate
Greenock burgher; mouth indicating sly humour and self-satisfaction" (J. A.
Froude, *Thomas Carlyle: A History of the First Forty Years of his Life*, edition London:
1908, II, p. 240).
[2] Maxim Gorky, *Fragments From My Diary* (London: 1940), pp. 138-9; Yeats,
Autobiographies, pp. 203, 219, 240. See also the suggestion, in *The Death of Synge*,
that Burns broke up Scotland's 18th-century idea of itself as "religious, moral and
gloomy" (*Autobiographies*, p. 520).

She is intelligently ironical about the provincial church-going set, but she does not fall into suggesting that the local makes up the whole genius of her country. To Galt it seems to come naturally to think and feel as though his own background were no longer by itself a sufficient source of experience for the observer or the moralist, and this reflects the inferior status of things Scottish in his day. Scottish students (for example the Glaswegians at Oxford) and Members of Parliament were exposed to a patronage which their dependent position, as incomers to the more powerful country, did not help them to resist. Alien manners as such were found amusing, and any action by one Scotsman was laid at the door of his countrymen as a tribe. Dr Johnson's famous jokes are merely the lighter side of what was for the many Scottish *émigrés* of that time a serious social obstacle. When John Home brought out a tragedy in London in 1769, David Garrick persuaded him to change its name from a Scottish one to something noncommittal and arranged for an Oxford student to pose as the author at rehearsals, to avoid the anti-Scottish violence of the London mob. According to Smollett, "From Doncaster northwards, all the windows of all the inns are scrawled with doggerel rhimes, in abuse of the Scotch nation".[1] Criticism of the Scottish caucus in England was no doubt often justified. The Scottish parliament since the 17th century had had so little experience of seriously influencing the central power, whether king or aristocracy, that English observers during Bute's ministry dreaded seeing constitutional power in Scottish hands; and as late as the Reform campaign Scottish Members still formed the only undiminished group behind the Tory government.[2] But the forces which tended to stereotype action and expression were also internal.

As we became absorbed into Britain, we naturally came to feel that if our culture had an essence, it lay in now bygone idiom and habits. Such an attitude is everywhere at this period. Allan Cunningham gives it as his motive for writing his *Traditional Tales*: he regrets the age when written literature was in touch with pagan mythology and "our oral or fireside verse and prose" abounded in "vivid presentment of action and character, an imagery fresh and green", and he observes that "with the diffusion of printed knowledge", "The oral wisdom, the

---

[1] Buckle, *History of Civilisation in England*, pp. 735-6, n. 100; Rae, *Life of Adam Smith*, p. 26; Mossner, *Life of Hume*, p. 550; Smollett, *Humphrey Clinker* (Everyman ed., London: 1943), 'Letter' of July 13, p. 188. See also note on Hume, p. 317.
[2] Mathieson, *Church and Reform*, pp. 4, 204.

unwritten sallies of wit and humour, the lyric compositions and legendary histories, have begun to vanish like all unrecorded things".[1] Similarly Sir John Sinclair, though anxious to groom away the uncouthness of the national speech, regretted losing the "full force, and genuine meaning" of the old "emphatic and significant" dialect; and the abject gaps, confusions, and unrealities on the practical side of his work on the preservation of the older Gaelic culture show how haplessly mixed the emotions of a patriot at that time were liable to be. He seeks to inspire Gaelic-speakers by reminding them that they are Scotsmen, with fine deeds to their credit such as the fighting at Quebec and in the French wars—a ghastly reminder of how the able-bodied men of the Highlands and Islands have been decimated in the ranks of the Royal and Merchant Navies and the Highland regiments, beyond any proportion that their small society could stand, while fighting Britain's wars. His policy for language is similarly wanting in an ordinary sense of social realities. Lairds and their sons are to learn Gaelic, a grammar and dictionary are needed—and Gaelic will be useful in wartime for shouts to rally Highland troops. But there is no word of teaching the language in school or of teaching *in* the language —indispensable conditions for well-rooted general use of any tongue.[2] Finally, in mid-century, Dean Ramsay notes how the country has improved "in common sense, in decency, in delicacy, and refinement"; but he cannot himself suggest much of these good qualities beyond temperance and nice behaviour generally. Certainly the country was changing for the better, or had at least set out on the track of progress. The more credulous superstitions were melting away before printed knowledge. Town gentlemen no longer ran each other through, on quite trifling pretexts, in the streets of the capital; and country gentlemen no longer took armed *possés* to plunder their neighbours' estates as a way of settling boundary disputes. There was less chronic drunkenness, at least among the upper classes; and children spent more of their time in schools, away from the vilenesses of the modern towns. But Ramsay has no word of such concrete changes; and the terms in which he describes what was lost in the 'refining' process reflect the concern of the period with the national types:

[1] *Traditional Tales of the English and Scottish Peasantry* (London: 1882), I, pp. iii–iv, vii.

[2] *Observations on the Propriety of Preserving the Dress, the Language, the Poetry, the Music, and the Customs of the Ancient Inhabitants of Scotland* (addressed to the Highland Societies of London and Scotland: 1804), pp. 5, 12–13.

If Scotland, in parting with her rich and racy dialect, her odd and eccentric characters, is to lose something in quaint humour and good stories, we will hope she may grow and strengthen in *better* things. . . . If Scotland has lost much of the quaint and original character of former lawyers, lairds, and old ladies, much of the pungent wit and dry humour of sayings in her native dialect, she can afford to sustain the loss if she gain in refinement, and lose not the more solid qualities and valuable characteristics by which she has been distinguished.[1]

The superficiality of summing up the changes in the quality of Scottish life in terms of relished quaintness and eccentricity might be just Ramsay, but his book of Scottish anecdotes was extraordinarily popular—it sold twenty-two editions in less than twenty years. He himself hoped that the book would become a standard volume in Scottish cottage libraries;[2] and it appeared during a sad gap in the line of notable Scottish fiction, that is, when there was a dearth of work which could have helped to keep the national ideas adult and 'all-round'. We find too that Robert Chambers, a literary publicist with a keen eye for the state of the country, is at this time anxious that the idea or type of Scotland should not be reduced to a narrow convention. He undertook a book of *Scottish Jests and Anecdotes* "to vindicate, for the first time, the pretensions of the Scottish nation to the character of a witty and jocular, as they are already allowed to be a painstaking and enlightened, race"; and in his *Domestic Annals* he argued, contrasting Dr Pitcairne, the early-18th-century wit, with James Steuart, a Lord Advocate, that the Scottish character was not one-track: "To nearly every idea associated with the word Scotsman, Pitcairne, like Burns and many other notable Caledonians, stands in direct antagonism: he was gay, impulsive, unworldly, full of wit and geniality, a dissenter from Calvinism, and a lover of the exiled house of Stuart".[3] The squeamishness of a publicist such as Chambers perhaps makes our morale seem lower than it was; but the defects of the leading novelists show that such qualms were more than the idiosyncrasy of a few.

In the end one wishes Scotsmen would have done with treating themselves as a special 'problem' and take their character, national or personal, for granted. Such self-consciousness

---

[1] *Scottish Life and Character*, pp. 131, 133, 134.
[2] See Preface to 1872 ed. (reprinted by T. N. Foulis, Edinburgh & London: n.d.), pp. 5-6.
[3] *Memoir of Robert Chambers*, p. 193; *Annals*, p. 384.

has dogged us even into an era of patriotism considerably more defiant than Sinclair's or Chambers's. A plank in the platform of the Scottish Renaissance movement headed by Hugh MacDiarmid has been a sort of synthetic national ethos, concocted from various sources, Celtic and Lowland, which we are to suppose could somehow be brought into being by an effort of will.[1] A regular critical approach to our arts is to rig out some common factors and make of these a criterion by which the success and true nationality of any work may be judged.[2] Of course our part of the world has its distinctive features, but one doubts, on the evidence of the fiction, whether the wisest way to realise is to think them into a finite ideal beforehand.[3] In his story 'A London Life' Henry James, the classic novelist of nationality and the way in which people of one nation venture on experience of another, shows us his American heroine, Laura Wing, brooding on the well-meaning young American who has fastened himself onto her in London society:

> . . . he still gave on her nerves when he asked if she continued to go by American usage and didn't find that if one lived there one had to 'do as the Romans did'. His very phrases made her wince, and she was weary of the perpetual opposition of the countries, was weary of the perpetual comparison; she having not only heard it from others but heard it a great deal from herself. She held there were certain differences you felt if you belonged to one or the other nation, and that this was the end of it: there was no use trying to express them. Those you *could* express were not real or not important, were in short not worth talking of.[4]

In practice James certainly does not play down his nationality; much of 19th-century America is concentrated in his fiction. What he brings home to us in that passage is that we must clear ourselves of over-consciousness if we are to get through in our

[1] This is too plain all over MacDiarmid's work to require much exemplification. See esp. his autobiography, *Lucky Poet* (London: 1943), e.g. the poetry in the chapter 'On Seeing Scotland Whole', pp. 303-4; the poems 'Kulturkampf' and 'Cornish Heroic Song for Valda Trevlyn': *A Kist Of Whistles* (Glasgow: 1947), pp. 11, 19; and the passages on the Scottish language's distinct "fields of consciousness": *At the Sign of the Thistle* (London: 1934), pp. 19, 28-9, 180, 195.

[2] See note 7.

[3] One of the more original living Scottish novelists, Robin Jenkins, recently filled in a gap in the presentment of one of his characters with that favourite scapegoat, "the deep-seated Calvinist conviction that sexual love, like all bodily pleasures, was sinful" (*The Thistle and the Grail*, p. 133).

[4] *The Spoils of Poynton* and Other Stories (London: 1947), p. 226.

literature to the real nature of the lives we live in our part of the world.[1]

It is true that some literatures have even been inspired by an aim consciously to create a nationhood: it is there in America (in Melville and Hawthorne's desire to free themselves of the English-literary influence), in Russia (in the constant remarks about 'the real Russia', 'the Russian character', made by writers such as Lermontov, Turgenev, Gorky, Blok). But in those cases the nations in question were either starting up or preparing to build themselves anew; they were triumphantly conscious of the powers of their people, ready for release, symbolised, for example, in the setting off into the virgin forest of Reuben Bourne's family in Hawthorne's 'Roger Malvin's Burial' or in Gorky's many stories of frustrated ability wishing it could only find its feet in a stable and humane society. In contrast, Scotsmen during this period could not but feel that the 'truly national' age of their country was now past.

[1] I realised on re-reading Mr John Speirs's essay 'The Contemporary Situation in Scotland' (*Scrutiny*, 1936: Vol. V, No. 2, esp. pp. 192-4) how much I owed to his diagnosis of 'cultural nationalism'. But the defeatism visible in his references to 'modern life' seems to me greatly to lessen the usefulness of his thought for modern needs.

CHAPTER VI

Religion in Scottish Fiction

> . . . seeing that novels must and will exist, and must and will exercise pro-
> digious influence, whether the religious world give its consent or no,
> we think the good people should by all means try whether they cannot con-
> scientiously patronise the good ones.—HUGH MILLER, 'Our Novel Litera-
> ture' *Essays*.

THE Scottish novelists seem to have been genuinely preoccupied
with their religious past and how their country's religious
traditions still affected the people. This concern stands out from
the general flatness of documentation and mimicry of 'manners'.
Some of the novels, it is true, hark pretty far back for their
subject-matter, and some do no more than 'recreate' history.
Hogg's *The Brownie of Bodsbeck* (apart from its ghost-story
trappings) merely recreates the Killing Time in the 1680's,
when the troops of an English monarchy inclined to the High
Church and Catholicism were hunting, slaying, and expropriat-
ing all over south-west Scotland those Presbyterians who
thought that true belief was incompatible with paying allegiance
to a head of state who did not share their faith. Galt's *Ringan
Gilhaize* recreates the period from the Reformation to Killiecrankie, the beginning of the end for Jacobitism. *Old Mortality*
renders the open warfare at the start of the Killing Time. In
Rob Roy, Andrew Fairservice is given as a typical High-flyer or
extremist of the period after the Establishment of Presbyterianism in 1690. Hogg's *Justified Sinner* is set at about the time of the
Revolution—but it no-one would charge with merely recreating
history. *The Heart of Midlothian* sets out, in part, to render the
unquenched moral severity, learned from a Cameronian
(Covenanting extremist) paternity, of a sectarian of the 1730's,
on guard against the backslidings of those around him. Lockhart's *Adam Blair*, Galt's *Annals*, and Stevenson's story 'Thrawn
Janet' (the first two of which are not felt to be distanced in
time) all concern the ministry. Scottish fiction, then—remembering Galt's *Betheral*, Mrs Oliphant's *Margaret Maitland*, and
the chapter 'Mrs Weir' in *Weir of Hermiston*—is concerned with
church and religion to a remarkable extent, a fact noticed by
19th-century writers who wanted to persuade the pious that the

novel was an unexceptionable kind of literature, and could even be a force for truth.[1]

Presbyterianism is essential to Scott's finest work, *The Heart of Midlothian*,[2] and it is perhaps the more successfully so in that it does not as such supply the centre of the drama. This novel gives us (as does no other Scottish novel till Stevenson and Brown) a complex situation worked out as a drama of individual lives the implications of which are something like fully realised by the author—not allowed to tail off into illustrations of history. Not that Scott hasn't here a deep interest in history, even taking from it some of his clues. But the centre of the novel—the conflict of religious and personal duties brought upon Jeanie Deans and her father by Effie's crime—could not have been as finely imagined as it is unless Scott had felt it directly as life, life which called out his deepest sympathies.

There are faults typical of the Scottish novel of religion. I ignore the deadwood of plot; it bulks large, but the central situation is so strong that the business of Effie's lover, of Madge Wildfire, even the clumsy farce of Dumbiedykes, Jeanie's gawky suitor, scarcely infringe on it. Nearer the centre is Davie Deans's often incredible loquacity; he gives a good run to Scott's flair for Covenanter rhetoric (learned from Patrick Walker), and the parody is often ridiculously broad. Yet Scott's sense of Deans's religion is also sure enough to produce the comedy of chapter 9: Davie, the trained believer, ruthless in his orthodoxy, confronting the motherly, scatter-brained Mrs Butler, too happy in her grandson's success ("'he has as decent a black coat as the minister'") to keep her mind on doctrine:

"And," continued Mrs Butler, "he can wag his head in a pulpit now, neibor Deans, think but of that—my ain oe—and a'body maun sit still and listen to him, as if he were the Paip of Rome."

"The what? the who, woman?" said Deans, with a sternness far beyond his usual gravity, as soon as these offensive words had struck upon the tympanum of his ear.

"Eh, guide us!" said the poor woman; "I had forgot what an ill will ye aye had at the Paip, and sae had my puir gudeman, Stephen Butler. Mony an afternoon he wad sit

---

[1] E.g. the essay by Hugh Miller quoted in the epigraph.

[2] This judgement is also made in F. R. Leavis's very suggestive footnote on Scott and in Arnold Kettle's excellent critique of *The Heart of Midlothian*, but these writers naturally do not relate the book to the Scottish social and literary tradition. (*The Great Tradition*: London, 1948, p. 5, n. 2; *An Introduction to the English Novel*: London, 1951, Vol. I, Part III, chap. 3.)

and take up his testimony again the Paip, and again baptising of bairns, and the like . . ."

Although the Presbyterians are here done broadly to the point of parody, we do feel that they take part in a real exchange, characters coming up against each other and affecting each other's feelings, as well as representing the varieties of belief (and non-belief) in that Scotland. Almost at once the drama broadens into the whole life of the Deanses. Davie's wife dies; he covers up his grief, and fortifies himself, by means of his unbending creed, given in the naturally poetic idiom of the Covenanters, seriously used: "'She's not to be forgotten on this side of time; but He that gives the wound can send the ointment . . . I have been this night on the banks of Ulai, plucking an apple here and there'".

This death leaves the daughters in the sole charge of their father. The events that follow work out the consequences of their intensive Presbyterian upbringing. Effie is as much a natural, feminine reaction to severity and sobriety as Jeanie is its dutiful product and Davie its enforcer with the inevitable limitations of humane understanding. This complex is given in the terse, perfectly dramatic and convincing exchange between the sisters at the start of chapter 10 (Effie is coming in singing from meeting her lover):

> " *The elfin knight sate on the brae,*
> *The broom grows bonny, the broom grows fair;*
> *And by there came lilting a lady so gay,*
> *And we daurna gang doun to the broom nae mair.*"

"Whisht, Effie," said her sister; "our father's coming out o' the byre." The damsel stinted in her song. "Whare hae ye been sae late at e'en?"

"It's not late, lass," answered Effie.

"It's chappit eight on every clock o' the town, and the sun's gaun down ahint the Corstorphine Hills. Whare can ye hae been sae late?"

"Nae gate," answered Effie.

"And wha was that parted wi' you at the stile?"

"Naebody," replied Effie once more.

"Nae gate! Naebody! I wish it may be a right gate, and a right body, that keeps folk out sae late at e'en, Effie."

Effie retaliates by making digs at Jeanie's suitors: "'And Dominie Butler—does he come to see our father, that's sae taen wi' his Latin words?'", and she taunts her with a bit of a song:

> " *Through the kirkyard*
> *I met wi' the Laird;*

The silly puir body he said me nae harm.
But just ere 'twas dark,
I met wi' the clerk . . ."

Jeanie breaks down, is consoled, and forgives her sister:

"... I canna be muckle vexed wi' ony thing ye say to me; but O dinna vex our father!"

"I will not—I will not," replied Effie; "and if there were as mony dances the morn's night as there are merry dancers in the north firmament on a frosty e'en, I winna budge an inch to gang near ane o' them."

"Dance!" echoed Jeanie Deans with astonishment. "O, Effie, what could take ye to a dance?"

Old Davie comes in in time to catch the word "dance", and delivers a heavy ban on "dissolute profane pastimes", thus stopping Effie from confiding further in her sister, and keeping her obediently in the house. So the tragedy is launched—by an accident, but not a melodramatic trick, rather an accident 'inevitable' from the nature of these people and what has conditioned them. It is written with a sensitivity which shows us all Scott's knowledge and experience coming together, under the pressure of a human crisis thoroughly imagined, for it has been chosen with an understanding of his types.

"She wad haud me nae better than the dirt below her feet," said Effie to herself, "were I to confess I hae danced wi' him four times on the green down-bye, and ance at Maggie MacQueen's; and she'll maybe hing it ower my head that she'll tell my father, and then she wad be mistress and mair. But I'll no gang back there again. I'm resolved I'll no gang back. I'll lay in a leaf of my Bible, and that's very near as if I had made an aith, that I winna gang back."

We see that religion touches these people all round, strengthening Jeanie, chafing Effie—for the best she can do to live up to the religion of her community is these pathetic resolves to 'be good' (that she is not just a petulant flirt, but has a natural happy emotion foreign to the others, is shown by the songs, officially frowned on, and other touches of imagination in that long dialogue). She goes off to service in Edinburgh, and the vulnerability which leads to her seduction is seen to be almost as much a result of her father's crippling innocence as of her weakness:

In the good man's security concerning the soundness of the theological doctrine which his daughter was to hear, he was nothing disturbed on account of the snares of a different kind to which a creature so beautiful, young, and wilful might be exposed in the centre of a populous and corrupted city. The fact is, that he thought with so much horror on all approaches to irregularities of the nature most to be dreaded in such cases, that he would as soon have suspected and guarded against Effie's being induced to become guilty of the crime of murder. He only regretted that she should live under the same roof with such a worldly-wise man as Bartoline Saddletree, whom David never suspected of being an ass as he was, but considered as one really endowed with all the legal knowledge to which he made pretensions, and only liked him the worse for possessing it.

There is a relevant comment on that in Yvor Winters's critique of the American novelists of Puritanism: "there can scarcely be virtue without a comprehension of sin, and the wider and more careful the comprehension the richer the virtue".[1]

Davie Deans's propensity to value religious orthodoxy above all else and to avert his gaze from the life he disapproves of is one of the main forces at work in Effie's crisis. He recoils from her because she is a sinner, and his words show us a Presbyterian conscience at the point of turning into self-righteousness and overgrown social pride:

"But the life of your child, goodman—think of that; if her life could be saved," said Middleburgh.

"Her life!" exclaimed David. "I wadna gie ane o' my grey hairs for her life, if her gude name be gane. And yet," said he, relenting and retracting as he spoke, "I wad mak the niffer, Mr Middleburgh—I wad gie a' these grey hairs that she has brought to shame and sorrow—I wad gie the auld head they grow on, for her life, and that she might hae time to amend and return, for what hae the wicked beyond the breath of their nostrils? But I'll never see her mair. No! that —that I am determined in—I'll never see her mair!" His lips continued to move for a minute after his voice ceased to be heard, as if he were repeating the same vow internally.

The bailie with whom he is reasoning replies in words which hint at a central issue of Calvinism:

"Well, sir," replied Mr Middleburgh, "I speak to you as a man of sense; if you would save your daughter's life, you must use human means."

This starts a religious argument—the reasonable, not very devout man exasperated by the seasoned sectarian who will

[1] *Maule's Curse* (Norfolk, Connecticut: 1938), p. 22.

not budge. The question is whether Davie should recognise any court set up by the present, 'uncovenanted' government and allow a daughter of his to go before it to testify on behalf of her sister. This leads naturally into a piece of retailed history—the development of the Presbyterian Kirk since the Establishment; but we put up with it and remain interested, not so much because it is intelligent history (there is nothing so close to the full facts in, say, *Old Mortality*), as because it increases our understanding of a situation in which we have been engaged by dramatic means.

The brunt of the trial of conscience which follows falls on Jeanie: should she or should she not save her sister by saying, untruthfully, that Effie had revealed her pregnancy—the only thing that could save her from the full guilt of child-murder. The exchange between Davie and Jeanie verges all the time on doctrinal debate, yet it is always felt as a crux in these lives. A misunderstanding, born of the fanatical scrupulousness natural to people with their background, is added to the dilemma. Jeanie has had her secret rendezvous with Effie's lover at Muschat's Cairn and been told what she must do to save her sister (chapter 15). In chapter 19 occurs Jeanie's crisis of decision: "'O father, we are cruelly sted between God's laws and man's. What shall we do? What can we do?'" Davie says to her, "'I perceive ye are aware of the matter'"— meaning the chief problem to him, whether or not to recognise the court. Jeanie assumes he means her crucial dilemma, to lie or not, and is terribly revolted at what seems his dishonesty in leaving her room to lie if she can see her way to do it: "'Wherefore descend into yourself, try your ain mind with sufficiency of soul exercise, and as you sall finally find yourself clear to do in this matter, even so be it'". The more he says the more he entangles her confusion and misunderstanding, for his thoughts are all for the niceties of Establishment, communion along with the indulged,[1] and the like; she even reasons with herself over the ninth commandment (could it possibly mean that false witness in *favour* of one's neighbour is not unlawful?). But her conscience, however beset, drives through clear to her fundamental duty:

> She remained in a state of the most agitating terror and uncertainty—afraid to communicate her thoughts freely to her father, lest she should draw forth an opinion with which she could not comply; wrung with distress on her sister's

---

[1] Congregations whose ministers, though Presbyterian, had been allowed to continue in office by the later Stuart kings because they had taken the oath of loyalty to the monarchy.

account, rendered the more acute by reflecting that the means of saving her were in her power, but were such as her conscience prohibited her from using; tossed, in short, like a vessel in an open roadstead during a storm, and, like that vessel, resting on one only sure cable and anchor—faith in Providence, and a resolution to discharge her duty.

We do not, I think, feel that this decision, with its horrifying consequences for her sister, involves any inhumanity which would kill sympathy for *her*, Jeanie, for her decision comes out of her character and its strong decency has been established. We shudder at the inflexibility of the inherited training which enforces such demands—the crisis of conscience is debated by Jeanie with minute scruples, simple girl though she is. Nevertheless we do not feel that she, Jeanie Deans, is grossly insensitive or selfish, and, in establishing this, the novel finely succeeds in its presentment of conscience and the right. The part of the novel that we take seriously ends as Jeanie goes innocently off to London to beg a reprieve from the Queen—driven to the last by the need to treat her decisions as moral dilemmas involving her father (the close of chapter 25). Scott has not the moral nerve to let Effie escape retribution for her 'sin'; the novel ends with her unhappiness in the grand life that follows her marriage to her seducer (chapters 49-52). But by then it has long ceased to be the fine fiction that we have in the first twenty or so chapters.

That part shows Scott living up to the reputation that has since been conventionally his—the master recreator of history. Balzac, for example (who had had similar creative interests himself), says of him:

When the latter [the great historical figure] does appear the reader already sees such a figure through the eyes of the minor characters in the story. Scott never chose great events as subjects for his pen, but he always carefully develops the causes which led to them, by depicting the spirit and morals of the age, and presenting a whole social *milieu* instead of moving in the rarefied atmosphere of great political events.[1]

One cannot say that *The Heart of Midlothian* uncovers the causes of any "great events"—by Scott's time Scotsmen no longer felt that there were any such events at home for them to participate in (and were half glad, half rueful as a result). But "the spirit

[1] Writing on Eugène Sue in the *Revue Parisienne*: quoted by George Lukács, *Studies in European Realism* (trans. Edith Bone, London: 1950), p. 70.

and morals of the age" are richly present in *The Heart of Midlothian*, and if we ponder what they amount to, we realise that what Scott uncovers is nothing less than the changes in moral and religious preoccupation which were the basis for the atmosphere of post-Union, pre-industrial Scotland, the sober concern with matters of piety and duty which had crystallised out of the turmoil of the 17th century. It is a rare case where the broad human condition of the Scottish people is expressed for us in a distinguished work of literature.

It will have been noticed that the art with which Scott evokes conscience is not quite sensitive enough. That key passage in which Jeanie's dilemma is given most inwardly is too much a sequence of ideas in an argument, too little the movement of feelings and ideas mingling in a person arguing with herself. For example, that inexpressive "conscience prohibited" (as though it were a simple command from outside) seems to evince the author's simplicity as much as his heroine's, and Scott apparently does not realise that he has got by without evoking directly any experience of choosing on Jeanie's part. There is nothing in Scott's art at the level of chapters 26-7 of *Daniel Deronda*, where Gwendolen Harleth swithers on the crux of committing herself to engagement to Henleigh Grandcourt. It is not only that Gwendolen is a less simple human being than Jeanie. George Eliot's art seems to work down, through every speech, rendered thought, and metaphor, to the very nerve of her character's consciousness. Beside this, Scott is nearer to illustrating a type from history through a kind of semi-personification. And if his theme, as has been suggested, is 'the nature of justice as it is in any age',[1] his exploration of it is far less radical than what is done in *Measure for Measure*, which *The Heart of Midlothian* (as we are reminded by Scott's epigraphs to chapters 18 and 20) at some points parallels. Shakespeare's poetry, where Isabella confronts Angelo in II, iv, and her brother Claudio in III, i, plays with extraordinary flexibility over not only the personal emotions involved but the principles of right and law ('What restrictive laws can natural humanity tolerate—how much freedom of personal life is tolerable in society?') which the persons must come to terms with. Of course Jeanie Deans of her nature (her puritan-like, Presbyterian nature) *cannot* feel, and hence recoil from, 'sin' with the intensity of an Isabella. Yet it seems inconceivable that Scott

---

[1] See Robin Mayhead, '*The Heart of Midlothian:* Scott as Artist': *Essays in Criticism*, ed. F. W. Bateson (Oxford: 1956), Vol. VI, 3, p. 277.

could have risen to an Isabella whatever his subject-matter. Here, indeed, we run up against the deep restrictions on his range as an artist.[1]

Perhaps the fairest and most thoroughly relevant comparison is with Hawthorne's *The Scarlet Letter*. Hawthorne was deeply versed in a religious background closely similar to the mixed or divided Scotland which can be symbolised by the two individuals, Burns and Scott. Writing on the "illiberal Protestantism" of the New England background, Van Wyck Brooks says: "The frontier was endemically prudish, odd as this seemed, in spite of all its wild outbursts of the natural man, for most of the settlers sprang from the evangelical Protestant sects that maintained the strictest taboos in sexual matters".[2] These mingling impulses in his background are at the core of Hawthorne's fiction, but he is able to imagine them with an artist's awareness which starts directly from life and hence gives reality to what he thinks essential in the history of New England. *The Scarlet Letter* is full of the experience of conscience, for example the superbly-done psychology of the secretly guilty Arthur Dimmesdale (the chapter 'The Interior of a Heart'), and in a stroke in the part of Hester which one feels could hardly go deeper. She stands beside the scaffold in the market place, scene of her former exposure as a sinful woman, while indoors Arthur, her lover, delivers the Election Sermon:

> If the minister's voice had not kept her there, there would, nevertheless, have been an inevitable magnetism in that spot, whence she dated the first hour of her life of ignominy. There was a sense within her—too ill-defined to be made a thought, but weighing heavily on her mind—that her whole orb of life, both before and after, was connected with this spot, as the one point that gave it unity.[3]

By this fine stroke Hester's moral fate is given as, in her life, something almost positive—the sum of what life has been to her, the meaning it has taken on.

The nearest equivalent to *The Scarlet Letter* that Scottish fiction has to show is Lockhart's *Adam Blair* (1822).[4] This novel stands slightly apart in the interesting Scottish fiction of the period; it is perfectly contemporary, not felt to be distanced in time—indeed, it represents the conventional moral feelings

---

[1] For Scott's depreciation of his own art and the motives for this see note 1.
[2] *The World of Washington Irving*, pp. 316-17.
[3] (First pub. 1850; edition London, introd. Moncure D. Conway: n.d.), chap. 22, p. 314.
[4] This comparison is touched on by Henry James: *Hawthorne*, pp. 114-17.

of the age. Blair is minister in a West of Scotland parish. His beloved wife has died bearing their only child. Blair is loved and honoured by the elders for his bravery under his loss. After some time Charlotte Campbell turns up, his cousin and the confidante of himself and his wife during their courtship. She has run off with a rotter and been abandoned by him; she is now married to a bone-selfish military man who buys a bleak estate in the West Highlands and is glad to go off with his regiment to the Continent whenever he can. Charlotte and Blair meet in an atmosphere of emotion heightened by their common memories. She is given the old bedroom of his wife and himself, never used since her death; and he comes upon her at night, all white in her night-dress, bending over his wife's grave. A climax of suppressed emotion (veiled from the reader as well as from the protagonists) is reached when Blair saves his child from drowning and is himself saved by Charlotte. She is taken from the water half-undressed by the struggle, and Blair frantically draws them both to him and begins "to kiss them alternately, cheek, and brow, and lip, and neck, hastily and passionately, as if ignorant or careless that he was within sight of anyone". The psychological consequence for him is a sleep full of nightmares: "Beautiful women's shapes, smiling eyes, and burning blushes, darted in glimpses here and there from amidst the thickest of tumults".[1]

A solicitor next turns up, sent by Campbell to remove his wife to the safety of Uigness, the remote estate. The canny local opinion of Blair's position is addressed to him by a neighbouring (Scots-speaking) minister, his advice clinched by the text, "'Let him that thinketh he standeth take heed lest he fall'". A sorrowful letter comes from Charlotte, and Blair resolves to set off after her and have it out with the insinuating lawyer who has escorted her to Uigness. He arrives at night and is greeted by Charlotte in a state of panic.

Mrs Campbell took Blair's hand, and withdrew him from the window. She reseated him by the table, pouring another glass of wine, and again forcing him to swallow it, began to tell him, in broken syllables, the story of her insults.

Had she never told that story, perhaps Adam Blair had never been a fallen man—nor

The moon hid her light
From his *heaven that night.*[2]

---

[1] 'New Edition' (Edinburgh: n.d.), pp. 75, 87.   [2] Pp. 104, 114.

Comes (in the first edition) a quadruple line of asterisks. The two wake up on Sunday morning—with the church bells sounding. Adam at once walks wildly off into the hills. When he is about to throw himself into a lochan, he is caught from behind by Charlotte. They exchange frantic speeches and say farewell. After more wandering through the hills, both given as though mad or diseased, she comes upon him again, seemingly ill. It 'might be' the result of exposure or physical weakness; as it comes out in the novel, it is a sort of moral-romantic retribution for their dire sin. Nothing is done to show a psychological link between their act and its aftermath; Lockhart is swept forward blinded by his assumptions about sin and conscience, for it is plain that he could not conceive (or dare to show) the 'sin' (which is not even clearly given) as anything but an enormity.

The vein of moral feeling of this kind running through 19th-century fiction is well known. Morbid repression is visible in many places. Charlotte Brontë in *Jane Eyre* has to blind Rochester before she can bring together a man who has desired a girl while his wife was still alive and this same girl; and there is a great deal of fiction on the lines of George Eliot's *Janet's Repentance*, in which it seems that virtue almost has to be accompanied by lingering disease as no other situation would give such fine opportunities for 'self-sacrifice' and the suppression of natural feelings. The peculiar Scottish interest of *Adam Blair*—akin to that of *The Scarlet Letter*—is that it is the minister who is picked for the role of sinner. "'I preached to others—myself am an outcast'", Adam exclaims to Charlotte.[1] In Adam, as in Hawthorne's Dimmesdale, is figured the moral pressure that a minister must bear all his life; he above all must live out the moral norms and fight the moral bugbears of the society he serves, whatever the cost to his vital feelings. At the time, indeed, this was used to justify the outcome of Lockhart's novel. In his review of it Henry Mackenzie wonders if "that utter prostration of mind and that long remorse, which are here so ably depicted", will seem adequately motivated by the crime in question, and concludes it is intelligible at least in Scotland, because of "the sanctity of the clerical character" which is "a part of the national belief and feeling".[2] In *The Scarlet Letter*, however, the after-tortures of conscience are not forced on us holus-bolus, to rush our moral judgement; they are presented

---

[1] P. 118.
[2] *Blackwood's Magazine* (Edinburgh: 1822), Vol. XI, No. 62, pp. 349-50.

with rare psychological delicacy. And the kind of feeling Hester and Arthur have for each other is allowed to be a value by which their society's judgement on 'adultery' may be criticised. Even Hawthorne gives in, in so far as he has to make his 'sinner' die after public revelation of his guilt (it is perhaps only realistic that he should call it a "sin" to Hester's face as he dies).[1] It is this element in the book which leads Lawrence to include it in his criticism of 'spirituality'.[2] But there are, weighing against that, elements such as the superb stroke of irony which concludes the passage in which Hester gets strange intimations of sin near at hand, from the most unlikely people, through her scarlet letter:

> Or, once more, the electric thrill would give her warning— "Behold, Hester, here is a companion!" and, looking up, she would detect the eyes of a young maiden glancing at the scarlet letter, shyly and aside, and quickly averted with a faint, chill crimson in her cheeks as if her purity were somewhat sullied by that momentary glance. O Fiend, whose talisman was that fatal symbol, wouldst thou leave nothing, whether in youth or age, for this poor sinner to revere?—such loss of faith is ever one of the saddest results of sin. . . .[3]

In contrast, Lockhart is simply at home amongst the prohibitions and inhibitions of the contemporary moral climate. Blair, like Hester, is committed to a life of servitude in humility. He confesses his guilt to the Presbytery in the Chapter-house of Glasgow Cathedral, and resigns himself to labour as a peasant. At the very end he is restored to his charge. In *The Scarlet Letter* the effects of time passing on Hester's standing in her community are given as an ironic reversal: "Individuals in private life, meanwhile, had quite forgiven Hester Prynne for her frailty; nay, more, they had begun to look upon the scarlet letter as the token, not of that one sin for which she had borne so long and so dreary a penance, but of her many good deeds since".[4] In *Adam Blair* the customary moral simplicities (I will not say decencies) are observed, and Mr Blair must help his community by publicly atoning for his sin to the bitter end:

> In those days, persons guilty of offences against the discipline of the church, were uniformly, after confession, and expression

[1] P. 330.
[2] D. H. Lawrence, *Studies in Classic American Literature* (edition New York: 1953), pp. 99-103.   [3] P. 111.   [4] P. 208.

of penitence, rebuked from the pulpit after divine service on Sunday in presence of the congregation. Whenever Mr Blair had occasion to discharge this duty, which is, perhaps, under any circumstances, one of the most painful that fall to the lot of the parish priest, he did it with deep earnestness and simplicity; but he never failed to commence his address to the penitent before him, by reminding him, and all present, of his own sin and its consequences.[1]

Lockhart's novel is not null; unlike most Scottish fiction of the time, it does have its theme or underlying concern, and there is a surprising amount of psychological insight hidden beneath the veiled style of the period. Yet *Adam Blair* does leave conventional morals undisturbed.

In the novels of Scott's age, the implications of religious conscience are not often shown as something which could move us now; they are usually set back in history. The proportion of attention given to the Covenanting period and other phases of extreme Presbyterianism is greater than might be expected of writers formed during an age which was strongly Moderate—sedate and rational in its devotions. Outside *The Annals of the Parish*, the more powerful side of 18th-century religion hardly appears—I use "powerful" to signify the religious party then in power in the centres of society.[2] What is more, the existing tension between uncompromising, 'High-flying' Presbyterianism, thinking of itself as the pure-bred product of the most testing times in the history of the Kirk, and a Moderatism which embodied the main secular ideas of the Augustan ethos—this tension makes little of a figure in the fiction. It was felt by Burns, felt intensely as part of his immediate experience, in such poems as 'Holy Willie', 'The Holy Fair', 'The Twa Herds', 'The Ordination'. But the novel has little to compare with that; Alexander Carlyle's autobiographical passage on his parishioners' hostility to the young, liberal minister is quite as interesting as most of the religious fiction of the time as a presentment of a crux in contemporary Kirk life.[3]

What the novelists seized on was, in the main, Presbyterianism in its extreme forms, with its striking features—the natural drama of the later 17th century, with the Crown troops hunting down the dwindling parties of Covenanters in the wild moors of the South-west, and the Biblical rhetoric of the Covenanters, which was for the novelist an effective style ready-made. One

[1] P. 173.   [2] See note 2.   [3] See above, pp. 66-7.

suspects that it was this literary exploitability, rather than any deeper affinity or idea of significance, which was at work. The Covenanting time did have its glamour for settled Regency Edinburgh. Jeffrey could write, under the influence of the gathering Disruption:

> You see the Tory lords are pressing Government now for an act to settle our despised Non-intrusion friends, and the bishops taking part in it too, and wishing the abuses of patronage to be repressed by the legislature in England, as well as in Scotland! Bravo! But if we in the north are not to get more protection from abuse than your English bishops will support for you, we must go to our hillsides and conventicles again.[1]

And Cockburn writes, on seeing the people of Menstrie at an outdoor service in the evening: "The mingling of the voices, at such an hour, in such a scene, combined with the recollections of the hill-folk, was solemn and delightful".[2] Such remarks are striking evidence of feelings still alive, especially coming from, respectively, an ex-Lord Advocate and the Solicitor-General for Scotland. Generally at this time the anti-Moderates were invoking the "old spirit" of the Kirk, the age two centuries back when "scriptural Christianity" was active amongst the people. In the Strathbogie case of 1838 the ministers who opposed the parish's candidate actually held meetings in the barns and fields; and those who were against government's being able to intervene in Church affairs "talked openly of the glorious days in which the blood of the Covenanters flowed on the hillside, and boasted that they were ready to let it flow again".[3] But of course such sentiments were not practical in that age. Even the ministers who left the Church at the Disruption settled down, after the first hardships of homelessness, into a well-financed establishment. The historian Mathieson observes that the opponents of the Moderates were genuinely appealing to popular passions, but in support of obsolete beliefs, and that the Moderates had a far more critical appreciation of history. He points out that patronage, the main cause of the Disruption, was never a vital issue in the puritan period, when the clergy were "more conspicuous as prophets than as pastors": "the historical background of the movement, to

---

[1] Cockburn, *Life of Jeffrey*, II, pp. 315-16. [2] *Journal*, I, p. 151.
[3] Hugh Miller, *My Schools and Schoolmasters*, p. 543; Thomas Chalmers quoted by Mathieson, *Church and Reform*, p. 315; *ibid.* p. 322; Cockburn, *Journal*, I, pp. 180-1.

which it owed most of its strength, was in great measure fictitious".[1]

This trend gets its direct reflection in the novels of the period. It was typical of the country that religion should have bulked large in its literature. But perhaps little inspiration could have been expected from the Church life of the novelists' own age. One of Scotland's best modern historians writes of the later 18th century: "It was in the purely secular sphere that Scotland now achieved what is set to her account by the world at large; religion, as it manifested itself in soul or mind, bore the stamp of mediocrity throughout the whole period".[2] Hume Brown is thinking of the leaders of Church opinion and the original thought on religious matters for which the Moderates were responsible. But we can see that for the novelist, too, no subject from his own time was such a natural as those from earlier periods. The cult of harking back to the Covenanters lent itself to obvious 'effects', for example Andrew Fairservice's speeches in *Rob Roy*:

> "Clauts o' cauld parritch—clauts o' cauld parritch," replied Andrew, with a most supercilious sneer; "gude aneuch for dogs, begging your honour's pardon. Ay! I might nae doubt hae heard the curate linking awa' at it in his white sark yonder, and the musicians playing on whistles, mair like a penny wedding than a sermon; and to the boot of that, I might hae gane to even-song, and heard Daddie Docharty mumbling his mass; muckle the better I wad hae been o' that!"[3]

However colourful such passages may seem after Osbaldistone or Diana Vernon, we cannot feel them as fully meant. They use their author's relish for idiom and 'character', but the other sides in such dialogue are mere feeds for the standard raciness. Fairservice is not a significant force in the drama, he is just Scott's kind of light relief, criticised by Coleridge: "One most characteristic quality of Sir Walter Scott's novels is the charm and yet the utterly impersonal and undramatic stuff of the dialogues".[4]

Much of this side of Scott, indeed, is no more than a compound of traits which Burns, and anti-extremist opinion in general, had taught Scotland to accept as the character of that

---

[1] *Church and Reform*, pp. 25, 315, 316, n. 2.
[2] *History of Scotland*, III, p. 265.　　　　[3] Chap. 17.
[4] *Coleridge's Miscellaneous Criticism*, ed. T. H. Raysor (London: 1936), p. 324. The passage Coleridge had marked in his copy of *Rob Roy* was Fairservice's speech in chap. 29 beginning "'Drink clean cap out, like Sir Hildebrand'".

element in its past. Compare, for example, 'Holy Willie's Prayer'—

> *Curse Thou his basket and his store,*
> *Kail an' potatoes. . . .*
>
> *L—d, hear my earnest cry and pray'r,*
> *Against that Presbyt'ry o' Ayr . . .*

with Davie Deans's speech in *The Heart of Midlothian* which begins "'though I will neither exalt myself nor pull down others'" and ends, "'avoiding right-hand snares and extremes and left-hand way-slidings, as weel as Johnny Dodds of Far-thing's Acre and ae man mair that shall be nameless'".[1] Or compare stanzas 13-15 of 'The Holy Fair'—

> *Smith opens out his cauld harangues,*
> *On practice and on morals,*

with Fairservice's speech in *Rob Roy*, "'There's but cauld-rife law-wark gaun on yonder . . .'".[2] Burns's parody of idiom springs from his main themes, and is taken over for his satirical style, whereas Scott puts in such material as so many isolated comic turns. Fairservice, the farcical-loquacious part of Davie Deans, the similar things in Hogg's *Justified Sinner* and *Brownie of Bodsbeck*, almost the whole of the extremists in *Old Mortality*, pieces like 'Placing a Scottish Minister' from Allan Cunning-ham's *Traditional Tales* and Stevenson's imitation of the suspicious and conservative-minded parishioner in 'Thrawn Janet'—it is in such places above all that we feel the national sense of the subject has too far set to keep it live as a theme which would justify quite so much attention.

The principal case of this is *Old Mortality*. Scott himself was a Moderate at heart; he became an Anglican, but the Edin-burgh Anglicans, such as the Rev. Archibald Alison, belonged to the same intellectual milieu as the leading Moderates. Rationality, decent restraint, and other of the motives which ranged themselves against fanaticism came as naturally to Scott as the old-time warfare and adventurousness which he roman-ticised. In his note to a Border ballad which retailed some of his material, 'The Battle of Loudon Hill', he reveals the attitude behind his novel: "Their indecent modes of prayer, their extravagant expectations of miraculous assistance, and their supposed inspirations might easily furnish out a tale, at which the good would sigh, and the brave would laugh".[3] In spite of

---

[1] Chap. 18.   [2] Chap. 20.
[3] *Minstrelsy of the Scottish Border*, ed. T. F. Henderson (Edinburgh: 1932), II, p. 250.

this leaning, Poundtext, the moderate-minded minister who has accepted the Indulgence, is a stock figure of canniness and lazy, homely pleasure-loving, more concerned for his own skin than working seriously for a civil settlement; and this travesty is admitted by Scott in a note:

> The Author does not by any means desire that Poundtext should be regarded as a just representative of the Moderate Presbyterians, among whom were many ministers whose courage was equal to their good sense and sound views of religion. Were he to write the tale anew, he would probably endeavour to give the character a higher turn. It is certain, however, that the Cameronians imputed to their opponents in opinion concerning the Indulgence, or others of their strained and fanatical notions, a disposition not only to seek their own safety, but to enjoy themselves. . . .[1]

It is indeed odd to find Scott taking some of his history from Cameronian views; but both his stated intentions and the novel itself show that, lacking an urgent sense of tension and divided tradition within the country such as inspired Hawthorne, he was not braced up to a faithful regard for history.

We know that Scott intended a faithful recreation of history. In a letter on the appeal of the subject he wrote that during the Covenanting period, "all human passions [were] stirred up and stimulated by the most powerful passions; and the contending parties as distinctly contrasted in manners and modes of thinking as in political principles. I am complete master of the whole history of these strange times both of persecutors and persecuted. . . ."[2] The novel is famous for its impartiality to all sides in the struggle; and Scott does earnestly intend this. Morton is always there to embody for us the decent sanity which we are to adopt in face of fanaticism on the one side and brutal military terrorism on the other. We are often prompted to take note of fair intentions: "And it is but doing justice to Mr Poundtext to add that, like most of his own persuasion, he was decidedly adverse to any such acts of unnecessary violence"; and again:

> Morton could not but strongly hope that these terms, which comprehended all that was wanted, or wished for, by the Moderate party among the insurgents, might, when thus cleared of the violence of fanaticism, find advocates even among the Royalists, as claiming only the ordinary rights of Scottish freemen.[3]

[1] Note 28.   [2] *Letters*, IV, p. 293.   [3] Chap. 27.

"Never trust the artist. Trust the tale." At such points, Scott seems to have to fill in from history, flatly retailed, the whole truth about the Moderates, and to *tell* us that the course of the historical events is tending towards a settlement based on reason and tolerance. But this ideal uniting all the forces in one state would be meaningful—would become something more than a preconception from the polite ethos—only if this complex of forces (sects, doctrines, degrees of political commitment) could be brought whole to the test of a fully imaginative rendering.

The debates before Bothwell Bridge (chapters 26-31) bring the main forces together. But where these are not ordinarily retailed history, they are set rhetorical exchanges which we cannot feel any outcome to depend on; they are being manipulated to a simply-preconceived, summary notion of the unrelieved bigotry of the extremists, the perfect good-sense and humanity of the moderates. Morton stands for decency; but a novelist whose imagination was engaged could not have conceived such speeches being addressed by an energetic, soldierly young man to tough veteran Covenanters:

> "Gentlemen," said Morton, "cease this irritating and unavailing recrimination; and do you, Mr Balfour, inform us whether it is your purpose to oppose the liberation of Lord Evandale, which appears to us a profitable measure in the present position of our affairs."

And Burley, a wild man and leader of the militants, speaks like this:

> "Thou errest," said Burley; "we must work by means, and these worldly men shall be our instruments. At all events, the Moabitish woman shall be despoiled of her inheritance, and neither the Malignant Evandale nor the Erastian Morton shall possess yonder castle and lands though they may seek in marriage the daughter thereof."[1]

Official statements issued by the Covenanters were couched in a strained jargon based on the Old Testament, but it is neither known nor likely that they spoke like that extempore in their discussions of tactics; indeed in that speech Scott seems to be shading into the Wardour-Street English of the 'historical novelist'. Parodying the devotional style of the Covenanters leads to much grosser implausibilities, for example the exclamations of the old peasant woman, Mause Headrigg, and the

[1] Chaps. 27, 30.

fanatical preacher, Kettledrummle, as they make a forced march to the hill of Drumclog in the hands of Claverhouse:

> "Through the help of the Lord I have luppen ower a wall," cried poor Mause, as her horse was by her rude attendants brought up to leap the turf inclosure of a deserted fold. . . .
> "I am sunk in deep mire where there is no standing; I am come into deep waters where the floods overflow me!" exclaimed Kettledrummle, as the charger on which he was mounted plunged up to the saddle-girths in a 'well-head'. . . .

Or Mause's exclamations as the Crown troops flee from Drumclog:

> "O, the false Egyptians, the proud Assyrians, the Philistines, the Moabites, the Edomites, the Ishmaelites! The Lord has brought sharp swords upon them to make food for the fowls of heaven and the beasts of the field . . ."[1]

In the first, Scott is perhaps (historian that he was) using the dying words of the famous English puritan, Major-General Thomas Harrison: "By God I have leapt over a wall, by God I have run thro' a troop, and by God I will go through this death, and He will make it easy to me".[2] But this fine formal utterance is merely out of keeping when put into the farm woman's mouth, at such a juncture; it is ludicrous in the wrong way.

Of a piece with this is the preaching we are shown. The young minister MacBriar's sermon after Drumclog is an elaborate concoction of Biblical rhetoric, the figures of speech and order of words highly contrived with no impetus or directness of speech.[3] Yet the field-preaching was traditionally colloquial and direct, and close to vernacular Scots. It is the tradition of Rutherford, in mid-century, and of the Covenanter preachers themselves, Peden, Cargill, Renwick. So far from using only an inflated, repetitious jargon, their style was close to life, calling up vividly the experience to which it appealed:

> The commodity is good, come away, we shall not cast out about the price: If ye have hearts to receive, I have an heart to give: Come away then, hearty good fellows, we will never stand upon it; for it is not with him as with the men of the world . . .
> O remember this! Ye who have any one predominant whose head ye clap . . . Remember this, ye moral civilians,

[1] Chaps. 15-17.
[2] Quoted from Christopher Hill, *Puritanism and Revolution* (London: 1958), p. vii.
[3] Chap. 18.

who are not chargeable with gross profanity in your private
walk, yet have your hands imbrued inblood, and have them
defiled with public land-sins, and which procure land-
judgements . . . do not think that he will sympathise with
any that are not his true members; for it is as if you should
tie a tree-leg to a man; let him wear it never so long he will
not find life in it . . .

O! how unconstant and unsure is he to lippen to! like a
loose tooth, or foot out of joint, that dow thole nothing.[1]

Renwick is full of the Old Testament and of technical theology;
but he is also worth reading as a man of lively convictions
exerting his whole powers in the great crisis of his Church.
Such men were fanatically anti-'curate' (the "abjured hire-
lings") and pro-Covenant, deadly in their enmities; but they
did not normally, like all Scott's extremists, vaingloriously
aggrandise themselves. Even in triumph, unlike Macbriar, they
were always quick to remind their congregations of vanity,
worldliness, and the brittleness of success.

Such reality had no chance with Scott. He here, in spite of
his gifts and interests, partakes of that alienation from popular
literature and thought which was typical of his class. Scott's
historical 'case', which his drama is framed to present, seems
openly rigged by introducing so wild a figure as Habakkuk
Mucklewrath, who is forced into the action against all credi-
bility, and given a fantastic presence and jargon which we are
expected to take as influencing the Covenanter army.[2] Yet the
facts of this stage in history could have been worked naturally
into a drama that went to the heart of the extreme Presbyterian
movement. These men lived by principles of religious sincerity
and independence, worked out and defended to the letter at
every single turn in their dealings with society. On the eve of
Bothwell Bridge, when their whole cause was in jeopardy, their
ranks were split, split, and split again by purist dissensions,
fanatically pursued, over the letter of the Indulgence. The
ministers who preached to the army carried their disagreements
and disputes onto the battlefield itself, where only united
generalship could have saved the cause. It is one of the phases

[1] *A Choice Collection of Very Valuable Lectures, Prefaces, and Sermons*, Preached upon
the Mountains and Muirs, etc., of Scotland. In the hottest Time of the late Persecution; by that faithful Minister and Martyr of Jesus Christ, The Reverend Mr
James Renwick (Glasgow: 1776), pp. 17, 24, 197, 496. For Peden see his letter of
1685 to the Covenanters imprisoned in Dunottar Castle: Walker, *Biographia Presbyteriana*, I, pp. 95-7. For Cargill see, e.g., *A Lecture and Sermon*, Preached at Different Times by that Faithfull and Painfull *Minister* of the *Gospel*, and now Glorified
Martyr, Mr Donald Cargill (no date or publisher: ? 1680), esp. pp. 15-16, 22.
[2] Chaps. 22, 31.

in Presbyterianism where we see the extremists, who genuinely thought that they alone stood for the only true religion, forced further and further out onto the limb until reality is lost sight of and catastrophe is reached.[1] Fidelity to fact could perhaps have made out of this an intense drama—if the forces converging at the crisis had been embodied in kinds of person and speech which had some credible imaginative life. But Scott is so sure of his 'case', he has made so little effort to imagine his way into the phenomenon he has chosen to present, that his types turn into grotesque puppets on his hands.

A contemporary review of the *Tales of My Landlord* (the series including *Old Mortality*) by Thomas McCrie, the biographer of Knox and Andrew Melville, rebuts Scott's history with evidence from contemporary records. For example, he objects to the "ridiculous and incoherent harangues" of the Covenanters, especially those on "points of religion, with which they had the best opportunity of being acquainted". He criticises Scott's bondage to the assumption that "in the opinion of all sensible men, they [the Covenanters] were completely indefensible . . . as if the truth of the facts which the author has brought forward, and the view which he has taken of them, were already placed beyond all reasonable doubt or contradiction". McCrie is perhaps less likely to have an acceptable or just view of fanatical religion than Scott—he was proud to consider himself the heir of the uncompromised Presbyterians. But my aim here is not so much to decide the historical case as to consider what quality of imagination Scott brought to his work, how far the meaning of *any* period, past or present, could be opened to him; and McCrie is more than a historian defending Presbyterianism, his sense of history enables him to see where *Old Mortality* weakens as a novel:

> Had he only introduced the leading facts in a conversation between Morton and a rational Presbyterian, (if such a personage could have entered into the author's conception) he might have given a higher tone to his work, and invested his nominal hero with the real character of a patriot, instead of making him a mere everyday person of romance.[2]

McCrie's historical scholarship is matched by R. S. Rait, who argues that Scott cannot be convicted of inaccuracy or unfairness as his Presbyterians are just one wing of that Church: "If the story had belonged to the year of Rullion Green instead

---

[1] See note 3.
[2] *Edinburgh Christian Instructor* (Edinburgh: 1817), XIV, pp. 176, 201, 55.

of the year of Bothwell Bridge, the characterisation of the insurgent Presbyterians would have been very different". He supports this with quotation from Scott's *Quarterly Review* article on Kirkton's *Secret and True History of the Church of Scotland*, an article written two years after the novel, where he describes the moderation of the Pentland Rising rebels who were routed by Dalziel's Royalist army while marching on Edinburgh, tortured, and hanged. Unlike the extremists who aimed to force the Covenant onto the whole country, they "limited their contendings and testimonies by declaring that they were only directed against the military law unjustly exercised on their own persons, and the tyranny to which their consciences were subjected" (Scott's words). Rait comments: "With such a protest Scott, like Henry Morton, was in full sympathy; those of whom he drew an unfriendly portrait in *Old Mortality* were enemies of that protest".[1] This rebuts some of McCrie's specific objections; but it ignores the critic's charge against the novel. For one thing, Scott's superficiality in re-creating history includes his moderate, Morton, as well as his extremists; and we can also see that he is swayed by an attitude to *all* Presbyterians, an assumption which weakened his grasp of their reality, for his indulged minister, who would have been detested by the extremists ("our old job-trot ministers is turned *curates*", as one said),[2] is yet treated with partisan caricature. Like Hume, Scott could barely credit that such beliefs had ever been held seriously.

McCrie complains that *Old Mortality* amounts to "a most unfair view of the common people of Scotland in point of intelligence",[3] a criticism which is in line with the general argument of this book. Mause Headrigg, for example, is implausibly ludicrous, and the only peasant worker in the book, her son Cuddy, is a blockhead. Yet there is one point even in Mause's scenes at which Scott shows how fine could be his sense of reality when his perceptions were sharpened through the direct speech of Scots-speakers. Mause has refused to let Cuddy go to the wappenschaw; the lady of the castle, their landlord, demands an explanation:

> . . . I am sure they belie baith Cuddie and me sair, if they said he wadna fight ower the boots in bluid for your leddyship

---

[1] 'Walter Scott and Thomas McCrie': *Sir Walter Scott To-day*, ed. H. J. C. Grierson (London: 1932), p. 37.
[2] Bruce, an early 17th-century minister quoted by Scott himself in the 'review' of his own *Tales of My Landlord* which he contributed to the *Quarterly* (1817), XVI, pp. 477-8.   [3] *Op. cit.* p. 176.

and Miss Edith and the auld Tower—ay suld he, and I would rather see him buried beneath it than he suld gie way; but thir ridings and wappenschawings, my leddy, I hae nae broo o' them ava. I can find nae warrant for them whatsoever.[1]

There is the intelligence of the common people—bringing judgement like that of a trained mind to the least decision in ordinary life. "'I can find nae warrant for them whatsoever.'" Such a touch shows us more of the sort of Presbyterian who refused the Indulgence than the whole of Balfour and MacBriar and the rest. But it was not until *The Heart of Midlothian*—less congealed into history—that Scott embodied that kind of religious conscience in a wholly convincing drama.

James Hogg's *The Private Memoirs and Confessions of a Justified Sinner* enables us to feel into the condition of a convinced Calvinist as *Old Mortality* does not. It is highly original—extraordinary, especially, as the work of a mainly self-educated shepherd, almost illiterate as late as eighteen, most of whose other work was imitation of fashionable *genres*. Extremes of self-righteousness, feelings of being the only saved individual in the midst of damned sinners, have occupied other novelists, for example the Hawthorne of 'Young Goodman Brown'. But Hawthorne, as Mrs Leavis puts it, 'explores the Calvinist sense of sin as a psychological state'.[2] Again, in *The Pilgrim's Progress* (staple reading among Hogg's class) Bunyan brings alive orthodox ideas of 'the Christian life' by vesting them, as a novelist would, in *personae* with fully human feelings (notably Mr Fearing). "Notwithstanding his condemnation of Free-willers and rejection of human righteousness, his practical ethics assume human freedom, and he is quite sure that imputed righteousness will show itself in right conduct."[3] Hogg is perhaps unique in taking a *theological* idea—the antinomian Calvinist one that those who are to be saved have been elected by God for all time, regardless of "right conduct", of how they live—and trying as it were to force this straight over into fictional terms. The brother Robert Colwan is conceived throughout as a man who is, by normal lights, conscienceless. Encouraged by his guardian, the zealous Calvinist minister Wringhim, to think of himself as one of the elect, he ignores, or

---

[1] Chap. 7. [2] 'Hawthorne as Poet' (*op. cit.*), pp. 197-8.
[3] H. J. C. Grierson, *Cross Currents in English Literature of the Seventeenth Century* (edition London: 1951), pp. 199-200.

RELIGION IN SCOTTISH FICTION

tries to ignore, his human conscience because the righteousness of what he does is ordained already by God.

Clearly this will put a great strain on the writer's powers of psychological invention, not only in keeping up interest in how such lives develop, but in at all realising them. Hogg could have known such types at first hand. Ingrained Calvinism seems to have produced people who resigned their responsibility for an action, however monstrous it might normally seem, because they felt their deeds were controlled by powers of good and evil beyond themselves. In his *Circuit Journeys* Cockburn describes the case of a fisherman from the Outer Isles whom he sentenced to death at Huntly, in Aberdeenshire, for the premeditated murder of his wife. The man told his story with anxious candour, describing his experience closely. Although he was "often under the influence of an odd mixture of wild religious speculation, and of terrified superstition", he was found perfectly sane and without delusions. "Haunted by some of his religious notions", he gave himself up; and after sentence said that "he has not been so comfortable for years, because he has got the better of the Devil at last, and is sure of defying him on the 11th of May".[1] Again, in his geography of Lewis and Harris Dr Arthur Geddes describes a Lewis woman of the 19th century who made and then destroyed clay figures of people she hated: "No doubt she persuaded herself that if the desired injury took place, natural or Divine law was at work and she herself was innocent or actually just".[2] Still closer to Hogg's *Sinner* is the story of a murder by a strict Presbyterian which Lockhart puts into his novel *The History of Matthew Wald*. The murderer, John McEwan, acts as though he had handed over to a power stronger than himself, and finally gives himself up, having told his own fate by *sortes* from the Bible ("'Whoso sheddeth man's blood, by man shall his blood be shed'"). He wants to plead guilty because he has so thoroughly reasoned out his case; and his extreme of preoccupation with the spiritual issues is finally shown passing into a kind of swollen pride at being so beset:

John, in a short speech of his own, expressed his sense of his guilt; but even then he borrowed the language of Scripture, styling himself 'a sinner, and the chief of sinners'. . . . The very agony of this man's humiliation had a spice of holy exultation in it; there was in the most penitent of his lugubrious glances still something that said, or seemed to say

[1] (Edinburgh: 1888), pp. 13-15.
[2] *The Isle of Lewis and Harris* (Edinburgh: 1955), p. 214.

—'Abuse me—spurn me as you will—I loathe myself also; but this deed is Satan's'. Indeed he always continued to speak quite gravely of his 'trespass', his 'back-sliding', his 'sore temptation!'

And in the death cell he still speaks as though he were in the power of a super-human system of good and evil:

He heard what they said [the consoling ministers] and instantly said something still stronger himself—but only to shrink back again to his own fastness with redoubled confidence. 'He had once been right, and he could not be wrong; he had been permitted to make a sore stumble!'[1]

Such cases show us in glimpses a state of something like complete possession by religious superstition such as it is difficult now for us quite to imagine. Hogg realises such a state by bringing it up against ordinary humanity, with comic effect, and by various ingenious symbols. His own position is that of an 18th-century man of sense, scornful of 'enthusiasm', and this he often conveys with a peasant's irreverent directness. Early in the novel, there is the scene of the marriage of a hard-drinking laird to an unco-pious young woman from Glasgow, the *protégée* of a Calvinist divine. When the laird goes up to bed on their wedding night, he finds his wife "engaged with the writings of the Evangelists, and terribly demure". When he tries to caress her, "she turned away her head, and spoke of the follies of aged men, and something of the broad way that leadeth to destruction".

The laird did not thoroughly comprehend this allusion; but being considerably flustered by drinking, and disposed to take all in good part, he only remarked, as he took off his shoes and stockings, that "whether the way was broad or narrow, it was time they were in their bed".

"Sure, Mr Colwan, you won't go to bed tonight, at such an important period of your life, without first saying prayers for yourself and me."

When she said this, the laird had his head down almost to the ground, loosing his shoe-buckle; but when he heard of *prayers*, on such a night, he raised his face suddenly up, which was all over as flushed and red as a rose, and answered:

"Prayers, Mistress! Lord help your crazed head, is this a night for prayers?"[2]

[1] Pub. with *Adam Blair* (Edinburgh & London: 1843), pp. 288-93.
[2] The novel was first published, anonymously, in 1824. Ed. used (London: 1947), pp. 5-6.

This kind of comedy comes straight out of that popular anti-clericalism—that often derisive antipathy to the discipline, solemnity, and self-righteousness which can accompany piety—which is typical of the most popular vernacular literature, Burns and the chapbooks.[1] This is the motive also of the excellent vernacular story, put in late in the *Justified Sinner*, about how the good people of Auchtermuchty are gulled by the Devil in the guise of a preacher. Preaching from the Old Testament, he delights the town by "proving all the people in it, to their perfect satisfaction, to be in the gall of bitterness and bond of iniquity. . . . 'He is a prophet of the Lord,' said one, 'sent to warn us, as Jonah was sent to the Ninevites . . .' The good people of Auchtermuchty were in perfect raptures with the preacher, who had thus sent them to Hell by the slump, tag-rag, and bobtail!" Finally a man of sense in the village lifts the Devil's robe and shows the cloven foot; "an' frae that day to this it is a hard matter to gar an Auchtermuchty man listen to a sermon at a', an' a harden ane to gar him applaud ane, for he thinks aye that he sees the cloven foot peeping out frae aneath ilka sentence".[2] This twist, whereby a morbid suspiciousness of evil is shown as the other side of piety, is like a comic or easy-going version of the close of Hawthorne's 'Young Goodman Brown':

> On the Sabbath day, when the congregation were singing a holy psalm, he could not listen, because an anthem of sin rushed loudly upon his ear and drowned all the blessed strain. When the minister spoke from the pulpit, with power and fervid eloquence, and with his hand on the open Bible, of the sacred truths of our religion, and of saint-like lives and triumphant deaths, and of future bliss or misery unutterable, then did Goodman Brown turn pale, dreading lest the roof should thunder down upon the grey blasphemer and his hearers. . . .[3]

Finally, Hogg conveys a 'normal' reaction to the maniacal convictions of a zealot through Scots dialogue which relates the action to history. The Calvinist brother has been imprisoned for taking it upon himself to chastise young gentlemen for playing at "vain, idle and sinful" games, and the whole scene in prison, from "I was not sorry at being thus honoured to suffer in the cause of righteousness", is admirably written:

> "Fat the deil are ye yoolling an' praying that gate for, man?" said he [the jailer], coming angrily in. "I thought the

---

[1] See note 4.   [2] Pp. 178-84.
[3] *Mosses From an Old Manse* (London: n.d.), pp. 80-1.

days o' praying prisoners had been a' ower. We hath rowth
o' them aince; an' they were the poorest an' the blackest
bargains that ever poor jailer saw. Gie up your crooning, or
I'll pit you to an in-by place, where ye sall get plenty o't."

"Friend," said I, "I am making my appeal at the bar
where all human actions are seen and judged, and where you
shall not be forgot, sinful as you are. Go in peace, and let me
be."

"Hae ye naebody nearer-hand hame to mak your appeal
to, man?" said he. "Because an ye hae-na, I dread you an'
me may be unco weel acquaintit by an' by."[1]

Hogg's novel is less successful when it tries to imagine more
subtly and closely into the consciousness of the zealot himself,
with his theological ideas and his tormented doubts whether
the power to which he has resigned his conscience is for the
good. There is some ingenious symbolism, for example the
contrast between the two brothers, sons of the laird: Robert, the
young zealot and minister's *protégé*, and George, the father's
favourite, the former "the best grammarian, the best reader,
writer, and accountant in the various classes that he attended"
and a prize-winner for essays on "controverted points of theology", and George, poor scholastically, "but greatly his
superior in personal prowess, form, feature, and all that con-
stitutes gentility in the deportment and appearance". This is
worked out dramatically in a scene in which we are consistently
made aware, as we take the actions, of the points in the theological theme which are being symbolised. The zealot badgers
the other as he enjoys himself at tennis:

> Instead of making him keep his distance, these rude shocks
> and pushes, accompanied sometimes by hasty curses, only
> made him cling the closer to this king of the game. He
> seemed determined to maintain his right to his place as an
> onlooker, as well as any of those engaged in the game, and,
> if they had tried him at an argument, he would have carried
> his point; or perhaps he wished to quarrel with this spark of
> his jealousy and aversion, and draw the attention of the gay
> crowd to himself by these means; for, like his guardian, he
> knew no other pleasure but what consisted in opposition.

The way in which the black-dressed Robert clings to the hand-
some George suggests that he personifies the conscience of the
homme moyen sensuel, shadowing him even amidst play. But other
touches, for example "he seemed courting persecution and

[1] Pp. 135-7.

buffetings, keeping steadfastly to his old joke of damnation'', suggests that Robert could be, too, the obsession of a religious man, getting perverted gratification from misunderstanding, adversity, and martyrdom.[1]

As the last sentence from that long passage suggests, Hogg tends to put in significance in explicit comments telling us what to think. At other points we have "'How delightful to think that a justified person can do no wrong!'" and "Should anyone think this picture over-strained, I can assure him that it is taken from nature and truth; but I will not likewise aver that the theologist was neither crazed nor inebriated".[2] Nor is any of the symbolism sustained; indeed the unsatisfactoriness of the novel is its swithering from mode to mode, not the switch from outside the sinner's consciousness to inside it (pp. 89 ff.), which has its obvious point, but such passages as the presentment of the crucial murder as a conventional mystery, like something out of Scott—coincidences, mistaken identity, melodramatic revelations.[3] Hogg is original at the cost of hammering out his form as he goes; and, further, he has perhaps too little fund of imaginative perceptions to rise to much evocation in concrete terms of the actual experiences that would be involved. In particular the temptation by the Devil-figure, Gil-martin, remains rather an external idea. The irony intended is that Robert has taken pre-destination to mean that he is helpless (because 'justified') even in doing what he feels to be wrong and that it is the Devil who persuades him, by will-power and casuistical arguments, that whatever he does must be right. Here is the Devil's first approach:

> That strange youth and I approached each other in silence, and slowly, with our eyes fixed on each other's eyes. We approached till not more than a yard intervened between us, and then stood still and gazed, measuring each other from head to foot. What was my astonishment on perceiving that he was the same being as myself! . . . as far as recollection could serve me from viewing my own features in a glass, the features too were the very same. . . .
> "You think I am your brother," said he; "or that I am your second self. I am indeed your brother, not according to the flesh, but in my belief of the same truths, and my assurance in the same mode of redemption . . ."[4]

This mirror-likeness or identity between devilish tempter and justified sinner no doubt symbolises the way in which, under

---

[1] Pp. 19, 21, 23.   [2] Pp. 14, 17.   [3] Pp. 51-84.   [4] Pp. 106-7.

pressure of Calvinist obsessions, the conscience may split itself off from the whole man and, dominating as a separate faculty, wind the zealot down into depths of moral confusion—arguing with himself only to square real doubts, perversely inciting himself to things his feelings recoil from, that he can approve only in his abstract intellect. Thus must witches have been tortured under the supervision of ministers, who solemnly catechised old women while four-inch pins were being stuck into their flesh. But Hogg's symbolism too much externalises temptation into the Devil-figure. The tussle of wills and feelings and the specific grounds for scruple are not present as evoked states of mind, they are no more than points in a general scheme:

> My mother began to lay down some of her old hackneyed rules of faith, but I turned from hearing her with disgust; for, after the energy of my new friend's reasoning, hers appeared so tame I could not endure it. And I confess with shame that my reverend preceptor's religious dissertations began, about this time, to lose their relish very much, and by degrees became exceedingly tiresome to my ear. They were so inferior, in strength and sublimity, to the most common observations of my young friend that in drawing a comparison the former appeared as nothing.[1]

As written, however, this aspect of the novel is blurred by being cast in a 'mysterious' style in the line of the Gothic novel and, later, Poe ("I can never describe the strange sensations that thrilled through my whole frame", "A sensation resembling a stroke of electricity came over me"). Something altogether more specific psychologically is wanted, but Hogg cannot supply it. He manfully undertakes to present detailed arguments, between natural human self and devilishly perverse 'conscience', concerning the necessity for the elect to pray, the justice of killing off 'sinners' in the name of God, and the like. But his imagination is not charged richly enough with experience of religion and Kirk: he is perhaps too limited to an 18th-century plain man's common-sense about fanaticism to get as deep into it as his conception demands. Too much of the crucial action comes down to plain crimes set side by side with flat generalisations against bigotry, where what is wanted is some inward presentment of how feelings, will, and ideas strive confusedly inside the zealot.

The novel ends, however, with Hogg once more in his *métier*.

[1] P. 117.

RELIGION IN SCOTTISH FICTION

At the end of the dialogue with the jailer, we have seen the last
extremes of that conviction of belonging to the elect taking its
course into mania:[1]

> "... I am the sword of the Lord, and Famine and Pestilence
> are my sisters. Woe then to the wicked of this land, for they
> must fall down dead together, that the Church may be
> purified!"
>
> "Oo, foo, foo! I see how it is," said he. "Yours is a very
> braw commission, but you will have small opportunity of
> carrying it through here. Take my advising, and write a bit
> of a letter to your friends, and I will send it, for this is no
> place for such a great man. If you cannot steady your hand
> to write, as I see you have been at your great work, a word
> of a mouth may do; for I do assure you this is not the place
> at all, of any in the world, for your operations."
>
> The man apparently thought I was deranged in my
> intellect. He could not swallow such great truths at the first
> morsel. . . .[2]

In the last powerful sequence (pp. 189-214), the sinner flees
south through the Border country, harried from farm to farm
by the peasant folk who have inklings that he is the Evil One.
Hogg's knowledge of these folk is such that he can present their
whole mixture of fears and beliefs—the confused experience,
part religious, part sheerly superstitious, of a still backward
people. It is recorded that in 1695 (the period of Hogg's novel)
a famous poltergeist, the Rerrick Spirit, haunted a farm,
stirring up cattle, and was heard to call out, "God gave me a
commission, and I am sent to warn this land to repent, for a
judgement is to come, if the land do not quickly repent". And
the chapbooks, those authentic pictures of the most primitive
countryfolk, show a similar welter of Christian and older superstitions. In 'Jockey and Maggy's Courtship' the mother
mentions Satan, then stops herself horrified: "'a sweet be wi'
us, we sudna speak o' the ill thief in the kirk, but it is a mercy
the minister's here an' he come'"; and in 'The History of the
Haverel Wives' Maggy, the stupid one, asks Janet, "'A sweet
be wi' us woman, is nit an unco thing they [the devils] dinna
a' flee on the minister, when he flytes and misca's them sae, do
ye think they hear him?'"[3] This is precisely the world of the
Justified Sinner. As the sinner flees south he hopes to pass himself

---

[1] It seems that the mania Hogg shows is psychologically true: see note 5.
[2] Pp. 136-7.
[3] Chambers, *Domestic Annals*, p. 113; *Writings of Dougal Graham* (*op. cit.*), II,
pp. 26, 138.

as a poor student of theology, going to Oxford, but this only makes matters worse: "I afterwards came to learn, that the term *theology* was by them quite misunderstood, and that they had some crude conceptions that nothing was taught at Oxford but the black arts. . . ." At one farm, moving about at night, he gets tangled in the crofter's loom, and the man comes out to him and begins to beat him, his wife protesting:

> ". . . Dear Johnny! I think ye be gaen dementit this morning. Be quiet, my dear, an' dinna begin a Boddel Brigg business in your ain house. What for ir ye persecutin' a servant o' the Lord's that gate, an' pitting the life out o' him wi' his head down an' his heels up?"
>
> "Had ye said a servant o' the Deil's, Nans, ye wad hae been nearer the nail, for gin he binna the Auld Ane himsel, he's gayan sib till him. . . ."

The sinner's possessed state is shown in something like a sequence of local tales of the supernatural: wherever he goes, the Devil is with him, the farm folk take fright at his looks, horses sweat and rear, noises from outside terrify the folk at night. The sinner himself no longer knows who he is or what is happening: "my body and soul were become terrors to each other; and, had it been possible, I felt as if they would have gone to war. I dared not look at my own face in the glass, for I shuddered at my own image and likeness." To his last ounce he fights the battle of thought. The Devil, dogging his steps, promises to protect him: "He then repeated an ejaculatory prayer, which I was to pronounce, if in great extremity. I objected to the words as equivocal. . . ." But he is now helpless and at his wits' end, and he resigns himself to God's will:

> Lord, thou knowest all that I have done for thy cause on earth! Why then art Thou laying Thy hand so sore upon me? Why hast Thou set me as a butt of Thy malice? But Thy will must be done! Thou wilt repay me in a better world. *Amen*.[1]

The novel has been uneven, often seemingly lost in its own complications; but through it there runs this thread of extraordinarily original and intense realisation of a departure from sanity to which fundamentalist Calvinism could run when followed out to the bitter end.

We may say, then, that the Scottish novel comes into its own when the dominating religiousness of the culture precipitates in

[1] Pp. 208, 196, 205, 215, 216.

the form of conscience (whether or not specifically theological) —intensely scrupulous conscience whose demands strain unbearably the individual psyche and the relations of family, parents and children, persons and community.[1] Driving or overbearing conscience is also at the back of the significant action in *Weir of Hermiston*, *The House with the Green Shutters*, and Lewis Grassic Gibbon's *Sunset Song*—three of the outstanding novels later in the tradition. The types of religion presented, the authors' attitudes to them, do not always avoid the unintegrated or backward ideas of the past and of the whole life of the people which, as we have seen, prevailed in the 18th century and the age of Scott. Yet the fiction of religion has behind it a dominating concern of the people, the main focus of their interests and energies in a pre-political age; and as a result these novels are alive, whereas the imitations of history and local life can do little more than supply material for the scholar.

[1] Compare Joseph Conrad's wonderfully independent-minded and forthright comment on Christianity: "Great, improving, softening, compassionate it may be but it has lent itself with amazing facility to cruel distortion and is the only religion which, with its impossible standards, has brought an infinity of anguish to innumerable souls—on this earth". (*Letters from Conrad*, ed. Edward Garnett: London, 1927, p. 265.)

CHAPTER VII

Fiction and the Scottish Reading-Public

Now I am ambitious that my compositions, though having their origins in this valley of Holyrood, should not only be extended into those exalted regions I have mentioned [the New Town], but also that they should cross the Forth, astonish the long town of Kirkcaldy, enchant the skippers and colliers of East Fife, venture even into the classic arcades of St Andrews, and travel as much farther to the north as the breath of applause will carry their sails.—SCOTT, *Chronicles of the Canongate*.

THE age of Scott, then, saw the rise of a literature which, unlike the vernacular poetry, attempted to picture the whole life of the country—all kinds of people, class, tradition, period, situation social and historical. The kind of currency fiction got in Scotland, and what author and publisher were aiming at, amount to a comprehensive example of the national morale during this period. Scottish fiction quickly grew into enough of an entity to knit and mould together a distinct public for itself; and the first significant works started up with an independence from each other which suggests a spontaneous movement, set going by some stir in the mind of the country. *Waverley*, the first of the famous 'Scotch novels', was begun in 1805, returned to in 1810, and finally rediscovered in a forgotten drawer and worked on for publication in the later part of 1813—the same year in which Galt was remembering early aspirations to fiction: "When very young, I wished to write a book that would be for Scotland what the Vicar of Wakefield is for England, and early began to observe, in what respects the minister of a parish differed from the general inhabitants of a country". As this refers to Greenock (whence he emigrated to London in 1804), he must have conceived the idea of rendering Scottish life in fiction simultaneously with Scott; and it was likewise in 1813 that his "intention of writing a minister's sedate adventures" occurred to him again, only to be rebuffed by the publisher Constable as *Waverley* had not yet appeared to legitimate novels about Scotland.[1] James Hogg claims that his Covenanter story,

[1] Lockhart, *Life of Scott*, II, pp. 52, 328; III, pp. 92-3, 124; Galt, *Autobiography*, II, pp. 226-7; Jennie Aberdein, *John Galt* (London: 1936), pp. 27-31. Galt's originality was claimed by 'Christopher North' (on behalf of the Blackwoodites) in answer to Jeffrey's assumption in a review of 'Secondary Scotch Novels' that these must all be camp-followers of the Waverley series; and Galt claimed, "I am the senior in Scottish historical sketches". (*Blackwood's Magazine*, 1824, XV, No. 85, p. 123; *Autobiography*, p. 268.)

The Brownie of Bodsbeck, was conceived independently of Scott's equivalent, *Old Mortality*, and would have come out first if Blackwood had been more oncoming; and what would have been Lockhart's first novel was conceived independently of *Waverley*: in autumn 1814 he writes to a friend that he has a Scottish novel "in hand", "a receptacle of an immense quantity of anecdotes and observations I have made concerning the state of the Scotch". Surprisingly he makes no mention of *Waverley*— then the latest successful novel—and a few months later he wrote: "Most of my novel was written before I read 'Waverley', but I fear the rush consequent to that popular work is such that mine is likely to be crushed among the row. I intend letting it sleep for a year or two and making use of it as a *drawable* for some more extensive thing."[1] So much did the 'Scotch novel' become a set *genre*, that by 1824 we find a skit called *Scotch Novel Reading; or, Modern Quackery* which parodies young English literary people so fascinated by Scottish ways that they try to cultivate the language. The book is full of jibes at Scott (some containing just points); one character complains that "'nothing now goes down but Scotch stories'"; and the common complaint about unintelligible Scots dialogue is repeated.[2] Presumably it is this public reaction that Scott makes fun of in the passage quoted in my epigraph: "As for a southward direction, it is not to be hoped for in my fondest dreams. I am informed that Scottish literature, like Scottish whisky, will be presently laid under a prohibitory duty."

This sudden growth of Scottish expression sprouted late in the day compared with the English (if one discounts Henry Mackenzie's fashionably tearful *The Man of Feeling*). The early English novelists, however limited, amount to a well-spring of contemporary life; they make available to us a sharp documentary impression of the ordinary scenes of their day, and they show the power of their culture to develop new forms of literature equal to the changing experience of their society. This Scotland had to do without until the early 19th century, when a pressing need was uncovered. It may be that the general paucity of creative work in Scotland accounts for this lag. But we must also question whether the Scottish public was less receptive to creative literature than, say, the English.

All over Britain since the Reformation, puritanism of various

---

[1] Hogg, *The Mountain Bard* (Edinburgh: 1821), p. 66; Andrew Lang, *The Life and Letters of John Gibson Lockhart* (London: 1897), I, pp. 71, 74-5.
[2] By A Cockney, a Mrs Green (London: 1824), e.g. I, p. 9.

shades had tried to enforce its disapproval of literary art not devoted to the glory of God, and to curtail even that which was. In *Fiction and the Reading Public* Mrs Leavis indicates the beliefs behind this as they impinged on fiction. She writes that leisure reading had by custom been 'improving', "of the 'Drelincourt's Book of Consolations against the Fears of Death' type". Thus Defoe had a problem:

> If fiction could be disguised so that it could be acceptable to the virtuous (for whom 'invention' meant lying, and more particularly the immoral literature and drama of the Restoration Court), fiction could be made to pay. Defoe therefore concentrated on literary devices which actually preclude the creation of a work of art.[1]

That was around 1719. A century later, in Scotland, Hogg was still forced to similar shifts to pass off his *Justified Sinner*,[2] and Galt's *Annals* was at first acceptable to the strict only because it seemed to be real history. Its publisher, Blackwood, wrote to Galt that his "worthy old mother read the book with great delight, and thought Micah an honest and upright minister of the Gospel. But, unfortunately, one of my little boys told her it was a novel, and thus it lost all its charms, and she was very angry with us for having deceived her."[3] Susan Ferrier, the author of *Marriage*, Scotland's nearest to a 'society novel', became in old age "so completely occupied with religious questions as to dislike and disapprove of the delightful works of her earlier days"; and Thomas Carlyle's father 'openly censured' neighbours of his for reading the *Arabian Nights*.[4] A record of the family of Macaulay the historian sums up the background of attitudes which worked against acceptance of fiction. The Macaulays came from a line of West of Scotland Presbyterian ministers. Zachary, the historian's father, finally settled in London as manager of a company which ran a settlement in Sierra Leone for freed slaves, editor of an Evangelical paper, and colleague of Wilberforce in the anti-slavery movement. The family used to read aloud, especially when Thomas Babington came home for the holidays: "Poetry and novels, except during Tom's holidays, were forbidden in

---

[1] P. 102. [2] See note 1.

[3] *William Blackwood and His Sons*, Vols. I and II by Mrs Margaret Oliphant, Vol. III by Mrs Gerald Porter (Edinburgh & London: 1897), I, p. 452.

[4] *Ibid.* p. 45: this may or may not be contradicted by the fact that she authorised a named edition of her novels in 1851, three years before she died (*Memoir and Correspondence of Susan Ferrier*, ed. John A. Doyle (London: 1898), p. 313); Carlyle, *Reminiscences*, p. 19.

the daytime, and stigmatised as 'drinking drams in the morning'".[1]

This long-standing suspicion of 'profane literature' spread out from the most uncompromising Presbyterians. It is perhaps pointless to speculate whether or not it was specifically due to Calvinism. The constant controversies on this problem have usually got no further than exchanging salvoes of prejudices, doughty supporters of old Calvin on the one hand, wholesale modern emancipators on the other. Calvin himself and his later Scottish followers certainly passed strictures on art and free imagination.[2] At the Reformation we find the *Gude and Godlie Ballates*, which were Presbyterian propaganda, eloquently recommending music and poetry for devotion. One ballad goes:

> *Play on your lute, and sweitly to it sing,*
> *Tak harpe in hand with monie lustie string,*
> *Tyrle on the ten stringit Instrument,*
> *And pryse our God with hart & haill intent.*
> *Sing na auld thing the quhilk is abrogate,*
> *Bot sing sum new plesand perfite ballat:*
> *Blaw up organis, with glaid & heuinlie sound,*
> *Joyfull in hart, quhill all the skyis resound.*[3]

That belongs to the time when Reformed religion was trying to take over something of the sensuous or artistic appeal of Catholicism. Unfortunately puritanism was in many aspects a hardening of the Reformers' principles (music was quickly expunged from Scottish churches, and to this day a minority of stricter Presbyterians forbid it); and in Scotland, by the 17th century, certain ministers were famous for their virulent mistrust of secular writings. In the General Assembly of 1644 one complained that "their schools and country were stained, yea pestered, with idle books, and their children fed on fables, love-songs, baudry ballads, heathen husks, youth's poison".[4] The Presbyterian historian, Wodrow, concerned about the growth of "unaccountable and loose principles", lamented the anarchy in the universities, where one teacher "stands not openly to tell the scholars that, next to the New Testament, Homer is the most religious book he knoues of in the world!",

---

[1] G. O. Trevelyan, *The Life and Letters of Lord Macaulay* (London: 1876), I, p. 60.
[2] See note 2.
[3] *Gude and Godlie Ballates*, ed. Mitchell, p. 93.
[4] Duncan Anderson, *The Bible in Seventeenth Century Scottish Life and Literature* (London: 1936), p. 262.

and he complains also about free, anti-Calvinist interpretation of the Greek New Testament.[1]

Wodrow was equally worried about Allan Ramsay's lending library, which lent out "all the villanous profane and obscene books and playes printed at London" to "young boyes, servant weemen of the better sort, and gentlemen":

> This, with the Playes and Interludes, come doun from England this winter . . . dreadfully spreads all abominations, and profaness, and leudnes; and a villanous, obscene thing, is no sooner printed at London, than it's spread and communicat at Edinburgh.

Ian Watt points out that this censorial attitude to the reading of the 'lower orders' was often motivated by the jealousy and antagonism of the educated classes.[2] But it was also a basic attitude of that severer Presbyterianism which found its strongest following among the lower classes themselves. Ramsay of Ochtertyre, one of the 18th-century gentlemen who championed liberal culture, wrote of Wodrow's successors, the Evangelical ministers who associated with the English Methodists:

> Nor were they more friendly to learning, or those pursuits that delight and ennoble the soul. They declaimed against all reading that had not their peculiar system for its object. The admired performances which either enforce the moral duties in a most persuasive strain, or which by a chain of deep reasoning illustrate the great truths of revealed and natural religion, were deemed useless, if not dangerous, by these new-fashioned ghostly fathers.[3]

The ministers themselves came to be thought of as peculiarly unliterary: writing secular works was improper to their profession. The Rev. John Skinner, the author of 'Tullochgorum',[4] writes in his 'Answer to an Epistle':

> *And yet may be some girnin gowks*
> *May tak the pett at harmless jokes,*
> *And think sic simple silly strokes*
> *O' poetrie,*
> *Far unbecomin sacred fowks*
> *The like o' me,*

[1] *Analecta* (*op. cit.*), III, p. 575. This 'censorship' points forward to the Church which in the later 19th century forced Robertson Smith, a pioneer of the 'Higher Criticism', out of the ministry and hence out of Scotland (see Donald Carswell, *Brother Scots*: London, 1936: chap. 2).
[2] Wodrow, *Analecta*, III, p. 576; *The Rise of the Novel*, p. 43.
[3] *Scotland and Scotsmen in the Eighteenth Century*, II, p. 20.
[4] See *The Oxford Book of Eighteenth Century Verse* (London: 1946), pp. 536-9.

and in a review of Lyte's religious poems the *Edinburgh Review* sarcastically contrasts the frivolous secularity of the English clergy with the narrow orthodoxy of the Scottish. "If Scott had become a minister of the Kirk, the proprieties of the Manse would probably have kept him down to about the level of Logan. We might have had Odes to Cuckoos, or melodies upon the 'Grave', but certainly no Marmions".[1]

Censorial principles were not confined to Scotland. English puritans such as William Law deprecated all secular works, scarcely discriminating between the cynical drama of Wycherley and Congreve and the plays of Shakespeare. Human learning, if not actually wicked, was good "only in so far as it may be the instrument of the religious emotions". Law wrote, "Whether a man die before he has writ poems, compiled histories, or raised an estate, signifies no more than whether he died an hundred or a thousand years ago".[2] Yet this philistine ban was specially severe in Scotland, for several reasons. The reputation of secular literature suffered, as we can see in Wodrow, because native work was scanty and England, the source of most of our supply of it in the early 18th century, was remote enough to be thought of darkly as a hotbed of vice—"the profane mint of London".[3] This is a disadvantage of a backward country with poor communications. Scott complains in a letter that new publications were very scarce in Edinburgh in the late '80's: after reading Crabbe's *Village* and *Library* in Dodsley's *Annual Register*, it took him many months to get hold of the complete poems; and the difficulty of getting German books even in Edinburgh was one of the final causes for Carlyle's emigrating to London.[4] Outlying towns were similarly handicapped. Although Peterhead (in Aberdeenshire) was by way of being a smart seaside resort for visitors from the south, it had no circulating library before 1770. In 1817 we find that it has several booksellers, though they do not themselves venture as publishers but rely on the lists of bookseller-publishers in the south.[5] By the time the 'Scotch novels' arose, the book trade in Scotland had begun to modernise its communications. Edinburgh papers, for

---

[1] Skinner, *Songs and Poems* (Peterhead: 1859), p. 14; *Edinburgh Review* (1834), LIX, p. 173.
[2] Stephen, *English Thought in the Eighteenth Century*, II, p. 398.
[3] See Graham, 'Janet Clinker's Oration': quoted in chap. 2, note 5.
[4] Scott, *Letters*, III, p. 181; Van Wyck Brooks, *The Flowering of New England*, p. 76, n. 2; Emery Neff, *Carlyle* (London: 1932), p. 41.
[5] *Blackwood's Magazine* (1820), VI, 34, p. 395. For Peterhead as a town see *James Beattie's Day-book, 1773–1798*, ed. Ralph S. Walker (Third Spalding Club, Aberdeen: 1948), pp. 15-16.

example, began to advertise books for London booksellers, and for firms in Paisley and Perth, early in 1795; and it was at about the same time (1790) that a bookseller started business in the country town in Galt's *Annals* and could get the minister any book published in London within a month of issue.[1]

This spread of modern reading habits had had to struggle against backwardness, such as the attitude of the cultivated mid-18th century laird typified by Scott in *Waverley*. The Baron of Bradwardine, though well-read in classic Scots poetry, "sometimes could not refrain from expressing contempt of the 'vain and unprofitable art of poem-making', in which, he said, 'the only one who had excelled in his time was Allan Ramsay, the periwig-maker'".[2] Here again the dearth of native work tells against literary tastes as a whole. Furthermore, religion was so devoted amongst the mass of the people, and ministers so revered and influential, that suspicion of the 'profane' could spread wide and deep. An example is Davie Deans's ban on "dissolute profane pastimes" in chapter 10 of *The Heart of Midlothian*: "'I hae often wondered, that ony ane that ever bent a knee for the right purpose should ever daur to crook a hough to fyke and fling at piper's wind and fiddler's squealing'", and he actually invokes Patrick Walker's thanks for hardship.[3] Many actual cases support this characterisation. In 1801 Scott wrote in a letter about his search for folk poetry in the Borders: "One of our best reciters has turned religious in his later days, and finds out that old songs are unlawful". Carlyle says that even at the height of Burns's fame his father never looked at the *Poems*: "The Poetry *he* liked (he did not call it Poetry) was Truth and the Wisdom of Reality". Alexander Somerville, author of the *Autobiography of a Working Man*, records that he had difficulty in getting sanction for his reading of Burns. Partly Burns was "coarse", and irreverent towards the ministers of his father's rigid sect; partly there was the general principle that "it was hardly fit for me to read poetry while so young". And there is no word of the better modern literature in Somerville's account of the circulating libraries for working-men that served the south-east; they were mainly 'improving', filled with "that silliest kind of literature—religious novels".[4]

These cases all belong to an extreme—the most severe censor-

---

[1] Daybook of Bell & Bradfute, Booksellers, for the 1790's, preserved in the Edinburgh Room, Edinburgh Central Public Library; Galt, *Annals*, p. 183.
[2] Victoria Edition (London: 1897), p. 73.   [3] See above, p. 169.
[4] Lockhart, *Life of Scott*, I, p. 332; Carlyle, *Reminiscences*, p. 8; Somerville, *Autobiography*, pp. 44-5, 47-50.

ship of the worldly, such as was laid down by the most rigid sects (to which Deans, Carlyle senior, and Somerville's father all belonged). And Somerville's experience belongs to the very poor, hardened against frivolous influences by a desperately bleak and scanty life. Yet the rather constrained earnestness of the Protestant tradition held good in a preponderance of religious works which applied to the whole of Britain. Throughout the 18th century, it has been estimated, two hundred religious works were published annually; and of roughly 45,000 books published in England between 1816 and 1851, well over 10,000 were religious.[1] Provincial parish libraries were mainly ecclesiastical in function and management; for example, in a Scottish scheme of 1817 it was laid down that a half to one-third of each box of books must be religious.[2] Private libraries reflect the same habit. According to Thomas Somerville, in the earlier 18th century books bought by the Scottish ministry were chiefly professional, and the "considerable libraries" collected by county gentlemen "together with the Greek and Latin classics, consisted, in great proportion, of voluminous works that treated of law and divinity". The *Lounger* gives details of one typical library, evidently of the earlier 18th century, which consisted mainly of theological and devotional works, along with some history and standard essays and a little English poetry. As late as 1820, *Blackwood's* emphasises, Peterhead's circulating libraries contained "a valuable collection of theology".[3] We have only to glance into the average religious work of the time, with its minute technicalities and utter lack of felt experience, to remind ourselves that at that time a high proportion of the more serious reading-matter was chokingly arid. Fiction naturally suffered from this tendency. Adam Smith, for example, had a strong interest in literature, yet his library contained no fiction apart from *The Man of Feeling* by his friend Henry Mackenzie and *Gulliver's Travels* in the works of Swift. Walter Stirling, the merchant who left his books to start a public library in Glasgow, "hated novels so heartily that he had not read one for forty years", and the 804 books he bequeathed included no fiction and not much creative literature of any kind.[4]

[1] Watt, *Rise of the Novel*, p. 49; Webb, 'The Victorian Reading Public' (*op. cit.*), p. 26.
[2] Raymond Irwin, *The Origins of the English Library* (London: 1958), p. 26.
[3] Somerville, *My Own Life and Times*, p. 350; *Lounger*, III, pp. 174-5; *op. cit.* p. 395.
[4] Rae, *Life of Smith*, p. 328; Mason, *Public and Private Libraries of Glasgow*, pp. 35, 45, 46-61.

That is, I think, as much as can be found to support the gloomier generalisations about the old reading-public. As the century wore on, even the most severe changed to more liberal tastes, or gave up the attempt at censorship. For one thing, a habit of religious reading did not necessarily rule out other types of book: one lady born in 1714 said of upper-class women in general that, "If they read any, it was either books of devotion or long romances, and sometimes both". Scott's catholic reading was disapproved of by his mother, "trammelled by religious scruples", and his tutor, who "thought it almost a sin to open a profane play or poem"; yet he managed to get hold of "the usual, or rather ten times the usual, quantity of fairy tales, eastern stories, romances, etc.". Maria Edgeworth was read aloud even in the Macaulay family:

> Morning or evening, Mr Macaulay disapproved of novel-reading; but, too indulgent to insist on having his own way in any but essential matters, he lived to see himself the head of a family in which novels were more read and better remembered than any household of the United Kingdom.

Carlyle's own literary work broke down his family's resistance to fiction. He inscribed his *Specimens of German Romance* to his father "though I know he will not read a line of it"; and his brother wrote him that the family were all reading his translation of Goethe's *Wilhelm Meister*: their mother

> is sitting here as if under some charm, reading 'Meister' . . . Though we are often repeating honest Hall Foster's denouncement against readers of 'novels', she still continues to persevere. She does not relish the character of the women, and especially of Philina: 'They are so wanton'. *She cannot well tell what it is that interests her* [my italics].[1]

It may be, then, that the development of a self-respecting Scottish fiction was held back by the drag of religious inhibitions. Literary art could not quite get through to a full, free recognition of its fineness and power for truth; it was liable to be belittled as frivolous. We see this in Carlyle's exaggerated reverence for his forebears who made things with their hands that would outlast any book, and in Stevenson's cult of the man of action, for example the poem on how his family has declined from lighthouse-building into literature, himself a mere man of

[1] Chambers, *Domestic Annals*, p. 571; Scott's 'Memoir' of himself, Lockhart, *Life*, I, p. 35; *Life of Macaulay*, I, p. 60; Froude, *Early Life of Carlyle*, I, pp. 393, 230.

letters, "playing at home with paper like a child".[1] But a free taste for literature was so natural an appetite that it could not be long held back. The evidence of private reading, libraries, and book sales contradicts some of the blacker generalisations. For example Stevenson says sweepingly of the reading of countryfolk in the 19th century: "To many people in his [an old gardener's] station the Bible, and perhaps Burns, are the only books of any vital literary merit that they read, feeding themselves, for the rest, on the draff of country newspapers, and the very instructive but not very palatable pabulum of some cheap educational series".[2] Any very general social situation can be made to seem unideal if one applies stringent standards to millions of people; and even so we must set against Stevenson's comment facts such as that observed by Burns's editor, Currie, that in the lists of the book-societies of the poorer classes in Scotland, works of "taste and fancy" (he has been discussing the *Mirror* and *Lounger*) tended to form a great part.[3] In any case Stevenson's is not a black picture as mass taste goes: compare with it the tawdry pastime reading, the yellow press and pulp fiction, which gluts the reading-public in Western Europe and America today.

There is also evidence that a boy with determined enthusiasm could get hold of richer material than the old gardener. The poet Michael Bruce was the son of a weaver; he and his parents were very pious and given to religious reading. Yet Bruce read in his youth *Candide* and *Gulliver's Travels*. Alexander Murray, the scholar and linguist (a shepherd's son, born at Dunkitterick in 1775), records that when he was ill, between the ages of nine and thirteen, he "'read, or rather studied daily, Sir David Lindsay, Sir William Wallace, the Cloud of Witnesses, the Hind Let Loose [Covenanter literature], and all the books of piety in the place', with any ballads he could either buy or borrow". That amounts to something like the gamut of native material readily available in Scotland which was either approved serious reading or permissible (the Scots poetry) through long usage. The scholar John Leyden (also a shepherd's son, born in Teviotdale in 1775) was taught by his grandmother "to read the Bible, which he held in life-long reverence, and whose

---

[1] Carlyle, *Reminiscences*, p. 24; *Early Life*, II, p. 259; Stevenson, "Say not of me that weakly I declined The labours of my sires" (*Poems, op. cit.* p. 44). In 'The Manse' he calls himself "only a man of letters" and invokes the stirring practical life of his father's family (*Memories and Portraits*: Tusitala ed., London, 1924: p. 57).
[2] 'An Old Scottish Gardener': *Memories and Portraits*, p. 41.
[3] *Works of Burns*, I, p. 112 n.

historical passages first caught and fixed his attention. On the shelves of neighbouring cottages he found some works of Scottish history, a translation of Homer, Sir David Lindsay's poetry, and Milton's Paradise Lost."[1] Fiction was often hard to come by for someone without access to a cheap library; but Burns early got hold of two odd volumes of *Pamela* and one of Smollett's *Ferdinand, Count Fathom* (possibly in the country, possibly when he was at the country town of Irvine, learning flax-dressing), as well as quite a range of other literature—Shakespeare, Locke, Pope, the *Spectator*.[2]

These readers were all exceptional men, with a personal passion for reading. But the evidence of libraries and book sales covers far more of the people. In the towns at least, fiction in plenty seems to have been available from mid-century onwards. A penny-a-night circulating library run by a bookseller-publisher in Aberdeen advertises in 1765 most of Fielding's novels, *Pamela* and *Clarissa*, Cervantes, *La Princesse de Clèves*, and Dryden's plays. This became standard stock for such libraries. A similar one in 1795 adds Fanny Burney, Rousseau's *Eloïsa*, and also Smollett and *Gil Blas*; and in 1821 the Public Library adds Scott, Hogg, Elizabeth Hamilton's *The Cottagers of Glenburnie*, Jane Austen, and Maria Edgeworth.[3] In 1763 James Beattie was disgusted to find that a Dundee bookseller stocked nothing but a circulating library of novels: "the man of the shop told me that nothing else was read in Dundee". In Edinburgh in the '80's Scott used the circulating library which the magistrates had earlier pried into, and he says it was peculiarly rich in works of fiction, with specimens of every kind. Towards the end of the century, in Peebles, the Chamberses used a bookseller's circulating library which contained *Don Quixote*, *Gulliver*, *Peregrine Pickle*, Fielding, Sterne, and Goldsmith; and Burns's letter on Riddell of Glenriddell's local library, from which anyone in the neighbourhood could borrow, records that it included (along with "a good deal of trash") *Joseph Andrews*, *Don Quixote*, and *The Man of Feeling*.[4] A very early poem of his

---

[1] James Mackenzie, *Life of Bruce* (London: 1905), p. 97; *Constable and his Correspondents*, I, pp. 214-17; *ibid.* p. 191.   [2] Chambers-Wallace, *Burns*, I, p. 18.
[3] Alexander Angus and Son's *Catalogue of Books for a Circulating Library* (Castlegate, Aberdeen: 1765), pp. 5, 8, 22, 24, 29; A. Brown, Bookseller and Stationer, *Catalogue of the New Circulating Library* (Homer's Head, Broad Street, Aberdeen: 1795), Nos. 98, 119, 122, 132-3, 154, 177; Public Library *Catalogue* (1821), Nos. 226, 235-6, 244, 252, 254, 266, 278, 285, 291.
[4] Margaret Forbes, *Beattie and His Friends* (London: 1904), p. 276; General Preface to the Waverley Novels; Chambers, *Memoir*, pp. 60-4; *Old Statistical Account*, III, p. 600. He himself presented *Humphrey Clinker* and Mackenzie's *Julia de Roubigné* to the Dumfries Public Library (Chambers-Wallace, *Burns*, IV, p. 55).

Mossgiel days, addressed to the "Mauchline belles", suggests that the local girls were reading Fielding and Richardson:

> *O leave novels, ye Mauchline belles,*
> *Ye're safer at your spinning-wheels;*
> *Such witching books are baited hooks*
> *For rakish rooks like Rob Mossgiel;*
> *Your fine Tom Jones and Grandisons,*
> *They make your youthful fancies reel;*
> *They heat your brains, and fire your veins,*
> *And then you're prey for Rob Mossgiel.*

For those bent on belittling it is always possible to hint that novels were read only because they were spicy (the same is still suggested to discredit the huge modern sales of D. H. Lawrence), or 'for the story'. But the fact remains that the majority of people are neither stupid nor depraved and that the novel was an extension of literature ideal for those who read because they have a deep interest in humanity.

William Chambers emphasises that his Peebles bookseller was "certainly something considerably superior . . . enterprising and enlightened beyond the common range of booksellers in small country towns"; and the experience of Alexander Somerville and Burns confirms that it was not quite so easy for country-folk to be sure of obtaining the best modern fiction. But there were certainly those copious sources of it in the towns. Novels made up about 20 per cent of the stock of such libraries—the same proportion as in English centres such as London, Newcastle, and Bath.[1] Much of this was indeed trash, of the *Love in a Nunnery* type; but the best works were also among the most popular: when William Chambers was a bookseller's apprentice in Edinburgh, he went to a bakehouse at five o'clock every morning and, in exchange for a hot roll, read to the men at work *Gil Blas*, Smollett and Fielding, which were the favourites for their picaresque action.[2] There are no Scottish records of a reception for fiction quite as free and whole-hearted as the English seems to have been: *Tom Jones* and *Roderick Random* kept in the farm bacon-racks; blacksmiths reading *Pamela* to the villagers, who rang the church bells to celebrate Pamela's marriage; Defoe's works given as school prizes.[3] But the evidence of the libraries proves that a widespread habit was in force quite early in the century.

---

[1] John and Muriel Lough, 'Aberdeen Circulating Libraries in the Eighteenth Century': *Aberdeen University Review* (1945), XXXI, 92, pp. 21-2.
[2] *Memoir*, pp. 103-4.
[3] A. S. Collins, *The Profession of Letters, 1780 to 1832* (London: 1928), pp. 83-4; Collins, *Authorship in the Days of Johnson (1726–1780)* (London: 1927), pp. 247-8.

Private libraries are less easy to assess, apart from isolated cases such as Adam Smith's. Marion Lochhead cites one belonging to an Edinburgh lawyer who died in 1758: it included *Arcadia, Don Quixote, Gulliver,* and books by Mrs Aphra Behn, as well as Ben Jonson's plays, Rochester, and Ramsay; and another writer cites as *atypical* of the 18th century Sir John Lauder's library, which included *risqué* plays such as *Marriage à la Mode* and *Epsom Wells,* as well as *Macbeth.*[1] No doubt at the start of the century money was tight, and private buying and leisure reading of English literature less common. But by the 1770's, as Edinburgh book sales attest, there was plenty traffic in contemporary fiction. *Gil Blas,* Defoe, Fielding, Richardson, Smollett, Sterne, Henry Mackenzie, Fanny Burney, Vanbrugh's plays, Rousseau's *Eloïsa,* and great quantities of the *Spectator* are constantly mentioned in the book-auction catalogues of the time.[2] Bell & Bradfute—whose day-book of sales for 1794 and 1795 has been preserved—were known as a very respectable firm, who sold little fiction and dealt mainly in law books; yet their trade in novels was as good as that in poetry (and much better than in contemporary poetry: the poetry sales would have been slender without Pope, Ramsay, Young, and Thomson). Their day-by-day record gives a thick cross-section of what was then most read: history, Greek and Latin classics, travels and topography, sermons and theology, a little politics (especially Paine and answers to Paine), English poetry, and the standard essays; and among these fiction is a prominent item. Much of their trade was supplying other booksellers—in Dumfries, Paisley, Perth, London, New York, and Philadelphia;[3] and fiction accounts for a good third of the average bulk order.[4] Even apart from orders sent abroad and to the

[1] *The Scottish Household in the Eighteenth Century* (Edinburgh: 1948), p. 348; Marjorie Plant, *The Domestic Life of Scotland in the Eighteenth Century* (Edinburgh: 1952), p. 234.

[2] E.g. those of W. Drummond (1773 and 1776), C. Elliot (1778 and 1792), W. Gordon (1791), and Peter Hill (1793): these catalogues are preserved in the Edinburgh Room, Edinburgh Central Public Library.

[3] American taste, like Scottish, had had to develop out of early narrowness: the people in the Eastern hinterland "did not care for stories. They thought that fiction was a fraud, and worse"; the "cultivated few" made an exception for Scott (and Richardson and Maria Edgeworth), and "in the East and South there had always been a gentry who were latitudinarian in taste, if not in conduct" and took "frank pleasure" in Smollett, Sterne, and Fielding (Brooks, *The Flowering of New England,* p. 56; *The World of Washington Irving,* p. 317).

[4] One order to Philadelphia gives a typical sample: fiction from Le Sage and Cervantes to Fanny Burney, standard essays, Ramsay's *Songs,* Young's *Night Thoughts,* Tillotson's works, Hervey's *Dialogues,* Pope's works, the *Scottish Register,* some theology, science, and reference books (22.9.1794)—the only main item missing from this order is Scotland's principal contribution to contemporary litera-

Scottish provinces there is local traffic in fiction; we even find one minister buying *The Mysteries of Udolpho* and another *Gil Blas*.[1] Bell & Bradfute's customers are mostly from the higher classes—lairds and their wives, judges, professional men. It seems that by that date censorial habits had little effect on their reading.[2]

The broadening of reading matter, and even the spread of reading, were deplored by the reactionary *Blackwood's*. In its polemics at the Reform period, it attacks working-class literacy —one might as well teach sheep or horses to fly as working-men to get the reading habit—and ridicules Lord Brougham's campaign for 'the diffusion of useful knowledge'. "The Bible", they say, "is fast yielding to the daily press" and is "the last book, as was well observed by Professor Wilson, of which we hear anything from the Reformers". It was the same reactionary piety which in an age of revolutions and reforms led bishops to mistrust Sunday schools for fear they would lend themselves to political propaganda. *Blackwood's* was concerned at the corruption of public thought, especially in serious reading: Pope and Dryden were almost unknown to the new generation, who were seduced by Byron and Tom Moore, and Hume, Robertson, and Gibbon lay neglected on the bookshelves, edged out by novels and travel. Richardson had gone out and "No great works intended to be durable" were any longer written; even the great Scott had depraved taste by over-writing. Finally the writer sighs for the old cultured taste in Addison, Johnson, and Mackenzie.[3] Certainly this points to some of the evils which have since come to a head in the age of Harmsworth, Beaver-brook, pulp-fiction and the best-seller. But *Blackwood's* is ignoring the real growth represented by some of these changes. Taste in the age of the Romantics could not stay tied to the Augustans, especially once Augustanism had stiffened into convention.

Furthermore, much of the new reading was instrumental to

ture, Blair's sermons, Robertson's histories, Hume's histories and essays, Beattie's and Reid's treatises, the legal commentaries of Kames, Erskine, and Dalrymple, which were usually much in demand.

[1] Daybook, 8.10.94 and 14.10.94. For Bell & Bradfute's usual law trade see *Publishers' Circular* (London: 15.7.1891), 1311, p. 171.

[2] We have seen already that P. F. Tytler read aloud *Gil Blas* and Maria Edgeworth to his father (see Appendix A). His own library finally included fiction by Smollett, Mackenzie, Edgeworth, Susan Ferrier, Jane Austen, Dickens, and Thackeray. (*Catalogue of Valuable Books including the Library of the late Patrick Fraser Tytler*, to be sold by Puttock & Simpson, Leicester Square, London: 4.4.1849, pp. 1-2, 7, 14, 23, 28.)

[3] *Blackwood's*, 'On Parliamentary Reform and the French Revolution', VI (1831), Vol. XXIX, p. 927; 'Remote Causes of the Reform Passion', I (1832), Vol. XXXI, pp. 11-13. Rae, *Life of Adam Smith*, p. 407.

the development of society. "Nothing in the interior economy of our country [is] so important to know, as the progress of instruction among the industrious classes." Late in the 18th century, popular political discussion was coming to the fore; and if religious controversy had been (as the older writers often insisted) mentally exercising, how much more so must have been controversy which bore directly on the life of the people? Tom Paine, according to the Paisley poet Wilson, was "read by mony a hunder"; he was carried by George Miller, a book-seller, librarian, and periodical-editor who fed much literature to the South-east; and in 1793 James Beattie was startled to learn that one Dundee bookseller had sold a thousand copies of Paine's works.[1] Literature for popular consumption is further seen at its best in Cobbett, and the circulation of his *Weekly Political Register* (with its keen-eyed and intelligent description of the whole life of the people) rose from 750 to between 40,000 and 50,000 when the price was lowered from 1s. to 2d. in 1816.[2] *Chambers's Journal*, with its flow of information on economics, handicrafts, history, science, and foreign countries, was handed from shepherd to shepherd, and it almost at once reached a circulation of over 40,000—about three times that of the *Edinburgh Review* at its peak.[3] Such reading-matter was, indeed, a necessity for the mass of the people in their effort to broaden their way of life, to give themselves a more actual understanding of the world beyond their own restricted experience; and in any case the rapid, widespread circulation of such writers as Scott, George Eliot, Hardy, and (though more slowly achieved) D. H. Lawrence has shown since that a public, even under conditions where publishing is run for profit, need not lose all taste for the best modern work.[4]

The outstanding trait of the fiction which grew up in Scotland

[1] Wilson, *Poetry and Prose*, II, p. 73; W. J. Couper, *The Millers of Haddington, Dunbar and Dunfermline* (London: 1914), p. 66; Forbes, *Beattie and His Friends*, p. 276.　　　　　　　　　　[2] *The Scotsman* (Edinburgh: 19.4.1817), p. 99.

[3] Chambers, *Memoir*, p. 228. This was for the first two numbers; when a London agent began distributing in England, the circulation rose to 80,000 and stayed there for many years, with hardly any advertising (*ibid.*).

[4] My implicit comparison is with socialist countries such as Poland and the U.S.S.R. where, it seems (according to even the hostile commentators), a high proportion of people in all walks of life are constantly reading the best literature, and pulp books and horror comics are almost unknown. Typical statistics supporting this are given in, e.g., Jürgen Kuczynsky, *The Condition of the Workers in Great Britain, Germany, and the Soviet Union, 1932–1938* (London: 1939), pp. 81-3. The organisation and enthusiasm of the Soviet reading-public is surveyed in detail by Sidney and Beatrice Webb in *Soviet Communism: A New Civilisation* (3rd ed., London: 1944), pp. 742-4.

along with this broadening and modernising of taste is that it was consciously national. The rendering of Scottish 'low' life had long been exposed to genteel dislike and depreciation; it had to justify itself either by rising above its subject-matter to some approved literary style or as propaganda meant to better a backward way of life.[1] James Ballantyne, dependent as a printer on Scott's success and therefore anxious to accommodate public tastes, was at first against the rendering of native life. He says of *Waverley*:

> . . . to my utter shame be it spoken, when I reached the exquisite descriptions of scenes and manners at Tully Veolan, what did I do but pronounce them at once to be utterly vulgar! When the success of the work so entirely knocked me down as a man of taste, all that the good-natured author said was—"Well, I really thought you were wrong about the Scotch. Why, Burns, by his poetry, had already attracted universal attention to every thing Scottish, and I confess I couldn't see why I should not be able to keep the flame alive, merely because I wrote Scotch in prose, and he in rhyme."

Ballantyne had not been imagining things. Jeffrey had had to apologise for Scottish novels in his review of *Waverley*, "composed, one half of it, in a dialect unintelligible to four-fifths of the country [Britain] . . . and published, moreover, in a quarter of the island where materials and talents for novel-writing have been supposed to be equally wanting". In 1827, after years of successful Scottish fiction, Scott still wrote (while working on *Chronicles of the Canongate*), "J. B. [Ballantyne] will, I fear, think it low; and if he thinks so, others will. Yet—vamos."[2] It was presumably a similar objection that led even the astute and patriotic Constable to refuse Galt's *Annals* in 1813 on the grounds that "Scottish novels . . . would not do".[3] Scott, however, was able to override Ballantyne, and go ahead to create his own public, with the confidence of one who knew his own powers of pleasing, one who was full of ideas and full, too, of the peculiarly national interests of the Scottish gentlemen of his time. Scott was even pioneering respectability for the Novel in general, for example in America, along with Richardson and Maria Edgeworth: "These novels, so moderate and elevating,

[1] Victorian writers allowed Ramsay's coarser poems to pass on the grounds that they were written to expose the evils of drinking and swearing, e.g. *Hogg's Weekly Instructor* for 1845 on 'Christis Kirk on the Green' (Ramsay, *Works*, III, p. 272).
[2] Lockhart, *Life*, III, p. 297; quoted from Jeffrey's *Contributions to the Edinburgh Review*, which contains all his criticism of Scott: III, p. 33; Scott, *Journal*, II, p. 7.
[3] Galt, *Autobiography*, II, p. 227.

served them [the East Coast gentry] as patterns of manners. Scott, who adorned and beautified all that was growing old and passing away, appealed to their conservative feelings."[1] Even in the Carlyle household, some time before 1820, novels had been allowed in in the form of Scott; and Beatrice Webb wrote as a girl in 1872 that if a child was let loose in a grown-up library, Scott's novels were recommended as 'books that cannot do any possible harm'.[2]

The success of the 'Scotch novel' added its weight to the idea of cheap literature on a catholic basis, beyond the strictly informative or devotional. Elizabeth Hamilton's *Cottagers of Glenburnie* (a novel about the Tytlers' model village at Wood-houselee, which takes up a typically Victorian soup-and-sanitation attitude to the working classes) was brought out as a 'Tale for the Farmer's Inglenook'. Published in 1808, it reached its seventh edition in 1822 and a 'People's Edition' in 1837. Inspired by the success of the Waverley Novels (and of the *Edinburgh Review* and other ventures), Archibald Constable planned that "'if I live for half-a-dozen years, I'll make it as impossible that there should not be a good library in every decent house in Britain as that the shepherd's ingle-nook should want the saut-poke. Ay, and what's that?' he continued, warming and puffing, 'Why should the ingle-nook itself want a shelf for the novels?'" Lockhart elsewhere records that *Old Mortality* was in fact to be found on the cottage shelf; and a Border shepherd wrote in to congratulate Scott on the excellence of his Scots dialogue.[3]

Such success (and the free hand it gave to Scott's colleagues in Scottish fiction) was partly aided by the new tendency to preserve records of the old Scottish *mores* and cultivate whatever was left of them. As early as 1802, before his long poems, Scott had caught onto the literary possibilities of this: "many of my countrymen . . . are charmed by the effect of local description, and sometimes impute that effect to the poet which is produced by the recollections and associations which the verses excite"; and in *The Lady of the Lake* and later in *Waverley* he exploited these 'local' possibilities, as he himself admitted.[4] Criticism of such 'effects' must be left aside for the moment; here we may

[1] Brooks, *Flowering of New England*, pp. 56-7.
[2] Froude, *Early Life of Carlyle*, I, p. 49; B. Webb, *My Apprenticeship* (Pelican ed., London: 1938), I, p. 82.
[3] Lockhart, *Life of Scott*, VI, p. 30; *Peter's Letters to his Kinsfolk*, III, p. 72; Wilfred Partington (ed.), *The Private Letter-books of Sir Walter Scott* (London: 1930), p. 323.
[4] Lockhart, *Life*, I, p. 351; Introduction to *Waverley*.

note how Scott's shrewdness was confirmed by the kind of currency he got. According to the publisher Cadell, *The Lady of the Lake* sent crowds to Loch Katrine, in Perthshire (thus founding the fame of the Trossachs):

> . . . from the date of publication of the *Lady of the Lake* the post-horse duty in Scotland rose in an extraordinary degree, and it continued to do so regularly for a number of years, the author's works keeping up the enthusiasm for our scenery which he had thus originally created.

St Ronan's Well by itself turned the little country place in which it was set, Innerleithen, into a crowded, highly successful Border resort; and the boom in tartan-making stimulated by the Waverley Novels contributed to the growth of Stirling between 1821 and 1841.[1] In 1821 the *New Edinburgh Review*, summing up its critique of the poems and novels, could write of

> a grand peculiarity of both classes of works, namely, the localising of the scenes . . . such is the effect of it, that multitudes, who never thought of it before, have, this summer, visited not only Kenilworth, but Cumnor, and the tomb of Anthony Foster, in its churchyard![2]

The Scott vogue is now a famous curiosity of the past. What is more important is that the works in which the Scottish novelists came to life were typically those in which they were on their native ground. This was regularly recognised by critics at the time,[3] but it is comments by Scottish readers, on both Scott and Galt, which are the most telling, for they show how moving for Scotsmen was the experience of realising that their life had found its voice. The *Inverness Courier* welcomes Galt's *Annals* as a record of Scotland worthy to be put beside David Wilkie's paintings and the *Statistical Account*; and a 'Letter of Thanks from an Occasional Contributor' in *Blackwood's* says of *The Ayrshire Legatees* (Galt's second novel published), "The author breathes freely—his face brightens—and his *whole nature is itself* when in the country, and that country is Scotland".[4] Cockburn is eloquent on the impact of *Waverley*: "The unexpected newness of the thing, the profusion of original characters,

---

[1] Lockhart, *Life*, II, p. 292; *ibid.* V, p. 316; P. R. Crowe, 'The Population of the Scottish Lowlands': *Scottish Geographical Magazine* (Edinburgh: 1927), XLIII, p. 155. In this Scott was of course both co-operating with and giving a boost to the new taste for the country and holidaying in remote places.

[2] (Edinburgh: 1821), I, No. 2, pp. 384-5.

[3] E.g. the many writers, American, English, and Scottish, cited by James T. Hillhouse, in *The Waverley Novels and their Critics* (Minnesota, 1936).

[4] Excerpted in *Blackwood's* (1821), IX, p. 210; *ibid.* (1822), XI, pp. 742-3.

the Scotch language, Scotch scenery, Scotch men and women, the simplicity of the writing, and the graphic force of the descriptions, all struck us with an electric shock of delight"; and, looking back over Scott while reading *Ivanhoe*, he says, "his genius never seems to find profusion of matter except in Scotland. See how the figures rush up into living life in any of his good Scotch novels [he exemplifies from *Waverley*, *Guy Mannering*, *Rob Roy*] . . . And so we may go on with nearly the whole works, each teeming with original life, exhibited in fresh, natural scenes." On Scott's death, he wrote that "Scotland never owed so much so one man", and this was the burden of the *Blackwood* review of *Chronicles of the Canongate*: "There can be no doubt that these works have made a great addition to the kingdom of Scotland. We have become, since their appearance, a more powerful people. For, does not the strength of a state consist in the quantity and quality of its national thoughts and feelings?"[1]

There is in *Blackwood's* a series of comments on Scottish work which shows how acceptance of it developed out of genteel distaste and inferiority-feelings (for why should it ever have been thought that "materials" for fiction were lacking in Scotland, or in any country?). An early challenge came from *The Heart of Midlothian*. Jeanie Deans was

> somewhat of a new character in novel writing, and certainly a very interesting one. Perhaps there is a little too much of it, as even with persons not very aristocratical, the attention may be too long, and too diffusely called to the concerns of a cow-feeder and his daughter. . . .[2]

This attitude contrasts with Jeffrey's—obviously conditioned by the gentility of his class, which cannot quite realise the existence of life outside its own, yet too intelligent himself to rest in that. He was at first defensive about Scottish fiction, and chary of filling the pages of his quarterly with it; but, two and a half years after *Waverley*, his recognition of *The Heart of Midlothian* is perfectly clear-sighted:

> . . . he has succeeded by far the best in the representation of rustic and homely characters;—and not in the ludicrous or

[1] *Memorials*, p. 281 (cf. pp. 211-12 on the impact of *The Lay of the Last Minstrel*); *Circuit Journeys*, pp. 348-9; *Journal*, I, p. 37; *Blackwood's* (1827), XXII, p. 552. Cf. Lord Meadowbank's toast to Scott at the charity-fund dinner at which he at last divulged his authorship of the Waverley series: "It is to him that we owe that our gallant ancestors and illustrious patriots have obtained a fame no longer confined to the boundaries of a remote and comparatively obscure country" (Lockhart, *Life*, VII, p. 18).   [2] (1818), III, p. 570.

contemptuous representation of them—but by making them at once more natural and more interesting than they had ever been before in any work of fiction . . . with affections not only stronger, but often as delicate as those whose language is smoother . . .

And he can use the *Blackwood* kind of class term without obscuring or belittling the life in view:

[Perhaps Scott's greatest triumph is Jeanie; she is] in the highest degree both pathetic and sublime; and yet she never says or does any one thing that the daughter of a Scotch cow-feeder might not be supposed to say . . . though acting always, and in very difficult situations, with the greatest judgement and propriety, she never seems to exert more than that downright and obvious good sense which is so often found to rule the conduct of persons of her condition.[1]

Such liberalisation of outlook was coming about all over Britain: for example, in 1828 the *Athenaeum* could say of Cobbett that his "personal consciousness of all which is concealed from our eyes by grey jackets and clouted shoes, has kept alive his sympathy with the majority of mankind".[2] Even the reactionary *Blackwood's* did not fail to catch up with this, and we can see that what eased the change in Scotland was the presence of a flourishing national literature which was also a fiction. In 1819 a general article on 'Novel Writing' says: "Since, in modern times, the different modes of national existence are no longer capable of being represented in epic poems, it has become the task of the novelist to copy, in an humbler style, the humbler features exhibited by human life", and he cites *Don Quixote*, *Gil Blas*, Fielding, Smollett, and Scott.[3] In time even the wistfulness for a more aristocratic culture fades out into the nationalist pride of the age. Finally, for the Scottish periodicals, Scott supplies a standard against which the reviewer can judge literature from other countries, whether American or English; and when the Waverley Novels came out collected in 1832 the *Edinburgh Review* could credit him with having established the novel (when it had seemed exhausted) "among the highest productions of human intellect".[4]

---

[1] *Contributions*, III, pp. 49, 76.
[2] Quoted by R. K. Webb, *The British Working Class Reader, 1790–1848*: Literacy and Social Tension (London: 1955), p. 51.
[3] Vol. III, p. 394.
[4] *Edinburgh Review* (1832), LV, p. 64. (In the word "exhausted" the *Edinburgh* is ignoring Jane Austen and treating the English novel as having lapsed between the age of Fielding and the 19th century.) The Romans in Addison's *Cato* are found wanting in 'reality' compared with Scott's moss-troopers; and the "cold and

The not unembarrassed pride of country at work in such
critics is typified by the following kind of thing:

> Our country is reflected in the mirror of imagination, and
> we are all proud to see Auld Scotia's weather-beaten face in
> such shadowy portraiture. We are an arrogant set of people,
> no doubt, even the humblest of us, and manly airs we give
> ourselves, down to the very fingernails, not always the
> cleanest of horn. But, after all, we have something to be
> proud of, going on in Auld Reekie, and elsewhere. . . .[1]

Thus the gawky countryman is allowed to stand for 'Scotland';
the national consciousness has altogether too many streaks of
the false and self-assertive in it for all-round cultural vitality.
What indeed emerges from the study of the reading-public
is that the very quality of Scottish fiction (and the national
morale it represented) is expressed, and a limiting judgement
of it suggested, by the kind of taste it both created and catered
for. This appears at the start, in the aims of the novelists. In
1814 Lockhart wrote, "It is to me wonderful how the Scotch
character has been neglected. . . . Now I think there is just as
great a fund of originality and humour in the Scotch character,
modified as it is, in the various ranks of life, as in the English or
Spanish, or any of those of which so much has been made." Of
course there was, but how was it to get expressed? According
to Andrew Lang, "In the matter of novel-writing, Lockhart's
ambition, at the age of twenty, was to be what Galt became,
the recorder of the Caledonian humours—of his own, not of
past romantic ages".[2] That is, Lockhart set out to write, not
with his imagination focussed upon some theme he felt essential
to humankind (whether or not he drew his experience of it
from the community around him), but in order to 'cover' a
restricted sector of life, there for the doing. Likewise Scott was
inspired by Maria Edgeworth, who had 'done something
towards completing the Union' between Ireland and England
by familiarising the English with the character of their neighbours:

> I felt that something might be attempted for my own country,
> of the same kind which Miss Edgeworth so fortunately
> achieved for Ireland—something which might introduce her

abstract" ideas in Fenimore Cooper's *Heidenmauer* are contrasted with Scott's ripe
characters (*Edinburgh Review*, 1831, LIII, p. 554; *Tait's Edinburgh Magazine* (1832),
VI, p. 663).
[1] Review of Galt's *The Entail*: *Blackwood's* (1823), XIII, pp. 85-6.
[2] *Life and Letters of Lockhart*, I, pp. 72-3, 75.

natives to those of the sister kingdom in a more favourable light than they had been placed hitherto, and tend to procure sympathy for their virtues and indulgence for their foibles.[1]

It is an acute concern with nationhood and the well-being of their common culture which thus feels that the country had until then lacked a complete image of itself. But in their particular comments on the sort of public they wanted for their work the Scottish novelists seem local, or at least provincial, rather than national.

The centre of this movement in Scottish public opinion was the Blackwood milieu. Blackwood's publishing enterprises gave Galt his natural platform, and were the spearhead of the movement to 'present Scotland'. The magazine serialised Galt, James Hogg's 'Pastoral Anecdotes', the *Noctes Ambrosianae* (that curious gallimaufry of Lockhart's and Wilson's), D. M. Moir's *Mansie Wauch*, and many other pieces in semi-vernacular prose. The publishing house brought out, for example, all the 'secondary Scotch novels' reviewed by Jeffrey in 1823.[2] A well-knit milieu, literary, academic, and business, was based on Blackwood's home.[3] Yet the spirit in which they did their work was hardly a strength to the culture, so given over were they to indulgence in reactionary and provincial cults. Galt's own letters to Blackwood contain little of what might have been hoped for in the way of discussion of what meant most to him as an exponent of the common language and experience of his country; but there is much word of how well his novels should go down in the localities they are based on. In 1820, sending in the first part of *The Ayrshire Legatees* (an epistle-novel about the ludicrous misunderstandings of an Ayrshire family on a jaunt to London), he writes, "Perhaps I ought to warn you that whatever change I may give to names and professions the persons described are all portraits, and I doubt not that some of them in the first part will be recognised by your Ayrshire readers". The following year, while serialising *The Steamboat* (an episodic

[1] General Preface to the Waverley Novels. See also his characteristically modest remark that "in what he had done for Scotland as a writer, he was no more entitled to the merit which had been ascribed to him than the servant who scours the 'brasses' to the credit of having made them . . . he had perhaps been a good housemaid to Scotland, and given the country a 'rubbing up'" (Lockhart, *Life*, VII, p. 221).
[2] Blackwood still held a similar position late in the century. Stevenson wrote to Charles Baxter, foreseeing difficulties in placing *Weir of Hermiston*, "there is one quarter in which the very Scotchness of the thing would be found a recommendation. . . . I mean Blackwood" (*Letters to Charles Baxter*, ed. DeLancy Ferguson and Marshall Waingrow: London, 1956: p. 314).
[3] See note 3.

'novel' on a plan "so free as to enable me to bring all my hear-says and actual observations whatsoever and howsoever made into play"), he writes Blackwood that he will resume the 'Responsive Notices' to the *Legatees* as they had created great interest in Greenock and Glasgow as well as Ayrshire.[1] The 'responsive notices' were gossipy pieces in which Galt made fun of readers who treated his characters as fictitious or defended himself with mild irony against readers who had written in protesting that a local personality or building had been mis-called. In one he mentions readers who had written in asking him to have his characters visit various other places and replies that he can hardly control the movements of real people.[2] It is a rather higher level of local interest that he thinks of himself as functioning at when he says of the *Annals* that certain episodes, not to be cut out, "are such events as are long remembered in country parishes" and refer to "real events which happened about the time in Ayrshire—and are calcu-lated, as I conceive, to give that degree of reality to the story which may induce *some* to think there has actually been an original chronicle". Concerning *The Last of the Lairds*, the novel whose reception showed that his particular vein was starting to give out, he explained to Blackwood: "The object and purposes of the plan were to exhibit the actual manners *which* about 25 years ago *did* belong to a class of persons, in Scotland—the west of it—but who are now extinct". And in a letter written after the publication of *The Provost* he shows that he did take local opinion into account when composing his novels: "I under-stand that the Provost is a good deal thought of in the West Country, you will do me a kindness if you will let me know the sort of points that are best liked, for that kind of knowledge has done me great service".[3]

As far as his sense of his public is concerned, Galt is thus hardly freer of a close community than Fergusson or Burns. Scott, of course, ranged far beyond the local, and he was not unfitted to serve as a source of types for a goodly range of his countrymen. Yet he can be remarkably local-minded for some-one of his status, for example in the 'Jedediah Cleishbotham' introductions which he wrote for some of his novels. These pretend that the novels have been communicated as tales at the

[1] National Library of Scotland Manuscript No. 4005, folios 82-3; No. 4006, f. 240; *ibid*. f. 219.
[2] Blackwood's (1820–1), VIII, Nos. 43, 45, 47; *ibid*. No. 47, p. 502.
[3] Nat. Lib. MS. 4006, f. 223; MS. 4017, f. 37; MS. 4008, f. 181. In this letter he tells Blackwood to announce *The Entail* with the motto, "Let Glasgow flourish".

local inn, and thus get heavy fun out of that common contrast between the local—village schoolmasters or farm folk ludicrously unaware of their own restricted experience—and the wider way of life in the cities or in England.[1] It is the tension which occurs again and again, like an obsession, in Scottish literature. Such things are mere trimmings to the Waverley Novels, yet they show that Scott never grew out of feeling his art as a kind of pastime, addressed in part to a small class with whom he was familiar, sharing the same antiquarian hobbies and little jokes. His art never quite wins through to a mature independence, sure of its own standing and level of approach to life. Galt is similarly conscious of the familiar public, out there ready to take his signals, as when he puts into the dialogue of *The Last of the Lairds*: "'That silly auld havering creature, Balwhidder o' Dalmailing [the hero of his own *Annals*], got a thousand pounds sterling, doun on Blackwood's counter, in red gold for his clishmaclavers'"; or again, about a surprise in the plot: "'. . . it's just a thing for playactors, and the likes o' Sir Walter to mak a clishmaclaver o'''".[2] No doubt *major* writers would have been less taken up with catering for immediate public tastes. But then it would be an essential of a major writer's situation to be unrestricted to any one small public—just as a larger, more varied society (Russian, French, English, American) might be more likely to throw up major writers.

Very rarely does one find in the statements of these Scottish novelists (or implicit in their work) an overriding concern with the life, whatever it might be, that moved them most in their dealings, as individual persons, with the world: no notes (such as there are in plenty in the work records of George Eliot or Henry James) of episodes, complexes of event and character, social observations, which absorb the author by the intensity of their human interest.[3] No-one gives us a keener sense of the emotions interacting in the religious life of the 18th century than does Burns; but he does so not out of a documentary intention but out of his own ironic exasperation and trenchantly humorous sense of the incongruous or false, which had to find expression. The equivalent motives or personal concerns in the novelists were too weak—not personal enough—as when Lockhart can let his observations of Scotland "sleep a year or two" because *Waverley* has captured public attention; or Galt

---

[1] E.g. *Old Mortality* (Victoria ed.), pp. xii, xvi.
[2] In two vols. with *The Provost* (*op. cit.*), I, p. 260; II, p. 140.
[3] *The Fair Maid of Perth* is a rare exception: see note 4.

can think it fruitless even to try to excel in "recreative stories" (of history) because Scott is in possession of that field; or Scott himself can speak of his potential subject-matter as a finite vein capable of simply being exhausted: "Novelty is what this giddy-paced time demands imperiously, and I certainly studied [in *Ivanhoe*, which broke the Scottish series] as much as I could to get out of the old beaten track, leaving those who like to keep the road, which I have rutted pretty well".[1] The Scottish novelists had this admirable aim—of writing out of the life of their fellow-countrymen; but it tended to go dead on their hands because they did not sufficiently work out for themselves what was significant in experience at large—they took it for granted that 'Scottish life' was a subject ready-made in itself.

Of a piece with this is that over-preoccupation with the past. It is the past that the *Blackwood's* writer thinks of when he discusses 'national thoughts and feelings':

> And how else are its national thoughts and feelings so thickly generated, and so genially nourished, as by Imagination bringing back the very dead—the good and the great of former ages—and brightening up from oblivion the incidents, events, changes, revolutions, customs, manners, morals, poetry, and religion that constituted the life of our ancestors, and gave them a distinctive character among the nations?[2]

Such an attitude tends to be unreal, or openly reactionary, about the needs of the present, especially in a country which feels it has now lost much of its identity. It is present achievements, present tendencies, that John Stuart Mill thinks of when he defines the workings of "national character" in his essay on Bentham.[3] In a passage such as that from *Blackwood's*, we sense a mind which feeds off its own past, thinks of that only as the great distinctive manifestation of itself. A reviewer of *The Entail* says (as though basing himself disinterestedly on an 18th-century ideal of culture), "To England we look, as to a country in advance of our native land, in the knowledge and power of civilisation", but his main point is to challenge England to produce anything like the popular works now triumphing in Scotland: "Are the peasantry—the people of England so poor as to afford no materials for gifted men to mould them into striking personifications, and to enrich thereby the possessions of English literature? . . . Scotland produces annually crops of

[1] Galt, *Autobiography*, II, p. 210; Scott, *Letters*, VI, p. 116.
[2] (1827), XXII, p. 552.
[3] See F. R. Leavis (ed.), *Mill on Bentham and Coleridge* (London: 1950), p. 73.

printed books, that smack of her fields and her atmosphere—redolent of spring", and he goes off into the extraordinary embarrassments quoted already—"manly airs we give ourselves, down to the very fingernails, not always the cleanest of horn".[1] "We take the liberty of wondering why England does not do more for herself in native literature than she is now doing": that is, the idea of 'native' literature on which he bases his claim for Scottish work means a literature of the rural peasantry. This was indeed in keeping with contemporary writing: Galt cannot take his heroes convincingly into the large towns, Scott cannot find the interest in people of his own class that he does in lower classes. Such a literature as that of the 19th-century Russian or English novelists is healthily 'native', not the less so for rendering types highly exposed to alien influences, for example Tolstoy's French-speaking gentry. But to the *Blackwood's* writer it is only the most obviously 'native' phenomena that count—for he would presumably not class as properly native such writers as Crabbe, Blake, Wordsworth, or Jane Austen.

To be sure there were other critics whose sense of the national was more than slogans. Jeffrey habitually discriminates amongst native work; the cases of it with which he deals are not, to him, just gratifyingly Scottish Scottishnesses, they make as searching demands on his mind as any of his other interests. For example he writes of *Rob Roy* that both the Bailie and Andrew Fairservice are "rich mines of the true Scottish language", but he does not make this an end in itself: "[they] afford, in the hands of this singular writer, not only additional proof of his perfect familiarity with all its dialects, but also of its extraordinary copiousness, and capacity of adaptation to all tones and subjects". He also had what was no doubt the needed coldness towards the Blackwood Scottishness.[2] It was, however, Blackwood Scottishness which prevailed, in letters, from that time on—in the 'Scottish life and character' books (which came flocking out during the 19th century, and seem to have been the origin of *Punch's* idea of Scotland as a nation of golf-caddies, ministers, and yokels), and in the popular line of writers including S. R. Crockett, Barrie, Iain Maclaren, and the comic side of Neil Munro. In general an alertly critical attitude to what was done with 'the Scotch matter' got lost in the

---

[1] *Blackwood's* (1823), XIII, pp. 85-6.
[2] *Contributions*, III, p. 70. Judging Galt's *Steamboat*, he writes that it has "really no merit at all" and "should never have been transplanted from the Magazine in which we are informed it first made its appearance" (*Contributions*, III, p. 123).

welcoming of it for its own sake, or for the sake of the happy, backward-looking irresponsibility which it licensed (the spirit of the *Noctes Ambrosianae*). It is another consequence of this direction taken by the Scottish tradition that the original novelists of modern times, Brown and Gibbon, should have written, not altogether freely out of their personal interests in humanity, but in reaction to a stereotyped Scotland that has needed to be challenged. *The House with the Green Shutters*, apart from its main themes, is full of little digs at the small community and unnecessary generalisations about Scotland and 'the Scot'.[1] It is as though behind the novel proper there were in Brown's mind a whole background of strained attitudes to the native country which he could not quite work out of his system and into a form of art. After its publication and the usual *furore* at its outrageousness, Brown diagnosed his own "personal animus"; antagonism to the "sentimental slop" of Barrie, Crockett, and Maclaren had made him "embitter the blackness", to "show the dogs what I thought of them". Finally he regretted this axe-grinding as a "gross blunder", yet he remained (rightly) convinced that his book was "more complimentary to Scotland" than theirs.[2] Finally in *Sunset Song* we are given a hint that Gibbon intends an all-round presentment of Scotland which will comprehend and replace the earlier partial ones, both the slop (Iain Maclaren's *Beneath the Bonnie Brier Bush*) and the blackness: it is symbolised in the incident of a minister's crowning discomfiture before an unsympathetic people:

> And then, when the porter had picked him up and was dusting him, the Reverend Gibbon broke down and sobbed on the porter's shoulder what a bloody place was Kinraddie! And how'd the porter like to live 'tween a brier bush and a rotten kailyard in the lee of a house with green shutters? . . . And the porter said it was awful the way the world went, he'd thought of resigning from the railway himself and take to preaching, but now he wouldn't.[3]

The circulation of the fiction of Scott's age depended on publishers as patriotic as the novelists and journalists. Lockhart wrote to Constable in 1814: "I have been amusing myself with

[1] E.g. "so flushed and riotous can the Scottish mind become over a commercial prospect that it sometimes sends native caution by the board, and a man's really fine idea becomes an empty balloon, to carry him off to the limbo of vanities. There is a megalomaniac in every parish of Scotland" (pp. 94-5).
[2] Veitch, *George Douglas Brown*, p. 153.   [3] P. 73.

writing a novel, and as it chiefly regards Scotland, I should wish
to have it published in Edinburgh"[1]—an unlikely choice now
when Scottish provincial publishing (for example in Paisley) is
more or less at an end and the Scottish writer looks to London.
Constable was indeed the natural choice in Scott's age for he
was himself devoted to the national literature. In an unfinished
autobiographical piece he wrote:

> My great ambition was to pick up curious and valuable works
> relative to the history and literature of Scotland, with which
> department of bookselling I considered no other at all to be
> compared, and I believe I was the first of the trade, at least
> in modern times, who took a deep interest in securing and
> preserving all books relating to Scottish literature.

To establish publishing on a national footing required something of a campaign. Elliot, one of the booksellers bent on
"retaining for his own advantage and the credit of his country
all the literary property he could acquire" in the works of the
18th-century writers,

> met with great opposition from the booksellers of London.
> These gentlemen had been accustomed to consider them-
> selves as entitled to a monopoly of all that was produced by
> Scottish literature, and looked upon Mr Elliot as an invader
> of the best branch of their trade . . . the booksellers of London
> were so illiberal as to enter into a combination not to receive
> into their shops any literary property published by him.

This drove Elliot to establish a branch in the Strand (London
had a magnetism positive as well as negative), and Constable
notes that the Scottish book trade was still so thin that Elliot
had no-one to partner him in Edinburgh or to continue his
trade (this was in the 1780's). He ends his *catalogue raisonné* of
the Edinburgh booksellers by saying, "There were few original
books published in Edinburgh, and intercourse with London
was consequently neither extensive nor important".[2] This is
perhaps innocent advertising of his own enterprise; Creech
alone had brought out a good many notable books, for example
the *Mirror* and *Lounger*, the Edinburgh editions of Burns's poems,
Tytler's life of Lord Kames, Forbes's life of Beattie, Beattie's
Scotticisms, Sinclair's *Observations on the Scottish Dialect*, the first
Statistical Account, and Jamieson's pioneering Scots dictionary.
But it is true that publication of native creative literature had
hitherto been insignificant, and it is also true that literary

---

[1] *Constable and his Correspondents*, III, p. 151.
[2] *Ibid.*, III, pp. 22-3, 533-4, 540.

business between the two countries expanded greatly in Constable's time with the arrival of saleable creative authors and of serious quarterlies (inspired so largely by the Scottish *literati*) with their kind of wide circulation. In the memoirs of the publisher John Murray (a Scotsman settled in London) we constantly hear of him getting wind of some success or likely item in Edinburgh; he thereupon writes up to Constable or Blackwood asking for a share in the work or at least the London agency for it.[1] Edinburgh was becoming a major publishing centre, able to do business with London on an equal footing. It had one of the two 'universally'-read reviews, the most popular encyclopaedias (the *Britannica*) and histories (Archibald Alison's), and, in Scott, one of the two great literary successes of the day (the other, Byron, being published by Murray). What Edinburgh specialised in putting out was the best native work; she had become 'the mart of her own literature', in the standard phrase.[2] This was due partly to her advantages as a centre, partly to the new constellation of talents. As the century went on, the publishers gathered momentum from their native successes. Mrs Oliphant wrote of William Blackwood:

> To so enthusiastic a lover of literature as Mr Blackwood, and one at the same time so patriotic and full of that love of his native country in all her manifestations which sometimes leads the Scot astray and confuses his judgement, Galt was at the beginning like the springing up of the most refreshing of fountains. I am disposed to think that our excellent founder would at any time have given all his goods and something to boot could he but have discovered another Scott among the many literary aspirants that crowded round him . . . I think I can see through his welcome of every new writer this glimmer of hope in his eyes.[3]

By the time the Chamberses started up in earnest with their cheap publishing in the 1820's, Scotland was a very ample field in itself, and they could bring out as their first ventures a whole run of Scottish works.[4]

---

[1] Samuel Smiles, *A Publisher and his Friends* (ed. London: 1911), pp. 22-3 (refusing all "country business" but *not* Constable's, who had just started the *Edinburgh Review*), 39-40 (to Scott, regarding the start of the *Quarterly*), 98 (agreeing to take *The Lady of the Lake*), an edition of Beaumont and Fletcher, and "a novel"), 103 (Hogg's new poems and the 4th edition of *The Queen's Wake*), 193 (his short-lived part share in *Blackwood's Magazine*).

[2] E.g. *Peter's Letters*, II, p. 156; Scott, Introduction to *The Fortunes of Nigel*; Cockburn, *Memorials*, p. 169.

[3] *Blackwood and His Sons*, I, p. 447.

[4] Songs of Burns, *Popular Rhymes, Scottish Ballads and Songs*, histories, a gazetteer, *Scottish Jests and Anecdotes*, a *Book of Scotland*, a *Dictionary of Eminent Scotsmen* (*Memoir*, pp. 149-51, 182, 186, 193, 212-15).

The heyday which this large output of Scottish material enjoyed, before it was incorporated into the mass of British letters, was fairly short. This appears both in the sales, returns, and circulation of the fiction and in the growing and waning of the publishers' activities. Details of sales and returns are given in Appendix B; what matters here is their bearing on the changes in social *mores* which have been the theme of this book. The productive spans of the novelists were rather short. Lang notes that Lockhart produced no creative work after leaving Scotland: his may have been a young man's creative burst, like Henry Mackenzie's.[1] Almost all Scott's significant work came out in ten years, from *Waverley* in mid-1814 to *Redgauntlet* in mid-1824. He began late, but the eight years from *Redgauntlet* to his death, which produced only 'The Two Drovers', seems long enough to register a distinct exhaustion. Hogg's serious fiction (in any case more a single item in a career of mixed letters than a creative flow) was confined to the early 1820's—a collection of tales, *The Brownie of Bodsbeck*, the *Justified Sinner*. Susan Ferrier brought out three novels at long intervals between 1818 and 1831. Galt's first published fiction, *The Ayrshire Legatees*, began serialising in 1820; what he himself recognised to be the last work from his true vein, *The Last of the Lairds*, came out only six years later, after five other novels in that *genre*. It is perhaps natural that these writers, working in what was almost a finite vein, should not have gone on developing their art through their own development as people, up to the end of their lives, as did Jane Austen, Dickens, George Eliot, James, and Lawrence.

This short curve of production is matched by the circulation Galt got and also by that of Scott, even in the midst of his great success. By the time Galt began to publish, the market for Scottish fiction had already been established by Scott's best work, that is, the novels up to *The Heart of Midlothian*.[2] Scott made a considerable success out of 'the Scotch novels'; his sales gathered momentum very quickly, he was able to keep satisfying and recreating his market, and his circulation kept up so well that eleven years after his death the sales of his works, now in collected editions, were still increasing.[3] But he could not *rely* on high sales and a good critical reception once the Scottish series was broken. His later circulation in fact depended to a great extent on the repute won by what the public recognised

---

[1] *Life and Letters*, I, p. 373.
[2] For the details behind the following paragraph see Appendix B, 'Sales and Returns of Fiction in the Age of Scott'.
[3] Jeffrey, *Contributions*, III, p. 32, n.

to be his *métier*, the works using his native and more-or-less first-hand experience (which had peopled everyone's fireside with inexpensive friends). With his flair for what would appeal he was able to produce an alternative line, the historical romance, and though there were critics enough to insist that this was of inferior interest, it found and kept a large public (as operas, Hollywood films, and school reading-lists still testify). Galt, with much less power and variety, could be "received with almost unfailing approbation" for his native work in the vein of the *Annals*, but his attempted alternatives, whether historical or contemporary (some based on his experiences pioneering trading settlements in Canada, where there is a town named after him), got no such popularity. Scott was able to get a hold on a peculiarly wide, mixed public which did not slacken for almost a century. The other novelists, with a few exceptions (the *Annals* and the *Justified Sinner* have in this century become different sorts of minor classic), found a circulation as confined and as short-lived as the veins from which they took their material.

Scottish publishing, too, did not long keep up its effective unity. The emigration of the publishers themselves is part of the trend detailed in the final chapter, but it must be glanced at here as it works in so closely with the history of the fiction itself. For one thing, Scottish men of letters had never been able—nor would it have been desirable—to keep independent of the English centres. Constable had been apprenticed in London and he apprenticed his son David there from 1811 to 1816. The house of Murray was founded by an *émigré* Scot (an Edinburgh lawyer's son who left the Royal Marines at Chatham and went into bookselling).[1] The same is true of Macmillan. Daniel Macmillan went to Stirling as a bookseller's assistant; but "'the place was too small and the boy was too big'. He had chafed against the confinement of it and suffered 'a most violent brain fever'." He went into a Glasgow bookshop, and regularly read weeklies, monthlies, and quarterlies into the small hours to fit himself for his business; fell ill again; and on recovering set off for London to join a Glaswegian, James Maclehose, already an assistant in a Fleet Street firm.[2] William Chambers thought of emigrating to London, on account of the "narrow scope for individual exertions" in Scotland,[3] but he

[1] *Constable and His Correspondents*, II, p. 108; *A Publisher and His Friends*, pp. 1-2.
[2] Charles Morgan, *The House of Macmillan, 1843-1943* (London: 1943), pp. 11-12.
[3] *Memoir*, p. 134.

knew nothing about London (such emigration usually depended on having contacts in the south). Edinburgh too was an attractive centre, and he stayed in Scotland and finally created his own scope. Two of William Blackwood's six sons were sent to London to learn bookselling; by 1840 the firm had a London branch, and their correspondence in the '40's is taken up with the problems of keeping up business in both centres. An agent would be unsatisfactory, there must be a branch, yet "the grand point is the business here [Edinburgh]". The solution will be the twelve-hour rail journey between the capitals, expected to come shortly: "This, whilst it will increase the facility, will also increase the necessity for your being frequently there"—a typical illustration of the emigration process. John Blackwood in London became an intimate of the Westminster politicians, and his firm became the publisher, in the '50's, of George Eliot, Bulwer, and Kinglake, in the '60's of Trollope, and also of R. D. Blackmore, Mrs Browning, and Mrs Hemans.[1] Thus this firm remained a centre of valuable Scottish enterprise (John was an intelligently helpful critic of George Eliot as her novels arrived in parts for the printer) and a source of money and employment to Edinburgh. But it was not to be a centre of native culture for much longer. Later, it published Neil Munro and John Buchan; but by then Edinburgh had ceased to be a commanding centre whose booksellers were key agents in its literary life.[2] The process was partly due to changing British practices; as Samuel Smiles writes:

> The old association of booksellers, with the accompaniment of trade-books [the practice of setting days aside on which special lots of books were offered wholesale at special rates to booksellers from all over the country], dwindled with the growth of the spirit of competition, so that, long before his [Murray's] death, the co-operation between the booksellers of London and Edinburgh was no more than a memory.[3]

At the same time the scatter of Scottish publishing talent was part of a widespread gravitation towards the richer opportunities of the south.

We see, then, that a point that emerged from criticism of the fiction itself—that, by the time it grew up, Scotland's sense of

---

[1] *Blackwood and His Sons*, II, pp. 254, 376-7, 379-83; *ibid.* chaps. 23-4; III, chap. 11 and p. 412.
[2] This dispersal also affected the leading reviews: see Appendix C, 'The Centralisation of Scottish Periodicals'.
[3] *A Publisher and His Friends*, p. 360.

itself had too far set into a repertoire of types, idioms, and styles from the past—is borne out in many aspects by a survey of the literary system as it affected the fiction. We may say that the Scottish novel arrived rather too late, for all the patriotic impulses that helped to give rise to it and assured its currency. Of course such a statement is highly general: it does not exclude the possibility of fine individual things (*The Heart of Midlothian, The Justified Sinner*) cropping up. But the interest in Scotland was such that it tended to keep the writer's experience fragmentary or unreal even as it moved him to get it down on paper. So Galt can write to *Blackwood's* approving "not only a general taste for the preservation of the national customs and antiquities, but even a growing fashion to revive many peculiarities that had either been proscribed [this was the year before George IV's visit to Edinburgh and the tartan gala organised by Scott] or become obsolete".[1] We may say that a nationalism has its back to the wall if it is forced to resort to *that*; for to 'preserve' a custom is merely to cling onto a way of behaving which no longer comes naturally to people. What is felt to be distinctively native has to be 'preserved', or recreated synthetically, it is not thought of as growing inevitably in whatever are the latest developments. 'Preservation' appears in a significant context in Cockburn's account of Jeffrey's speech and Scottish tastes:

> Our mere speech was doomed to recede, to a certain extent, before the foreign wave, and it was natural for a young man to anticipate what was coming. But our native *literature* was better fixed; and Jeffrey knew it, and enjoyed it. He was familiar with the writers in that classic Scotch, of which much is good old English, from Gavin Douglas to Burns. He saw the genius of Scott, and Wilson, and Hogg, and Galt, and others, elicited by the rich mines of latent character and history with which their country abounds, and devoted to the elucidation of the scenes which awakened it; and, of all their admirers, there was not one who rejoiced more, or on better grounds, in the Scotch qualities that constitute the originality and the vivid force of their writings. He felt the power of the beautiful language which they employed, and were inspired by; and, as many of his subsequent criticisms attest, was most anxious for the preservation of a literature so peculiar and picturesque.[2]

The words which give Cockburn's notion of the distinctively Scots—"peculiar", "picturesque"—suggests a sense of litera-

---

[1] (1821), X, pp. 665-6.   [2] *Life of Jeffrey*, I, p. 48.

ture as almost a curio, a fascinating specimen whose basis in real life is no longer his own main environment. The literature was "fixed", yes; but all that means is that there was the literary past. Given the faltering of serious literary production before mid-century, the intelligent Scottish critic—however strong his faith in the 'mines of latent character'—could hardly carry on thinking of the literature as growing, not fixed, just as Blackwood was forever tantalised by the need of another Scott to carry on the literature to which he was committed. Odd works by George Macdonald and Stevenson, *The House with the Green Shutters*, Gibbon's *Scots Quair*, Hugh MacDiarmid's poetry from *Sangschaw* to *Stony Limits*—certainly these amount to as fine a body of work as that of the ages of Burns and Scott. But, considered for its continuity as a tradition, Scottish culture during the past century has only in isolated phases afforded us the experience of minds of a fine quality working in creative literature. Whether deep matters in Scottish life have been left unexpressed, or whether our public has been genuinely satisfied by the literatures of England and America, can only be a matter for speculation.

PART III
LANGUAGE

CHAPTER VIII

Literature and Native Language

It is easier to think in a foreign language than it is to feel in it. Therefore no art is more stubbornly national than poetry. A people may have its language taken away from it, suppressed, and another language compelled upon the schools; but unless you teach that people to *feel* in a new language, you have not eradicated the old one, and it will reappear in poetry which is the vehicle of feeling. . . . A superior language can seldom be exterminated except by the extermination of the people who speak it. When one language supersedes another it is usually because that language has advantages which commend it, and which offer not merely a different but a wider and more refined range, not only for thinking but for feeling, than the more primitive language.—T. S. ELIOT, 'The Social Function of Poetry' (1943): *On Poetry and Poets.*

IT has been an article of faith with Scottish Renaissance criticism that Scots—that is, a Scottish speech or language, of whatever kind—is a *sine qua non* for Scottish writers. The grounds for this are obvious, and have been formulated repeatedly by Hugh MacDiarmid and others. But the critical valuation it implies needs closer questioning. In his *Golden Treasury of Scottish Poetry* MacDiarmid quotes Edwin Muir: "No writer can write great English who is not born an English writer and in England", and comments: "I cannot see that any Scottish writer, writing in English, has managed to write first-class work or to contribute anything essential and indispensable to the central tradition, the main stream, of English literature", and again: "No recent Scottish poet writing in English has written poetry of the slightest consequence; their contemporaries who write in Scots have shown a far higher creative calibre".[1] This, however, though broadly true, is only a comparative way of judging the literature in Scots—that it is better than certain second-rate work. MacDiarmid is meeting a further argument of Muir's, regarding the limitedness of Scots poetry, the cramped base it affords for future work; and this critical challenge is precisely dodged by MacDiarmid's reply: "Whatever the truth may be regarding Scottish poetry *vis-à-vis* English poetry, certainly recourse to the medium of the English language has availed Scottish poets little" (p. xxix). For surely the literature MacDiarmid is speaking for must prove its worth, not by comparison with some weak, Anglicised offshoot of itself, but at the test of our sense of what is finest in any language.

[1] (London: 1946), pp. xvi, xxiv.

It is true that MacDiarmid's comparative case is unanswerable. To shift the argument to fiction, Scott rarely comes to life except when he changes to Scots from literary English, Hogg writes curiously uncertain, mixed literary English outside his Scots dialogue, Galt is null when he deserts the staple of thin Anglo-Scots which he invented for himself. The best things in Scottish fiction are almost all founded on Scots: Bailie Nicol Jarvie from *Rob Roy*, the Deanses from *The Heart of Midlothian*, Cuddie Headrigg from *Old Mortality*, the Mucklebackits—the fisher-folk from *The Antiquary*; the Moderate and commercially-minded ethos of *The Annals of the Parish*, *The Provost*, and *The Betheral*; Stevenson's 'Thrawn Janet' and the opposition between Archie and his father in *Weir of Hermiston* (chapter 3); Gourlay and 'the bodies' in *The House with the Green Shutters*; the direct speech and echoed comments in Lewis Grassic Gibbon's trilogy. Yet, when all this is said, we must also recognise that these authors never use a full Scots (as full as they can use with masterly effect in snatches) for their *medium*: for that they must make the best of English. The vernacular they draw on comes from a society with its own strong character, which lives to a great degree in its language—its spoken tongue—and a tongue which is close to the movements of an alert feeling for life. But the general truth to be derived from the existing creative achievements in this language seems to be that what it can do for literature is rather to give unusual life to a writer who does not produce sustained art on major subjects than to appear the inevitable medium to a great originating talent—especially in an age when the major literature is fiction, requiring a staple of prose, which Scots does not possess.

This, however, only marks out the limits of the subject; it leaves untouched the kind of resources and inspiration which the poets and novelists actually found in their native language. As the process through which a writer brings into play his native language is easy to simplify or distort, I propose first to discuss it in general terms, to consider on what grounds one can properly judge a language as a vehicle of expression.

A recent authority on language finds three speech-groups among educated Scotsmen of Allen Ramsay's time: "those who, like Allan Ramsay, preferred Scots dialect, but could probably Anglicise a good deal when they chose"; those who spoke English like that of the official records the writer analyses, "English with a sprinkling of Scotticisms" and a Scots pronunciation, these people being able also to use dialect "for a change"; and those who despised dialect but were perhaps not more Anglicised in practice than the rest.[1] On the usage of the authors themselves, the writer says:

> The fact that Ramsay, Fergusson, and Burns all succeeded better in Scots than in English poetry has also been interpreted as evidence of lack of knowledge of English. Again, this seems to be the 18th-century sense of 'knowledge of English' [i.e. ability to write polished Augustan prose]. These writers may indeed have been more familiar with Scots—none of them came from the same social class, or received the same education, as most of the writers of letters and records . . . but I cannot accept poetry written in good English as evidence that the authors could not write English without great difficulty.[2]

This, however, merely answers a minor point as to whether Scots-speakers were actually hard put to it to manage English at all. That these poets had adequate 'knowledge of English' is perfectly obvious. Burns, for example, wrote hundreds of letters in quite fluent (though rarely very personal) 18th-century English. But as they were poets, the writing of theirs that matters—and exposes the issue most fully—is their poetry; and their verse-English, though good in the sense of grammatically correct, is as expression null—devoid of any sharp fidelity to something experienced at first hand. For example, compare Burns's set-piece, "Edina! Scotia's darling seat":

> *Thy sons, Edina, social, kind,*
> *With open arms the stranger hail;*
> *Their views enlarg'd, their liberal mind,*
> *Above the narrow, rural vale . . .*

with the lines on Edinburgh from the 'Epistle to William Simson':

> *My curse upon your whunstane hearts,*
> *Ye E'nbrugh gentry!*
> *The tythe o' what ye waste at cartes*
> *Wad stow'd his pantry!*

Burns may not have been knowingly hypocritical when he wrote the first; but what stands out is that when he was just performing dutifully, he took to English, and when he was writing from the whole of himself, he felt in Scots.

[1] On Anglicisation, see also below, Chapter VIII, note 4; Chapter IX, note 3.
[2] Lillian E. C. MacQueen, unpublished Ph.D. thesis (University of Edinburgh: 1957), *The Last Stages of the Older Literary Language of Scotland*: A Study of the Surviving Scottish Elements in Scottish Prose, 1700–1750, Especially of the Records, National and Local, pp. 291, 241.

It is, therefore, meaningful to say that these poets 'could not write English'—in the sense that Donne or Pope could. So that even if they could switch languages 'for a change' in their daily business, this still does not mean that the less accustomed dialect, English, could release and bring to definition the fullness of their experience. A rare explicit testimony to this is given in the biography of John Wilson already quoted:

> [It is] the common language of the country, in which he expresses himself with most ease and vivacity, and, clothed in which, his earliest and most distinct impressions always arise to his own mind. He uses a species of translation, which checks the versatility of fancy, and restrains the genuine and spontaneous flow of his conceptions.[1]

The creative employment of a language is thus a delicate thing, and it seems that it is a critical sense of what words do in poetry that best enables us to do it justice. On Scots usage in poetry Robert Fergusson's recent editor writes:

> For both Ramsay and Fergusson, therefore, their use of Scots was a symbolic act. It no more meant a rejection of English as a literary medium than their nationalism meant a denial of their British patriotism. It was like their Jacobitism, the most obviously available way of showing their feelings for the national past and of asserting the Scottish part of their inheritance. Fergusson most probably wrote the one-half of his poetry in Scots, more because it was the traditional language than because it was the more natural or more satisfactory medium to use.[2]

"Most probably"—but there is a body of admirable evidence on the matter, Fergusson's poetry, and it brings home that the poet's use of language works at a level deeper than the kind of superficial, conscious 'choice' and 'rejection' suggested by the reference to "British patriotism". Mr MacDiarmid is mistaking how expression arises in a poet's mind, the way in which his perceptions of what means most to him rise up into clear vision as they take on their right wording—wording supplied by the idiom in which alone they can become articulate. The inevitable rightness of Scots for what was most alive in Fergusson is apparent in countless touches, for example the beginning proper of 'Auld Reikie':

> *Now morn, with bonny purpie-smiles,*
> *Kisses the air-cock o' St Giles . . .*[3]

---

[1] John Leyden (ed.), *Scotish Descriptive Poems*, p. 14.
[2] *Poems*, ed. Matthew MacDiarmid, I, p. 139.   [3] *Ibid.* II, p. 109.

This is one of those places in poetry in which every suggestion seems to run together to create something immediately sensuous, beyond a set of words; and it is clear that in this case the coming-together takes place in the medium of a feeling innate in the vernacular, that buoyant familiarity, here enhanced by the rich colouring of the new day. Therefore, if it is true that "the vernacular had come to be considered as old language" and that the poetry of Ramsay and Fergusson was affected by an antiquarian tendency in using it,[1] nevertheless it is often strikingly evident in Fergusson's (and Ramsay's and Burns's) poetry that, whatever forms and styles they took over from English literature, it was Scots that welled up in them as the right medium, and the only right medium, for whatever they felt at a creative level.

When they were working at the top of their bent, the Scottish poets were no more proceeding by deliberate choice and rejection than was Joseph Conrad in writing in English rather than French. Conrad said that *"had I been under the necessity* of making a choice between the two, and though I knew French fairly well and was familiar with it from infancy, I would have been afraid to attempt expression in a language so perfectly 'crystallised'"; but he stresses that there was no deliberate choice: "it was I who was adopted by the genius of the language, which directly I came out of the stammering stage made me its own so completely that its very idioms I truly believe had a direct action on my temperament and fashioned my still plastic character . . . if I had not written in English I would not have written at all".[2] Conrad is describing a peculiar case— writing literature in a language wholly alien to that of one's native country. But his comment is not the less applicable to Scotsmen. For them, Augustan English must indeed have seemed too 'crystallised'; and if they had not written in Scots they would not have written at all—significantly.

We may now expand our idea of how far Scottish writers needed to be in touch with Scots to express their experience. Hugh MacDiarmid does well to insist that languages have their own fields of consciousness, "psychological qualities capable of, or requiring, under their superficial Anglicisation, expression in very different forms"—it is this which makes perfect translation impossible—and he goes on to say of Scotland: "Confinement to the English central streams becomes a sort of

[1] *Poems of Fergusson*, I, pp. 149-50.
[2] *A Personal Record* (edition London: 1919), pp. ix, x, xii.

self-infliction of an extensive spiritual and psychological blind-
ness . . . a struggle with media and traditions so radically un-
suited to their psychologies".[1] Probably the Scottish 'field of
consciousness' is less distinct from the English than MacDiarmid
(for flag-waving purposes) has to assume, and his idea must be
less close to actuality now than it may have been in the 18th
century. Yet it is valuable because it brings in that side of
language, its organic connection with the life of the speaker or
writer, which is ignored by absolute standards of what language
is 'best' for a people. Speech has its being in the mass of individuals who use it, with the run and stress, the direction, depth,
and force of feeling at work as they live out their kind of life.
The sounds and content of the language in which a speaker is
brought up will affect his psyche, will to some extent select
which elements in it become dominant. Similarly, a change in
his experience which begins as the imitation of sounds and
idioms not originally present in the speech familiar to him will
work back to affect the sources of his feelings. Speech can never
be a fixed standard, like the standard foot; it is a force of life in
action, alternately affecting and itself being played upon by
particular phases of experience.

   This side of language, then, must go to form our idea of what
is the 'best—the most expressive—language for a particular
people. Some writers have tried to lay down minimum qualities
for such a language. One historian, writing on the Scottish
courtiers of the 16th and 17th centuries who took to English for
its advantages in diplomacy and social life, says that "consciously or unconsciously, they turned towards English as the
more convenient, and it may be, the more perfect mode of
expression".[2] Miss Bald does not say what such a 'perfection'
might consist of; she merely argues back from the fact of a
social change, as did William Robertson and the first *Edinburgh
Review* in taking it for granted that cultural benefits would
accrue to Scotland from the Union.[3] More convincing is the
idea of a 'superior language' suggested by T. S. Eliot in the
epigraph to this chapter, which is the more persuasive in that
it has behind it his ideas of the quality of emotional life necessary
to poetry. At this point we need not either reject or accept his
idea that people can be 'taught to feel' in a new language, that
a true 'superseding' of a native tongue can take place. Here I

---

[1] 'The English Ascendancy in Scottish Literature' and 'The Case for Synthetic
Scots': *At the Sign of the Thistle*, pp. 28-9, 19, 195.
[2] Marjorie Bald, 'The Pioneers of Anglicised Speech in Scotland': *Scottish Historical Review* (Edinburgh: 1927), Vol. XXIV, p. 193.   [3] See pp. 54-5.

want rather to establish a kind of paradigm of thought on language which can be applied to Scotland.

Some other language (say, English) may have a 'wider and more refined range for feeling and thinking' than the native Scots. Scots, which at a certain period was the only natural expression for Scotsmen, may get displaced—not wiped out, but mixed and made intermittent. The new usage may enable a speaker to express *more*; but (at first anyway) it stresses feelings and thoughts other than those in his old range. Of course, if these elements of feeling and thought had been natural to the speaker previously, then his language would have been *different* (he would, perhaps, have belonged to a society whose literature gave expression to a greater range of the life lived there). *As it was*, however, Scotsmen belonged to a country without an extensive major literature—one, therefore, whose language was perhaps narrow-ranging and unrefined in Eliot's sense. Such a line of speculation verges at its next stage on specifically literary questions. Is it likely that writers of the superseded language will be able so to make the new language their own that what can be put in it is really felt by them? How much of their experience so harks back to the old speech for its full expression that it will only blunt itself or go underground when it comes up against the sounds, tones, vocabulary, and syntax of the new medium which has become most acceptable, or even obligatory, in the community of readers he now has to address?

When we are considering the significant 18th-century poetry in the light of these ideas, we must remember that the Scots used in it was not the language used for all purposes by everyone in the society, or even by the authors themselves. Its basis is almost wholly colloquial; for example it does not represent the whole usage of a widely-experienced man with a major say in the affairs of his country, and it also differs from the written usage of even the broadest speakers—the letters of the Carlyle parents, peasant folk born in the middle of the century, are not exactly Standard English, but neither are they transcripts of their own speech.[1] This is said not to disparage the dialect poetry but to underline the fact that the language favoured for creative purposes did not draw on the whole gamut of expression extant in the country. Yet when these writers were experiencing their subjects at first hand, it was some sort of Scots that they inclined to use; hence the language characteristics present

[1] See note 1.

in their poems do represent some traits of their ordinary usage.

We can see at once from the poetry of Burns, and of Ramsay, Fergusson, and the rest, that there existed a language strongly distinct from the one it most resembled, Standard English. This includes its total character as a medium which rose to the lips of someone deeply enough moved to want articulation. The distinctive nature of this language strikes one especially in syntax, for the relation between clauses and between the parts of a clause, especially the relations given in verbs, are mainly responsible for the movement—the flow onwards, if the poem does flow—of the whole meaning. Vocabulary is not difficult to piece together, as we see nowadays in the more synthetic verse of the Scottish Renaissance, because it is easy to compose in a language so akin to Scots as English is and then simply to put in some 'Scotsness' in the form of Scots synonyms for nouns, adjectives, etc. But transposition of syntax would demand alteration of the very basis of each sentence or unit of meaning, making a sharp difference in the run of the meaning, say in emphasis or tone. To think up a Scots synonym (or, strictly, near-synonym) may call for little revision of the language in which the English-speaking, would-be Scots poet normally expresses himself. Thus we have this from Sydney Goodsir Smith's 'My World in Nether Winter':

> *My world in nether winter is the sun*
> *Barred in a cell and dernit dull in yerth*
> *The cache is tint, the road unmapt*
> *And dumb wi babban-quaas its dule and rime—*
> *Sol is dowsit dim, deid not but hapt . . .*

or this from Maurice Lindsay's 'Munelicht':

> *Nichtirtale a siller net*
> *cast oot bi the mune*
> *dods upo the blirtie swaul*
> *affshore frae Dunoon,*

or this from Tom Scott's 'The Paschal Candill':

> *Thon leaman lowe wes seen*
> *Abuin the altar-claith and priest up-standan*
> *By callant and by queyn,*
> *Lyart carle and carlin,*
> *And purpour skugs fell back frae aa it shone on.*[1]

---

[1] *Honour'd Shade*, selected and edited by Norman MacCaig (Edinburgh & London: 1959), p. 121; *Modern Scottish Poetry*, ed. Maurice Lindsay (London: 1946), p. 129; *New Statesman & Nation* (London: 30.10.54).

The curious limping flatness of such verse—the lack of vital movement, or of real vividness for all the display of adjectives—feels as though it were due to piecing together sentences from words which are not second nature to the writers. "Dods upo the blirtie swaul", for example, would be even more obviously the very ordinary line that it is if it were written out as "Rocks upon the squally swell". It is not unfair to treat the line like this because the poet himself has had no thoroughly Scots language-forms working in his head; all he has done is to start from the usual, superficially fresh sea-description and Scotticise it by means of synonyms, perhaps from the dictionary, perhaps from memory, but not from his own habitual tongue.[1]

The 18th-century poets, as we can see, must have thought and felt quite differently from their 20th-century followers. Scots was the long-accustomed channel in which their thoughts ran, and departing from it would have meant, not just excising a few nouns and adjectives, but disrupting their whole syntax. This comes out even in Ramsay. We have seen what he was willing to do with Scots to exploit it for its folk colour. Yet for a part of him Scots was natural usage, and the poems which make up his significant work, for example the verse epistles, contain many instances of speech which is native through and through. The vernacular enables him to move at ease within stanza or couplet, and to get emphasis, say on the rhyme-word, when he wants it, as in the 'Epistle to Mr James Arbuckle':

> *They wha have never seen't are bissy*
> *To speer what like a carlie is he.*[2]

"What like" is simply brief (compared with 'what sort of a') and therefore convenient for the four-beat couplet; and "is he" (for English 'he is') enables the tripping light-ending. Similar easy brevity marks the epistles to Hamilton of Gilbertfield:

> *Ye'll quat your quill! that were ill-willy,*
> *Ye'll sing some mair yet nill ye will ye,*
> *O'er meikle haining wad but spill ye,*
> *And gar ye sour;*
> *Then up and war them a' yet, Willy,*
> *'Tis in your pow'r.*[3]

"Sour" used intransitively exemplifies the flexible grammar possible to such a poet when he is working at ease in his own dialect, and helps him with his informal style. Hamilton, of a higher social class than Ramsay, sometimes seems not at ease

---

[1] For Hugh MacDiarmid's *successful* use of non-spoken Scots see note 2.
[2] *Works*, III, p. 52.   [3] *Ibid.* p. 31.

in Scots (a Scots much fuller than the gentry used for their
Scottish songs), and he often writes what is really near-English
forced into Scots by means of single words; but he can also
write a Scots which is genuinely colloquial:

> *Tho', Sir, sae high ye compliment me*
> *Ye might deferred,*
> *For had ye but haff well a kent me,*
> *Some less wad ser'd.*[1]

The double auxiliary in the second last line—"had" plus "a"
—is not a mistake; it belongs to the looseness of speech, impro-
vising as it goes along. Fergusson, though controlling his Scots
as fluently as Ramsay, is less rich in points of Scots syntax; he
is also prone to slide into literary English even in his Scots
poems. Yet he too constantly gets effects by a free, rapid movement from point to point for which, we feel, he is released by
familiar usage, for example the rapid succession of principal
clauses, with their terse, off-hand effect, in

> *The day looks gash, toot aff your horn,*
> *Nor care yae strae about the morn.*

And a concentration into succinct couplets is got by the Scots
adjective-form in

> *Still making tight wi' tither steek,*
> *The tither hole, the tither eik,*
> *To bang the birr o' winter's anger,*
> *And had the hurdies out o' langer.*[2]

Such examples do little more than show the ordinary
naturalness or effectiveness which is possible to a writer working
in his native tongue. They do not show how a writer of powerful
originality might take to Scots as the right medium for his kind
of experience. What we have in Ramsay and Fergusson is the
minor writer helped past the anonymously literary or poetical
by access to a language which came naturally to him. Burns
does much more with Scots than that. John Speirs speaks of the
"irrepressible flow on" of the Kilmarnock-volume poems, and
shows how this flow is of the essence of their meaning, what
Burns stood for in his Scotland: "what is reasserted in Burns's
poetry (in the very rhythm of it, I mean) is a human normality
older than Calvinism. . . . The rhythm of Burns's poetry is never
essentially depressed."[3] Mr Speirs is suggesting that Burns's
native idiom "is itself almost poetry", in its concreteness, its

---

[1] *Works*, p. 33.   [2] *Poems*, II, p. 215.
[3] *The Scots Literary Tradition*, pp. 116, 136.

metaphors, and racy turns (p. 126). What I want to emphasise is rather Burns's sheer command of the whole body of his language, the accustomed turns of syntax, grammar, and the rest, which is what enables him to release his vitality into his writing. One can read hardly a stanza of his better work without feeling that one is responding to a distinctive *speech*, for example these lines from 'A Poet's Welcome to his Bastart Wean':

> *The mair they talk, I'm kent the better,*
> *E'en let them clash.*

Contemptuous self-assurance is got by the abrupt succession of clauses, and the off-hand confidence, scarcely bothering to meet the charge, by the free run of the long line, not worrying about any 'correct' order of adverb-verb, adverb-verb. In the first 'Epistle to Davie' winter is concentrated into the lines:

> *. . . winds frae aff Ben-Lomond blaw,*
> *An' bar the doors wi' drivin' snaw,*
> *An' hing us owre the ingle.*

The personification of the weather, made the subject even of the word "hing", is an ordinary poetic device, but it needs the imaginative agility possible to these poets only in their own language. So 'Death and Dr Hornbook' ends:

> *But just as he began to tell,*
> *The auld kirk-hammer strak the bell*
> *Some wee short hour ayont the* twal,
> *Which rais'd us baith:*
> *I took the way that pleas'd mysel,*
> *And sae did* Death.

The style is perfectly effortless and concise ("the *twal*", "rais'd us"), and it is also everywhere pointed with neatly-caught tones, for example the faintly ironic matter-of-factness of "And sae did *Death*". This writing has, in fact, the firm, emphatic rhythm and deftly-realised metaphor which we still notice in Scots-speakers whose dialect is perfectly sure of itself.

Burns is so good that ease of speech does more than supply an adequate basic style. In contrast to Ramsay and Fergusson, it concentrates even occasional pieces into intense poetry:

> *Had I to guid advice but harket,*
> *I might, by this, hae led a market,*
> *Or strutted in a bank and clarket*
> *My cash-account;*
> *While here, half-mad, half-fed, half-sarket,*
> *Is a' th' amount.*

('The Vision')

245

The poet, thinking freely in Scots, can render his whole situation in the form of actions (given in those verbs and verb-parts) which seem to act themselves out before us: "strutted in a bank". Generally, intensified speaking-idiom enables him to play upon his subject with an endless fusillade of invention, exuberantly playful or attacking from all angles in rapid succession, as in 'Tam o' Shanter':

> *That ilka melder wi' the miller,*
> *Thou sat as lang as thou had siller;*
> *That ev'ry naig was ca'd a shoe on*
> *The smith and thee gat roarin' fou on . . .*

> *They reel'd, they set, they cross'd, they cleekit,*
> *Till ilka carlin swat and reekit,*
> *And coost her duddies on the wark,*
> *And linket at it in her sark!*

Here the 'flow on' of the words, especially the momentum which seems to gather in "They reel'd, they set, they cross'd", is at one with the action. It is as though a writer whose speech habits were mainly colloquial, with little intervention of a printed standard, ran straight from speech through into poetry. This gives not only a physical kind of impetus; it is at the bottom of his very original idea of making over Kirk ceremonies into popular jollifications, as in 'The Holy Fair':

> *See, up he's got the word o' God,*
> *An' meek an' mim has view'd it,*
> *While 'Common-sense' has taen the road*
> *An' aff, an' up the Cowgate*
> *Fast, fast that day,*

or 'The Ordination':

> *Nae mair by 'Babel's streams' we'll weep,*
> *To think upon our 'Zion';*
> *And hing our fiddles up to sleep,*
> *Like baby-clouts a-dryin'!*
> *Come, screw the pegs wi' tunefu' cheep,*
> *And o'er the thairms be tryin';*
> *Oh, rare! to see our elbuck's wheep,*
> *And a' like lamb-tails flyin',*
> *Fu' fast this day!*

Spoken idiom can also create the variety of ironic tones through which Burns creates his most intelligent satire of self-righteousness and snobbery, notably in 'To a Louse', where the poet's mock complicity and almost sporting interest in the doings of

the wee parasite are defined by pointed switches of tone like those
of direct speech:

> Ha! whaur ye gaun, ye crowlin' ferlie?
> Your impudence protects you sairlie;
> I canna say but ye strunt rarely,
>   Owre gauze and lace;
> Tho' faith! I fear, ye dine but sparely
>   On sic a place. . . .
>
> I wadna been surpris'd to spy
> You on an auld wife's flannen toy;
> Or aiblins some bit duddie boy,
>   On's wyliecoat;
> But Miss's fine Lunardi! fye!
>   How daur ye do't?

Scots is by its nature fitted to express main virtues of Burns's
class, in all its downright conviction and directness, as we can
see in both the manner and the content of 'A Man's a man for
a' that', for example the abrupt emphases of the first stanza,
which ignore the tidy sequentiality of a written language:

> Is there for honest Poverty
>   That hings his head, an' a' that?
> The coward slave, we pass him by,
>   We dare be poor for a' that!

Such poetry is almost purely colloquial; it is much nearer the
Byron of *Don Juan* than even, say, the Pope of the 'Epistle to
Arbuthnot'. Much of it consists of a kind of dramatic mono-
logue, and even 'Tam o' Shanter' is strongest not in the narrative
parts but where Tam is addressed by the poet. Such poetry,
however, is colloquial not just to imitate a given class of speaker,
probably other than the writer's (as was Scott and Galt's way),
but because the colloquial is what arises naturally out of the
poet's experience. The poetic qualities it makes for—ease of
movement, directness, freedom to desert strict prose logic—are
qualities other than those we are most likely to acquire through
training in printed matter. They belong, of course, to other
dialects as well as the Scots. Adrian Bell writes of English
country speech in his essay 'English Tradition and Idiom':

Sustainedly, the emotional and muscular content of his [the
countryman's] idiom is almost equal to that of poetry, for he
possesses that same instinct by which the poet places words
in striking propinquity; the urgency of his feeling causing his
mind to leap intermediate associations, coining many a

'quaint' phrase, imaginatively just, though superficially bizarre. Local idiom is actually terse, inventing ellipses of its own.[1]

Burns so commanded such an idiom that its qualities themselves became the motive-force for poetry of rare intensity. Thus the ideal of free social intercourse, the absence of privilege and false dignity, implicit in 'To a Louse' *is* the ironic insouciance of the speech used; and the dual style of 'Holy Willie's Prayer' shows that bilingual usage, with the insincerity which it may let in, has been brought to consciousness by the poet as part of his subject-matter. Burns was limited, in the ways suggested in Chapter III. Yet his poetry—thought of as a whole—stands for a power of spontaneously frank, whole-hearted emotion such as, one imagines, only a basis in familiar speech could have embodied.

Now, the evidence is that Burns worked at what was in many ways an oral level, in his most considerable poetry just as much as in his songs. For example, he is said to have composed 'Tam o' Shanter' in his head. Mrs Burns told Cromek, the English folk-song collector, that her husband spent most of the day of composition on his favourite river walk; when she joined him in the afternoon,

> He was busily engaged *crooning to himsel*; and Mrs Burns, perceiving that her presence was an interruption, loitered behind with her little ones among the broom. Her attention was presently attracted by the strange and wild gesticulations of the bard, who now, at some distance, was agonised by an ungovernable access of joy. He was reciting very loud, and with the tears rolling down his cheeks, those animated verses which he had just conceived. . . .[2]

and the passage concerned was indeed the finest in the poem, "Now Tam, O Tam! had thae been queans, / A' plump and strapping in their teens!" Furthermore, it is clear from memoirs that Burns was an outstanding talker, and in a style very similar to that of his best poetry. Dugald Stewart wrote that "Nothing, perhaps, was more remarkable among his various attainments than the fluency, and precision, and originality of his language, when he spoke in company". Apparently this was not even in Scots, "as he aimed at purity in his turn of expression, and avoided, more successfully than most Scotchmen, the

---

[1] *Scrutiny* (1933), II, No. 1, p. 47.
[2] Lockhart, *Life of Burns*, p. 208 and n. 2.

peculiarities of Scottish phraseology".[1] That is, one sign of his genius with words was his ability to cut out of his speech the idiom of which he was the great master. Switching into English was of course typical of his time. Sir James Wilson points out that, as Scots has never had a stable written standard, "Even a Scotch reader of Burns's poems is apt to pronounce them as if they were a mixture of standard English and Scotch", and he suggests that "probably he [Burns] himself would make them more English in reading them to a refined Edinburgh audience than to his friends and cronies in central Ayrshire".[2]

It is clear, however, that Burns was not holding *himself* back in polite company. Stewart takes exception to his social manner rather as Jeffrey did to his poetic attitude to women; he found him lacking in "gentleness and accommodation", owing to his having been "accustomed to give law in the circle of his ordinary acquaintance" and to his "dread of anything approaching meanness or servility".[3] From some of the poems and letters one would indeed judge that this 'dread' of Burns's was an unsound thing, giving rise to rather shaky self-assertion and bravado; but the "decided and hard" manner Stewart disliked sounds like the natural attitude of the working-man, to whom it does not occur to speak in euphemisms and evasive social formulas.

It is equally significant that Stewart's account of Burns's social manner would apply as well to his poetry as to his speech:

> Among the subjects on which he was accustomed to dwell, the characters of the individuals with whom he happened to meet was plainly a favourite one. The remarks he made on them were always shrewd and pointed, though frequently inclining too much to sarcasm. . . . His wit was ready, and always impressed with the marks of a vigorous understanding; but to my taste, not often pleasing or happy.

Likewise a Dumfries school-teacher wrote in a letter that Burns's conversation "was playful or caustic by turns, following an allusion through all its windings; astonishing by its rapidity, or amusing by its wild originality, and grotesque, yet natural combinations".[4] That is the very kind of language which Robert Heron described as appealing to peasant readers in the poems. Such comments, like all the records of Burns's talk, and also of

[1] Currie (ed.), *Works of Burns,* I, p. 137.
[2] *Scottish Poems of Robert Burns in his Native Dialect* (Oxford: 1925), pp. 4, 6.
[3] *Op. cit.* p. 137.
[4] *Ibid.* p. 140; Peterkin, *Review of the Life of Burns (op. cit.),* p. lxxxvi.

Ramsay's and Fergusson's,[1] show that powers as a talker were specially useful to a poet who used the mainly colloquial Scots language for written work.

Stewart notes that Burns fell forwards not to be a servile peasant; and a woman who met him at a ball, apparently in Edinburgh in 1787, wrote of his speech that "It seemed as if he affected a rusticity or *landertness*".[2] These instances mark the dangers of inhibition and artificiality which were rife in that Scotland. Burns became aware of the writer's problems over language as soon as he began to work for a British (or English-dominated) market. Early in his exchanges with the song-editor Thomson, we find him pleading to be allowed "at least a sprinkling of our native tongue" in the words he wrote or arranged for traditional tunes; and two years later he wrote to the same man: "These English songs gravel me to death. I have not that command of the language that I have of my native tongue. In fact, I think that my ideas are more barren in English than in Scottish. I have been at 'Duncan Gray' to dress it in English, but all I can do is deplorably stupid."[3] Burns's awareness and diagnosis of the problem is thus complete; we could hardly have more direct evidence of the impediment suffered by a creative writer who has to work in a language foreign to him—even if it is one so akin to his own that the two may be classed as cognate dialects. Had Burns come a little later—say, in the age of fiction, when a staple of English had been set up in Scottish literature [4]—he might well have tried to succeed as one or other type of English versifier; and it seems certain that in that case his feelings would have been choked, misdirected, at a loss for the right wording as they rose to the point of articulation. That is to say, Scots was at that time deeply enough ingrained and distinctive enough in its forms, idioms, and rhythms to make a norm any lapse from which would tend to stop the writer short of creative expression.

We have seen that Scots in literature was being forced onto the narrowest possible ground, appearing mainly in imitations of speech. This is not by itself a critical judgement, but it marks

---

[1] See note 3.
[2] On this occasion he was perhaps drunk; the woman noted that "when he said the music was 'bonie, bonie', he spoke almost like a child" (Chambers-Wallace, *Burns*, II, p. 137).   [3] *Letters*, II, pp. 122, 268.
[4] This would also have meant that he was writing in an age when literature was becoming more and more exclusively printed and losing its direct communications with oral sources. The oral tradition in Scotland has, naturally, remained much more Scots than the printed.

the changes which were grounding themselves ever deeper in the country and were bound to act on the writer's media. Prose was overwhelmingly English, owing to official usage and to the supremacy of English literary prose, in the Authorised Version, in journalism (the periodical essayists and Scottish newspapers and magazines), and in the early novelists (Bunyan and the 18th century). The Scots prose writings which circulated in chapbooks, notably Dougal Graham's very popular tales, are written in the vernacular of the still broad-spoken lower classes. Much of the language in them is taken straight off speech, no printed standard intervening, and is thus a close transcript of contemporary spoken usage, down even to 'phonetic' spelling of the kind of Scots word-forms which were usually (e.g. in the Kilmarnock Burns) printed as though they were mistakes in Standard English.[1] 'The Ancient and Modern History of Buckhaven' (a fishing village in Fife) has spellings rendering the east-coast fisher dialect: 'tu' for 'you', 'dat' for 'that', 'ting' for 'thing'; and also forms which are found in most Scots dialects: 'a' for 'have' (cf. the more usual 'ha'' or 'hae') and 'it' for 'that' (cf. the more usual ''at'). The dialogue of this tale keeps close to a peasant speech whose rhythms, tones, forms, and vocabulary make up a medium quite distinct in character or whole physical entity from Standard English, for example:

> . . . it wada been four good bannocks and a scone, and a sair'd our Sunday's dinner, sae wad it een, but an ye keep a reeking house and a rocking cradle three eleven years as I hae done, less o' that will sair ye yet, baggity beast it tu is, mair it I bore thee now, a hear ye that my dow.[2]

Such writing, indeed, needs to be sounded to oneself if it is to be fully 'got'; and if the reader has rarely heard Scots spoken, it will help to give him a sense of it.

The narrative of tales such as 'Buckhaven' is not pure Scots; it usually wavers between Scots and English. (Some English forms may have been slipped in unconsciously by the compositor in later reprintings.) But the nearer it comes to the actions of Scots-speaking characters, or presentment of their attitudes and ways of thinking, the more Scots it gets. In fact the style of

[1] Scots would seem much more of a distinct tongue and less of an illiterately garbled dialect if it were printed, as it ought to be, with the Scots sounds and forms rendered straight and not punctuated as though they were lapses from correct English, e.g. in 'bidin' or 'bidan' (for 'biding') the 'g' is not elided through slovenliness; the Scots participle is in fact a distinct form.
[2] Graham, *Collected Writings* (*op. cit.*), II, pp. 213, 228.

Dougal Graham is largely colloquial. Narrative is never for long distanced from the characters themselves, and the narrator's style is, either as a convention or spontaneously, that of an oral story-teller, holding the attention of a crowd around him. 'The Young Coalman's Courtship to a Creel-wife's Daughter' begins:

> All you that's curious of Courtship, give attention to this History of Mary and her son Sawny, a young Coalman, who lived in the country a few miles from Edinburgh.
> Mary, his mither, was a gay hearty wife, had mair wantonness nor wealth; was twelve years a married wife, nine years a widow, and was very chaste in her behaviour, wi' her ain tale (for want of charging:) for a' this time of her widowhood, there was never a man got a kiss o' her lips, or laid a foul hand on her hind quarters.

Hence the style is able, in a primitive way, to keep close to the run of the action and the way the characters feel it:

> . . . well might ony body see there was a storm in Sawny's nose, light where it like; for no sooner had he sell'd his coals than he left his horse to come hame wi' a nibour callen, and gade keeking up the Cow-gate, and thro' the closes, seeking auld *Be-go* his good mither to be. . . .
> So Sawny came swaggering through a' the shell wives, but she was nae there, but coming down the town beneath the guard, meets auld *Be-go* just in the teeth, and crys, hey laddie my dow, how's your mither honest Mary? I thank you co' Sawny, she's meat-heal, and ay working some, how is a' at hame, is Kate and the laddie well? [1]

Thus the narrative style runs with little break into the dialogue which makes up most of such tales (the comic strips of their day). The characters being mostly peasant, of the labouring and crofting classes, the speech is very broad; but it is also differentiated into shades of Scots, English with Scots rhythm and idiom, and pure English for various higher classes—the minister, the justice, and the laird. Scots, however, predominates, and the idiom is especially suited to oral delivery, for example the alliteration accompanying the stringing together of proverbial tags, as in 'The History of John Cheap the Chapman' or 'Janet Clinker's Oration' (which oddly resembles *Piers Plowman*):

> But when she married she turns a madam, her mistress did not work much, and why should she! Her mother tell'd at she

[1] *Writings*, II, p. 53.

wad be a lady, but cou'd never show where her lands lay; but when money is all spent, credit broken, and conduct out of keeping, a wheen babling bubly bairns, crying piece minny, parich minny, the witless waster is at her wit's-end....[1]

Some of the conditions which made it possible for a literature so oral, and therefore so broad, to get into print appear in the little that is known of Graham himself. He had little education: according to Fraser his parents were too poor to send him to school, although MacGregor says "he had nothing beyond the common education of the time", which would mean at least a few terms off and on at a parish school in intervals of work for bread-and-butter.[2] (The same is said of Patrick Walker, the Edinburgh packman who wrote down lives of Covenanters early in the 18th century. And he too is unusually Scots in his narrative-style. In this he is partly echoing the usage of famous Covenanting ministers such as Cameron, Peden, and Renwick. His standard phrases and Covenanter rhetoric often alliterate ("hash and hag off", "pawky-witted primitive Trucklers"), as does Peden himself in the snatches of sermons, letters, and talk which Walker records: "And that Plough has, and will gang Simmer and Winter, Frost and Fresh-weather, till the World's End".[3]) Furthermore, Dougal Graham was a master of quick retort, droll or caustic, and acted as a kind of jester when working at his job of skellat bellman (advertising town-crier) in Glasgow. He also did his own printing, and it is possible that he composed straight into type.[4] So we see in these cases too the powers as a speaker which were necessary to bring forth prose-writing in Scots. Almost the whole weight of printed prose went to impose Standard English, and a strong impulse from the oral side was needed to break through that practice.

Thus the Scottish novel had, when it appeared, little basis of all-round Scots, and the vernacular appears in it mainly as imitation of lower-class speech. Indeed, by that time due rendering of the various shades of language spoken in the country was a natural part of any novelist's subject-matter, say in rendering relations between the classes. Language was a theme or problem in itself, and was often commented on by the novelists.[5] But when we put Burns side by side with Scott, we realise that language appears in concentration in poetry as it does not necessarily in fiction. "It is easier to think in a

---

[1] *Ibid.* p. 149.
[2] *Humorous Chapbooks of Scotland*, p. 157; Graham, *Writings*, I, p. 11.
[3] *Biographia Presbyteriana*, I, p. ix; pp. 51, 283, 287.
[4] Fraser, *Humorous Chapbooks*, pp. 191-2; 194.   [5] See note 4.

foreign language than it is to feel in it. Therefore no art is more stubbornly national than poetry." Hence it is futile to expect a *Scots* literature in the age of fiction—a point that has never been admitted, or even recognised, by Douglas Young and the other Scottish 'linguistic nationalists'. The distinctively native content of our literature since Burns has perforce had to take other than purely linguistic forms.

It is noticeable that Scott writes what are almost two separate languages, and he does not manage to give the one, English, what Beattie called a vernacular cast. Even in the strong part of *The Heart of Midlothian* he regularly puts in clumsy English glosses on what the dramatic Scots of the dialogue has already created to perfection: for example, in spite of Effie's songs and direct speech we have to be told that she is an "untaught child of nature, whose good and evil seemed to flow rather from impulse than from reflection". For all his fondness for swift actions and adventures, Scott never gets through to an easy-moving English style; he hobbles along by means of clichés and the intellectual vocabulary of 18th-century English. What his dual style exemplifies is the point made earlier, that a writer not a great originating talent may be helped to unusual intensity or sensitivity by writing in the dialect still familiar on the tongues of his countrymen. The significant part of the Bailie in *Rob Roy* consists almost wholly of masterly direct Scots, for example the conversation with Rob Roy in the tolbooth, with its shifts, second thoughts, and wavering from attitude to attitude:

> "Na, na," said Bailie Jarvie; "he's nane o' your great grandees o' chiefs, as they ca' them, neither; though he is weel born, and lineally descended frae auld Glenstrae. I ken his lineage: indeed he is a near kinsman, and, as I said, of gude gentle Hieland blude, though ye may think weel that I care little about nonsense; it's a' moonshine in water—waste threads and thrums, as we say; but I could show ye letters frae his father, that was the third aff Glenstrae, to my father Deacon Jarvie—peace be wi' his memory!—beginning, 'Dear Deacon', and ending, 'Your loving kinsman to command'. They were amaist a' about borrowed siller, sae the gude deacon, that's dead and gane, keepit them as documents and evidents. He was a carefu' man."

Scott can never hold our interest in this way from phrase to phrase when he is working in English; his English is ponderous stuff taken from books, devoid of natural life, whereas speech like the Bailie's has tone and nuance at every point. Scots, indeed, enables Scott to get through stagey trappings to life itself. Class-consciousness leads him into contortions of embarrassment when he is making, in *The Antiquary*, distanced English comments on the fisher-folk, the Mucklebackits (chapter 31 opens, "In the inside of the cottage was a scene which our Wilkie alone could have painted . . ."), but once he is into the direct speech of the fisher-folk themselves, the naturalness of the language asserts itself. After the drowning of the son, the antiquary says to the father, who is repairing his shattered boat on the beach:

> "I am glad," he said in a tone of sympathy—"I am glad, Saunders, that you feel yourself able to make this exertion."
> "And what would you have me to do," answered the fisher, gruffly, "unless I wanted to see four children starve, because ane is drowned? It's weel wi' you gentles, that can sit in the house with handkerchers at your een when ye lose a friend; but the like o' us maun to our wark again, if our hearts were beating as hard as my hammer."

Similarly Cuddie Headrigg in *Old Mortality* gives us more of a man's experience of civil war and battle, in his few spoken comments, than all the historical manœuvres and official heroes of the book, for example:

> "To be sure, it is no right to speak evil o' dignities. . . . But deil a dram, or kale, or ony thing else, no sae muckle as a cup o' cauld water, do thae lords at Edinburgh gie us; and yet they are heading and hanging amang us, and trailing us after thae blackguard troopers, and taking our goods and gear as if we were outlaws. I canna say I tak it kind at their hands."

And during and after Bothwell Bridge:

> "The head's taen aff them, as clean as I wad bite it aff a sybo!" rejoined Cuddie. "Eh, Lord! see how the broadswords are flashing! war's a fearsome thing. They'll be cunning that catches me at this wark again. But, for God's sake, sir, let us mak for some strength!"

The ordinary man's mixture of excitement and unashamed urge to escape is beautifully caught, as is the sensible-stoical tone of his final comment:

> "I fell into Claverhouse's party when I was seeking for some o' our ain folk to help ye out o' the hands of the Whigs, sae being atween the deil and the deep sea, I e'en thought it best to bring him on wi' me, for he'll be wearied wi' felling folk

the night, and the morn's a new day, and Lord Evandale awes ye a day in har'st; and Monmouth gies quarter, the dragoons tell me, for the asking. Sae haud up your heart, an' I'se warrant we'll a' do weel eneugh yet."[1]

Cuddie is what the Augustan critics (including Scott himself) called a 'boor', and he is certainly meant to be a figure of fun; yet that admirable simple actuality is typical of his speeches. Likewise Mrs Saddletree in *The Heart of Midlothian* is one of the racy chorus who supply the lighter side of the drama; yet her Scots comments regularly pierce to the core of the issues of right and conscience which are central to the novel, for example the dialogue which ends, "'Then, if the law makes murders, the law should be hanged for them; or if they wad hang a lawyer, the country wad find nae faut'", or her comments after Effie's trial and condemnation: "'It was a burning shame to see sae mony o' them set up yonder in their red gowns and black gowns, and a' to take the life o' a bit senseless lassie'".[2] These characters, with their natural speech, are disabused and direct, they are close to reality—a reality such as it is the novelist's duty to present.

Scott had (like Burns and Dougal Graham and the others) the exceptional powers of speech seemingly necessary if one was to use Scots successfully for literature. Cockburn, speaking of the popularity of Scott's talk, mentions "the bur in the throat . . . and the general plainness of appearance, with the Scotch accent and stories and sayings"; and Lockhart mentions that "he used many words in a sense which belonged to Scotland not to England, and the tone and accent remained broadly Scotch". "He had strong powers of mimicry—could talk with a peasant quite in his own style, and frequently in general society introduced rustic *patois*, northern, southern, or midland, with great truth and effect." The many examples of his Scots scattered through the *Life* show that it was indeed as much his own natural speech as a turn or performance.[3] Further, it seems that fluency in the vernacular was indispensable to the writing of his novels. Like Gorky, he had in him, though he was an educated man and professional writer, the talents and inclinations of a folk story-teller, that kind of prodigious memory and extempore fluency. On one occasion he

continued for an hour or more to walk backwards and forwards on the green, talking and laughing—he told us he

---

[1] Chaps. 14, 32, 33.   [2] Chaps. 5, 25.
[3] Cockburn, *Memorials*, pp. 267-8; *Life*, I, pp. 88-9; *ibid.* II, p. 174, III, p. 377, IV, pp. 171, 353, 365.

was sure he should make a hit in a Glasgow weaver, whom he would *ravel up with Rob*; and fairly outshone the Cobbler, in an extempore dialogue between the bailie and the cateran —something not unlike what the book [*Rob Roy*] gives us as passing in the Glasgow tolbooth.

That is to say, one of Scott's most significant scenes began as a piece of oral improvisation in the dialect; and he worked the same way in *Redgauntlet* and *St Ronan's Well*.[1] This will indeed have been almost a necessity, for such language survived almost wholly by word of mouth, and to get all the vivacious turns as in life he might well have to take it as it sprang to his lips.

Scott was, however, with his reading-public and his own mixed usage, committed to a staple of English—the medium of which he was *not* a master. Only in *The Heart of Midlothian* does he venture to make the central actions depend on Scots-speakers. *Rob Roy* has already been discussed. In *Old Mortality* the hero, supposedly a 17th-century laird in an outlying part of the south-west, speaks literary English. Touches of fidelity to the process of Anglicisation are perhaps meant by making Lady Margaret Bellenden speak English on public occasions and Scots to her servants (although she says "weel", "ain", and the like to Claverhouse); and at the torturing of MacBriar (chapter 36) the character of Lauderdale is admirably got through his kind of Scots—the gentleman unbending to his victims in a vulgar familiarity which expresses no real fellow-feeling. But the main events, for example the passages between Morton and Balfour, are acted out in literary English. *Redgauntlet* shows something like the complete variety of Scots which Scott used. In the famous 'Wandering Willie's Tale' (set in the 1690's) the laird speaks Scots; so does his son (who votes in Parliament for the Union), but when he becomes 'serious', he speaks stilted English.[2] In the novel proper (set in the reign of George III), Alan Fairford's father speaks an idiom in which, realistically enough, the lawyer's pedantries are Scots, but Alan —the hero—of course speaks pure, literary English. In chapter 10 the Provost of Dumfries speaks a thin Scots which is, like the elder Fairford's, a passable rendering of the speech likely in his social position. But the old Jacobite Summertrees speaks Scots only when delivering a racy set-piece (chapter 11); it abruptly thins into literary English when he comes to ordinary dialogue.

---

[1] *Life*, IV, p. 69; VI, p. 116.
[2] In fact members of the Union Parliament spoke quite broad Scots: see Ramsay of Ochtertyre in Currie (ed.), *Burns*, I, pp. 280-2.

In such usage, then, we have, not rendering of shades of real speech, consistently carried out, but a literary habit in which Scots may be taken up for favourite effects but is not felt to be feasible as the language of the hero or moral centre of a book. This is typical of the period. In Lockhart's *Adam Blair* the hero speaks English, although his elder colleague in the ministry speaks Scots. In the case of Hogg's *Justified Sinner*, Presbyterians of the late 17th century, such as Robert or his guardian, would certainly have spoken a tongue full of Scots—as does the laird, Robert's father; but Hogg makes them speak pure literary English, and we can sense that the thickest Scots in the book is grafted on as a kind of purple patch, for example the way in which the Auchtermuchty story is foisted into the main narrative.[1] Such writers, although their actual Scots practice is often masterly, are partly eroded by a feeling like that of the Anglicisers, Beattie, Pinkerton, and the rest, that Scots will not quite do for a 'serious' character, one supposed to feel deeply or meant to carry the moral weight of the book.

Not only Scottish authors show this (in effect snobbish) lapse from realism. Even Hardy, for example, does not use dialect consistently; he flinches from putting it in the mouth of figures meant to have the reader's fullest sympathy. Tess of the D'Urbervilles speaks literary English even to her dialect-speaking mates on the farms—she has to, for she is a full-blown heroine. That a realistic sense of working-class speech is a gauge of a novelist's intelligence we can see in George Eliot. She has no qualms in her presentment of dialect; it is just part of her general intelligent grasp of speech. She is specially interested in the logic and the often comic incongruities of ordinary usage; and this, along with her deep feeling for the lives of country-folk—deeply sympathetic, yet undisturbed by any sentimental investment in them or wishfulness about their way of life—enables her to keep dialect under control. In *Adam Bede* Mrs Poyser's speech is sometimes implausibly thick; but usually it is masterly in its use of an idiom which draws its rich material from the things such a woman knows and owns and works with: for example, her appreciation of her favourite minister:

"Pleasant! and what else did y'expect to find him but pleasant?" said Mrs Poyser, impatiently, resuming her knitting. "I should think his countenance *is* pleasant indeed! and him a gentleman born, and 's got a mother like a picter. You may go the country round, and not find such another

[1] See especially pp. 174-5 and 177-8.

woman turned sixty-six. It's summat-like to see such a man as that i' the desk of a Sunday! As I say to Poyser, it's like looking at a full crop o' wheat, or a pasture with a fine dairy o' cows in it; it makes you think the world's comfortable-like. But as for such creatures as you Methodisses run after, I'd as soon go to look at a lot o' bare-ribbed runts on a common."[1]

The life of the novel is not exclusively vested in such a style; it is just one of the author's resources. She can comment wittily on Mrs Poyser's "confidence in her own powers of exposition", and later she even analyses the Poyser speech through the mouths of other characters: "'Sharp! yes, her tongue is like a new-set razor. She's quite original in her talk, too; one of those untaught wits that help to stock a country with proverbs.'" George Eliot also comments, through the mouth of the 're-fained' inn-keeper, on the class-factors inseparable from speech:

"They're curious talkers i' this country, sir; the gentry's hard work to hunderstand 'em. I was brought up among the gentry, sir, an' got the turn o' their tongue when I was a bye. Why, what do you think the folks here say for 'heven't you?' —the gentry, you know, says, 'heven't you?'—well, the people about here says 'hanna yey'. It's what they call the dileck as is spoke hereabout, sir. That's what I've heard Squire Donnithorne say many a time; it's the dileck, says he."

George Eliot does not shrink from having a hero who speaks the 'dileck':

"Donna thee sit up, mother," said Adam, in a gentle tone. He had worked off his anger now, and whenever he wished to be especially kind to his mother, he fell into his strongest native accent and dialect, with which at other times his speech was less deeply tinged.[2]

Unfortunately Adam is not consistently interesting enough to show to the full what might be done in the way of casting in dialect a figure who is felt to be the height of awareness for the novel (this indeed very rarely happens in first-class literature[3]). But *Adam Bede* does in the main render dialect as the natural language of human beings who, if to some extent 'characters', are nevertheless human beings with whom we can feel full imaginative sympathy.

[1] Chap. 8.   [2] Chaps. 6, 33, 2, 4.
[3] One outstanding case where it is done successfully is Lawrence's *Lady Chatterley's Lover*: see note 5.

Characters from all classes should come into any considerable novelist's range; but if lower-class speech is so distinctive as to amount to a dialect, rendering of it is apt to tend to the virtuoso and away from the real. This is specially dangerous in the Scottish case because, as we have seen, such speakers were felt to be peculiarly national, embodiments of 'the real Scotland'. One of Scott's worst traits is fustian-romantic stylisation, and this occurs in the celebrated Scots of Meg Merrilies as well as in the (much worse) English fustian of *The Bride of Lammermoor*. Coleridge speaks of the "falsetto" of Meg Merrilies—thinking presumably of such passages as her premonition of ruin in chapter 53 of *Guy Mannering*: "'Do you see that blackit and broken end of a sheeling . . .'" Such things as this and Edie Ochiltree's vision of his death have often been admired for their 'universality', their moving evocation of fundamentals of life.[1] To my ear they are, rather, literary workings-up, through artificial rhythms and over-elaborated metaphors, of what is given with terse irony and truly grim juxtaposition of life and death in ballads such as 'The Twa Corbies', or in Scott's own 'Proud Maisie'. It is true that fidelity to usage is difficult to decide for certain; and there is a clue to such a 'high' style in real life in Stevenson's essay 'An Old Scots Gardener': "In boyhood, as he told me once, speaking in that tone that only actors and the old-fashioned common folk can use nowadays, his heart grew '*proud*' within him to see foxgloves".[2] In the 17th and 18th centuries the culture of countryfolk was still based on oral usage rather than printed matter, but their oral usage was affected by classic literature: poems in a high style such as the Middle Scots were known by heart, peasants could preach fluently and had the Bible by heart, and there were professional speakers (such as Wandering Willie and Edie themselves) who would perfect, like ballad-singers, certain tropes and styles of delivery more elaborate than ordinary speech. But the danger for someone of a later period, whose own usage is mixed, is that this high style will run away with him, and that he will not be able to conceive of such speakers as fully real, sharing in a normal society.

John Galt was a conscious advocate of Scots for creative uses; there is a postscript to *Ringan Gilhaize* which discusses the Scots available to the novelist and defends his own practice.[3]

---

[1] Coleridge, *Miscellaneous Criticism*, p. 329; Edwin Muir, *Essays on Literature and Society* (London: 1949), pp. 81-2.
[2] *Memories and Portraits*, p. 39.   [3] See note 6.

But his own virtuoso Scots resembles Ramsay's: he puts in vernacular gems for their own sake. Leddy Grippy, the 'character' of *The Entail*, is often no more than a vehicle for displays of language, for example:

> ". . . it's well-known, and I dinna misdoot ye hae found it to your cost, that she is a most unreasonable, narrow, contracted woman, and wi' a' her 'conomical throughgality—her direction-books to mak grosart-wine for deil-be-licket, and her Kate Fisher's cookery, whereby she would gar us trow she can mak' a fat-kail o' chucky-stanes and an auld horse-shoe—we a' ken, and ye ken, laird, warst o' a', that she flings away the peas, and maks her hotch-potch wi' the shawps, or, as the auld by-word says, tynes bottles gathering straes . . .
>
> ". . . So, if ye dinna like to tell your son to gang for a minister, I'll do it myself; and the sooner it's by-hand and awa', as the sang sings, the sooner we'll a' be in a situation to covenant and 'gree wi' Beenie's father. . . ."[1]

Here the points where Galt decides to lard on another Scots tag are actually visible. Scots idioms are piled up for their own sake and not to advance a natural drama of Scots-speaking people. Galt's manipulatory attitude to the language is unconsciously noted by Jennie Aberdein:

> Here are two directions in which he never doubted his skill: his power to make truthful and recognisable portraits, and his command of West Country Scots. Meddling with his work on these points he would not tolerate; they were to him the important matter, and a story was a mere peg on which to display them to the best advantage.[2]

Galt would hardly have turned to such exploitation of the language, in dissociation from the other sides of his fiction, if his own usage had been integrated, but of course he had had to Anglicise to get on and as a natural result of leaving his country. He was thus artificially distanced from the sources of his own experience, and Miss Aberdein even mentions a trip to Scotland (while *The Entail* was writing) to "add to his Scots vocabulary".[3]

Galt's Scots is at its best where he attempts to make of it his very medium. In *The Annals* and *The Provost*, the first, fresh output of his native inspiration, and in the later sketches, *The Betheral* and *The Howdie*, he makes up a kind of Scoto-English

[1] Galt, *Works*, ed. Meldrum (*op. cit.*), *The Entail*, II, pp. 128-9.
[2] *John Galt*, (London: 1936), p. 97.   [3] *Ibid.* p. 117.

which creates something no other usage could have managed. In *The Annals* the English of the Bible and the pulpit, the doublets (Latinate plus Saxon or Scots) of legal usage, and the Scots of the country mingle in the minister's style, suggesting both his background and character and the naïve provincial self-importance which Galt always shows us as belonging to such people. For example, a diluted religious sense of the brittleness of worldly things is shown to be inseparable in the Moderate minister from ordinary canniness ("'he was a carefu' man'"):

> At the time of the stoppage, however [of the mill], we saw that commercial prosperity, flush as it might be, was but a perishable commodity, and from thence, both by public discourse and private exhortation, I have recommended to the workmen to lay up something for a reverse; and showed that, by doing with their bawbees and pennies what the great do with their pounds, they might in time get a pose to help them in the day of need.[1]

In *The Provost* this Scoto-English evokes a community dominated by trade and law, its self-respect and self-righteousness based on the Bible and the morality inherited from Presbyterianism. The provost speaks, even of his own ambitions and manœuvres, as though he were the people's appointed shepherd rather than their temporary, elected representative:

> I did not secede from the council. . . . In a word, I was persuaded that I had, at times, carried things a little too highly, and that I had the adversary of a rebellious feeling in the minds and hearts of the corporation against me. . . . But the matter which did most service to me at this time was a rank piece of idolatry towards my lord, on the part of Bailie M'Lucre, who had again got himself most sickerly installed in the guildry. . . .[2]

Galt's language is not broad; indeed, it imitates the rather stilted, Latinate English such as is still typical of Scotsmen (rather than of Englishmen) as much as it imitates the vernacular. In this idiom his perceptions are concentrated as they never are in Standard English. Touches in *The Betheral* suggest sharply another typical attitude to the 'worldly', the close watch kept by the village on anything new or independent, for example: "And certainly, when she was seen to shoot out her horns in the shape of a new bonnet on Sunday, there was an expectation.

[1] *Op. cit.* p. 267. [2] *Op. cit.* I, p. 75.

But when the bairn died of a kinkhost, there was the end of all her bravery."[1] The grim piety common among the people is caught perfectly in many touches there and in *The Howdie*, for example, "the generality of the people being mediocres, and more given to see what a shilling is made of, than to sing anthems", which recalls what T. F. Powys made of the language of English puritanism; or this: "Home with you said Nanse, ye mud that you are, to think yourself on a par with pipeclay, with other hetradox brags, that were just a sport to hear".[2] Here his language moves incisively where his English would sprawl and hobble.

At the same time, using Scots as a medium has grave drawbacks; it was bound to, as it was no longer the all-round usage of anyone engaged in serious literary work. The *personae* whom the author must use as the consciousness of his fiction are so limited, or backward, or absurd, that we can't help feeling amused *at* them—we are meant to. The limitation put upon *The Annals* by the *persona* of the Rev. Micah Balwhidder has been discussed already. Such diminishing of life is the rule in Scottish fiction cast in a medium less than the author's whole usage. Mrs Oliphant's *Margaret Maitland* is told as though by a pious old woman. One passage in which she recalls her brother's first sermon runs:

> But when Claud lifted up his head in the pulpit, and preached his first sermon on the grand text, "Who is He that cometh from Edom, with dyed garments from Bozrah?", there was a glance from below his brow that shot into your heart. I had near said it was a proud day for us, that day that Claud preached his first sermon, and truly it is not to be denied that carnal pride is ill to mortify. . . .[3]

Here the actual use in life of the old Kirk idiom is not brought home to us, for such phrases as "carnal pride" merely hit off the famous clichés of the subject, they do not take us deeper into the moral preoccupations they are meant to represent. And as the life in the novel is wholly enclosed in the mentality of the God-fearing old woman, no other kind of experience can be brought up against it; simple-minded piety remains the sum of what is presented.

A vernacular need not subdue an author's fullness of life, if cultural conditions are satisfactory. In *Huckleberry Finn*, for

[1] *Literary Life and Miscellanies*, III, p. 55.
[2] *The Betheral*, p. 80; *The Howdie: Tait's Magazine* (1832), VI, p. 709.
[3] Margaret Oliphant, *Margaret Maitland of Sunnyside*, Written by Herself (London: n.d.—1st ed., 1849), pp. 7-8.

example, there is no simply-established suggestion that the author and reader are all the time a level above the hero, the uneducated lad who has never before ventured out of his district. Huck has, indeed, live qualities which constitute values in themselves, for example his perfectly shrewd, unawed attitude to the patrician Grangerfords—whose pride of caste and military distinction, it is suggested by means of Huck, run too much to insane feuds, and whose 'sensibility' is the morbid soulfulness of the daughter, with her tearful verses and paintings and scrapbook of "patient sufferings". I say Huck's "live qualities" because his spoken idiom, which is the medium of the novel, is felt to be a wholly contemporary language, bubbling up with endless resources of humour and first-hand knowledge, as did Burns's. In comparison with the Scots novelists, Mark Twain transcends the 'limitations' of an unsophisticated vernacular by means of the subtlety of genius which is really an extra insight into all there is to life. Though Huck is 'limited', still, whenever his innocence or acceptance of some value we know to be limited is being shown, some twist adverts us that the natural shrewdness of the boy is even stronger than he knows himself:

> Col. Grangerford was a gentleman, you see. He was a gentleman all over, and so was his family. He was well born, as the saying is, and that's worth as much in a man as it is in a horse, so the Widow Douglas said, and nobody ever denied that she was of the first aristocracy in our town; and pap he always said it, too, though he warn't no more quality than a mud-cat, himself.

There is no need to analyse the double-edged suggestions there, or the way in which each successive phrase further deflates the opening notion; the whole book consists of such rich, many-sided humorous irony. And this works in with one of its most serious themes, the colour question. At first Huck just accepts the white, property-owning attitude to the negro, not for a moment conceiving that the slave is a human being:

> Jim talked out loud all the time while I was talking to myself. He was saying how the first thing he would do when he got to a free State he would go to saving up money and never spend a single cent, and when he got enough he would buy his wife, which was owned on a farm close to where Miss Watson lived; and then they would both work to buy the two children, and if their master wouldn't sell them, they'd get an Ab'litionist to go and steal them.

It most froze me to hear such talk. He wouldn't ever dared to talk such talk in his life before. Just see what a difference it made in him the minute he judged he was about free. It was according to the old saying, 'Give a nigger an inch and he'll take an ell'. Thinks I, this is what comes of my not thinking. Here was this nigger which I had as good as helped to run away, coming right out flat-footed and saying he would steal his children—children that belonged to a man I didn't even know; a man that hadn't ever done me no harm.[1]

Here the reader may realise that Huck is bounded by an outlook he himself is free of; but his response is not superior amusement, it is to realise the more deeply how unconscious inhumanity can be. Thus Mark Twain manages an unsophisticated—but not unsubtle—idiom so that it helps to convey a profound moral theme. The treatment of colour in *Huckleberry Finn* is, it seems to me, more penetrating and more equal to the complexity of the problem from life than the rather contrived formula of the substituted babies in his *Pudd'nhead Wilson*, told in 'good English'.

Throughout his work we can see that he has the advantage not only of literary genius but of being able to feel his 'Americanness' as live experience, not something congealed in the past. Scots was, of course, still alive, and as distinct from Standard English as the American dialects; the Scottish National Dictionary now being compiled has to record about 50,000 Scots words in use since the early 18th century. But a language depends on the state of mind of its speakers as well as on its repertoire of words, and that 'national self-consciousness' whose development has been traced already seems to have made against the use of Scots as a medium in its own right.

We have seen that anyone writing during this period was harassed all round by the mixed nature of the usage amidst which he lived and the assumptions and expectations it set up in the public. Scots was still strong enough to be present, at least at the back of the mind, as a medium from which one might have to translate or into which one might slip. And English had to be held at the front of the mind as the proper usage, deviations from which came in for peculiarly close attention. We can see that the stress would be worse than for a writer from the English provinces, because in Scotland there

[1] *Tom Sawyer* and *Huckleberry Finn* (Everyman ed., London: 1944), pp. 271-3, 274, 260.

was the awareness of having had, not long ago, a self-contained nation with a language much more distinctive than the English regional vernaculars in its literary uses and in vocabulary, syntax, and (specially important for their immediate physical sensations) in sound and cadence. Thus while Wordsworth's Cumberland upbringing will have helped him to recognise that the Augustan staple had to be broken down by recourse to the speech of countryfolk (in which "the essential passions of the heart . . . are less under restraint, and speak a plainer and more emphatic language"), yet he did also have, to give him something to push against, the broad mass of previous poetry in English. He also could have less inhibition about taking up common speech than Scots writers, for English vernaculars, belonging to an ascendant nation, had never come in for the acutely self-conscious criticism and grooming-away which the Scots had applied to their own speech. It is true that there were cases such as that of the man from the North Riding of Yorkshire, in the 1860's, who was intended for the local grammar school because the family could afford only one son at Eton. Coal was discovered on the estate, the younger son too was sent away to school, and "He had to begin by *learning English* in place of the North Riding dialect which was his native speech" (my italics).[1] Yet the tensions and falsities which must have spread over English society as a result of such centralisation and the monstrous regiment of the public schools seems almost unheard-of in the literature, presumably because Englishmen had no consciousness of an old *national* habit being lapsed away from.

Now, a Scotsman may often have been able to switch usages simply 'for a change', in Miss MacQueen's words, and as she further said, he may well have had no difficulty (especially as late as our period) in speaking correctly and making himself understood. Yet this does not cover the whole speech-experience involved in using a language creatively—in the effort to be as faithful as possible to one's deeper personal experience. A standard taken over, as contemporary writers again and again insisted,[2] more from books than from living would tend to act as a line to be toed, the author keeping his inward eye on that instead of being able (in Lawrence's phrase) to 'yield to the perfectest suggestion from within'. To apply another idea of his, there is nothing deadlier for a writer than 'emotional self-

[1] G. M. Young, *Victorian England: Portrait of an Age* (London: 1936), p. 96, n.
[2] E.g. Ramsay, *Scotland and Scotsmen*, I, p. 168; Beattie, in Forbes, *Life and Writings of Beattie*, II, pp. 16-17; William Craig, *The Mirror (op. cit.)*, III, pp. 72, 74-5.

consciousness': "any form of emotional self-consciousness hinders a first-rate artist: though it may help the second-rate";[1] and everyone knows how checking and putting-on the sounds we make in speech can work back to the roots of our feelings. May it not be that the flow of unself-conscious perceptions vital to the writer was liable to be stopped or distorted deep down by the imposed unfamiliar usage?

Finally there is no way of telling whether or not potential literary powers have been repressed in Scotland. But there are outstanding facts to account for. The Scottish part of Britain yielded no poetry of significance (or even interest) between Burns (1796) and MacDiarmid (1925); and serious novels about this part of the country were warped by provinciality soon after they began to appear in force and have been few and far between ever since. Such a dearth is not unlike other phases in the Scots literary tradition, but with the difference that this period, which is one of serious, conscious falling-away from the language, is also a period of abortive talent—the deficiencies and tailings-off in Burns and Scott and Galt, as compared with (say) the solid achievement of the Middle-Scots poets. Carlyle, discussing Jeffrey's speech, thinks he detects in it an unfulfilled talent:

> I used to find in him a finer talent than any he has evidenced in writing: this was chiefly when he got to speak Scotch, and gave me anecdotes of old Scotch *Braxfields*, and vernacular (often enough, but not always, *cynical*) curiosities of that type ... I used to think to myself, "Here is a man whom they have kneaded into the shape of an *Edinburgh Reviewer*, and clothed the soul of in Whig formulas, and blue-and-yellow; but he might have been a beautiful Goldoni, too, or something better in that kind, and have given us beautiful Comedies, and aerial pictures, true and poetic, of Human Life in afar other way![2]

Even allowing for Carlyle's usual curmudgeonly biases, we do seem to glimpse here a Scots kind of talent in the very act of being moved off rendering the native life, because the idiom this would need is losing status, becoming no more than the medium for funny stories. Carlyle himself, the most important talent of Scottish origin working around 1850, seems to show some wrongness of development, for his prose is not that of one native to English (which his parents wrote with difficulty), nor is it anything else native. His inability to be straightforward,

---

[1] *Phoenix*, ed. Edward D. Macdonald (London: 1936), pp. 671, 248.
[2] *Reminiscences*, p. 340. "Blue-and-yellow" were the colours of the *Review's* cover.

his contorted syntax (which yet is trying to follow thought and speech), the air his prose has of being fabricated from a mixture of roots (colloquial, German, Biblical English) all suggest that he has no secure basis in any speech.

To put it positively, a poet needs (as Burns shows) the effortless run of idiom, the natural rhythm and profusion of turns of phrase, which he is hard put to it to get, as he needs them, from an unfamiliar tongue. As late as the present day, this is still so for some Scottish writers. Our only significant living writer, Hugh MacDiarmid, has written as finely in English as in the Scots of which he has (or had) such mastery; yet his English is often fabricated from clichés, as in the superb 'Lo! A Child is Born' from *Second Hymn to Lenin*. It ends:

A strategic mind already, seeking the best way
To present himself to life, and at last, resolved,
Springing into history quivering like a fish,
Dropping into the world like a ripe fruit in due time.—
But where is the Past to which Time, smiling through her tears
At her new-born son, can turn crying: "I love you"?

MacDiarmid's Scottishness is so integral to the man that his English is not an easy taking-over of some current style, it is an idiom which, in its perfect seriousness—unmannered, with little flexibility of tone—represents the effort of someone who is (in his case, unlike so many Scotsmen, to good effect) not at ease in the foreign tongue.

Fiction need not use language in such concentration as poetry. Yet fidelity to different usages is indispensable in fiction which, for example, presents differences in class; and the importance of a vernacular element is demonstrated by much of major English fiction—Dickens, George Eliot, Hardy, Lawrence, Powys. We know that Scots of various degrees was on the tongues of millions of people in the 19th century; yet, as used by novelists, it had set into stock raciness at the start, and it later even became—for example, in D. M. Moir's *Mansie Wauch* (1828), in William Alexander's *Johnny Gibb of Gushetneuk* (1871), and in W.P. Milne's *Eppie Elrick* (1955)—the subject of specialised rendering. These novels are written to exhibit 'good Scots' for its own sake, aside from serious life-interests of which speech would be only one aspect.

At the same time there was, during these decades following the intensified Anglicisation detailed already, no writer in Scotland who saw life whole. Apparently there have recently been forces keeping Scottish minds from developing for their part of the world the artist's concern with humanity which is so plenteous in fictions such as the Russian, the American, and the English. Clearly, inhibitions about language will not be the only force making against that kind of articulateness; but in Scotland the shrinking of distinctive speech has, demonstrably, accompanied not only difficulties in using that speech seriously but lack of general intelligent interest in this part of the world. For why should it be that a nation so alive and various as Scotland was figured to the world at the turn of last century through *Punch*'s jokes about golf caddies, ministers, and gawky housemaids, the soft-headed ruralising fiction of the Barrie-MacLaren school, and the century-old genius Burns?

This state of affairs, however, can hardly be permanent. Indeed, the shrinking of Scots is clearly a phase in the development throughout the United Kingdom towards a more or less standardised English. We may surmise that it will take acceptance of our language change, put into practice in a realistic fiction—rather than a poetry which attempts to keep Scots as its whole medium—to put Scottish literature on a sound basis again. Language habits are not something which can be legislated for. It is true that in the last century there have been examples of languages built up synthetically from colloquial or ancient roots, and catching on securely—*landsmaal* in Norway, Hebrew in Israel. At present in Ceylon linguists are preparing to equip Sinhalese with words which the language requires if it is to be equal to modern education and technology; and authorities are disputing as to which Sinhalese—colloquial or written-scholarly—should be decided on as the national medium. But in all these cases the initiative and the solid social basis for the change have been socio-political (the setting up of an independent state), rather than literary. Furthermore, there is no natural law, or overwhelming likelihood, that a separate nation must have its separate language: America has not required it, and Ibsen became Norway's literary hero although he wrote almost pure Danish. In these circumstances, to entertain the idea of establishing synthetic Scots seems no more than a hobby, a piece of wishful thinking, or a substitute for seriously effective political interests. Thus it seems to me right that people in Scotland should be concerned that the speech of all classes in their society should contribute to their literature, but wrong—a wasteful delusion—to treat Scots as a *sine qua non*, or a guarantee, of adequate native literary achievement.

PART IV

CONCLUSION

CHAPTER IX

Emigration

IN the mid-19th century the Scottish literary tradition—the writing by Scotsmen of fiction and poetry of more than parochial interest—paused; from 1825 to 1880 there is next to nothing worth attention. This was also a period of heavy emigration—a landslide of people away from Scottish soil. It seems, *prima facie*, likely that the literary break was connected somehow with the social force which was then bursting in on thousands upon thousands of Scottish lives. The loss of a high proportion of the most vigorous men and women to countries abroad has been a sore problem to the Scottish people for nearly three centuries. Only in this century, following the changes of mind due to regular census-taking, for example, and belief in government planning and subsidy, have attempts been begun on anything like the large scale necessary to improve the livelihood in the home country which is the basis of the problem: for example, by subsidising transport in the Highlands and Islands, by beginning the revision of farm tenure in the crofting areas and direction of industry from the British centres into Scotland. As it is Scotland loses about 22,000 people annually by emigration—many of them the most able-bodied, in the 25-35 age-group. According to the most recent authority the net loss by migration from 1861–1951 was 1,585,000 people, or 43 per cent of the natural increase. This ruinous phenomenon is fairly recent, and it has fallen unusually heavily on Scotland. From the Union to 1801 Scotland and England were increasing their population at an approximately equal rate; but whereas at the Union Scotland had about one-fifth the population of England and Wales, she now has about one-ninth.[1] The records show how severely this bleeding process affected the country towards the end of the period covered by this book. Between 1841 and 1851 about 50,000 Scotsmen went to England, whereas only about 17,000 Englishmen came to Scotland; and Marx shows in his article of 1853, 'Forced Emigration', that four-fifths of the total current emigration from the United Kingdom (excluding

[1] D. J. Robertson, 'Population Growth and Movement': A. S. Cairncross (ed.), *The Scottish Economy* (Cambridge: 1954), pp. 9, 13.

Wales) was from Scotland and Ireland.[1] It seems that about 52 per cent of the (mainly Highland) emigrants of the earlier 19th century were aged 20-35; and several examples show that outstanding practical talent was being creamed off, for example farmers who could instruct the growing colonies in new methods of agriculture, and 'mechanics', i.e. skilled industrial workers.[2] Both Macdonald and the most recent writer on emigration are agreed that perennial, grinding poverty was the main cause of mass emigration. "The movement which inevitably resulted [from turning arable farms into sheep pasture] was quite unorganised. . . . Frequently, no provision was made for the displaced tenants, who had to choose between migration to the Lowland towns and emigration, usually to North America." This choice was usually made according to the capital at the victims' disposal; it was said that people from the Western Highlands went to America if they had "spirit or wealth", to the Scottish Lowlands "if they be poor".[3]

> Glen after glen had been turned into sheep-walks, and the cottages in which generations of gallant Highlanders had lived and died were unroofed, their torn walls and gables left standing like mourners beside the grave, and the little plots of garden or of cultivated enclosure allowed to merge into the moorland pasture.[4]

The author of *Colonists from Scotland* says that "At no time before the Peace of Paris did 'depopulation' alarm the Scottish gentry as it did after that event", when it truly became 'mass migration'.[5] Even at the turn of the 17th and 18th centuries, however, there had been leading Scotsmen who were worried about emigration. Clerk of Penicuik, the Union Commissioner, wrote in a dispatch on the Union that thousands of Scotsmen in England might return if they thought there was a livelihood for them but that the exodus of the landowners to London after the Union might scare them off by depressing employment on the land.[6] Andrew Fletcher of Saltoun, the fervid

[1] Donald F. Macdonald, *Scotland's Shifting Population, 1770–1850* (Glasgow: 1937), p. 9; Marx and Engels, *On Britain*, p. 372.
[2] Macdonald, pp. 150, 151-2.
[3] Macdonald, pp. 37-8; I. C. C. Graham, *Colonists from Scotland*: Emigration to North America, 1707–1783 (Cornell University Press: 1956), p. 4.
[4] Donald Macleod, *Farewell to Fiunary* (1882): quoted by Alexander Mackenzie, *The History of the Highland Clearances* (Glasgow: 2nd ed., 1946), p. 236.
[5] *Op. cit.* pp. 185-9.
[6] *A Letter To A Friend Giving An Account of How the Treaty of Union Has Been Received Here* (with some remarks on what has been written by Mr Hodges and Mr Ridpath), attributed to Clerk in his *Memoirs* (*op. cit.*), p. 244: *Letter*, pp. 17-18.

anti-Unionist M.P., who made one of the earliest estimates of the number of unemployed poor in Scotland, looked to the return of *émigrés* as one of the great benefits that would follow from a more settled state in the country.[1] At the turn of the 18th and 19th centuries, the *literati* showed a like concern. Francis Horner, the economist, reviewing (in the first number of the *Edinburgh*) a book by a Rannoch minister on the causes and effects of emigration from the Highlands and Islands, points out that the problem affects all districts of the country, not just the Highlands, and is due to difficulties in industry as well as on the land.[2] Thomas Chalmers, the minister, corresponded with Wilberforce about the Emigration Societies. He was concerned that the government should have granted land in Canada and thus raised hopes when there was still no money to pay for passages to America. His sermon in aid of a parish collection to help emigrants discourages emigration but hopes that money will be forthcoming to help people already committed to leaving the country. Chalmers is plainly right in thinking that getting rid of a few poor people will not "have any great effect, economically speaking, on the state of matters here". But his own position is shamefully *laissez-faire*—the government, he says, should not 'interfere' in any way with the economics of the country "save for the purpose of a revenue to itself", and when sermonising all he can recommend is humble resignation to one's lot.[3] *Laissez-faire* plus 'Christian' resignation was of course what had opened the running sore of emigration in the first place. A few years later Thomas Carlyle at least shows the influence of the growing movement for social legislation. In *Sartor Resartus* he ends a Swiftian passage on 'overpopulation' ("Perhaps in the most thickly-peopled country, some three days annually might suffice to shoot all the able-bodied Paupers that had accumulated within the year. . . . Have them salted and barrelled") with the suggestion that the unemployed should be given the virgin areas of the earth to cultivate; and in *Past and Present* he helpfully proposes an 'Emigration Service' for that end.[4]

Such emigration affected literature directly in depriving the country of writer after writer. It also worked more insidiously

[1] *Political Works (op. cit.)*, pp. 68, 75.
[2] *Edinburgh Review* (1802), I, No. 1, pp. 61-3.
[3] Rev. William Hanna, *Memoirs of the Life and Writings of Thomas Chalmers* (Edinburgh: 1850), I, pp. 258-60, 522-7.
[4] *Sartor Resartus* (bound with *Lectures on Heroes, Past and Present*, and *Chartism*: London, n.d.), p. 141; *ibid.*, pp. 278-9.

CONCLUSION

and pervasively by helping foster the nostalgia which has un-
manned much of Scottish writing since the 18th century.

During the 19th century the country was emptied of the
majority of its notable literary talents—men who, if they had
stayed, might have thought to mediate their wisdom through
the rendering of specifically Scottish experience. Of the leading
British 'sages' of the time an astonishingly high proportion were
of Scottish extraction—the Mills, Macaulay, Carlyle, Ruskin,
Gladstone. That is, if the balance of power in Britain had been
different, there would not have been the movement of population which carried along with it the intelligentsia as well as
those whom the ruling-class were ready to regard as 'redundant
population' (in the standard callous phrase of the time).
During the 18th century the Scottish intelligentsia were so
frequently in England that they came to have their set resorts.
The British Coffee-house in London, kept by a sister of Bishop
Douglas (one of a number of Episcopal *émigrés*), was the
meeting-place of such men as William Hunter, the surgeon,
John Home, the dramatist, Robert Adam, the architect, and
Gilbert Elliot, the politician, and of Adam Smith, Alexander
Carlyle, and William Robertson when they were in the south.[1]
Edinburgh was losing its snug self-sufficiency as a milieu: Cock-
burn observes that about the end of 1802 the "delightful
brotherhood" of Edinburgh intellectual lights began to be
"thinned by emigration". Within two years Francis Horner,
Thomas Campbell, John Leyden, and Sydney Smith all left,
mostly for London, Leyden for the Far East.[2]

It is necessary to concentrate on authors and men of letters;
but a word on the variety of talent that was sucked out of the
country will suggest the scope of the process. During this
period Scotland lost the painters William Aikman, Allan
Ramsay (the poet's son), David Allan (for a time), Gavin and
William Hamilton, Jacob More, and David Wilkie; Gillray
the cartoonist; the architects James Gibb, the Adam brothers,
James Stuart, and Robert Mylne; Telford the engineer;
William and John Hunter the surgeons and anatomists; and
Horner the economist.[3] We also came within an ace of losing
William Robertson, Adam Smith, Hume, Henry Mackenzie,
Burns, William Chambers, John Leslie the scientist, Jeffrey,
and Thomas Chalmers.[4] We lost quantities of first-rate practical

[1] Rae, *Life of Adam Smith*, p. 267.   [2] *Memorials*, p. 176.
[3] The details of the many emigrants mentioned in this paragraph would be
unwieldy in the text, and have therefore been put into the Notes at the end:
see note 1.   [4] See note 2.

men, for example gardeners and farm bailiffs.[1] In the case of the artists especially, travel, apprenticeship, and study somewhere abroad were indispensable. The evil for Scotland was that an artist who passed through London on his way to the Continent, or found patrons in England, was apt to stay away from his country for good. As in these and many other cases, we see that emigration was made the less of a wrench by the fact that Scotsmen already settled in London formed a beachhead for later emigrants; thus the process gained momentum as it went on.

How inferior was Scotland's socio-political position is shown by the fact that in response to the Union, young men intended for ruling-class careers were sent to school in England to learn the polished English without which, it was thought, they could not get to the top.[2] We know today how much it is the rule for such men to be sent either south or to one of the Scottish branches of Eton. At that time, however, it was still rather exceptional, and the majority of the men who rose to the top in the professions or as rulers were content with the education at the Scottish grammar and other schools and the universities.[3]

Some traffic abroad was of course a natural condition of belonging to Europe. Such men as Boswell, Adam Smith, Francis Jeffrey, Lockhart, William Hunter, and Bishop Douglas took advantage of the higher education to be had abroad.[4] Furthermore, this traffic was not all one way. Scotland had a high reputation for teaching in subjects in which it then led thought, especially the sciences and philosophy; and men came to Scotland to study under such thinkers as Smith, for example an eminent Geneva doctor sent his son to study under him because of his admiration for the *Theory of Moral Sentiments*.[5] Then during the Napoleonic Wars, when the Continent was closed to England, Edinburgh came into its own as a British centre; Cockburn gives this, "along with the blaze of that popular literature which made this the second city in the empire for learning and science", among the reasons why talented young men—Sydney Smith, Brougham, Palmerston—resorted to Edinburgh in the first decade of the 19th century.[6]

---

[1] Alexander Carlyle, *Autobiography*, pp. 379-80; Cobbett, *Tours in Scotland*, p. 761: "many gentlemen in England have Scotch bailiffs", often principal witnesses at trials of labourers for machine-breaking, where they would tell the court how docile the peasantry were in Scotland.   [2] See note 3.
[3] For a selection of names see note 4.   [4] See note 5.
[5] Élie Halévy, *England in 1815* (2nd ed., London: 1949), pp. 540-3; Rae, *Life of Smith*, p. 59: see also pp. 154, 161.
[6] *Memorials*, pp. 212-13; see also note 6.

Furthermore, Scotland's universities always catered more for the whole of the people than did, say, the English (the proportion of the population which attends the universities in Scotland is still much the highest in the United Kingdom); and in the 18th and 19th centuries Scotland attracted English students who had not the money or social standing to go to Oxford or Cambridge—a fact George Eliot notices with typical shrewdness in *Felix Holt* and *Middlemarch.*[1]

This was partly, however, an artificial phase within the main process of emigration. The Napoleonic War ended, London reasserted its pull. Brougham, for example, was much sought after in London for his 'charm and talents',[2] and Edinburgh had not the prestige or positive inducements to compete with the London Court, seat of government, and sheer crowds of talented company. The position of London reminds us that the process was also one of centralisation inevitable inside any state blessed with a metropolis. In England, too, the provinces were losing men such as Johnson to London.[3] But London was at least England. It is surely for this reason that the English writers, wherever they come from, show little sign of the emotional strain, harking back, and ordinary practical disadvantages of displacement from their own part of the world.

The Scottish authors and men of letters emigrated for a number of main motives, but these so overlap and mingle that it is best to take the cases chronologically and generalise on their motives at the end. Emigration was in force early in the period. Episcopalians were of course forced out during the 17th-century troubles and after the Presbyterian Establishment in 1690. Archbishop Leighton, who had always disliked the intolerance of Scottish belief (he had the same outlook as Wotton, Chillingworth, and their set in England), retired to Sussex when he resigned the see of Glasgow. Bishop Burnet, the historian, was, like Leighton, more at home with some of the English ways of life but he was a minister in Scotland for many years. He was often at the London Court on political business, and finally resolved to settle in England on being warned that Lauderdale would try to ruin him if he went back to Scotland for good. John Arbuthnot, the author and friend of Swift, Pope, and Gay, was the son of an Episcopal minister who lost his church because he would not accept the Presby-

---

[1] *Felix Holt*, chap. 4; *Middlemarch*, chap. 40.
[2] Mathieson, *Church and Reform in Scotland*, p. 135.
[3] Stephen, *English Literature and Society in the Eighteenth Century*, p. 103.

terian Establishment. Both Arbuthnot and his brother shared
their father's High Church principles (the brother fought at
Killiecrankie and later became a banker and helped to finance
the 'Fifteen), and both decided they would have to make their
lives abroad.[1]

As communications between Scotland and the south improved,
for reasons both political and practical, emigration exerted its
pull on a greater and greater variety of people. James Thomson,
author of *The Seasons*, typifies many of the motives at work
among men of letters. He was discouraged by the native attitude to poetry. The natural profession for him at home was the
ministry, but (like William Hunter, James Mill, and Thomas
Carlyle later) his heart was not in that. He went south with
introductions to Scottish nobility resident in London, was
helped with subscriptions and employment by some of the
many monied literary aristocrats, and (like David Malloch,
Adam Smith, James Mill, and Carlyle) became a tutor in an
upper-class family.[2] The loss of writers such as Thomson and
Malloch led Ramsay of Ochtertyre to imagine what might have
been: "an opportunity was lost of enriching the Scottish
language with classical productions which would have maintained their ground as long as there was a ray of taste and
common-sense in Scotland".[3] In the 1730's Smollett, too, set
out for London with introductions in his pocket.[4] J. M. Robertson's idea that 'the Scottish polity would die unremembered or
but dimly inferred from our idealistic novelists' comes home to
us if we think of the realistic impressions of Scottish life that we
might have had if Smollett had stayed and written in Scotland.

Such emigration was not yet in full force. Edinburgh,
Glasgow, Aberdeen in the 18th and early 19th centuries made
sufficient milieux for leading literary men. There was, however,
a steady drain of lesser men—John Home and John Logan;[5]
John Campbell, according to Johnson "the richest author who
ever grazed the common of literature"; Robert Jamieson the
antiquary, who taught in London and tutored in Latvia before
Scott got him back to Scotland to work on the national records

---

[1] Leighton, *Whole Works*, with Life by Rev. J. N. Pearson (London: 1825), I,
pp. cxiii, cxvi-vii; Burnet: biography by his son in *History of My Own Time*, ed.
Osmund Airy (Oxford: 1897), II, p. 58; Arbuthnot: Lester M. Beattie, *John
Arbuthnot*, Mathematician and Satirist (Harvard: 1935), pp. 20-1; *Dictionary of
National Biography* (ed. 1908–9), I, p. 534.
[2] Douglas Grant, *James Thomson*, pp. 30-5, 37, 45, 49-50, 69, 73-4, 89, 93, 95.
[3] *Scotland and Scotsmen*, I, pp. 24-5.
[4] Lewis Melville, *The Life and Letters of Tobias Smollett* (London: 1926), pp. 16-17.
[5] See above, p. 130.

in the Register House; George Chalmers, the scholar of Scottish literature, who spent three-quarters of his life out of Scotland in posts in London and America, and was forever writing Constable for Scottish books; John Richardson, another friend of Jeffrey's, who wrote lives of Scott and Campbell, and became "one of the most distinguished of the respectable body of Scotch solicitors" in London.[1] A little later the journalist Rintoul, who had edited the Radical *Dundee Advertiser*, was got to London where he founded the *Spectator*.[2] The loss through the centralisation of journalism has been especially serious. J. M. Robertson was got to London by Bradlaugh after making his name in Scottish newspapers; and George Douglas Brown and Lewis Grassic Gibbon both went to London to live by journalism and died prematurely there after writing fiction marked by strained emotions for the country they had left.

So the draining-away continued. G. R. Gleig, the minister who wrote *The Subaltern*, was another Episcopalian who sought his fortune abroad, first as an Army chaplain and then in the English ministry. James Mill was licensed to preach after studying and tutoring in Scotland but failed to get a church (according to his son, he also found that he could not accept Christian doctrine). He went to London with introductions, to make his way by writing for the reviews—a few months before the *Edinburgh* started up in Scotland. Lockhart was invited south to edit the *Quarterly*—and went. Sir James Mackintosh had a notable career as a judge in India, and on returning to Britain he wrote that if he were to devote himself to literature he would want to live in Edinburgh; but this never came to pass.[3]

In the early 19th century a succession of creative writers left the country. Alexander Wilson, the Paisley weaver poet, emigrated to America, sickened by the persecution of the Radicals, himself among them. Thomas Campbell was educated in Edinburgh but, after difficulty in fixing on a career, he settled in London. He long wanted to have a cottage near Edinburgh, where the nucleus of his friends was, but he felt, even

---

[1] Boswell, *Life of Johnson*, p. 119 and n.: there used to be "' shoals of Scotchmen'" at Campbell's London house; Jamieson, *Constable and His Correspondents*, I, pp. 505, 512, 517; Chalmers, *ibid.* p. 405; Richardson: Cockburn, *Life of Jeffrey*, I, p. 170.

[2] *Blackwood and His Sons*, I, p. 512; Mathieson, *Church and Reform*, p. 165.

[3] Gleig: *DNB*, VII, p. 1303; *Blackwood and His Sons*, I, p. 483; Mill: John Stuart Mill, *Autobiography* (London: 1873), p. 3; Alexander Bain, *James Mill* (London: 1882), chap. 1 and pp. 36-46; Lockhart, *Life and Letters*, I, pp. 359, 363, 370, 373; for Mackintosh see note 7.

in the age of the *Edinburgh Review*, that London was the great field for literary opportunities.[1] The cases of Galt and Allan Cunningham perhaps typify best the whole circumstances of the emigrant writer. Galt went off to London at the age of twenty-five, hoping for a business future. He had quarrelled with a customer in Greenock, where he was a junior in a trading business; a man who knew him there believed that his 'high ideas' had estranged him from the townsfolk, although he could have risen to lead the town if he had stayed. The disadvantage of displacement for a writer whose real element is wholly native is marked by that return trip to Scotland in 1822, while *The Entail* was writing, "undertaken so that he might add to his Scots vocabulary, and so that the atmosphere might help him to work out his conception".[2] In just the same way David Wilkie the *genre* painter, whose subjects at first were almost wholly from Scottish village life, had from time to time to return to Scotland from London (where he had become a fashionable success), to replenish his store of Scottish sights and details.[3] Cunningham's career shows how London was getting the upper hand as a centre of the profession of letters. Cromek got him to London to help in bringing out the *Remains of Niths-dale and Galloway Song* (Scott is said to have "wished to God we had that valuable and original young man fairly out of Cromek's hands again"). Cunningham avowed in a letter that he was "unacquainted with any other nature save that of the Nith and the Solway", and although he had an urge to "write and think like a man of the world and its ways", Thomas Carlyle found him little altered by London: "he got at once into *Nithsdale*, recalled old rustic comicalities (seemed habitually to *dwell* there). . . . His resort seemed to be much among Scotch City people; who presented him with punch-bowls, etc."[4] But his Scots poetry had dried up; henceforth he was, like Campbell ("Ye mariners of England"), what one can only call a 'British' poet—the author of "A wet sheet and a flowing sea". One

[1] Campbell, *Life and Letters*, ed. William Beattie (London: 1850), II, pp. 19-20 and n. He was invited to London by Lord Minto, a Scottish landowner settled in England.
[2] *Autobiography*, I, chap. 10; Aberdein, *John Galt*, pp. 26-31, 117; after publishing his *Life of Byron* Galt thought of returning to Scotland but he finally stayed in England for the sake of his sons' careers (*ibid.* p. 181).
[3] Cunningham, *Life of Wilkie*, I, pp. 117, 338, 459 ff., II, p. 116, III, pp. 246 ff. See also note 8.
[4] Hogg, *Songs and Ballads*, p. cxiii; Cunningham, *Poems and Songs* (London: 1847), introduction by his brother Peter; *Memoir of Robert Chambers*, p. 237; Carlyle, *Reminiscences*, p. 117: compare *Early Life of Carlyle*, II, p. 213: "Allan was, as usual, full of Scottish anecdotic talk. Right by instinct: has *no* principles or *creed* that I can see, but excellent old Scottish *habits* of character."

cannot say that talents like Galt and Cunningham would have been likely to produce distinguished work if they had made their homes in their own country. Yet, at the least, they were adding to that snowballing process which was laying waste the Scottish literary milieu; and, even at their own level, the work for which they drew on first-hand, Scottish experience is incomparably more interesting than their later placeless, characterless, wholly derivative kinds of writing.

I mentioned at the start that a high proportion of the most influential literary figures of the 19th century were of Scottish extraction. Byron had a Scottish mother, lived in Aberdeen as a child, and went to school there for some years; but when he was ten he succeeded to the titles and estates of the fifth Lord Byron and lived from then on amongst the English aristocracy.[1] Ruskin's family were well-off merchants who had moved from Perthshire to London in search of business opportunities; and Ruskin himself had "many links of association with the 'auld town' [of Edinburgh]".[2] Macaulay's family had been West of Scotland ministers; the historian's father went abroad on missionary work and then settled in London to supervise similar work and be at the centre of the anti-slavery movement.[3] The emigration of the Mills has been detailed already. Thomas Carlyle's case is worth considering most fully, because it embodies so many elements in this experience of emigration. In his case we feel with special acuteness that he came within an ace of staying, that significantly Scottish writing might have come from him if he had stayed—but that he was bound, for what he wanted in life, to leave his own country.

The various memoirs of him in the 1820's and early '30's show him becoming gradually inured to the feeling, part real dilemma, part pose of being ill-used, that Scotland could not be other than a bleak desert for him. This arose from his situation as an original-minded man who could not at first find his *métier*—his function or his literary medium.[4] But many particular conditions conspired with this. German literature was his first original field, but he could not find a tutor, speakers of German, or German books in Edinburgh; finally he imported books direct from Germany through an acquaintance in Kirkcaldy who did business with the Baltic and North Sea ports. He was living by review writing, and while Jeffrey had been an

[1] Galt, *Life of Byron* (London: 1830), pp. 9-13. Efforts to trace Scottish influences on Byron seem never to have found anything tangible: see note 9.
[2] John Ruskin, *Præterita* (ed. London: 1905), I, pp. 4-5, 15, 42, 80-92, 143.
[3] See above, p. 200.   [4] See note 10.

accommodating editor on the *Edinburgh*, he had to dun Macvey Napier for his money, whereas *Fraser's Magazine* in London paid him, and promptly, five guineas more than the average for an article. Jeffrey could help him to find publishers—and Jeffrey was in London in the early '30's as Lord Advocate.[1] Above all, London had strong positive attractions of its own, especially the set of "Radical notabilities" including John Stuart Mill, who were then projecting a new review which Carlyle at first hoped to edit; whereas Edinburgh, as Cockburn again and again observes, was long a centre of repressive Toryism, and even the more advanced men of the higher classes, such as Jeffrey and Cockburn, were reforming rather than radical in their thinking about society.[2]

Carlyle thus felt that he would have to go abroad for elementary facilities and for the company of sufficiently advanced men. In a letter of 1833 to a brother in Rome, he even—along with another brother who, like Burns, was struggling with an infertile upland farm—turns his thoughts to America as a possible place for a new start, realising that "thousands and millions must yet go" there from Scotland. In the end it was London that could satisfy him most, or exacerbate him least: according to Emerson he liked the "huge machine" in which each being "keeps its own round", leaving each other alone and working away efficiently. He often returned to Scotland, especially until his mother died, but

> the thorn in his heart, which the solitudes of Scotland could not remove, was his utter inability to bring his intellect into any harmony with the faith and ideas of the people. After he had come to London, where he was scandalised by the frivolous and tippling habits of so many even of the literary men, he saw the old folks and friends of Scotland in rosy tints. Again and again he went back there, but, as Mrs Carlyle told me, the majority of them were so narrow that Carlyle hardly drew a peaceful breath till he got back to Chelsea.[3]

That Carlyle might fruitfully have written about Scotland, or mediated his world-view through specifically Scottish experience, is of course speculation. Yet his scattered notes on

[1] Brooks, *Flowering of New England*, p. 76, n. 2; Emery Neff, *Carlyle* (*op. cit.*), p. 41; *Early Life*, II, p. 361; *ibid.* e.g. II, pp. 170-1; Jeffrey also helped to get a needy brother, John Carlyle, a job as travelling physician to one of the nobility (*ibid.* p. 184).
[2] *Early Life*, II, pp. 452-3.
[3] *Ibid.* pp. 401, 373; Moncure D. Conway, *Thomas Carlyle* (New York: 1881), p. 129.

Scottish matters are rivalled only by Cockburn for their pene-
tration, seriousness, and independent, unprovincial judgement.
Here, for example, is the criticism in his journal of Scott's kind
of history:

> A series of palace intrigues and butcheries and battles, little
> more important than those of Donnybrook Fair; all the while
> that *Scotland*, quite unnoticed, is holding on her course in
> industry, in arts, in culture, as if 'Langside' and 'Clean-the-
> Causeway' had remained unfought . . . For the rest the
> 'Scottish history' looks like that of a gypsy encampment—
> industry of the rudest, largely broken by sheer indolence;
> smoke, sluttishness, hunger, scab and—blood. Happily, as
> hinted, Scotland herself *was not there.*

And no-one has criticised Scott's novels more decisively.[1]

Further, Carlyle had more comprehensive experience of his
country than any other man of letters. From his early days he
knew the humblest, hardest life of the country workers. He
had seen the semi-nomadic casual labourers on the trek for employment. His father had hunted hares for food, and in later
life was both crofter and craftsman, and a devoted religious
sectarian. He used to give Thomas "little sketches of Annan-
dale biography"; and as Carlyle himself moved up through the
social levels, he could observe the life of all the classes. In his
memoirs these are again and again noted with the immediacy
of a novelist. In his memoir of the preacher Edward Irving
(another *émigré*[2]), he describes the Dumfriesshire yeoman
farmers, and details the kinds of character and the social dis-
tinctions represented in the different shades of Presbyterianism:

> Breakfast (wholesome hasty porridge) was soon over; and
> next in course came family worship, what they call "Taking
> the Book" (or Books, i.e. taking your *Bibles*, Psalm and
> Chapter always part of the service): David was putting on
> his spectacles, when somebody rushed in, "Such a raging
> wind risen; will drive the stooks into the sea if let alone!"
> "Wind!" answered David; "Wind canna get ae straw that
> has been appointed mine; sit down and let us worship God"
> . . . Adam and a select group were in the habit of pilgrimage
> for Sermon. Less zealous brethren would perhaps pretermit

[1] *Early Life*, II, p. 87. The criticism of the novels is well known, and to my
mind unanswerable: "your Scott fashions them [his characters] from the skin
inwards, never getting near the heart of them . . . much of the interest of these
Novels results from what may be called contrasts of costume. . . . Opinions, emotions, principles, doubts, beliefs, beyond what the intelligent country gentleman
can carry along with him are not to be had" (*Essays on Burns and Scott*, pp. 174-9).
[2] See note 11.

in bad weather; but I suppose it had to be very bad when Adam and most of his group failed to appear. The distance, a six miles twice, was nothing singular in their case; one family, whose streaming plaids, hung up to drip, I remember to have noticed one wet Sunday, pious Scotch weavers, settled near Carlisle . . . were in the habit of walking fifteen miles twice for their Sermon, since it was not to be had nearer.

In the chapter on his wife we feel the impact on him of a more monied, tasteful, genteel class than he had moved amongst before, and he gives his impression of this easier and richer life with a feeling for its physical presence as well as for the personal assurance and punctilio, contrasting with his father's utter plainness of manner, that belonged to the elegant home at Haddington, "Clean, all of it, as spring-water; solid and correct as well as pertinently ornamented: in the Drawing-room, on the tables there, perhaps rather a superfluity of elegant whimwhams". Glasgow he observed with equal keenness, its bourgeoisie "sauntering about in trustful gossip, or solidly reading their newspapers,—I remember the shining bald crowns and serene white heads of several", and their daughters more gaudily dressed than their counterparts in Edinburgh. His unerring eye for the 'essential history' of Scottish Toryism has already been shown: "old powdered gentlemen in silver spectacles talking with low-toned but exultant voice about 'cordon of troops, Sir'".[1]

We do not know what could have come of this experience in the way of literature. When he was groping for his right literary medium, he several times projected some kind of fiction, and in an early letter to Jane he sketches a 'discussion-novel' which they were to write together.[2] In *Sartor Resartus* he occasionally verges on a fiction-like presentment of the themes that possessed him; and he did have leading thoughts—for example, the unfulfilment of people in the working-classes— which could have been taken up into creative work. Inveterately, however, the interest of a scene or theme is turned into more fodder for his deaving moralisings. Life no sooner begins to open out before his mind than he seizes on it as just one more scapegoat for the near-phobias which he had projected onto the world before his experience of it was anything like full.

[1] *Reminiscences*, pp. 18, 23, 26; *Early Life*, II, p. 468, n. 2; *Reminiscences*, pp. 172, 176-9; *ibid.* p. 99; *ibid.* p. 214.
[2] *Early Life*, I, pp. 395, 397, 426; *Early Letters of Thomas Carlyle*, ed. C. E. Norton (London: 1886), II, pp. 135 ff.

Froude opined that an ingrained puritanical bent warped him away from the 'invention' which fiction would have demanded, and that may well be true.[1] Yet we may speculate that a final achieved integration with a native way of life might conceivably have put him into a more practical, outward-looking relation to society, and so opened his imagination more freely; for it is clear that it was partly his sights of England and its industrial battlefields which set him into rankling opposition to modern life, made him think of it as nothing but a welter of money-greed, shoddiness, and dirt. At the least, what Scotland lost in Carlyle was a mind of rare power, one which, if it had been able to stay in its native place, might have devoted itself to the native history—to the Reformation (Knox and Queen Mary), the religious troubles of the 17th century, or the 'Enlightenment' of the 18th, instead of to the history of France, Prussia, and England; or, again, his autobiographies might have been nearer to being for Scottish nationality what Yeats's are for Irish. As Robertson observes in *Modern Humanists*, Carlyle always raged against the 'narrow and dogmatic' Scots amongst whom he could not live, "yet he never sought to enlighten the bigots".[2]

This range of examples, then, suggests the host of talent which abandoned the country, and the complex causes which were at work. These men were moved, in varying degrees, by dissatisfaction with hardship, narrowness, or lack of opportunity at home—though in some cases they were projecting onto Scotland a subjective malaise; or by attraction to the riches available abroad—though in some cases they were falling in with a tendency rather than knowing clearly what they were after. Some lost touch with the only experience they were at home in and able to understand; some got through to a kind of work for which there was not the scope, the facilities, or the monied patrons at home (notably the painters and architects who required commissions from the wealthy). Many of them, in any case, contributed to the literature of Britain (and thus of the world) as well abroad as they would have in their native country. The loss suffered by Scotland itself, however, was not such as could be made good. Such losses do not merely reduce numbers; they weaken cumulative strength. They undermine the sense that one's country offers a feasible environment, an adequate field for one's thought and work. Amongst the people one talks to in Scotland nowadays, a West-Highlander is

[1] *Early Life*, I, p. 385. [2] *Op. cit.* p. 25, n. 1.

expressing the real problem when he says of the young people who are leaving the neighbourhood, "There's nothing for them here". But the Lowlander uneasily conscious of England's greater prestige is fancying disadvantages when he says, "What —you mean to stay in a country as small as this—with your education!" That is to say, once the tendency is there, it can itself become a cause, both through the natural magnetism of a movement once it has got a hold and for the practical reason that once some Scotsmen are settled in the south or in America they make a beach-head of contacts, influence, and introductions through which still more can make their way abroad.

Robertson, writing in the 1880's, observed that as "our literary men have since [the days of Scott and Galt] tended to drift to London, so has our fiction tended to disappear"; and, thinking of Carlyle's move south to be near, for example, the London libraries, he made the crucial diagnosis:

> . . . we lost the culture-force of a local literary atmosphere; and defect superinduces defect, till it becomes almost a matter of course that our best men, unless tethered by professorships, go south.[1]

In earlier chapters we have followed a tradition which, if often intermittent in creative work, did have its communities of very distinguished men of letters, working together, and supplying their country with much of its serious literature. After the decline of the Edinburgh of the *Review* and of Scott, Scotland does not again have a resident literary class who can be taken as representing the best mind of their society. The great drain of talent detailed above suggests that the main cause of this quite abrupt change was emigration.

Cockburn, as we have seen, was losing through emigration many of his best-loved colleagues; and he writes, in his passage on the perpetuation of "Scotch peculiarities", on the evils of centralisation—"the insatiableness of the London maw that irritates its distant compulsory feeders". (He is thinking also of the injustice that London services, e.g. parks and police, should have been paid for out of national taxation whereas all other— and poorer—towns had to pay for themselves.[2]) What Cockburn regrets losing is "Scotch peculiarities", "local manners". This rather minimises the loss in satisfaction from work and leisure,

[1] 'Belles Lettres in Scotland': *Criticisms*, II, p. 67.
[2] *Journal*, II, p. 301.

and in the actual viability of the whole economy, likely in a country whose communities large and small are losing so many of their liveliest people. That is, Cockburn's attitude shows up the weak position of Scotsmen at that time: what they were left cherishing was an inadequate object for their still ardent patriotism.

Cockburn himself is too sensible to lapse into the nostalgia which began to well up to fill this gap. *His* patriotism is above all practical: "This is all very sad, but it is the natural course; and foolish associations, with their nonsense about Bannockburn and the Union, only hasten the progress by bringing the taste for averting it into discredit". Generally, however, nostalgia for the old country was now becoming part of the emotional strain suffered by thousands of emigrants.[1] Carlyle felt it (though it did not pervade him). On one return trip to Dumfriesshire, "two Girls, with their Father for *octave* accompaniment, sang us 'The Birks of Aberfeldy' so as I have seldom heard a song; voices excellent and true, especially his voice and native expression given; which stirred my poor London-fevered heart almost to tears". Such remarks occur by the hundred as the century wears on, culminating in the acute mixed emotions of Stevenson's *The Silverado Squatters*:

> I do not know if I desire to live there, but let me hear in some far land a kindred voice sing out, 'O why left I my hame?' and it seems at once as if no beauty under the kind heavens, and no society of the wise and good, can repay me for my absence from my country. . . .[2]

During the period covered here such nostalgia had not yet developed into the full cult-emotion represented by the 'Canadian Boat Song':

> From the dim shieling on the misty island,
>   Mountains divide us and a world of seas,
> But still our hearts are true, our hearts are Highland,
>   And we in dreams behold the Hebrides.
> Tall are these mountains, and these woods are grand,
>   But we are exiled from our father's land.[3]

[1] I was first put onto this matter of nostalgia by John Manson's article 'Scottish Literature and the Scottish Community': *Fox*, a review (Aberdeen University: 1953), p. 34.

[2] Carlyle, *Reminiscences*, p. 113; Stevenson, quoted by J. B. Caird, 'Fergusson and Stevenson': *Robert Fergusson, 1750–1774*, p. 116.

[3] Quoted from Mackenzie, *History of the Highland Clearances*, p. 237 (corrected in accordance with the often-quoted version).

But such nostalgia was already recognised as typical of Scotland. The 18th-century English traveller, Thomas Newte, remarked on the tendency of the Scottish youth to leave their country, their "enterprising and wandering disposition". "Scotchmen, but particularly the Highlanders, are well known to be subject, to that *maladie du pais,* that longing desire of revisiting their native country, which characterises still more strongly the natives of Switzerland."[1] Indeed the nostalgia of the *émigré* was now coming to be catered for by producers of Scottish literature as a basic part of the needs of their public (as it still is by advertisers of calendars, dialect novels, and tartan editions of Burns). Even the most robust poetry was subjected to this treatment. Currie recommended Burns for his "tender appeal" for the 150,000 Scotsmen abroad—a need which the literary men in Edinburgh cannot judge; and *Tait's Magazine,* reviewing an illustrated edition of 'Auld Lang Syne' in 1860, recommends it as "one of the best books that could be sent to the colonies or to India as a reminiscence of the braes and burns of youth, and the braid seas that roll between old friends".[2] Scott aims his prologue to *The Family Legend* at the same audience:

> *Chief, thy wild tales, romantic Calydon,*
> *Wake keen remembrance in each hardy son;*
> *Whether on India's burning coasts he toil,*
> *Or till Acadia's winter-fetter'd soil . . .*
> *He hears with throbbing heart and moisten'd eyes,*
> *And as he hears, what dear illusions rise . . .*
> *Tradition's theme, the tower that threats the plain,*
> *The mossy cairn that hides the hero slain,*
> *The cot, beneath whose simple porch was told*
> *By grey-hair'd patriots the tales of old . . .*

Here, as commonly, the Scotland which is summoned up for the exile is archaic, wholly rural, or *passé.*[3]

Such nostalgia was not caused by emigration alone. It is also another aspect of that harking back to the older life of the country which was now melting down into the British. When

---

[1] *Tour in Scotland and England in 1785 (op. cit.),* pp. 268-9. Newte also reckons that "This spirit of wandering will, however, abate of course, in proportion to the improvement of their own country, which, at present, appears to be in a state of rapid progression" (p. 277). But it has not abated yet.

[2] Burns, *Works,* I, pp. 329-30; *Tait's Magazine* (1860), XXVII (New Series), p. 182.

[3] Joanna Baillie, *Dramatic and Poetical Works (op. cit.),* p. 481. Compare Stevenson's reference to Scotland (in a letter to Barrie from Samoa, while he was writing *Weir of Hermiston*) as "the cold old huddle of grey hills from which we come" (*Letters,* ed. Sidney Colvin (London: 1911), IV, p. 122.).

Lockhart describes Cockburn's use of Scots in the courts—appealing to the jury on behalf of a prisoner from a poor background—he observes that the pathos would be weakened if cast in "any other than the same speech to whose music the ears around him had been taught to thrill in infancy". Wilson, writing on Burns, says that his poems "awaken in a moment all the sweet visions *of the past*" (my italics); and Jeffrey, after making the sensible point that Scots is, historically, a language rather than a dialect, says:

> ... though it be true that, in later times, it has been, in some measure, laid aside by the more ambitious and aspiring of the present generation, it is still recollected, even by them, as the familiar language of their childhood, and of those who were the earliest objects of their love and veneration. It is connected, in their imagination, not only with that olden time which is uniformly conceived as more pure, lofty, and simple than the present, but also with all the soft and bright colours of remembered childhood and domestic affection.[1]

Notice how far this takes us from the poetry of Burns himself or of Fergusson—written in an idiom particularly real, close to the present and to a Scotland of streets and markets, sociable communities, rather than moors and lonely cottages. Yet Scots and the life behind it was bound to become, for men in the higher classes, a medium solely of childhood and country, and a haven of wistful memories, for the towns were centres of Anglicisation and they themselves had had to lose their Scots as they grew up and as they rose to be public men.[2]

Thus much of Scotland was forced out into a kind of remote ideal image, distanced in place and time. Yearning for regression to a place where life (it was imagined) would be simpler and more peaceful than the present tended to become an overriding emotion in such men's sense of their origins. Such nostalgia, in this 'national' form, was strong in many 19th-century literatures—in English poetry, for example Arthurian romances and 'Merrie England' work, and in the German equivalents. It is indeed one form of Romantic escapism. What matters for integrity of feeling is the place or value this emotion is allowed to have in the whole experience, how far it is understood, and perhaps resisted. In Scotland there is some work in which it is

---

[1] *Peter's Letters*, II, pp. 70-3; from *Blackwood's* (May 1829): reprinted in J. D. Ross (ed.), *Early Critical Reviews on Robert Burns* (Glasgow: 1900), p. 212; *Contributions to the Edinburgh Review*, II, pp. 175-6.

[2] For details of this process see note 12.

at least clearly focussed. In his unfinished novel *The Young Chevalier* Stevenson describes admirably the Young Pretender in exile at Avignon, at the mercy of a "debilitating cycle of emotions"—nostalgia, and disgust at the ineffectual feeling itself.[1] And at his tragically premature death George Douglas Brown was sketching a second novel, *The Incompatibles*, whose theme he gives as

> that thing you know yourself so well, the power to forget, to let the past slide, the dislike to open communication with it when once you have entered on a new world. Get this very vividly from your own experience in relation to Ayr in particular and Scotland in general since you have been up here in London.[2]

To dislike and turn one's back on a meagre past might be another kind of escape, but Brown's wording suggests a self-knowledge of the motives bound up in displacement such as is rare in Scottish writing.

Nostalgia was a potent thing in Stevenson's own life, and it weakens *Weir of Hermiston*, for example the way in which the glamour of "old, unhappy far off things" is used (in chapter 6) to cover up the failure to show in an adult way the love-relation between Archie and Kirstie. Again, the feelings in Barrie's *A Window in Thrums* are typically mixed. The author cocks snooks at the old village for its small-minded obsession with gossip but at the same time uses it as a pretext for appealing pathos: "You may climb and look into the attic, as Jess liked to hear me call my tiny garret-room. I am stiffer now than in the days when I lodged with Jess during the summer holidays I am trying to bring back, and there is no need for me to ascend. Do not laugh at the newspapers with which Leeby papered the garret. . . ."[3] The main family described in the novel is on its last legs: the energetic young folk going south, burdened with the mother's fondest hopes, the old folk falling ill, bed-ridden, dying off. We sense that behind Thrums there is the real history of small weaving towns gone stagnant, but this is not brought into full realisation through any suggestion of objective social change; it is enough that the old summer holidays should be wistfully described. Above all, nostalgia pervades through and through Lewis Grassic Gibbon's *A Scots Quair*—with MacDiarmid's poetry, the most significant literature of

---

[1] Stevenson, *Works* (Swanston Edition, London: 1912), Vol. XXI, pp. 263-4.
[2] Veitch, *George Douglas Brown*, p. 172.
[3] *Works* of Barrie (London: 1936), pp. 3-4.

the present age in Scotland. The trilogy of novels is experienced through the woman Chris Guthrie who leaves the upland farm for the village, the village for the town, and finally (at the close of *Grey Granite*) ends her symbolic journey in the Aberdeenshire farm where she was born.

> . . . And she'd open her eyes and see only the land, enduring, encompassing, the summer hills gurling in summer heat, unceasing the wail of peesies far off.
> And the folk around helped, were kind in their way, careless of her, she would meet them and see them by this road and gate, they knew little of her, she less of them, she had found at last the road she wanted and taken it, concerning none and concerned with none. . . .
> Crowned with mists, Bennachie was walking into the night: and Chris moved and sat with her knees hand-clasped, looking far on that world across the plain and the day that did not die there but went east, on and on, over all the world till the morning came. . . .
> Time she went home herself.
> But she still sat on as one by one the lights went out and the rain came beating the stones about her, and falling all that night while she still sat there, presently feeling no longer the touch of the rain or hearing the sound of the lapwings going by.[1]

This plangent emotion pulses through the three novels (although by *Grey Granite* it is decidedly out of control). In *Sunset Song*, the first, it is given good grounds by some of the main actions—the break-up of the farm community which loses its men to the Great War, its woods to the timber profiteers. But in the later two, especially in the evocation of time passing in *Cloud Howe*, it swamps all firmness of feeling other than what is done (which is a great deal) in the vernacular direct speech. The author, an *émigré* in London, writing just before his early death, is possessed by nostalgia for the countryside of his birth, and we can feel in the mechanical metre of his prose that it is out of control. The effect on the meaning of the trilogy is that any historical point which the return of the heroine to the countryside might have symbolised is quite undermined. Her return has no place in a pattern representing an idea of how the country is developing, it is no more than an ideal refuge for the author's sorely-tried emotions. He hands over to his nostalgia, lies back and lets it carry him along. Such emotion unfits an

[1] See *A Scots Quair* (separately paged), p. 144.

artist to make sense of his experience even as it moves him to get it down on paper. For the reader, if he responds, it touches off a terrible thrill, only to leave him desolate and useless when it ebbs.

It is a mark of the uncertain foothold for a national literature in Scotland that this weak ground of nostalgia should crop up in so many places. Emigration of our most notable talents thus both creates gaps in the imaginative records of the country and tempts our writers into indulgence of their weaker sides. Not many of them could be regarded (as could the major Russian and English) as figuring for us wholeness and strength of being and genuine efforts to achieve it. What again and again weakens them (apart from individual flaws of talent) is the feeling that the ground in their country is shifting under their feet, and this perhaps gets worse the greater the determination to *have* a national vantage-point, to take up one's stance inside exclusively Scottish territory. It is for this reason among others that one comes to think that a freer spirit, facing up more openly to experience at large whatever its origins, might better enable the Scottish writer to cope with the problems of living in this place at this time.

APPENDIX A

Scottish Great Houses as Literary Centres[1]

AN interesting observation on Scotland's potential of this kind—applying to
a period a little earlier than what is covered by this book—is made by Ian
Finlay. After the mid-17th century,

> patronage had swung away from the people back to something like Court
> circles. . . . But the men who indulged in the great new classical mansions
> were king's men and haters of the Kirk. . . . It was a cultivated taste, and
> there is a vast amount of it and of good scholarship shown in their
> patronage. It can indeed match up pretty well to the contemporary
> standards of Evelyn's London. But it is unreal and aloof compared with
> the healthy clamour for more modest but widespread amenities which
> an increase of trade had brought about at the beginning of the century.[2]

In the 18th and 19th centuries Scotland did have its big houses, especially
in the Lothians, which were gathering-places for the most influential groups
of literary and public men. There was Jeffrey's Craigcrook, then outside
Edinburgh, on the north-eastern slopes of Corstorphine Hill. Cockburn
wrote of it: "No unofficial house in Scotland has had a greater influence on
literary or political opinion. . . . Their rural festivities are dignified by his
virtues and talents, by all our Edinburgh eminence, and by almost every
interesting stranger."[3] Craigcrook was evidently the centre for confabula-
tions on the *Edinburgh Review*, and it was there that Carlyle, still young, shy,
and unknown, met Jeffrey's circle. There was also the Tytler seat, Woodhouselee, on the slopes of the Pentlands, south-west of the city. The village
on the estate was made an experiment in model land-owning, in housing,
dairying, sanitation, and the like; and constant guests at the big house included Henry Mackenzie, John Gregory, Dugald Stewart, John Playfair, the
law lords Abercrombie, Craig, and Meadowbank, Sydney Smith, Sir James
Mackintosh, Jeffrey, Scott, John Leyden, and Adam Ferguson: "all those
who were most distinguished in Edinburgh for their manners, their talents,
and their accomplishments". "In his [Lord Woodhouselee's] very ambition, there was always something domestic. . . . The eyes in which he
desired to read 'his history', were not those of 'a nation', but those of his
family and friends."

> For about ten years his great delight had been to embellish his grounds,
> to extend his plantations, and to improve the dwellings of his cottagers,
> 'an occupation in which he found himself every day rewarded by seeing
> the face of nature and of man brightening around him'. He enlarged his
> house in order 'to render it more adequate to the purposes of hospitality;
> and in the course of a short period', writes Mr Alison, 'he succeeded in
> creating a scene of rural and domestic happiness which has seldom been
> equalled in this country, and which, to the warm-hearted simplicity of
> Scottish manners, added somewhat of the more refined air of classical
> elegance.'[4]

[1] See above, Chapter IV, p. 135.   [2] *Art in Scotland* (Oxford: 1948), pp. 77-8.
[3] *Life of Jeffrey*, I, pp. 236-7; *Memorials*, p. 294.
[4] John Burgon, *The Portrait of a Christian Gentleman* (London: 1859), pp. 8-9, 10,
11, 13, 29-30, 34-9, 175.

Literature had its place: Patrick would read aloud in the evenings to the family *Gil Blas* and Maria Edgeworth; and at his father's request he wrote a *Comus*-like *Woodhouselee Masque* which the family were to perform. The improvements on the estate inspired one of the first Scottish novels, Elizabeth Hamilton's *The Cottagers of Glenburnie*, which aimed to instruct the farmers of other districts in the same methods.[1]

With all this, however, an element of amateurish dabbling in 'old Scotland' runs through the picture, which suggests that the Tytler circle were not bearers of civilisation of the stature of Sir Henry Wotton or Viscount Falkland in England. Scott was a dominant influence, forever telling his tales of ghosts and Covenanters. Members of the household would pen pale Burnsian lyrics. Patrick finally became a founder-member of the Bannatyne Club, which went in for olde Scottishe antiquarian fun.[2] It is difficult not to feel that the Scottish gentry were by then radically *passé*—lacking a full present-day function and culture. As Lockhart and Cockburn often observe, they were now pulled away south from their old capital by the magnet of London. Scotland became for them more of a haven or a holiday-place than the scene of their most pressing activities. Cockburn's own intense devotion to preserving old Edinburgh smacks rather of lapsing contemporary concerns, for all his important work in, for example, helping to draft the Scottish Reform Bill. His own obituary comment on the elder Tytler ends: "there is no kindness in insinuating that he was a man of genius, and of public or even social influence, or in describing Woodhouselee as Tusculum".[3] Those homes played their part in knitting together Scotland's distinguished intellectual upper-class at the turn of the century. But no Scottish members of it could imagine them as centres of ideal literary and rural society, as Ben Jonson could Penshurst, Carew Saxham, or Marvell Nun Appleton, possibly because the creative talents were lacking, possibly because our culture was no longer self-sufficient.

[1] John Burgon, *The Portrait of a Christian Gentleman* (London: 1859), pp. 20-1, 69, 77.
[2] *Ibid.*, pp. 24 ff., 29-30, 37, 162-3.
[3] *Memorials*, p. 276.

Sales and Returns of Fiction in the Age of Scott[1]

SCOTT soon reached a regular basis with his publishers of 10,000 copies for the first impression of a novel.[2] Lockhart computes his annual income from fiction, after the first four novels, at £10,000. Galt, starting as an unknown, got only 60 guineas for the copyright of *The Annals*. But *The Ayrshire Legatees*, according to *Blackwood's Magazine*, "increased our sales enormously"; *The Annals* sold 500 in three or four days in London and 400 in Edinburgh; and *The Provost* sold 2,000 in a fortnight (another equally large impression was soon melting away "like snaw off a dyke"). This compares favourably with *Waverley's* 3,000 in two months or *Guy Mannering's* 2,000 the day after publication, although it does not approach *Rob Roy* (a first impression of 10,000 in a fortnight) or *Ivanhoe* (a first impression of 12,000). Galt's reward, accordingly, was a payment of £300 on account of the copyright of *The Provost, Sir Andrew Wylie*, and articles for *Blackwood's Magazine*. In the same year, negotiating with Blackwood, he could say that Murray had offered him five hundred guineas after reading two-thirds of *Sir Andrew*, and finally accept for it from Blackwood £200 plus credit on the sale of copies after the first 1,500. Longmans had a quick sale of *The Entail*—a novel which also had something of a *succès d'estime* in London—and Galt got his highest money for it, £525 for the copyright from Blackwood.

After this, however, Galt had a break with Blackwood (no evidence exists to explain it). When he returned to him with *The Last of the Lairds*, we find him protesting at the reduction of the first impression from 3,000 to 2,000 while the book was in proof; and in 1829 he leaves it to Blackwood to decide whether or not 'My Landlady and her Lodgers' would be better brought out in the magazine considering "the present state of the novel market" (which was in fact very good). Galt's money is all along oddly low compared with, say, Lockhart's (1,000 guineas for the copyright of *Reginald Dalton* in spite—or because?—of the rumpus over the immoral *Adam Blair*, and 400 guineas for his last novel, *Matthew Wald*) or Susan Ferrier (£1,000 from Blackwood for *Inheritance* and £1,700 from Cadell for her last novel, *Destiny*). Galt does not seem to have risen in the eyes of his publisher beyond the status of a magazine regular, in spite of the hopes Blackwood once held for him, and perhaps this indicates a quick slackening of sales. He was included along with Scott in the novelists who made up the biggest class of serious fiction in the returns of circulating libraries in working-class London for the 1830's; but it seems likely that it was Scott who dominated this class, by means of his huge posthumous editions. In 1837 the *Edinburgh*, reviewing Galt's *Life of Byron*, placed him in a sentence: "He is favourably known as a novelist of a certain class. . . ."[3]

[1] See above, Chap. VII, p. 227.

[2] The references to this Appendix would be so tiresomely numerous if given detail by detail that I will mention here all the sources from which the information has been taken: on Scott, Lockhart's *Life*, III-VII, Scott's *Journal* and *Letters*, *Constable and His Correspondents*, III; on Galt, *Autobiography, Literary Life*, National Library Blackwood MSS., and *Blackwood's Magazine*, 1820–1832; on Lockhart, *Life and Letters*, I, and Blackwood MSS.; on Hogg, 'Memoir of Himself', *Blackwood and His Sons*, and Blackwood MSS.; on Susan Ferrier, *Memoir and Correspondence*, Collins, *The Profession of Letters*, and Blackwood MSS.

[3] R. K. Webb, 'The Victorian Reading Public' (*op. cit.*), pp. 35-6; *Edinburgh Review* (1837), LII, p. 230.

APPENDIX B

Scott alone made a considerable success of 'the Scotch novels'. James Hogg claimed when negotiating with Blackwood that Oliver & Boyd had sold 1,500 copies of his 1820 *Tales* in five months; but *The Justified Sinner*, which had to come out anonymously, sold poorly, in spite of its powerful originality. Scott's work, on the other hand, so commanded the public that it could be turned into successful stage-plays which seem in turn to have boosted the sales of the book (as happens nowadays when a book is filmed or serialised on the radio). *Rob Roy* was produced in the theatre on an average once per month for eighteen years up to 1837 (it was still a constant favourite, along with versions of *The Lady of the Lake* and *The Heart of Midlothian*, in the late 1880's), and the book had the exceptional sale of 40,000 in twenty years after the first two impressions amounting to 15,000. Scrutiny of these sales, however, shows that not much fillip was given to them by the works after *The Fortunes of Nigel* (7,000 in the first ten hours). *Ivanhoe*, the first break in the Scottish series, was a great success, and the last great success, *The Crusaders* (including *The Talisman*), was also in the historical-romance kind; but *The Abbot*, the second novel after *Ivanhoe*, was the first to be counted a failure, and *Redgauntlet*, which before publication aroused the interest of lovers of *Waverley*, was received "somewhat coldly". Later collected editions, therefore, had to carry several unsuccessful items (in spite of which they sold immensely). In 1821 Constable, having found that an octavo edition of the early novels (which were purely Scottish) was "extremely well received", proposed a similar edition of *Ivanhoe*, *The Monastery*, *The Abbot*, and *Kenilworth*, but this included two of the mediocrities. Thus 'the Scotch novels' made a stir in their day, and were accounted a distinct *genre*, but with a few exceptions they have not proved permanent classics in the way of Jane Austen or Dickens.

The Centralisation of Scottish Periodicals[1]

In the middle of the 19th century the Scottish periodicals suffered the same wasting process as the literature itself, due mainly to the fact that they were powerless to resist the general centralisation of British literary affairs on London. *Blackwood's* has stayed in Scottish hands till the present day, and *Chambers's Journal* did so until its very recent death. The *Edinburgh*, however, the first and best of Scottish reviews, was taken over *in toto* by Longmans in 1826, and the editorship passed out of Scotland for the first time in 1847, on the death of Macvey Napier. It was then edited for a while by Jeffrey's English son-in-law Empson, and remained thenceforth out of Scotland.[2] The Scottish content of the main periodicals also dwindles as the '30's go by, after the thriving time when Scott and Galt were being almost continuously reviewed and the functions of a national literature, the problems of writing in Scots, etc., discussed.

The Scottish works reviewed by the *Edinburgh* after Scott's heyday were of secondary importance—Cunningham's *British Painters* and *Songs of Scotland*, Carlyle's *Burns*, James Montgomery's *Poems*, an edition of *Ancient Scottish Melodies*, lives of Telford and Watt.[3] The more important reviews were of reprints—the complete Waverley Novels with Scott's Notes, McCulloch's edition of *The Wealth of Nations*; there was also Jamieson's dictionary of Scots.[4] The review of *Ancient Scottish Melodies* discusses over-patriotism, and opines that nowadays (1839) 'nationality' is "much less prominent and prevailing". Only "the simple and unsophisticated" think everything Scottish is best, music and mountains, dancing and dishes, language and laws. At the same time the reviewer warns (as Scotsmen so often do) against affecting the exotic, '*Di tanti palpiti*' or '*Una voce poco fa*', instead of cultivating native work, 'Low down in the Broom' or 'Logie o' Buchan'.[5]

The journals that published creative work, notably *Blackwood's*, *Tait's* and *Chambers's*, also tail off—necessarily, with the exhaustion of Galt and the dearth of fruitful new writers. *Blackwood's* concerned itself for its first two decades with Scottish affairs (from the rankest Tory point of view) in the form of comment on current Scottish elections, legislation, and the like. But it was not long before it died out as a vehicle of Scottish literature: the 'Noctes Ambrosianae' feature, in which Lockhart and Hogg had enjoyed themselves, stopped after January 1835, a series on 'Ancient Scottish Poetry' which began on Dunbar in the next number got no further, the serials (which had included in the '20's Galt, Hogg, and D. M. Moir) became purely English. In the end only reviews of minor poetry and

[1] See Chap. VII, p. 229.
[2] Cockburn, *Journal*, II, p. 175; *Constable and His Correspondents*, I, p. 56.
[3] 1831–40: vols. XLVII, XLVIII, XLIX, LXI, LXIX, LXX.
[4] Vols. LV, LXX, XLVII.
[5] LXIX, pp. 209-10. Compare Fergusson's 'The Daft-Days':

> Fidlers, your pins in temper fix,
> And roset weel your fiddle-sticks,
> But banish vile Italian tricks
>   From out your quorum:
> Nor *fortes* wi' *pianos* mix,
>   Gie's *Tulloch Gorum*.

patriotically-worded reports of Burns festivals distinguish it, on the literary side, from other British magazines;[1] and it devotes itself mainly to the Victorian jingoism which helped it to become the light reading of old-fashioned British imperialists, tea-planters and the Indian Army.

Tait's had a much more progressive attitude to modern affairs, for example the antipathy declared in the first editorial to "cock-and-bull stories about the abominations of the French Revolution, as if every movement in favour of liberty and equal laws were necessarily and inseparably connected with brutality". *Tait's* serialised one of Galt's shorter fictions told through the *persona* of a Scots-speaker, *The Howdie*, but it had started rather late to get much from him. For literature it mostly had to make do with pale songs by William Motherwell, long revaluations of Scott, and the like, although it never descended to the trivial 'human interest' of *Chambers's*. It became, in fact, an adequate British periodical, and among the English writers it published were Ebenezer Elliott, de Quincey, and Harriet Martineau.[2]

Chambers's, which started in 1832, at once established a rather trifling level in literature—'Peculiarities of Authors', anecdotes of Scott, the 'background' of Burns poems.[3] In short the Chamberses were assuming that they must write down to their public. They were also out to help the working man. An article on 'Scottish Manufacturing Conditions' congratulates Scotland on growing beyond its primitive beginnings, for example developing a silk industry at Paisley through the "patient labour of workmen" and the "cheapness of labour at the time"—this at a time when skilled weavers were starving was nothing short of an insult to the class to whom its readers belonged. An article on the 'Results of Machinery' proves that the expansion of industry and foreign trade has been simply splendid all round—while at the same time an article by Adam Ferguson on Canada is addressed to the "humbler classes" as it is they, "it is evident", who will have to emigrate. In No. 22, 'A Chapter of Political Economy, Written for the British Peasantry' informs the humbler classes that they are "redundant population" who must run off to America "in the same manner as fluids find their level".[4] In this context even the enthusiasm of Robert Chambers cannot make of Scottish culture a live subject.

[1] XXXVI; 1844, LVI.
[2] (April, 1832), I, p. 11; (1832), VI-VII.
[3] (February–May 1832), Nos. 2-16.
[4] No. 16, pp. 23-4; No. 10, pp. 79-80; No. 1, p. 3; No. 22, p. 169.

NOTES

Chapter I

1 (p. 28): Thomas Chalmers, a famous writer and preacher active early in the 19th century, wrote that "the greatest palliation for the misconduct of the poor, especially in the great towns, is the cruel neglect and abandonment of them by the upper ranks of society"; and W. L. Mathieson remarks (discussing the great number of pubs in the crowded Glasgow of the early Industrial Revolution) that "the severe and protracted labour to which they were accustomed from childhood left them little leisure for anything but a propensity to drink" (*Church and Reform in Scotland*, pp. 248, 245). *Blackwood's Magazine*, in one of its diatribes on the depravity of the lower orders, objected to the law which allowed any £10 householder to sell drink on his premises—many pubs, they alleged, were also brothels; and Engels quotes evidence that in Glasgow 30,000 working men got drunk every Saturday night. In 1830 one house in twelve and in 1840 one house in ten was a pub (*Blackwood's*, Edinburgh: June 1831, Vol. XXIX, pp. 925-6; Marx and Engels, *On Britain*, p. 159).

2 (p. 34): For place-seeking and how deeply it affected the social life of the Stuart milieu, see G. M. Trevelyan, *England Under the Stuarts* (London: 1904), pp. 15, 17; L. C. Knights, *Drama and Society in the Age of Jonson* (London: 1937), pp. 327-9; Christopher Hill, *The English Revolution, 1640* (London: 1955), pp. 18-19, 31; Marjorie Cox, 'The Background to English Literature, 1603-1660': Boris Ford (ed.), *From Donne to Marvell* (London: 1956), p. 21.

For "cultured nobility and arranged marriages", see L. C. Knights, 'On the Social Background of Metaphysical Poetry'; *Scrutiny* (Cambridge: 1944), Vol. XIII, No. 2, pp. 44-9; *England Under the Stuarts*, pp. 11, 13; Rhodes Dunlap (ed.), *The Poems of Thomas Carew* (Oxford: 1949), pp. xv-xvii, xxxv.

"Candour and naturalness" is from Edmund Wilson, *Axel's Castle* (New York: 1936), p. 39.

F. R. Leavis refers justly to the "urbane grace" of Carew's poetry; but he is perhaps assuming too much when he says that in his "sophisticated gallantry" there is "nothing rakish or raffish", and that his Court culture "preserved, in its sophisticated way, an element of the tradition of chivalry" (*Revaluation*, pp. 16-17, 30). Dunlap shows that Carew was known in his day as "a great libertine in his life and talk", a specialist in "scandalous discourse" (*op. cit.* p. xli); and Izaak Walton in his *Life of Carew* says that one of the most popular poems in the manuscript 'anthologies' current in his set was 'A Fly that Flew Into My Mistress her Eye', which shows us Carew's ingenious suggestiveness at its most futile (*Lives* bound with *The Compleat Angler*, London: 1906, p. 231). Arranged marriages and the idle Court life inevitably produced promiscuity; and many poems of the time, e.g. Donne's 'Womans Constancy' and 'The Undertaking', take promiscuity for granted.

Gentlemen not publishing their poetry: Knights, *Drama and Society*, pp. 325-6; Marjorie Cox (*op. cit.*), p. 18.

3 (p. 39): Even experts find it almost impossible to be sure of the population of Edinburgh at any period. The rough-and-ready counts taken in the 18th century are usually approximations or else do not define how much

of the town they take in. As far as I can make out, what may be called the Old Town proper contained 20,000 in 1687, 25,000 in 1722, and 35,000 in 1755 (the year of the minister Webster's census). A figure of 60,000 is given for Edinburgh minus Leith in 1790, but that might include non-Old-Town districts such as St Cuthbert's (James Anderson, *A History of Edinburgh*, Edinburgh & London: 1856, pp. 394, 607; Creech, *Edinburgh Fugitive Pieces*, p. 88).

Chapter II

1 (p. 51): The Edinburgh Philalethic Society would discuss all questions except those "of an abstruse, theological, or political nature". A Glasgow club run by the University Professor of Mathematics, whose members included James Watt, Adam Smith, and Joseph Black, debarred only one subject—religion. The Easy Club decided that they "shall never be acters or intermedlers in politicks as a Society" (McElroy, *op. cit.* p. 298; Rae, *Life of Adam Smith*, p. 98; Andrew Gibson, *New Light on Allan Ramsay*, Edinburgh: 1927, p. 57).

2 (p. 52): In the 19th century working-men's clubs had no such inhibitions, for they had become conscious of the need to struggle for their rights. Q. D. Leavis mentions that Thomas Cooper, the Lincolnshire Chartist, ran a mutual improvement society in Leicester which was equally political, religious, and literary. "Unless there was some stirring local or political topic", Cooper lectured on or recited poetry (*Fiction and the Reading Public*, London: 1932, p. 116).

3 (p. 53): Stories recorded of the older kind of believer regularly show their extraordinary and whole-hearted literalness of belief. A Scottish painter J. H. Lorimer, who painted subjects from Kirk life with local people as his models, records a story told by his mother about one of these people: "Mrs Lorimer expressed her sympathy with the old man in his loneliness, to which he replied—'Me lonely? What for should I be lonely wi' the Father, the Son and the Holy Ghost in the bed beside me?'" (*The Scotsman*, Edinburgh, 8.12.56). Dean Ramsay tells of an old woman dying in bed during a storm: "with no thought of profane or light allusions, she looked up, and, listening to the storm, quietly remarked . . . 'Ech, sirs! what a nicht for me to be fleeing thro' the air!'" (E. B. Ramsay, *Reminiscences of Scottish Life and Character*, Series 2 (1-vol. ed., London: n.d., p. 53). Cockburn records many such, and characteristically approves of them; but writing at a time when Augustan decorum was developing into Victorian gentility, he has to say: "It is remarkable that though all these female Nestors were not merely decorous in matters of religion, but really pious, they would all have been deemed irreligious now. Gay hearted, and utterly devoid of every tincture of fanaticism, the very freedom and cheerfulness of their conversation and views of sacred subjects would have excited the horror of those who give the tone on these matters at present" (*Memorials*, p. 67).

4 (p. 54): Lord Kames's biographer says of his writings that "We are not infrequently offended by a colloquial vulgarity of expression . . . which probably the author has mistaken for an ease and freedom of composition, or imagined to give a pleasing variety"; and the humble idioms which he singles out include "Selfishness . . . eradicates patriotism, and leaves not a *cranny* for social virtue", "To enter *bluntly* on a subject of such intricacy, might *gravel* an acute philosopher", and "I shall *draw out of my budget* one

instance" (*Life*, by Tytler, II, pp. 157-60). Kames was in fact writing as he spoke—he was known for his broad or near-Scots language (Ramsay of Ochtertyre, *Scotland and Scotsmen*, I, pp. 211-12, 475, n. 1; and Kay, *Edinburgh Portraits*, I, pp. 323-4). Similarly Sir John Sinclair comes down on any idiom which departs from a dead level of 'correctness' for the sake of being expressive, e.g. 'put the horses into the carriage' is a "ridiculous phrase" and 'strapping' a "ludicrous word" (*Observations on the Scottish Dialect*, pp. 96, 108). It is significant that he should sigh a little for the lost expressiveness of the improper Scots: "it is difficult to find words in the modern English capable of expressing their full force, and genuine meaning. But what our language has lost in strength, it has gained in elegance and correctness" (pp. 78-9).

5 (p. 54): Broad Scots was identified, even militantly, with the Low Kirk, anti-Moderatism, and uncontaminated Presbyterianism generally. The 17th-century Church historian Kirkton said of the Episcopal Burnet (who settled in England), "though he speaks the newest English diction, he spoke never the language of ane exercised conscience", and this attitude was equally prevalent in the 18th century when correct English was gaining ground. Patrick Walker, the Covenanter annalist, complains, "And in our Speech our Scripture and old *Scots* names are gone out of Request; instead of *Father* and *Mother*, *Mamma* and *Papa*, training children to speak nonsense, and what they do not understand". In 1767, an anti-patronage minister wrote criticising "the smarts [*sic*] and clever fellows . . . the flimsy superficial gentlemen, who having pick'd up somewhat of the English language, can read another man's sermon with a becoming grace"; and McKerrow in his *History of the Secession Churches* records that the Anti-Burgher Synod warned candidates for the ministry "against an affected pedantry of style and pronunciation and politeness of expression in delivering the truths of the Gospel" (J. H. Millar, *Scottish Prose of the 17th and 18th Centuries*, Glasgow: 1912, p. 58, n. 2; Walker, *Biographia Presbyteriana*, I, p. 140; Rev. James Oswald, *Letters Concerning the Present State of the Church of Scotland*, Edinburgh: 1767, p. 23; Mathieson, *Awakening of Scotland*, p. 234).

There is rich evidence of this cultural clash in the literature of the time. The popular chapbook lampoon, 'Janet Clinker's Oration', by Dougal Graham, parodies an Old-Testament-like lament on the degeneracy of the times:

> They will not speak the mother language of their native country, but must have southern oaths, refined like raw-sugar through the mills of cursing, finely polished, and fairly struck in the profane mint of London, into a perfect form of flunkey-language; even the very wild Arabs from the mountain-tops [i.e. Highlanders], who have not yet got English to profane his Maker's name, will cry, *Cot, cot*; hateful it is to hear them swear who cannot speak. (*Collected Writings of Dougal Graham*, ed. George MacGregor, Glasgow: 1883, II, p. 152.)

Similarly Burns writes in his subtly double-edged evocation of the Moderate preacher:

> What signifies his barren shine,
> Of moral powers an' reason?
> His English style, an' gesture fine,
> Are a' clean out o' season. . . .

The *moral man* he does define,
But ne'er a word o' *faith* in
That's right that day.
('The Holy Fair')

6 (p. 57): Carlyle records of Hume and Jardine: "One night Hume having declined to be lighted down the turnpike stair from his friend's lodging, fell in the darkness. Jardine rushed for a candle, and as he lifted the bulky body of his guest slyly said, 'Davie, I have often tell't ye that "natural licht" is no' sufficient'" (*Autobiography*, p. 285, n. 1). Broad-Scots sentences by Hume are on record (Mossner, pp. 370-1). Cockburn says of a leading Edinburgh minister, John Erskine (died 1803), "His language (like that of his colleague Principal Robertson) was good honest natural Scotch" (*Memorials*, p. 55). Scott was evidently quite broad. Lockhart records the publisher Constable speaking broad to Tom Purdie, the working-man who companioned Scott: "'Be sure, Tam . . . that ye egg on the Dominie to blaw up his father—I would na grudge a hundred miles o' gait to see the ne'er-do-weel on the stool'", and Scott replies, "'Na, na, let sleeping dogs be, Tam'"; and he also spoke Scots more or less to himself, e.g. when looking at Chantrey's bust of himself: "'Ay, ye're mair like yoursel now!'" (Lockhart, *Life of Scott*, IV, pp. 353, 365).

It is not always clear what these men meant when they said 'Scots' or 'Scotch'; but Dean Ramsay says conclusively of one unusually broad speaker of the 18th century, a lady: "Many people now [in the mid-19th century] would not understand her" (*Scottish Life and Character*, pp. 39-40); and the *literati* themselves felt the language division to be deep: "the foreign language, which the English is to us" (Carlyle, *Autobiography*, p. 232).

7 (p. 59): Song, whether folk- or art-song, has not been studied in this book, as it should properly be considered either in its musical settings or as it exists in practice among the people. This is of course being done by the students of music and by the folk-lorists working in the field with tape-recorders.

Here it will be enough to note how the native songs were taken up by contemporary taste. The beginnings of the fashion for folk-songs among the gentry are recorded by Ramsay of Ochtertyre (*Scotland and Scotsmen*, I, p. 19 and n.) and Chambers (the fashion for Scots songs in England as well as Scotland: *Domestic Annals* under 1718, pp. 473-5). Pinkerton mentions folk tunes which were fashionable as full of 'feeling' (*Scottish Tragic Ballads*, London: 1781, p. xxxi). The communication of songs also worked in the opposite direction socially. William Chambers describes Peeblesshire farmers at home in the evening telling stories and singing the songs of Ramsay and Hamilton of Bangour while the women spun (*Memoir of Robert Chambers*, p. 41).

8 (p. 61): Catering for a British public regularly led to both exaggeration of the outlandishness of Scottish *mores* and playing down of whatever was overtly Scottish in the native work. In his review of Burns, Jeffrey half apologises because although "all his best pieces are written in Scotch"; he has quoted few of these, "guided more by a desire to exhibit what may be intelligible to all our readers"; and in 1820, reviewing *Ivanhoe*, again in the *Edinburgh*, he begins by saying that he has been abused "for the abominable nationality of filling up our pages with praises of a Scottish author, and specimens of Scottish pleasantry and pathos" (*Contributions*

to the Edinburgh Review, II, p. 156; I, p. 74). In the very Anglicised *Lounger,* Mackenzie, reviewing Burns, alleges that the "provincial dialect" of Ramsay and Burns is now read, even in Scotland, "with a difficulty which greatly damps the pleasure of the reader", and in England is quite unintelligible without using a glossary and so destroying one's pleasure. His former point is contradicted by evidence of how broadly even the upper-classes still spoke; and his latter point would be an argument against reading literature in *any* foreign language.

9 (p. 62): Robertson's account of the stultification of Scots is standard. It occurs in his review of the state of the nation since the accession of James VI and I:

> The English and Scottish languages, derived from the same sources, were, at the end of the 16th century, in a state nearly similar, differing from one another somewhat in orthography, though not only the words, but the idioms were much the same. The letters of several Scottish statesmen of that age are not inferior in elegance, or in purity, to those of the English Ministers with whom they corresponded. . . . Scotland might have had a series of authors in its own, as well as in the Latin language, to boast of. . . .
>
> But, at the very time when other nations were beginning to drop the use of Latin in works of taste, and to make trial of the strength and compass of their own languages, Scotland ceased to be a kingdom . . . the Scots, being deprived of all the objects that refine or animate a people, of the presence of their Prince, of the concourse of nobles, of the splendor and elegance of a court, an universal dejection of spirit seems to have seized the nation . . . no domestic standard of propriety and correctness of speech remained; the few compositions that Scotland produced were tried by the English standard, and every word or phrase that varied in the least from that, was condemned as barbarous; whereas, if the two nations had continued distinct, each might have retained idioms and forms of speech peculiar to itself; and these rendered fashionable by the example of a court, and supported by the authority of writers of reputation, would have been considered in the same light with the varieties occasioned by the different dialects in the Greek tongue, would have been marked as beauties, and, in many cases, used promiscuously by the authors of both nations.

He then asserts that the changes in the language during the 17th century were all 'corruptions', resulting from the loose usages of ministers preaching popular sermons and lawyers pleading: hence those "vitious forms of speech, which are denominated *Scotticisms*". Thus his standard of language is wholly courtly or ruling-class; but one can hardly doubt that his theory of the decay of Scots as an *educated* medium is substantially right. (See his *History of Scotland, op. cit.* II, pp. 301-7.)

Chapter III

1 (p. 85): The comically deflating folk attitude to death is responsible for some of Ramsay's most graphic and subtly-toned Scots, e.g. from the 'Elegy on John Cowper, the Kirk-Treasurer's Man':

> SHAME faw ye'r Chandler Chafts, O Death,
> For stapping of *John Cowper's* Breath;
> The Loss of him is publick skaith:

I dare well say,
To quat the Grip he was right laith
This mony a day.

2 (p. 88): Thomson's career is worth detailing; it is typical of that popular literary culture discussed in this and the following chapter. When herding as a boy, he always carried with him "some ballads, or book of songs", especially Ramsay's songs and *The Gentle Shepherd*, which he soon knew by heart. To his friends he seemed a "prodigy of learning", but he abandoned his hopes of "higher pursuits" to become a weaver, at the age of thirteen, to support the grandparents he lived with. "As nobody could read what he wrote, he seldom was at the trouble to use the pen"; he would memorise his poems, and his schoolfellows used to pester him to repeat them. Some of his poems he "contrived to write so as they could be read"; they were handed about by local farmers, and came to the attention of the minister, who circulated them amongst the gentry and thus got Thomson patronage (the dedication of his *Poems* says that the Leith merchants had always been good friends to him).—'Life' by George Maclaurin, reprinted from *Scots Magazine*, LXXV, pp. 647 ff.: see *Poems* (*op. cit.*), pp. iv–ix; Dedication, pp. xxi–xxiii.

3 (p. 95): Familiarity with practical, working life is what constantly supplies Burns with his deft or witty turns, e.g. in the 'Epistle to James Smith' friendship is given thus:

Ye've cost me twenty pair o' shoon,
Just gaun to see you;
An' ev'ry ither pair that's done,
Mair taen I'm wi' you.

In 'The Ordination' he thus writes off one of the ministers:

Or, nae reflection on your lear,
Ye may commence a shaver;
Or to the Netherton repair,
An' turn a carpet weaver,
Aff-hand this day,

and farm imagery is used to create his mock celebration of the triumph of Low Kirk extremism:

Now auld Kilmarnock, cock thy tail,
An' toss thy horns fu' canty;
Nae mair thou'lt rowte out-owre the dale,
Because thy pasture's scanty;
For lapfu's large o' gospel kail
Shall fill thy crib in plenty,
An' runts o' grace the pick an' wale,
No gi'en by way o' dainty,
But ilka day.

And at the start of 'Tam o' Shanter' communal work is seen to be at the heart of his zestful sociability:

. . . ilka melder wi' the miller,
Thou sat as lang as thou had siller;
That ev'ry naig was ca'd a shoe on
The smith and thee gat roarin' fou on . . .

4 (p. 95): Unfortunately Burns's only offer of a decent competence for literary work would have taken him out of Scotland. Lockhart comments

that had he published some "newspaper squibs upon Lepaux and Carnot,
or a smart pamphlet 'On the State of the Country'", he might have been
patronised by the influential London set (*Life of Burns*, p. 238). The proprietor of the *Morning Chronicle* offered him a salaried post, but he would
not be drawn into London journalism (Cromek, *Reliques of Burns*, pp.
161-2, n.). Compare the speed with which Pitt and Fox responded to *The
Lay of the Last Minstrel* (Lockhart, *Life of Scott*, II, p. 34). Scott's Romantic
tale was a full-dress literary performance, perfectly fitted for fashionable
success, whereas Burns's seemingly local kind of poetry was easy to
dismiss to a lowly class.

5 (p. 107): Typical of what Lowland writers made of Highland life are the
plays which use the Highlands as a misty scene for the full-blast stage-
heroics of 18th-century Tragedy, e.g. those Edinburgh successes, John
Home's *Douglas* (1757) and Joanna Baillie's *The Family Legend* (1823).
Scott helped to put on *The Family Legend* with correct Highland costume
and an audience of chieftains (Harold W. Thompson, *A Scottish Man of
Feeling*: Oxford, 1931: pp. 174-5), and wrote for it a prologue picturing
how these "wild tales" of "romantic Calydon" would fill Scotsmen
abroad with nostalgia (Baillie, *Dramatic and Poetical Works*: London, 1851:
p. 481). The final speech in the play, an idealised picture of Highland
regiments raised by Pitt for the Napoleonic Wars, shows at least one use
that the central powers had for the Highlanders. Scott himself succumbs
to the usual Highlandising in *The Highland Widow*, in which a Highland
crofter woman and her son address each other in Ossianic rhetoric, and
the MacIvors in *Waverley* are similarly unreal, where they are not just
walking folk-lore. But in *Rob Roy* and 'The Two Drovers' Scott rises above
such glamour and sets himself to imagine what really happens when
Highland and Lowland ways of life are opposed in the same community
or the same person. (For *Rob Roy*, see chap. V, p. 150.)

6 (p. 108): The great hit of the stage *Rob Roy* was Bailie Nicol Jarvie, but
Scott had to warn the character-actor Mackay against overplaying the
part. Finally he was delighted with the "national truth and understanding" of Mackay's acting, but he doubted if it would be "broad enough,
or sufficiently caricatured" for a London audience (Lockhart, *Life of
Scott*, IV, pp. 227-30; V, pp. 82-3). Even in Scotland itself the theatre was
liable to show up the shaky status of the native dialect. Most professional
actors in Edinburgh in the 18th century were English, and audiences
"were wont to go into fits of laughter over the ill pronunciation" of actors
in *The Gentle Shepherd*. One manager advertised in the *Caledonian Mercury*
in 1758: "Application has been taken to learn the Scots Dialect in this
Piece as perfectly as possible", to do justice to "this excellent Pastoral"
(James C. Dibbin, *The Annals of the Edinburgh Stage*: Edinburgh, 1888:
pp. 96-7). This may well have been carried out: Henry Mackenzie recalls
hearing an English actor in the play speak Scots 'like a native' (*Anecdotes
and Egotisms*, p. 15).

Chapter IV

1 (p. 113): The first (Kilmarnock) edition numbered 612; the first Edinburgh (1787), 2,800 (with 1,500 subscribers); and the 1793 Edinburgh
(one of the last in his lifetime), 1,000. Currie's edition of the *Works* (1800),
which had reached its eighth printing by 1815, sold 2,000 copies of each
of its first four printings, and these came out within four years. (Chambers-

NOTES

Wallace, *Burns*, I, p. 388; II, p. 91; III, p. 260, n. 1; IV, p. 294; Kilmarnock *Bibliography*.)

2 (p. 120): Hamilton of Gilbertfield Augustanised the *Wallace* in 1722. Neither Hamilton nor Blind Harry has much interest for us now, but the medieval poet tells his story with some immediacy, and points it with the genuinely weighty realisation of fate and time natural to his age, whereas Hamilton deals glibly in routine couplets. The difference is between a style influenced by Chaucer and a style affected by Ramsay's kind of 'homeliness'.

I doubt if, as is often assumed, the mass of readers were usually using Hamilton's version. It is true that many contemporary editions of the *Wallace* and of Barbour's *Brus* were in black-letter, which only scholars could read with ease, e.g. *Wallace*, Edinburgh 1648, Edinburgh '1758' (supposedly 1716), uniform with a *Brus*; *Brus*, 1670, 1672, 1737, '1758'. But a great many more editions were in ordinary type, and it is of these that a writer on 19th-century Glasgow libraries (who is careful to distinguish between Hamilton and the original) remarks: "No other books were more read, and consequently it is extremely difficult to get hold of clean and perfect copies" (Thomas Mason, *Public and Private Libraries of Glasgow*: Glasgow, 1885: p. 275). John Pinkerton wanted the Middle-Scots spelling of the old poems rigidly preserved to keep them out of the hands of "the vulgar"; their own Scots would then wither away, a desirable end as "few modern Scotticisms are not barbarisms" (*Ancient Scotish Poems*, I, pp. xvii-xviii). He would scarcely have bothered about this if the peasants' copies of the poems had been in the modern recensions.

3 (p. 127): Gentlemen such as Sir Robert Aytoun and Lord Gordon wrote pale imitations of the English poets—Wyatt, Donne, Vaughan, Marvell. On the other hand, Sir Thomas Maitland (a son of the compiler of the famous MS. collection) has a coarse vernacular flyting which is really a word-game with Scots ('Satyr upon Sir Niel Laing': Watson, *Choice Collection*, Part II, p. 54). One long-drawn-out piece of very local humour, the anonymous 'The Mare of Colingtoun', switches from rough vernacular,

> I leave the Creash within my Wame,
> With a' my Heart to *Finlay Grame*,

to a parody of Middle-Scots poetic diction,

> I leave my Tongue Rethorical,
> My duice Voice, Sweet and Musical . . .
> (*Choice Collection*, Part I, pp. 60-1).

Laing collects occasional poetry—panegyrics on the birth of royal children, events such as Killiecrankie and the Darien Expedition. His two collections register the take-over of run-of-the-mill Scottish verse by the couplet of Dryden. Scots is rarely used. Such as there is ranges from the folk-doggerel of 'Killychrankie',

> And Clinkim Clankim on their Crowns,
> the Lads began to claw then,

(Series I, Poem 27) to 'New Lessons for the Kirk of Scotland' (Series 2, Poem 12), written in that far from broad Scots (marked by a few spellings and religious and legal technical terms) which survived in formal and upper-class usage till a late date.

Chapter V

1 (p. 141): Tannahill belonged to one of a "considerable number" of Paisley tradesmen's clubs which met for various kinds of discussion. His club discussed "Essays, Songs, and Musical Compositions", and in the case of poetry "each stanza, verse, line, and word was keenly discussed". The members considered themselves "the cream of the intellectual tradesmen of the town". Tannahill himself was a weaver (Robert Tannahill, *Poems*, ed. D. Semple, Paisley: 1900, pp. xlvii, lii).

2 (p. 142): This basic history (where references have not already been given) has been taken from the *Old Statistical Account*; Hume Brown, *History of Scotland*, III; Mathieson, *The Awakening of Scotland* and *Church and Reform in Scotland*; Johnston, *History of the Working Classes in Scotland*, chaps. 9-11; L. J. Saunders, *Scottish Democracy, 1815–1840* (Edinburgh: 1950); and Thomas Ferguson, *The Dawn of Scottish Social Welfare* (London: 1948), esp. chap. 4.

3 (p. 146): There are *The Provost* (discussed later in this chapter); Barrie's *A Window in Thrums*, although he deliberately presents his small Angus weaving town as having more of a village mentality; and Lewis Grassic Gibbon's *Grey Granite* (1934), the first serious Scottish novel to be based on a sense of the large town with its variety of classes, its industrial work, and its affiliations with the country. Many modern writers, of course, have rendered the Scottish town—George Barke, George Blake, Robin Jenkins—but novels such as *The Shipbuilders* hardly ask to be taken as literature. Two recent novels, Robin Jenkins's *The Thistle and the Grail* and David Lambert's *He Must So Live*, catch admirably the racy backchat of the Glasgow tenement-dweller; but their narrative style, plot, and general level of insight are disappointingly close to the usual library-novel.

4 (p. 146): Examples will emerge during this and the following chapter. Leddy Grippy in Galt's *The Entail*, and in Scott Caleb Balderstone (*The Bride of Lammermoor*), Andrew Fairservice (*Rob Roy*), and even the Head-riggs in *Old Mortality* are overripe 'characters'; and Morton and Lord Evandale (*Old Mortality*), the Master of Ravenswood (*The Bride of Lammermoor*), Alan Fairford (*Redgauntlet*), and even Reuben Butler (*The Heart of Midlothian*) are stock heroes from romance.

5 (p. 149): This essay also criticises current Scottish drama: "We no longer attempt to represent Scotch life on the stage at all. 'Rob Roy', the 'Lady of the Lake', and 'Jeanie Deans', those compositions out of compositions, conventionalised at the second remove from imagination, keep our boards with a perdurable hold . . . for a number of years one of the most popular representatives of Jeanie Deans in the minor theatres has been a lady who does not even pretend to speak Scotch" (pp. 63-4); historiography: "the century and a half since the Union, or the century since the Rebellion—remains much less familiar than the corresponding period of English life to the Scottish generation which has grown up with Mr Stevenson" (p. 66); the fixation on the country: "what tolerable Scotch fiction we have tends to deal only fragmentarily with rural lives and never with the collective life of our larger towns" (p. 68); and general taste: "our attention to our preachers is the measure of our neglect of our literary men"—Burton and Skene, Masson, even Lang and Stevenson

get less attention than published sermons and "the last new preacher" (pp. 68-9).

6 (p. 153): Certainly the 'Forty-five drastically affected the lives of many thousands of people. It brought about the virtual suppression of the ancient Highland social unit, the clan. It led to the massacre of some thousands of Highland folk who had set off south at the call of traditional loyalties, enticed by a prospect they could barely grasp, and led by a nobleman whose cause was half a century out of date. The state administration of the lands confiscated from Jacobite chieftains was good in that it ended the feudal dues and services which the crofters had previously owed to their landlords, bad in that the Crown put in factors (managers) who had no hereditary respect for the people. In all, the 'Forty-five brought about rapid, widespread *modernisation* of the Highlands (in dress, communications, land tenure). But this process was already well under way—for example British troops had been building roads and bridges there since the 1720's. Any novelist who was to do more than glamorise the Rising as the noble swansong of a heroic age would have had to bring out this phase in a gradual process, and show something of the ordinary life of the society which was thus disrupted.

7 (p. 164): Forced Scotticising can be found daily in our belles-lettres, e.g. in the many writings which try to make out that an unusual sense of colour, or detail, or description is distinctive to Scottish painting, or literature, or architecture. This approach is comparatively restrained by a critic's sense of the concrete in John Speirs's *The Scots Literary Tradition*, Ian Finlay's *Art in Scotland* (Oxford: 1948), and John Tonge's *The Arts of Scotland* (London: 1938)—although it peeps out again and again in shaky generalisations such as Tonge's "Scottish art as a whole . . . is much more involved and restless and dynamic than English art", which he relates to our Celtic roots (p. 16). The tendency runs amok in Kurt Wittig's *The Scottish Tradition in Literature* (Edinburgh: 1958). Dr Wittig, a German, never hesitates to distort, prune, explain away, or silently overlook whole sections of his subject if that is the only way to fit it into his small model of the 'truly Scots'. His governing assumption comes out, for example, in his argument that if certain architectural features, such as crow-stepping, open spires and crowns, and stone-slabbed roofing, occur frequently in Scottish buildings, then it can only be because "they reflect an underlying, essentially Scottish conception of beauty, and that the same essentially Scottish conception of it is to some extent reflected in certain other Scottish arts" (pp. 4-5). No word of either the practical needs which threw up such features or of the quite other cultures in which they also occur. The literary effects of riding this theory are too numerous to detail (they include arguing that Dunbar has more humour than Burns).

Chapter VI

1 (p. 174): Scott constantly spoke as though art were an inferior activity, e.g. (to Maria Edgeworth) "no brain but a madman's could have invented so much stuff" (*Letters*, VIII, p. 165), and to Lockhart (when he was flogging himself on after his bankruptcy), "You know I don't care a curse about what I write or what becomes of it" (*Letters*, IX, p. 368). This carelessness was not just the fatigue of a trying period; he was from the first so reckless a writer that he used to send the first version of his

novels straight to the printer and publish them as they stood. Lockhart
noted that he prided himself more on the manures he had compounded
than on his poems and novels (*Life*, V, p. 133). In fact Scott was not
capable of, and even shied away from, the intense psychological engross-
ment, the exploration of himself and others, essential to creative work.
Apart from the unmistakable impression we form from Lockhart's *Life*,
there is a remark by his acquaintance Captain Basil Hall: "By concealing
even from himself, as it were, every unkindly emotion, he ceases to feel
it" (*Life*, V, p. 417).

2 (p. 178): 18th-century Church history, from the revoking of the Act
against patronage by the London government in 1712, is a series of victories for Moderatism. In the General Assembly they won most of the
key decisions, e.g. the Abjuration Oath imposed in 1719 was unsuccess-
fully resisted by the High-flyers; the Marrowmen (opponents of the "cold
morality" of the Moderates) were defeated, and rebuked by the Assembly,
in the Marrow Controversy of the 1720's; and the first Seceders, under
Ebenezer Erskine, who resisted the various degrees of patronage imposed
by the government, were at first supported by the Assembly but finally
ejected (Hume Brown, *History of Scotland*, III, pp. 236-42).

3 (p. 186): For the manœuvres of the splinter parties before Bothwell
Bridge, and the disastrous policy of the extremist preacher Blackader,
who persuaded the prisoners not to free themselves by signing a harmless
indemnity (they were finally deported, and drowned in a wreck off
Orkney), see Wodrow, *History of the Sufferings of the Church of Scotland*
(edition Edinburgh: 1829), III, pp. 118 n., 125-6; Mathieson, *Politics and
Religion in Scotland*, II, pp. 277-82. In 1690 the Covenanters were trying
to raise an army to protect the Parliamentary Convention in Edinburgh
against the still active Catholic forces who held the Castle. The "jangling
debates" on the make-up of the army, the fanatical determination of the
extremists to insulate themselves against all possible 'corruption' and to
refuse all officers except those of known religious zeal, are recorded in
Faithful Contendings Displayed, collected and kept in record by Mr Michael
Shields, Clerk to the Societies [of Covenanters] (edition Edinburgh:
1780), pp. 393-401.

4 (p. 191): Pennecuik of Edinburgh published in his *Collection of Scots Poems*
(a favourite work, constantly reprinted) two poems, 'The Presbyterian
Pope' and 'Elegy on Robert Forbes', which feed popular resentment of
Church discipline by suggesting with much dirty detail that the kirk-
treasurer's man (who supervised the people's morals) was in league with
the prostitutes to make money from the townsfolk (*op. cit.* pp. 108 ff.,
133 ff.). In Dougal Graham's 'Jockey and Maggy's Courtship', Jockey's
mother flytes at 'Whigry'—Presbyterian puritanism—which makes no
practical provision for bastard children and would rather punish the
parents: "'a' your mortifying o' your members, and a' your repenting-
stools; a wheen papist rites an rotten ceremonies, fashing fouks wi' sack
gowns, and buttock-malls, an' I dinna ken what'"; and she accuses the
Kirk Session of excusing the laird the cutty stool—the seat on which
swearers, fathers of illegitimate children, and the like had to sit for several
Sundays in full view of the congregation—although "he's continually
riding on the hussies to this day, and them that wadna let him, he rives
their duds, and kicks their doups" (Graham, *Collected Writings*, II, pp.
21-2, 30).

NOTES

5 (p. 195): Norman Cohn, a recent writer on the psychology of religion, observes, "In the popular eschatology of the Middle Ages, as in the phantasies of a paranoiac, the world is seen in terms of a mortal struggle waged by good parents and good children against bad parents and bad children", and again: "The megalomaniac view of oneself as the Elect, wholly good, abominably persecuted, yet assured of ultimate triumph . . . these attitudes are symptoms which together constitute the unmistakable symptoms of paranoia" (*The Pursuit of the Millennium*, London: 1957, pp. 69, 309).

Chapter VII

1 (p. 200): Hogg had to bring out *The Justified Sinner* anonymously, and he got nothing for it. He wrote to Blackwood asking that as the 'Noctes Ambrosianae' feature in his magazine would probably be the first 'efficient noticer' of the book, it should conceal the authorship and ascribe it to a Glasgow man: "This will give excellent and delightful scope and freedom". At its start (p. 3) the novel is made circumstantially realistic, rather in the way of Defoe; and the third-person, 'editor's' narrative closes similarly: "this is all with which history, judiciary records, and tradition, furnish me relating to these matters" (p. 85). The sinner's diary is rounded off with a supposedly authentic account of finding the corpse of a suicide, perfectly preserved; the 'editor' prints one James Hogg's account of the last days of this unfortunate (which was actually printed in *Blackwood's* (1823), XIV, pp. 188-90), and then recounts his own imaginary visit to the grave and his finding the diary in it (pp. 217-30). (For Hogg's letter to Blackwood see National Library MS. 4012, f. 184.)

2 (p. 201): In *Calvin and Art* Dr Mary P. Ramsay argues that Calvin's "abhorrence of all materialistic anthropomorphism" does not mean that he thought there was anything "intrinsically inferior" about non-didactic art. Her case depends, it seems to me, on special pleading. Calvin wrote in his *Institutes* that historical and representational pictures "have some use in teaching and admonishing a man" but 'purely imaginative and decorative art' had no such justification: "what profit the second can bring save only delectation, I see not. And yet it is evident that even such were almost all the images that heretofore have stood up in churches. . . . Only I speak to this end, that though there were no fault in them, yet they do nothing avail to teach." Surely this implies some disparagement of "delectation" and hence an even graver undervaluing of the imaginative? Here as elsewhere Calvin blocks off certain experiences by his narrow and artificial psychology and for anti-Catholic propaganda ends. The arguments of both him and Sir William Mure of Rowallan, the Scottish Calvinist, suggest an idea of the whole feelings and of art which—like Plato's—dissects experience into detached parts which are not in fact true to experience, e.g. treating painting as an actual illusion which is meant to, and does, deceive (*op. cit.* Edinburgh: 1938, pp. 18-27, 59-70).

3 (p. 219): The Blackwood set were close knit by marriage, as were many such in that Edinburgh—William Robertson, the Adam brothers, the Broughams, and the lawyer Clerk of Eldin; Dundas, Cockburn, and the Hermands; the Tytlers, Sir James Mackintosh, and Henry Mackenzie; Scott and Lockhart. Amongst the Blackwoodites, a daughter of John Wilson was married to a nephew of Susan Ferrier (a philosopher, who

edited the *Noctes Ambrosianae*) and Wilson's youngest daughter married
William Aytoun, John Blackwood's closest friend among the second
generation of contributors to the magazine. (*Blackwood and His Sons*, I,
p. 42; III, p. 20). The first generation, when William lived in Princes
Street, was the heyday of this circle (Hogg, Lockhart, Galt, Wilson); but
a second close group of contributors, including Wilson, Aytoun, de
Quincey, D. M. Moir, and Lord Neaves, frequented John Blackwood's
house (*ibid*. II, p. 454; III, p. 20).

4 (p. 221): Scott did conceive of *The Fair Maid of Perth* at a morally subtler
level. When preparing for it he wrote in his journal: ". . . it may be possible to make a difference betwixt the old Highlander and him of modern
date", and again, "Suppose a man's nerves supported by feelings of
honour, or say by the spur of jealousy supporting him against constitutional timidity to a certain point, then suddenly giving way—I think
something tragic might be produced" (*Journal*, II, p. 78). But he had
hardly the consistent delicacy of touch to bring off such a subject. In
practice Conachar is far too much a thinly-personified embodiment of
one set trait, cowardice, for the novel to get deeper than the historical
surface.

Chapter VIII

1 (p. 241): Carlyle's mother was naturally colloquial in her writing, e.g. to
Thomas: "Oh, man, could I but write! I'll tell ye a' when we meet, but
I must in the meantime content myself . . . and tell me honestly if you
read your chapter e'en and morn, lad. You mind I hod if not your hand,
I hod your foot of it." His father wrote a careful, bookish language
learned from religious usages, e.g. "before long we must leave the place
we now occupy for a place in eternity, and only one of two places can we
look for, as there is not a third"; and recalling a chapel-door argument
about which body rose at the day of judgement, "I observed that I thought
a stinking clogg of a body like Robert Scott the weaver's would be very
unfit to inhabit those places". Carlyle himself often resorts to Scots, esp.
in family letters, usually in the form of standard idioms which he sometimes italicises as consciously not Standard English, e.g. "She has . . . a
bit *nimblegawn* tongue", or "He has need to have a lang ladle that sups
with the Deil, and he has need to have a long head that predicts the movements of aught depending on Mrs Buller" (*Early Life*, I, pp. 100-1; 180;
190, 212-13).

2 (p. 243): In many poems of Hugh MacDiarmid's words lifted from non-
spoken Scots (for example from Jamieson's *Dictionary*) are used with con-
summate success, notably in the first stanza of 'The Eemis Stane':

> I' the how-dumb-deid o' the cauld hairst nicht
> The warl' like an eemis stane
> Wags i' the lift;
> An' my eerie memories fa'
> Like a yowdendrift
>
> (*Sangschaw*, Edinburgh: 1925, p. 23)

Here the verbal *trouvailles* are so used that each takes on sufficient meaning from its context to *become* meaningful for the reader as the poem un-
folds; they do not just add to a new poetic diction. "How-dumb-deid",
for example, is quite as expressive as Shakespeare's "dead vast and middle

of the night". Yet MacDiarmid's poetry hardly alters my argument, as it has taken his very unusual genius to give life to dead words.

3 (p. 250): Fergusson was the recognised wit and speech-maker of the Cape Club, and Ramsay was much sought after for his talk in the Edinburgh of the 1720's (Chambers, *Traditions of Edinburgh*, p. 25). An old Irvine man told Robert Chambers that he remembered Burns's talk for its "sententious brevity"—what Burns himself claimed as his "countra wit" (Lockhart, *Life of Burns*, p. 36). Similarly Mrs Dunlop describes his unwillingness in conversation to 'suppress an arch and full-pointed bon mot'—again a quality that went straight through into his poetry (Currie, *Burns*, I, pp. 254-5). Such powers of talk gave Burns a special place in his community: Scott says that "it was no easy task to deal with Burns. The power of his language—the vigour of his satire—the severity of illustration with which his fancy instantly supplied him bore down all retort"; and this is confirmed by a local minister. He speaks of Burns in company —"the acuteness and originality displayed by him, the depth of his discernment, the force of his expressions", and recalls his own sudden "tremor and embarrassment" when in mid-sermon he suddenly noticed that Burns was in the congregation (*Quarterly Review*, 1809, I, p. 26; Lockhart, *Life*, p. 51).

4 (p. 253): Two cases in the fiction illuminate key aspects of the language difficulties, the Anglicisation resulting from 'getting on in the world' and the stiffness produced by Anglicisation. In Galt's *Sir Andrew Wylie* the hero speaks unusually broadly when he returns to his native village, and the comment is made (although it has not been shown in the body of the novel), "He had, indeed, resolved in his own mind to resume his former familiarity, as well as the broad accent of his boyish dialect; not that the latter required any effort, for he had carefully and constantly preserved it, but he had unconsciously adopted a few terms and phrases purely English; and in the necessity of speaking intelligibly to his clients and fashionable friends, had habitually acquired, without any of the southern tone [i.e. accent], considerable purity of language" (*op. cit.* p. 375). This reads as though it might be an account of Galt's own experience.

In *Rob Roy* Scott makes the Northumberland hero notice, on first meeting a Scotsman, "the national intonation and slow pedantic mode of expression, arising from a desire to avoid peculiarities of idiom and dialect" (Victoria ed., p. 33). This agrees with contemporary accounts of Scotsmen's speech from mid-century (Scott, indeed, is perhaps describing usage of his own time rather than of the Union period), e.g. "their pronunciation and accent is far from being agreeable; it gives an air of gravity, sedateness, and importance to their words; which, though of use sometimes in an harangue or public discourse, in common conversation seems dull, heavy, stupid, and unharmonious", and makes them take the sting out of anecdotes (Captain Topham, *Letters from Edinburgh*, Written in the Years 1774 and 1775, London: 1776, pp. 54-5. I am indebted to Tony Inglis for this reference). A letter in Ruddiman's *Weekly Magazine* for 17.9.1772 remarks that "an itch of Englifying prevails among us, which, being for the most part an uncouth mixture of bad English with Scots, has the stiffest and most absurd appearance" (p. 361; my attention was drawn to this letter by J. W. Oliver's article 'Fergusson and *Ruddiman's Magazine*' in *Robert Fergusson, 1750–1774*).

It is significant that such stiltedness, typical of what we would now call 'Morningsaide' or 'pan-loaf', was thought to be *atypical* of Scotsmen at an earlier period—before intensive Anglicisation. Sir George Mackenzie in the preface to his *Pleadings* contrasts Scots with the English 'gravity' and 'slowness' of speech: "The Scots pronunciation, on the other hand, is, like ourselves, fiery, abrupt, sprightly, and bold", "brisk, smart and quick" (quoted from Millar, *Scottish Prose*, p. 128). It seems unlikely that the Scots of average countryfolk was ever "fiery, abrupt, sprightly", i.e. Mackenzie is giving evidence of an important side of the language change: Scots was not just shrinking indiscriminately, it was ceasing to be the usage of the *urbane cultivated class*. Many 18th-century writers claim that there was at one time a more civilised Scots than any now known; they must mean the speech of a sophisticated upper-class. E.g. Scott describes a Mrs Bethune Baliol, an old woman of 'good family' whose "juvenile recollections stretched backwards till before the eventful year 1745". "Her speech was Scottish—decidedly Scottish, often containing phrases and words little used in the present day", but—the typical qualification—it was as different from "ordinary Scotch *patois*" as the speech of St James's from Billingsgate"; it had no "disagreeable drawl", the vowels were no broader than Italian, and it was accompanied by a "lively manner and gestures", suggesting an origin in old Scottish court speech (*The Highland Widow* and *Chronicles of the Canongate*, Victoria ed., pp. 379, 387; see also Ramsay of Ochtertyre, *Scotland and Scotsmen*, I, pp. 18-19, and in Currie (ed.), *Burns*, I, pp. 280-2; and Lockhart on an aunt of Scott's, perhaps the model for Mrs Bethune Baliol: *Life of Scott*, I, p. 75).

5 (p. 259): In this final novel of Lawrence's, Mellors, the gamekeeper, tied by marriage to a randy in the village, becomes the lover of Lady Constance Chatterley, from the big house. After his experience of war and of marriage, Mellors periodically craves to retreat into himself and hold off emotional insistences from other people. These tensions are expressed simultaneously in his deliberately coarse use of dialect (which he can also use tenderly) to hold Connie off; and this is even argued out between them, she charging him with an offensive use of common talk. " . . . he took no notice of Constance or of Lady Chatterley; he just softly stroked her loins or her breasts. . . . His 'tha mun come' seemed not addressed to her, but some common woman. . . . After all Mr Winter, who was really a gentleman and a man of the world, treated her as a person and a discriminating individual; he did not lump her together with all the rest of female womanhood in his 'thee' and 'tha' " (Ed. Stockholm: 1946, pp. 154, 161, 163; and see esp. chaps. 10 and 15, *passim*).

6 (p. 260): There had been objections to the style of *The Provost*, which Galt answers by appealing to his proper, Scottish audience: "What has thus been regarded as a fault by some, others acquainted with the peculiarities of the language may be led to consider as a beauty". He maintains that Scots is as appropriate in a historical work as in "a composition so local as 'THE PROVOST' " because there can be no bad taste in using Scots to express "sentiments and feelings entirely Scottish". He also notices the distinction between vocabulary and thoroughly Scots syntax: "there is such an idiomatic difference in the structure of the national dialects of England and Scotland, that very good Scotch might be couched in the purest English terms, and without the employment of a single Scottish word" (*Ringan Gilhaize*, in *Works*, ed. Meldrum and Roughead, Edinburgh: 1936, II, pp. 325-6).

NOTES

Chapter IX

1 (p. 276): Aikman studied in Rome after selling off a paternal estate in Angus; he was persuaded to settle in London by the Duke of Argyll, and there became a fashionable portrait painter (*DNB*, I, p. 187).

Allan Ramsay's career was similar. He settled in London to paint portraits after a Grand Tour and study at Rome. Four of the six main patrons mentioned by his biographer were Scottish noblemen who spent some of their time in London, and he was also, through the Argyll family, one of the many Scotsmen in London who got patronage from Bute (Alastair Smart, *The Life and Art of Allan Ramsay*, London: 1952, p. 37).

David Allan spent some time in Russia: according to Cunningham, "he was determined to go abroad somewhere or other . . . to try his fortune" (*Life of Wilkie*, I, p. 78).

For the Hamiltons and More, see Ian Finlay's comment on *émigré* artists of the 18th century, with their typical frigid and derivative classicism (*Art in Scotland*, pp. 80-1).

For Wilkie, see below, note 8.

Gillray's father was a Lanark man, who served as a trooper in Flanders under Butcher Cumberland and was later a Chelsea Pensioner in London, where the cartoonist was probably born (*DNB*, VII, p. 1253). In London Gillray found a subject unavailable elsewhere—the personalities and decisions of the central government.

For Gibb, the Adams, Stuart, and Mylne, see John Holloway, 'Scotland's Émigré Architects': *Saltire Review* (1955), No. 4, pp. 18-24. Dr Holloway ends with the hope that someone will go into "the fundamental cause of this steady emigration of genius".

Telford emigrated from Eskdale in the Borders in search of better opportunities for his building skills than he could find at home. There was the less inducement to stay because many of his friends had already left; when Samuel Smiles asked what all the Eskdale children did for a living, he was told, "Oh, they swarm off". Telford went south with letters of introduction to various members of landed Eskdale families already settled in London (L.T.C. Rolt, *Thomas Telford*, London: 1958, pp. 6-8; Sir Alexander Gibb, *The Story of Telford*, London: 1935, p. 5).

William Hunter was meant for the Church but could not accept the Articles and studied medicine instead, in Glasgow, London, and Edinburgh. He was invited south by James Douglas, one of the first notable Scottish doctors and anatomists settled in England, as an assistant dissector. He had succeeded to an estate in Lanarkshire, but he never took it up. His brother John went south to assist him, and was a student at Oxford and an Army doctor in Portugal before entering on his great London career. Douglas had studied in Rheims before settling in London (*DNB*, X, pp. 382-3; 287-8; V, p. 1234).

Horner was dissatisfied with Scotland for many reasons. "To one resident in the stagnation or poverty of Edinburgh conversation, the *beaux-esprits* of London are entertaining and instructive novelties." "I become daily more averse to the practice of the Scots Court"—this was the period when young Whigs could not get briefs and only political truckling paid, Many motives for emigrating 'occurred daily to his meditation', and Dugald Stewart seems to have advised in favour of it. In 1802 he left

Scotland. On revisiting Edinburgh in 1812, he enjoyed the company of Jeffrey, Henry Erskine, John Playfair, Dugald Stewart—but he still hankered after the Hollands and Foxes and the top-level discussion of political affairs in the London great houses (*Memoirs and Correspondence*, I, pp. 173, 174, 178; II, pp. 110-11).

2 (p. 276): For Robertson, see above, p. 131.

Adam Smith went to England, like the historian Adam Ferguson, as tutor to nobility, a rich inducement for a Scottish professor as he rarely got more than £300 a year for his Chair (plus the 'sale' of it when he retired), whereas for tutoring he got as big a yearly salary plus the same as a pension for life on giving up the post. Smith spent some time in France in the company of Quesnay and the new economists, the Encyclopedists, and at the provincial capital, Toulouse. Strahan (a publisher of Scottish extraction) hoped that he would be persuaded to settle in London, where he was a close friend of the Scottish circle and of Johnson, Burke, Reynolds, and Gibbon at the Literary Club. But in 1778 he settled in Edinburgh Old Town, where he had many friends (the nucleus of the *literati*), and stayed there till his death (Rae, *Life*, pp. 165-6, 197-217, 315, 325).

Hume's wanderings are complicated and need not be given here; his movements and motives can be followed in detail in his *Letters* and Mossner's *Life*. We may note that he first left Scotland as a tutor to a Scottish nobleman settled in the Home Counties. Ministers' prejudice kept him out of several Scottish jobs, e.g. the Glasgow Chair of Moral Philosophy. He had to stay in London for a time studying material for his *History of the Tudors*; and thenceforward we find him periodically wondering where he should settle—in Paris for good? in London for good? return to his native country? He spent twenty months in London after Paris, but the virulent anti-Scottish prejudice of the time wore him down, and at last, his diplomatic commission having expired, he forswore "ambition" and settled in Edinburgh, "without casting the least Thought of Regreat to London, or even to Paris", resolved to stay in Scotland except for 'jaunts' south. His Scottish friends in London had included many of the *émigrés* mentioned elsewhere in this chapter, e.g. John Home, Adam Ferguson, Gilbert Elliot, Allan Ramsay the painter, Wedderburn, the Adams, and the publishers Strahan and Millar (Mossner, *Life*, pp. 162-3; 247 ff.; 390 ff.; *Letters*, I, p. 264, II, p. 83; Mossner, pp. 401, 504-5; *Letters*, II, p. 208; Mossner, p. 556; *ibid.* pp. 392-3).

Henry Mackenzie went to London to study English Exchequer practice, and a friend wanted him to stay and qualify for the English bar; but the wishes of his family and his own lack of legal ambition decided him to stay in Scotland (Scott, *Lives of the Novelists*, pp. 163-4).

Burns, like many small farmers in the south-west (e.g. the Carlyles), was worn down by the hardship of winning a decent life from poor land, and this, along with his troubles with women, made him think of emigrating to the West Indies. He had arranged a passage, and was hurrying the publication of the Kilmarnock volume to pay for it, when Mary Campbell died in bearing his child, and it seems that this release from responsibilities, along with the success of the *Poems* a little later, decided him to stay (Snyder, *Life*, pp. 140-52).

For William Chambers, see above, pp. 228-9.

Leslie went to America as a tutor in 1789, in 1790 he went to London 'in search of fortune', and he then spent two years in Etruria as a tutor to the Wedgwood family, some of whom had been fellow-students in Edinburgh. He returned to Scotland as Professor of Mathematics at Edinburgh against the "united opposition" of the town ministers, who considered his endorsement of Hume's theory of causation a piece of blasphemous freethinking (*DNB*, XI, p. 984; Mathieson, *Church and Reform*, pp. 95-100).

For Jeffrey, see below, note 3.

Chalmers was offered the Chair of Moral Philosophy at London and at first thought that the imminent Royal Commission decision on the Scottish Universities would decide him whether or not it was worth staying on as a university teacher in Scotland. He was then enabled to postpone his decision for a year, and in the meantime he was elected to the Edinburgh Chair of Divinity (*Memoirs*, III, pp. 155-7, 159, 205-8).

3 (p. 277): Sir John Clerk sent his son to Eton: "I thought it wou'd be an additional qualification to him that he understood the English Language, which since the Union wou'd always be necessary for a Scotsman in whatever station of life he might be in [*sic*], but especially in any publick character. . . . I had no more to expect from an English education but that he should learn the English language" (*Memoirs, op. cit.* pp. 86-7, 99).

David Dalrymple (later Lord Hailes) went to Eton: "Perhaps his father intended him for the English Bar, or expected him to get a seat in the House of Commons, where his being master of the language would be of great advantage to him" (Ramsay, *Scotland and Scotsmen*, I, pp. 393-4).

Gilbert Elliot was sent, after private schooling, to Oxford for the sake of "advancement" in England (Chambers, *Dictionary of Eminent Scotsmen*, I, p. 528).

Wedderburn, later a Lord Chancellor, "was sent a winter to the Temple to study English law and to acquire a thorough knowledge of the English pronunciation, which his father considered as a matter of great consequence to a public speaker. He had, with that view, taught his children from their early years to avoid Scotticisms in phraseology and elocution" (Ramsay, *Scotland and Scotsmen*, I, pp. 438-9). Ramsay remarks that Wedderburn managed when speaking to be 'natural' in spite of his 'correctness'; and James Mackintosh, in an article on the first *Edinburgh Review*, to which Wedderburn contributed, cites one of his mistakes in grammar as showing "the difficulties he had had to surmount in acquiring what costs an Englishman no study" (Mackintosh, *Miscellaneous Works*, London: 1846, II, p. 472).

Francis Horner's father sent him to read with a minister in the Isle of Wight, "thinking it desirable that he should be freed from the disadvantages of a provincial dialect to a public speaker". At the age of 19 he writes his father minute letters on his progress in Anglicisation: "I am now and then detected in a Scotch inflexion, but hardly ever without previously detecting myself". In later life he writes of the 'composition' of a travel book by a Scotsman that it is "very Scotch in the cast and all the thinking of it; but very good, for all that" (*Memoirs*, I, pp. 5-6, 16; II, p. 298).

Lord Woodhouselee sent his son Patrick Tytler to an English school "chiefly for the improvement of his scholarship", although he had been at a Scottish one himself (Burgon, *Portrait of a Christian Gentleman*, p. 44).

Jeffrey "thought frequently of the English bar" but, like many of his friends, decided against it because it was expensive, it demanded a longer wait without practice than the Scottish, and he had more contacts in his own country. He too, "always contemplating the probability of public speaking being his vocation . . . was bent upon purifying himself of the national inconvenience"—his dialect and accent (Cockburn, *Life*, I, pp. 50, 46-7).

4 (p. 277): For example, among the lawyers Cockburn, Dundas, Jeffrey (though he did some further study at Oxford), James Mackintosh, and Henry Erskine; among the ministers Sir Harry Moncrieff, Robertson, Chalmers, Thomas McCrie, another man of letters Thomas Thomson, John Jamieson the lexicographer, John Home, and Alexander Webster who made one of the first censuses of Edinburgh; among the literary men Henry Mackenzie, Hume, Scott, Beattie, and Dugald Stewart; the 'commonsense' philosopher Reid; and among the scientists Joseph Black and the geologist Hutton.

5 (p. 277): Many Scottish literary men went to Oxford to study Classics, some (like Smith and Lockhart) on the Snell Exhibition to Balliol College. Boswell was one of many Scotsmen training for the law who went to study in Holland (*Boswell in Holland*, pp. 2-5). Bishop Douglas, the son of a Pittenweem merchant, studied at Oxford, and was then an Army chaplain and a curate in the Home Counties before Lord Bath, whose son he had tutored, gave him sinecure livings; he became a political pamphleteer and controversialist against Hume (*DNB*, V, pp. 1242-3).

6 (p. 277): Lord Lansdowne sent a son to Edinburgh at this time; he took part in debates at the Speculative Society along with Jeffrey, Brougham, and Horner, as did Lord Webb Seymour. Horner wrote that the idea of legal practice in England kept occurring to him "chiefly, perhaps, in consequence of the intimacies which I have successfully formed with the young Englishmen who have come to the University of Edinburgh to finish their education" (Halévy, *England in 1815*, p. 543; Cockburn, *Life of Jeffrey*, I, p. 107; Horner, *Memoirs*, I, p. 199).

7 (p. 280): Mackintosh at first thought of bookselling in London but had no capital. He studied medicine in Edinburgh, and then went to London for no particular reason save that there was the trend south and he already had relatives in London and Bath. When he went into Parliament he was given a Scottish constituency but London had, of course, become his base. After his Indian career, he hankered after Scotland, and thought of 'retiring' to the Professorship of Moral Philosophy at Edinburgh; but he decided against deserting the Whigs in London at a critical period in their affairs. He later regretted missing his last chance of settling in his native country (*Memoirs of the Life of the Right Hon. Sir James Mackintosh*, ed. R. J. Mackintosh, Boston: 1853, I, p. 20; II, pp. 372-3; *Constable and His Correspondents*, II, p. 176).

8 (p. 281): Everything seems to have been against Wilkie's start as a painter in Scotland. Born in Fife, he soon ran out of patrons and sitters in his own district and went to the Fife coastal towns and to Aberdeen in search of more; but he could get no supplies of brushes, colours, canvas, or ivory outside Edinburgh. Finally he decided that he had better go to England to study at the Royal Academy. In London he soon sold one or two pictures by exhibiting in the windows of print-sellers (Cunningham, *Life*, I, pp. 70-4).

NOTES

9 (p. 282): In his essay 'Byron' T. S. Eliot suggests, authoritatively, but with no show of argument, that Byron's diabolism could have come only "from the religious background provided by a nation which had been ruined by religion. It was a monstrosity, of course, for Scotland to bring forth; but it could come only from a people who took religion more seriously than the English" (*From Anne to Victoria*, ed. Bonamy Dobrée, London: 1937, pp. 602-3). There is no word, however, of how this religiousness might have been passed on to Byron, whether by the atmosphere of mother, neighbours, and school at Aberdeen or by deliberate upbringing; and a very similar diabolism was surely in vogue in France, Italy, and elsewhere.

10 (p. 282): The evidence for this is all over the *Early Life*. The essence of it is also to be found in *Sartor Resartus*, in the contorted presentment of the thinly externalised Teufelsdröckh, with his inability to find regular work and his eccentric habits. He is given as 'difficult' because he is "not without some touch of the universal feeling, a wish to proselytise", i.e. the habit which made editors mistrust Carlyle himself. Carlyle also parodies Jeffrey's orthodox objections to his style (*op. cit.* pp. 5-6, 10, 18, 179). The immediate cause of the eccentricity of the book itself, in which Carlyle comes right onto his almost pathologically indirect and far-fetched manner, is surely this literary frustration.

11 (p. 284): See Carlyle, *Reminiscences*, chap. 'Edward Irving', esp. p. 231: "Theological Scotland, above all things, is dubious and jealous of *originality*; and Irving's tendency to take roads of his own was becoming daily more indisputable". He was finally deposed from the Church of Scotland for the heretical doctrine of the Human Nature of the Divine Man (*ibid.* p. 288); but by that time he had been invited to the more latitudinarian London to preach, and there (before he became a kind of spiritualist) he had a great fashionable success—like Chalmers and, later, the curious Henry Drummond (*Memoirs*, III, p. 161; IV, p. 39; Donald Carswell, *Brother Scots*, pp. 31-7). Thus men like Irving might have had more normal and socially useful Christian careers if their native Church had been less narrow.

12 (p. 290): Children could hold their Scots longer because there was less social pressure on them and because (even if upper-class) they might mix freely with working-class children in the streets or (in the country) at school. Thus about 1810 Scott's son spoke very broad Scots to his English-speaking mother; and in 1817 Jeffrey's little daughter could speak "the nicest broad Scotch"—presumably imitating servants or country children (*Life of Scott*, II, p. 302; *Life of Jeffrey*, II, p. 173). But by 1844 Anglicisation had spread so widely that the children of an upper-class man such as Cockburn could not be got to "do more than pick up a queer word" of Burns here and there, whereas he himself, an old man representing an age of far more Scotticism, spoke "more Scotch than English throughout the day" and English had "made no encroachment" on him (*Journal*, II, pp. 88-9).

GLOSSARY

(The definitions given here apply only to the meanings of the words as used in the passages quoted in this book. They by no means cover all possible uses of these words in Scots.)

A

A', aa: all
aboon, abuin: above, up
aff: off
aff-hand: on the spur of the moment
agains: against
ahint: behind
aiblins: perhaps, possibly
air: early
aits: food, i.e. desert, due
als: as
ane: a, one
arselins: bottom first, on one's bottom
aught: eight
aughtlins: at all, in the least
Auld Reikie: 'Old Smoky', i.e. Edinburgh
ava: at all
awes: owes

B

Babban-quaas: quaking bogs
baggity: greedy
bairn: child
banes: bones
bang: overcome
bawbees: halfpennies
beaking: warming
beas' (i.e. beasts): vermin
beck: curtsey, do obeisance
beddle: beadle, church-officer, and grave-digger
bendis: jumps, clumsy heavings up and down
bicker: wooden cup or dish
bield, beild: shelter
bike: nest (bees' or wasps')
binna: be not, i.e. are not
bir, birr: force, violence
birk: birch
birkie: lively lad
birkin: birchen
birle: spin
birse: bristle
bizz: sizzle, buzz

blackit: blackened
blate: bashful, simple; unpromising
blaws: blows
blear: dim the vision
bleezing: blazing
blirtie: (of weather) changeable, squally
bobbit: bobbed
bodle: small coin; (pl.) pence
bolt: arrow
bonnock: bannock or cake
bonny, bonie: pretty
bowses: drinks
brae: hill
brags: challenges
branks: bridle with wooden curbs
brats: small pieces, rags
braw, brawly: fine, finely
broo: liking, opinion
brugh: town, burgh
bubly: running at the nose
bum: hum, buzz, drone
Burnewin: 'Burn-the-wind', i.e. blacksmith
buttock-mall: fine for fornication imposed by Kirk Session
bye: out-of-the-way
by-hand: finished, settled, over
bynge: bow obsequiously, cringe

C

Ca': call
cald, cauld: cold
caldrife, cauldrife: chilly
callant: lad
cant, canty: cheery, lively, frisky
carl: man, old man
carlin, carline: old woman, shrew, hag, witch
cartes: cards
cateran: Highland robber or freebooter
caup: cup, bowl
cautionrie: suretyship
cawsey: causeway, street
chafts: jaws

chappit: struck
chiel: man, fellow
choppies: (dimin.) shops
chuckie-stanes: small pebbles, used in a game
claise, claes: clothes
Clark-plays: popular dramatic shows, originally on Scriptural subjects
clash: tattle, gossip, tell tales
clattering: chatting
clauts: handfuls
cleekie: crafty
cleekit: link arms; *cleikit:* struck up
clinks: coins, cash
clishmaclaver: idle talk, gossip
clogg: (lit.) block of wood
cloots (baby-cloots): nappies
"Cot, Cot": imitation of Highlander pronouncing "God"
couli: boy, (contemptuously) man
couth, couthy: homely
crack: (*v.*) chaff, talk; (*n.*) tale, speech, say-away
crambo-jingle: ready or extempore rhyming
cranny: crevice
crap: crept
craws: crows
crazed: weakened, decrepit
creeshie: greasy
cuist: cast
cumit: come (past tense)
custock: cabbage stem
custron: rogue, vagabond

D

Dacent: decent
darigies: dirges
daurna: dare not
daws: dawns
dazit: dazed
decoir: adorn, decorate
deid: dead
deil-be-licket: damn all
dernit: hidden
diein': dying
dinna: do not
dis: does
dods: jolts, rocks
dominie: schoolmaster
doup: bottom

dow: (*v.*) is able to; (*n.*) dove (often term of endearment)
dram: small measure (usually of whisky)
dreech: long, slow, tedious
drumlie: thick, muddy, turbid
dub: puddle, gutter; (pl.) mud, filth
duds: rags; hence *duddie:* ragged
dwal: live (dwell)
dwining: dwindling, declining, wasting away
dyke: low wall; ditch
dyvor: bankrupt; debtor; ne'er-do-well, trouble-maker

E

E'e: eye (pl. *een*)
eemis: unsteady
e'en: even
eik: addition
eild: old age
eithly: easily
elbuck: elbow

F

Fa': fall
fain: eager
fairlie, ferly: curiosity, novelty, wonder
fash: bother, worry
fat-kail: broth made with fatty stock
fauld: fold
faut: fault
fawsont: attractive, becoming
feckly: mainly, for the most part
fen': (i.e. fend) manage, subsist
fidge: fidget
fient a: devil a (as in devil a bit)
figmagairie: (usually *figmaleery, whig-maleerie*) whim, caprice
flaff: flap
flannen: flannel
flee: (*v.*) rout; (*n.*) fly
flingin'-tree: flail
flyte: abuse, scold; *flyting:* (lit.) formal abusive rhetoric
fock: folk, people
forcasten: neglected
forgie: forgive
fother: fodder
fou, fu': full; drunk

GLOSSARY

foul a: devil a
frae: from
freath: froth
fresh: (of weather) open, thawing, wet
fure: went
fyke: fidget, flirt
fyle: soil (defile)

G

Gaed: went
gait, gate: way, distance; *nae gate:* nowhere
gane: gone
gang: go
gar: make (i.e. compel, bring about)
gash: spruce, lively; (of weather) bright, pleasant
gaudsman: ploughman
gaun: going
gayan, gey: pretty much, rather
gaylies: pretty-well, well enough
geyzen'd: parched, warped with drought
gi'e: give
girn: grin; snarl; whimper
glowming: twilight
goavin: looking vacantly; throwing the head up and from side to side
gooly: large knife (gully-knife)
gowden: golden
gowk: fool, blockhead
graith: gear (harness, etc.)
gravel: harass, wear down; confuse
greet, greit: cry (weep), moan
grein'd: longed
grey nick quill: (obsc.) Burns's MS. reads "grey neck still", poss. metaphor from sheep-breeding, to suggest a hybrid, or sitter-on-the-fence
grosart: gooseberry
guid: good
gurling: shimmering or swimming in heat-haze (usually used of water)
gyte: mad

H

Ha'—"*big ha' Bible*": hereditary copy belonging to house ("*ha'* ": house or principal room)

had, haud: hold; keep
hae: have
haff: half
hag: hack, chop
haining: saving, hoarding; economising; abstaining
hairst, har'st: harvest
hallion: rogue
hame: home
hap: wrap up
harl: gather, rake together
hash: slash
havering: drivelling, chattering at random
heid: head
herriet: plundered
hie: high
hirdsel: flock
hizzie: hussy
hod: ("I hod if not your hand, I hod your foot of it"): hold (phrase meaning "I am interested in all you do, even if I cannot help directly")
holt: wood
hough: leg, thigh
howdie: midwife
how-dumb-deid: silent middle of night
howff: inn, pub
huff: fit of temper
hurdies: haunches, buttocks
hurle-barrow: wheelbarrow, hand cart

I

Ilk, ilka: each
in-by: in inner part of house
ingle: hearth
intil: into
ither: other

J

Jad: lass, girl; jade
jowler: heavy-jawed dog

K

Kail-yard, -yaird: small kitchen garden, cabbage-patch
kinkhost, -hoast: whooping-cough
kin'les: kindles
kirk: church
kist: box, chest

L

Laigh: low
lang: long
langer: weariness (languor)
lass: girl
leaman: gleaming, shining, blazing
lear: knowledge, learning
leeze me on: (phrase of enthusiasm) give me! cheers for!
leive: ("*micht as leive*"): might as well
leuche: laughed
liein': lying
lift: sky
liket: liked
linking: tripping along
lippen: rely, depend
loon, loun, lown: lad, boy
lounder: buffet, wallop
loup: jump
lowe: flame, blaze
lug, lugget: ear, eared (i.e. with handles)
luikit: looked
luppen: jumped
lute: allowed (let)
lyart: grey (of hair), hoary

M

Madinis: girls (maidens)
maid: made
mailing: farm, holding; rent
mair: more
maist: most
mak: make
mald: girl's name—Mollie
mark: dark
mart: market
maun: must
meat-heal: with a good, healthy appetite
meir: mare; hence *play meir:* hobby-horse in morris dancing
melder: quantity of grain ground at one time
men: mend
merkat: market
merry-dancers: northern lights (*aurora borealis*)
mim: prim, demure, quiet
minny: mummy
mirrie: merry

misdoot: misdoubt
mistaen: mistaken
mony: many
moss: area of boggy moor from which peat could be cut
mottie: full of motes or smuts
muck to lead: dung to cart over the field
mumlingis: mumbled prayers for the dead
myght: might

N

Na, nay: no
naig: horse
neuk: nook, niche, corner, crevice
nichtirtale: by night
Nickie-ben: the Devil
niffer: exchange, bargain
nimble-gawn: garrulous (of a tongue)
nocht: nothing
nokkis: notches
noo: now
nowt: cattle

O

Oe: grandchild
orrow: odd ("*some orrow ouk*": some week or other)
ouk: week
oulklie, owklie: weekly
owre: over

P

Pang: cram, stuff
parich, parritch: porridge
pawky: sly; slyly humorous; shrewd
pease-scon: scone of pease-meal (i.e. ground dried peas)
peblis: Peebles (town)
peesie: lapwing
peety: pity
penny-wedding: wedding of poor folk at which guests brought small contributions of money
perfite: perfect
pett: "*tak the pett*"—take offence, sulk
pick-an-wale: very best choice
piece: something to eat, usually bread or bun

pike: *"Pike yer Bain"*—'pick your bone', i.e. finish off your meal and get down to the game

pingle: combat, struggle

plainstanes: pavement; sometimes town Exchange paved with flag-stones

platfut: flat-footed, clumsily

play (*"peblis to the play"*): merry-making

playit: played

poind't: distrained, expropriated

poortith: poverty

pouch: pocket

preen: pin

purpie, purpour: purple

Q

Quat: leave (quit)

quean, queyn: lass, girl

queff: two-handled drinking-cup (cf. *quaich*)

quene: queen

quha: who

quhilk: which

quhill: while

quod: said

R

Rae: roe-deer

ravel: tangle, twist together

raw: row

rax: stretch

reaming: frothing

reeking: smoking

renk: bold or strong man, 'warrior'

requeist: request

rive: tear apart; eat up ravenously; rob

roset: rub with resin or cobbler's wax

routh, rowth: plenty

rowte: roar, bellow

ruf: lusty, vigorous

runt: hard stalk of kail or cabbage

russet coat: traditional peasant dress

S

Sae: so

sairing: fill (*n.*), sufficiency

sairlie: greatly (used intensively)

sang: song

sanit: blessed

sarkit: dressed in a shirt (or *sark*)

saunt: saint

saut-poke: pouch or bag for keeping salt

scaldin': scolding

scantly: scarcely

scho: she

sconner, scunner: disgust, be disgusted

screigh: shriek

se: see

sen: since

ser'd: served, sufficed

seventeen hunder linen: linen of specially fine quality (*hunder*: hundred)

shaul': shallow

shaver: barber

shawps: pods

shell wives: women who sold mussels, oysters, etc.

sheugh: ditch, drain, small ravine

shoon: shoes

sib: akin, closely related

sic, siccan: such

siclike: suchlike

siller: silver

simmer: summer

skaith: harm

skirl: high-pitched, somewhat *tremolo* sound (as of bagpipes)

sklent: look sideways; fib

skugs: shadows

slump: *"by the slump"*—the lot, in a lump

smiddie: smithy

smolt: (of weather) fair, clear, mild

snell: sharp, keen; bracing; fierce, severe; tart, sarcastic, acrimonious

soup, sowp: mouthful (sup), small helping

souple: supple, limber

spail: splinter

spear, speer, speir: ask

spence: parlour

spile: spoil

stane: stone

stang: sting

stank: pond, pool; slow-flowing or stagnant ditch; open drain

sted: placed

steek: stitch

GLOSSARY

steid: place
stendis: strides
steppand: stepping
stert: started, suddenly appeared
stewin: Stephen
stinted: left off, stopped
stoure: dust; *stour'd:* hurried (raising a dust)
strae: straw
straik: stroke
strength: strong vantage-point (as in battle)
stroan'd: pissed
strunt: strut; walk sturdily or with dignity
sum: some
swack, swak: supple, limber
swat: sweated; *swats:* new ale, small-beer
swaul: swell
swinge: whip
swith: quick
sybo: young onion, Spring onion
syke: small stream
syne: ago

T

Tack: bargain, agreement; promise; lease; holding
tae: toe
tak: take
tawted: matted
tent: look after, attend to; herd
teugh: tough
thai: they
thair: their
thairms: fiddle-strings
thame: them
than: then
thigging: begging
thole: bear, endure, put up with
thon: that (demonstrative)
thrasher: thresher, hand taken on or paid extra for threshing grain
throughgality: frugality
thrums: threads (usually in spinning and weaving)
till: to
tint: lost (cf. *tyne*)
tirl: strip
tooly: brawl
toom: empty; shallow

townis: town's
toy: woman's cap, usually woollen, with deep shoulder-piece
tram: shaft of barrow, cart, etc.
tree-leg: wooden leg
trental: series of thirty masses for the dead
trig: smart, spruce
trin'le: wheel
trow: believe
tulchin: calf-skin stuffed with straw used to make a cow give her milk (hence nickname for 17th-century bishops who accepted a bishopric with the aim of assigning the temporalities to a secular person)
tulzie: cf. *tooly*
twa: two
twal: twelve (o'clock)
tyke: dog
tyrit: wearied
tyrle: vibrate, touch strings
tythe: tithe, tenth part

U

Unco: too, very (used intensively)

W

Wabster: weaver
wad: would
waefu': sad (woeful)
wan: won
wappenschawing: review of small arms once held in every district
war: better (*v.*), excel
ware: stock
wark: work, job
warl': world
warst: worst
warth: worth
wats: knows
wauken: waken
wedder: weather
weel: well
weighbauk: beam of weighing machine
weir: war
wes: was
weym: stomach, belly
wha: who
whan: when
whang: flog

whim-whams: kickshaws, *bric-à-brac*
whunstane: whinstone
wi': with
wilyart: shy, bashful, awkward
withoutten: without
woody: halter; the gallows
wrang: wrong
wylie-coat: under-vest, flannel shirt
wyly, wylie: wily

Y

Yae: a
yerth: earth (cf. *yird*)
yestreen: last night
yett: gate
yill: ale
yird: earth (cf. *yerth*)
yon: that (demonstrative)
yowdendrift: wind-driven snow

(This Glossary is much indebted to Chambers's *Scots Dictionary*, compiled by Alexander Warrack (edition 1955).)

INDEX

Titles are not normally indexed separately, but under author; fictional characters, editors, compilers and editions are not indexed as such. Page numbers in italics refer to quotations.

INDEX

Caledonian Mercury, The, 128, 307
Calvin, John, *Institutes, 312*
Calvinism, 66, 75-6, 130, 189-94, 201, 244, 312
Cambuslang, 70
Campbell, George, *On Pulpit Eloquence,* 55 n.
Campbell, Islay, 30
Campbell, John, 41 n., 279-80
Campbell, Mary, 317
Campbell, Thomas, 276, 280-1
Candide, 207
Cape Club, the, 33
Carew, Thomas, 34, 296, 301; *Life of Carew, see* Walton; *Poems of Thomas Carew, see* Dunlap
Cargill, Rev. Donald, *49,* 184
Carlyle, Alexander, 276; *Autobiography,* 40, *41-2, 56, 66-7,* 178, 277, *304*
Carlyle, Thomas, 276, 279, 317; on Cunningham, 281; early life, 284; Emerson on, 283; emigration and its effects, 203, 282-8; on his father, *15, 86,* 204-5, 284; on Galt, 160 n.; on Edward Irving, *284-5,* 320; and Jeffrey, 56, 267, 295; language and dialect, 56, 313; his parents, 241, 313, 317; religious influence, 126, 320; and Scott, 214, *284;* his wife, 285; his development as a writer, 267
Works:
 Burns, 40, 88, 299; *Burns and Scott,* 110; *Carlyle, see* Neff; *Thomas Carlyle, see* Conway; *Early Life, see* Froude; *Past and Present,* 275; *Reminiscences,* 87-8, *154,* 200, *204, 267,* 281 n., *284-5;* 320; *Sartor Resartus, 275,* 285, 320; *Specimens of German Romance,* 206; translation of *Wilhelm Meister,* 206
Carnot, Lazare, 306
Carswell, Donald, *Brother Scots,* 202 n., 320
Catholicism, 64, 68, 201, 311-12
Cervantes, *Don Quixote,* 120, 208, 210, 217
Ceylon, 269
Chalmers, George, 280; *Life of Thomas Ruddiman,* 127 n.; 128 n., *Works of Allan Ramsay,* 21 n.
Chalmers, Thomas, 179, 275-6, *301,* 318-20; *Life, see* Hanna
Chambers, Robert, 66, 164, 208, 226, 300; 'A Trait in Public Affairs', *50; Domestic Annals,* 29 n., 31 n., 33 n., 35 n., 36 n., *50-1,* 63 n., 122 n., 127 n., 128 n., 129 n., 130 n., 163, 195 n., 206 n., 304; *Eminent Scotsmen,*

318; *Scottish Jests and Anecdotes,* 163, 226 n.; *Traditions of Edinburgh,* 36 n., 39 n., 45, 314
Chambers, William, 209, 226, 228, 276, 317; *Memoir of Robert Chambers,* 45, 51, 66 n., 113-14, 118, 163 n., 212, 281 n., 304
Chambers's Edinburgh Journal, 36 n., *47,* 114, 299-300
Chantrey, Sir Francis, 304
Chaucer, Geoffrey, 308; 'Prologue', *75, 95-6*
Chillingworth, William, 50, 278
Church of Scotland, 63-5, 178-80
Clapham, J. H., *Economic History,* 29 n., 82
Clare, John, 100, 105
Clerk, Sir John, 312, 318; *Memoirs, 69,* 274
Cobbett, William, 141, 217; *Political Register,* 212; *Tours in Scotland, 29,* 36 n., 83, 142 n., 277 n.
Cochrane, Andrew, 141
Cockburn, Lord Henry, 40, 155, 160, 312; Anglicisation, 57, 296; and elections, 71; on Jeffrey, *319;* language, 290; on 'manners', 151-2; his patriotism, 288
Works:
 Circuit Journeys, 43, *189; Letters,* 44, 143; *Life of Jeffrey,* 43, *44,* 68 n., 70, *102, 179, 230,* 280 n., 283 n., *290,* 295, 319-20; *Memorials, 15,* 35, 37-8 n., 43, *45,* 146-7, *154-5,* 215-216, 217, 226 n., *256,* 276, 277, *284,* 295, *302, 304; Journals, 43,* 68, *80-1, 98-9,* 142, *179,* 287, 299, 320
Cohn, Norman, *Pursuit of the Millennium, 312*
Coleridge, Samuel Taylor, *180,* 260
Collins, A. S., *Authorship in the Days of Johnson,* 129 n., 209 n.; *Profession of Letters,* 209 n.
Congreve, William, 203
Conrad, Joseph, *197 n.,* 239
Constable, Archibald, 213-14, 224-5, 298, 304; *Literary Correspondents,* 32 n., 112 n., 208 n., *225,* 228, 280, 297 n., 299 n., 319
Conway, Moncure D., *Thomas Carlyle,* 283 n.
Cooper, Fenimore, *Heidenmauer,* 218 n.
Cooper, Thomas, 115, 302
Couper, W. J., 212
Cowley, Abraham, 127
Cox, Marjorie, in *From Donne to Marvell,* 50 n., 131 n., 301

330

INDEX

INDEX